C000056498

The 12 Pillars
of Project Excellence

A Lean Approach to Improving Project Results

THE 12 PILLARS OF PROJECT EXCELLENCE:
A Lean Approach to Improving Project Results

The 12 Pillars of Project Excellence book represents a highly pragmatic guide to project management. In this sense, it's an experience-based "how to" book, not a collection of academic theories. Not only does the book provide the fundamental tools that leaders need to get better project results, it lays out the way of thinking that underpins success. Owing to this, the book represents a simple, manageable, actionable, repeatable and teachable body of knowledge that everyone could benefit from.

> — **Mikel J. Harry, Ph.D.,** *Co-Creator of Six Sigma, National Best Selling Author, Consultant to World's Top CEOs*

The 12 Pillars of Project Excellence provides the most significant contribution for leaders to mitigate the project risks, assure sustainable growth and guarantee survival in a global economic scenario full of uncertainties.

> — **Carlos Alberto Briganti,** *General Manager of Eaton Europe and Japan (2001–2003), Vice President of Eaton South America (2004–2007), Currently Managing Director of Power Systems Research, South America; Associated Partner of MB Consultants*

Very few books talk about project leaders and **The 12 Pillars of Project Excellence** is one of the best books I have ever read on project leadership. The book has extraordinary concepts on leading a project, which are unique and exceptional. This book reveals the facts behind project failures and the approaches to overcome those failures by leading all projects to a successful close. I highly recommend this book for all project managers and executives who are serious about building successful project leaders in their organization.

> — **John Salazar,** *CIO Department of Work Force Solutions, State of New Mexico, Ex-CIO Department of Taxation & Revenue Department, State of New Mexico*

The 12 Pillars of Project Excellence is definitely a thought-provoking book which will accelerate an intrinsic cultural change within your business operations. This book bridges the worlds of academia and business ventures. It provides a step-by-step guidance in managing programs and projects that will result in your overall business success! Leading successful innovations always comes with inherent risks and obstacles. In my 30+ years experience in Defense, Space and Academia I have observed that several great opportunities fail due to lack of proper tools and processes. Following the steps outlined in **The 12 Pillars of Project Excellence** will not only allow program and project leaders to overcome these challenges but also provide managers and leaders checks and balances for total business transformation. I am confident that **The 12 Pillars of Project Excellence** is a comprehensive guide that will assist any business leader within an organization to consistently achieve excellent business results! A Must Buy—get it Now!

> — **Billy Billimoria,** *Director, Customer Applications, BAE Systems, Program Director, Lockheed Martin; Manager, Hughes Aircraft (acquired by Raytheon Corporation), Project Engineer, Space Shuttle and Support Equipment Design*

Buy this book! Your business is dead in the water with unfinished projects… they're like cinderblocks tied to your feet. **The 12 Pillars of Project Excellence** breathes life back into your project teams. It motivates them to think BIG and then actually DELIVER. Great book, great methodology.

> — **Karl Wadensten,** *President, VIBCO Vibrators, Host of the Radio Talk Show **The Lean Nation** on 790AM-WPRV*

Dalal's **The 12 Pillars of Project Excellence** book is a true innovation in leadership and the human-side of project management. This book provides some simple yet extraordinary tools to help project managers and organizations understand and transform their culture. I highly recommend this book to individuals who wish to be excellent leaders, organizations who wish to consistently run profitable projects and universities who wish to develop future leaders and executives. I strongly recommend this book as the "must-read and apply" for anyone desiring growth and profits through perfection in leadership and project excellence.

> — **Professor Dr. Vijay Mahajan,** *John P. Harbin Centennial Chair, McCombs School of Business, University of Texas, Austin, Associate Dean of Research, Graduate School of Business, University of Texas, Austin (1991–1994); Dean of the Indian School of Business (ISB) (2002–2004)*

U.S.A. has lost its leadership in manufacturing to other countries because we did not heed our own words to make quality in projects the top priority, especially when we design and manufacture product. The innovative approach laid out by Adil Dalal in his book **The 12 Pillars of Project Excellence**, which pioneers combining Lean concepts with project management, and focusing on human assets to achieve excellence, takes project leadership to its ultimate pinnacle and will result in Six Sigma type results or "zero failures" on all projects. I strongly urge all executives aspiring for top quality in manufacturing, software, service or other projects, to make **The 12 Pillars of Project Excellence** a mandatory workbook for all levels within their respective organizations.

> — **Manny Chavez,** *President & CEO, Aristos Technologies, Inc., Former President/CEO of Harvard Technologies (HT) and former Executive at IBM, Businessman of the Year, Graduate of University of Texas, Harvard University*

The uniqueness of Dalal's book, **The 12 Pillars of Project Excellence**, is integrating lean, strategic, and behavioral thinking into project management, so it's a book on leadership, emphasizing projects. Once you are familiar with the tools and techniques of modern project management, this is the book to get, and to digest. And as Dalal notes, as a leader you need to practice new habits of thinking and leadership; otherwise, no book will be of much help.

> — **Robert W. "Doc" Hall,** *Author of **Zero Inventories** (1983) and **Compression** (2009), One of the first examiners for the Malcolm Baldrige National Quality Award. Recipient of AME's and SME's lifetime achievement awards, Editor Emeritus of AME's **Target Magazine***

The 12 Pillars of Project Excellence is a very inspiring text of learning. Adil covers the span of the project management body of knowledge and leadership attributes that one can learn and directly apply to enhance their project management skills. This is formatted with an easy-to-read, easy-to-follow array of critical points of learning followed up with an excellence array of case studies and exercises that will give the reader reinforcement of their understanding. This is a "must read" from the novice to the skilled project leader.

> — **Dewey Butts III,** *CQPA, CQA, CQE, CMQ/OE, Continuous Improvement, Senior Lean Six Sigma MBB, Harley-Davidson Motor Company, York, PA*

The **The 12 Pillars of Project Excellence** book provides a systematic coverage of project management and project leadership based on practical nuggets of over 300 successful projects by Adil Dalal. The book is comprehensive, simple and has a best practice focus. I would highly recommend this book to anyone who is serious in achieving success with their projects.

> — **Manu K. Vora, Ph.D.,** *MBA, ASQ CQE, and Fellow, Chairman and President, Business Excellence, Inc., Recipient of U.S. President's Call to Service Award (2011)*

In my career as a professor, a manager, and a consultant, I have observed scores of leaders over the past 40 years. Adil is among the best. I observed him leading a group of professionals, all volunteers, tasked with turning around the fortunes of an organization that has been declining for years. Adil is an excellent leader: patient but firm, flexible but always headed in the direction of his vision. His humility left me unprepared for the outstanding quality of **The 12 Pillars of Project Excellence**. It is a must read for anyone who aspires to improve as a leader. While the book is specifically directed to project leadership, it generalizes to all types of leadership. It was so well conceived and well written that I could not put it down.

Once when Dr. Deming was asked why particular stories were included in his book **Out of the Crisis**, he told the audience in his most emphatic voice "Because I was there!" Based on my personal experience of having attended several seminars conducted by Dr. Deming I can say that Adil, like Dr. Deming, shares some great stories in his book, because Adil was also there! The analysis in Adil's book is all the more powerful because it forms that basis of his successful leadership of over 300 projects. It is a book with lots of theory backed by Adil's 15 years of experience as a successful leader. I strongly suggest you read it.

> — **Brooks Carder, PhD,** *Author of **Measurement Matters: How Effective Assessment Drives Business and Safety Performance**, Consultant to the world's largest corporations including ExxonMobil, IBM, Hewlett-Packard, Abbott Laboratories, IBM, Intel, Bayer, Monsanto*

Having worked in project "management" for years and seeing the carnage of leaders who have tried to do the right thing, Dalal's book, **The 12 Pillars of Project Excellence**, truly summarizes the anatomy of the project "leadership" process. He then helps the reader to functionally address the issues to enable success. This innovative book in written to enable people at all levels to successfully effect project leadership. If you are serious about achieving results in your organizational teams, as a leader, an interactive member or as a sponsor, then Dalal's **The 12 Pillars of Project Excellence** book will help you meet that objective. Many thanks to Adil for making this resource available to us all.

> — **Jd Marhevko,** *ASQ Fellow, CMQ/OE, CQE, MBB, Chair ASQ-QMD, Principal, JQLC Inc.*

The 12 Pillars
of Project Excellence

A Lean Approach to Improving Project Results

Adil F. Dalal

 CRC Press
Taylor & Francis Group
Boca Raton London New York

CRC Press is an imprint of the
Taylor & Francis Group, an **informa** business

A PRODUCTIVITY PRESS BOOK

CRC Press
Taylor & Francis Group
6000 Broken Sound Parkway NW, Suite 300
Boca Raton, FL 33487-2742

© 2012 by Taylor & Francis Group, LLC
CRC Press is an imprint of Taylor & Francis Group, an Informa business

No claim to original U.S. Government works

Printed in the United States of America on acid-free paper
Version Date: 20110810

International Standard Book Number: 978-1-4398-4912-5 (Paperback)

This book contains information obtained from authentic and highly regarded sources. Reasonable efforts have been made to publish reliable data and information, but the author and publisher cannot assume responsibility for the validity of all materials or the consequences of their use. The authors and publishers have attempted to trace the copyright holders of all material reproduced in this publication and apologize to copyright holders if permission to publish in this form has not been obtained. If any copyright material has not been acknowledged please write and let us know so we may rectify in any future reprint.

Except as permitted under U.S. Copyright Law, no part of this book may be reprinted, reproduced, transmitted, or utilized in any form by any electronic, mechanical, or other means, now known or hereafter invented, including photocopying, microfilming, and recording, or in any information storage or retrieval system, without written permission from the publishers.

For permission to photocopy or use material electronically from this work, please access www.copyright.com (http://www.copyright.com/) or contact the Copyright Clearance Center, Inc. (CCC), 222 Rosewood Drive, Danvers, MA 01923, 978-750-8400. CCC is a not-for-profit organization that provides licenses and registration for a variety of users. For organizations that have been granted a photocopy license by the CCC, a separate system of payment has been arranged.

Trademark Notice: Product or corporate names may be trademarks or registered trademarks, and are used only for identification and explanation without intent to infringe.

Library of Congress Cataloging-in-Publication Data

Dalal, Adil F.
  The 12 pillars of project excellence : a lean approach to improving project results / Adil F. Dalal.
      p. cm.
  Includes bibliographical references.
  ISBN 978-1-4398-4912-5 (pbk. : alk. paper)
  1. Project management. 2. Leadership. I. Title. II. Title: Twelve pillars of project excellence.

HD69.P75D347 2012
658.4'04--dc23   2011031364

Visit the Taylor & Francis Web site at
http://www.taylorandfrancis.com

and the CRC Press Web site at
http://www.crcpress.com

To

The pioneers of the field of project management:
As we stand tall on your shoulders today, we are ever grateful
for your service to the field of project management;

and

To

All project professionals and executives of our new world:
I hope this book lights the fire of undying passion and yearning
for project excellence and provides a roadmap for success in
your quest to be legendary and visionary leaders.

Contents

Foreword

Adil Dalal's *The 12 Pillars of Project Excellence* can be described in one word—*"Enlightening!"* Dalal's book should revolutionize the field of project leadership. Just as Deming's concepts have universal applications far beyond the field of quality, Dalal's concepts will reach far beyond the field of project management. Why am I qualified to make these bold statements? I was with Dr. Deming, my good friend and my mentor of over 20 years and in Dr. Deming's own words—*"Bill was my student, and there's none better in the world ... It takes a little ingredient called profound knowledge, and he's got it."*

The profound insights I acquired by working with gurus like Dr. Deming, Joseph Juran, Philip Crosby, and others are that the framework of permanent change is broadly based on a combination of physical, logical, and emotional activities by people working as individuals and as members of an organization, team, or family; and the fact that theory without action is useless and action without theory is costly. Dalal's profound insight, knowledge, and drive for excellence in leadership and in project management are evident by the way he not only integrates all three levels of physical, logical, and emotional aspects into a "holistic framework" but also by how he provides a blueprint of the pathway to the pinnacle by incorporating pioneering and revolutionary concepts with action-oriented tools.

Dr. Deming once told me, *"We are here to learn, have fun and make a difference."* He was right—he captured the minds of millions of people around the world and gained global recognition as a *"Guru"* and the *"The American Who Taught the Japanese about Quality."* The "12 Pillars" book *"creates a brand new corporate world"* and takes the field of project management into a new era of project leadership built on the foundation of sophistication, elegance, and simplicity.

What struck me about this book and the reason I decided to write this foreword is the simple, no-nonsense, practical, and enlightened advice Dalal provides to transform individuals and corporations. Dalal also backs up that advice with case studies from his own experience, and powerful practical tools of self-assessment. His simple yet powerful balance of process and results concepts of the *"science of simplicity™,"* *"appreciating assets,"* the *"power of visualization™,"* *"dynamic risk analysis"* are truly pioneering and are equally applicable to leaders aspiring for excellence as well to every corporation aspiring to leap from good to great.

As the impact of this book spreads globally and the importance of this work is recognized, I hope Adil Dalal will be recognized as the *"Guru of (Project) Leadership."*

William Scherkenbach[*]
Austin, Texas

---

[*] Mr. Scherkenbach is recognized as one of the world's foremost authorities on the subject of quality and its implementation and is a recipient of the prestigious Deming Medal and the Engineering Society's Gold Award.

Preface

Excellence is a mind-set built on the foundation of precision, perseverance, and passion. Project management is a skill-set based on the foundation of nine knowledge areas and five process groups. The purpose of the "12 pillars of project excellence" is to share with you a practical blueprint that will allow you to convert the skill-set into a permanent mind-set.

The purpose of the "12 pillars of project excellence" is to share with you a practical blueprint that will allow you to convert the skill-set into a permanent mind-set.

Mount Everest is the highest peak in the world, soaring more than 8848 meters or 29,028 feet. Reaching the summit seemed "mission impossible" and resulted in fatalities of a number of the world's strongest climbers, until one morning of May 29, 1953, when a beekeeper from New Zealand, Edmund Hillary along with the Nepali-Indian Sherpa mountaineer guide Tenzing Norgay, set foot onto the pinnacle of the world. This pioneering feat earned them instant immortality in the history of the world. Although our corporate projects, in general, are significantly less adventurous and precarious than that undertaken by Sir Edmund Hillary and his Sherpa guide, Tenzing Norgay, every project we undertake is like an expedition to reach the pinnacle of success and can have a significant impact on the future of our organization. There are basically two types of projects—successful and failed. If leading successful projects is not your passion, then project management is not your career, it is just a hobby. If you truly want to make leading projects a career choice, you need to be successful in every undertaking. However, to be a successful project manager, it is critical to make excellence a permanent attitude. Also, it is important to understand that excellence is not perfection—perfection is a requirement for robots; humans aspire to excellence.

It is important to understand that excellence is not perfection—perfection is a requirement for robots; humans aspire to excellence.

However, to achieve excellence and be considered a legend, even Sir Edmund Hillary needed a "guide" or a Sherpa. Thus, to achieve excellence as a legendary mountain climber or as a champion athlete, one needs a coach or a "guide" to highlight his or her strengths and diminish flaws. If you wish to follow in the footsteps of Sir Edmund Hillary and scale to the summit of project management, have you selected your guide or coach? This book is written with the intent that it will play the role of Sherpa Tenzing Norgay and serve as a "guide" for you and your organization and show the most efficient and safest path to the pinnacle of the field of project leadership.

How is the book qualified to be your guide? The reason it qualifies as a guide is that includes the lessons, wisdom, and the stories gathered from almost a decade and a half of leading more than 300 "challenging corporate expeditions" from the base to the high summits. The "expeditions" or projects and programs ranged from major acquisitions, strategic IT implementations (hardware/software), software development, capital equipment purchases, and Lean and six sigma implementations to complete transformations of divisions and corporations. The 12 pillars are a direct result of this amazing experience gained by working in the trenches with thousands of talented individuals on teams who rose to the challenge each time by stretching their abilities to make the impossible possible.

The 12 pillars are a direct result of this amazing experience gained by working in the trenches with thousands of talented individuals on teams who rose to the challenge each time by stretching their abilities to make the impossible possible.

At the start of my career, I was fortunate to have studied the fundamentals of project management directly from some of the gurus in the field, namely, Dr. Harold Kerzner, Eliyahu Goldratt, and others, and received a PMP certification when most did not know what it even meant. I had a true zest for leading projects, but I did not have a formula for success in this field. In every project, from every mentor, I tried to identify the formula for its success. I asked myself, "What is that 'extra' characteristic within them which makes them 'extra' ordinary?" For example, I honed my leadership skills by closely observing my mentor, "the leader of leaders," Lonny, who is currently a president in a Fortune 500 corporation. Lonny's leadership and motivation style, described in Pillar XI, helped me develop my own project leadership style on the basis of five "magic" powers described in Pillar I. Thus, the practical principles of the 12 pillars were very carefully collected during the early part of my career. Applying the lessons of the 12 pillars to my projects was the turning point in my career. After almost a decade and a half of being involved with leading more than 300 small, medium, and supersized projects in numerous industries, internationally, I can boldly affirm to have a proven formula called the "12 pillars of project excellence" for success in project leadership. Thus, this book distills the formula that has provided consistent breakthrough results for me and my project teams and is thus well-qualified to be at your service. I share my formula with you so that you can benefit from my project trials, tribulations, and lessons learned—by adopting my formula directly or by using my lessons learned you can discover and design your very own formula—tailored perfectly for your success. Also, I hope that those of you who have already discovered the right

This book distills the formula that has provided consistent breakthrough results for me and my project teams.

formula for success in project management may be able to use this book to validate and fine-tune your discovery. Project management has been a very satisfying career choice for me, and I see this book as an opportunity to give back to this discipline. Thus, this book is the fruit of my 15 years of excitement, experience, and experimentation in the field of project leadership. This book is written from my vantage point of leading projects. I openly share with you my ideas, successes, and lessons learned using case studies from my own experience and from those I consider my true heroes. I hope you enjoy it and can gain from it some useful nuggets of knowledge that you can use for your own successes. The primary goal of this book is to motivate aspiring and/or established project leaders to "dream big" and to teach those project leaders some key principles of project leadership that are based on my own experiences in this field. This book is dedicated to all project leaders, project managers, team members, executives sponsors, stakeholders, and other individuals who want to move beyond their comfort zone and achieve something that they, too, can one day share with others.

Get involved with the movement of the 12 pillars by joining the LinkedIn Group "12 Pillars of Project Excellence" or contact me directly with your questions, concerns, or comments at *adil@pinnacleprocess.com* or at (512) 289 7080.

Acknowledgments

Thank you:

To my precious dad, who recently moved to his heavenly home, and who will be loved forever for his steadfast support and pride in all my endeavors.

To my wife and three children for putting up with me for a year and a half while this book was being written and fine-tuned through several revisions.

To all the people who have played a major role in making this work possible, including my publisher; my editor Lenin Kamma, and my illustrator Kyra Kauschel for their help in significantly enhancing the value of this book.

Introduction

> The quality of a person's life is in direct proportion to their commitment to excellence, regardless of their chosen field of endeavor[1]
>
> Vince Lombardi

1.1 Origin of the Term "Project"

The word "project" has its roots in the Latin word *projectum* and Latin verb *pro-icere*. *Proicere* means "to throw something forward." Originally, the term project meant "something that comes before anything else happens." The modern definition of project is "a temporary endeavor to create a unique product, service or a result."[2] By definition, project leaders and teams are required to "plan something truly original" new "voyages in unchartered waters."

From time immemorial, the human race has evolved by taking on and completing challenging projects—inventions like the automobile, electricity, computers, Internet, satellites; defining processes like coal and oil exploration; manufacturing technology; and undertaking incredible journeys like discovering America, exploration to Antarctica, and journey into space.

Sir Edmund Hillary, who undertook and successfully completed the project of reaching the summit of Mount Everest in 1953, remarked, *"The explorers of the past were great men and we should honor them. But let us not forget that their spirit lives on. It is still not hard to find a man who will adventure for the sake of a dream or one who will search, for the pleasure of searching, not for what he may find."*[3]

1.2 Project Management as a Career Choice

John F. Kennedy once said, *"We need men (and women) who can dream of things that never were."* I think this is directly applicable to project managers. I truly believe that project management is one of the "coolest careers" in this world as it is a field that binds together those individuals who share the spirit of adventure to go where "no one has gone before" and those who have the courage to "preserve on this journey against all odds." Project management allows individuals and teams to dream up an idea, then to innovatively execute and create something unique every time. All project managers have a potential to make a significant impact on people's lives. For example, President John F. Kennedy's audacious vision of "landing a man on the moon and bringing him back to planet earth" during his May 25, 1961, speech to the Congress was not only accomplished by the project managers of NASA within the decade (July 20, 1969) but inspired the ailing United States to believe that dreams do come true. This "daring dream" of a President and the "successful execution" by the NASA project managers not only inspired a nation but had a major impact on trust and belief in human potential, for the entire world.

1.3 Current State of Project Management

Let us discuss the good, the bad, and the ugly state of project management because it is critical to understand this for all project managers.

I.3.1 The Good News about the State of Project Management Today

Since 1985, The Standish Group has been collecting and analyzing project success and failure data. According to the article by Jorge Dominguez, "The Curious Case of the Chaos Report 2009" based on the data on project success rate from The Standish Group, project success rate has doubled since 1994.[4]

The following can be concluded on the basis of the statistics shown in Figure I.1:

   i. The failed projects are definitely trending downwards and show a 23% drop since 1994.

  ii. The challenged projects are also trending downwards and show a 17% drop since 1994.

 iii. The successful projects have shown an improvement of 100% since 1994.

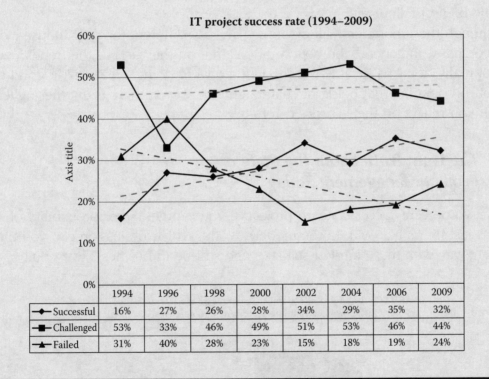

	1994	1996	1998	2000	2002	2004	2006	2009
◆ Successful	16%	27%	26%	28%	34%	29%	35%	32%
■ Challenged	53%	33%	46%	49%	51%	53%	46%	44%
▲ Failed	31%	40%	28%	23%	15%	18%	19%	24%

Figure I.1 IT project success rate trends (1994–2009).

That seems very upbeat news for project management, doesn't it? It seems that the millions of dollars spent on project management education and development of thousands of new PMP's each year is finally paying off? Is it time to pop the champagne? Well, I would hold off till we get to the part about the "bad news."

I.3.2 The Bad News about the State of Project Management Today

The summary of CHAOS Report 2009 states, "This year's (2009's) results show a marked decrease in project success rates, with 32% of all projects succeeding which are delivered on time, on budget,

This year's (2009's) results show a marked decrease in project success rates, with 32% of all projects succeeding which are delivered on time, on budget, with required features and functions

with required features and functions," says Jim Johnson, chairman of The Standish Group, "44% were challenged which are late, over budget, and/or with less than the required features and functions and 24% failed which are cancelled before completion or delivered and never used."[5] Figure I.2 graphically shows these data.

"These numbers represent a downtick in the success rates from the previous study, as well as a significant increase in the number of failures," says Jim Crear, Standish Group CIO, "They are low point in the last five study periods. This year's results represent the highest failure rate in over a decade."[6]

Although these numbers will obviously be very different for your industry or your company, in general, the bottom line is that on the basis of the trends, we are not really doing as great as we thought we were doing. Now, isn't it good we held off on opening that bottle of champagne? However, there is another uglier truth if you reflect on the statistics carefully.

I.3.3 The Ugly Truth about the State of Project Management Today

Thirty-two percent success rate on projects—you can get better probability of success just flipping a coin. In the modern world, which profession can you think can get away with these kind of statistics and still be in business? Even our

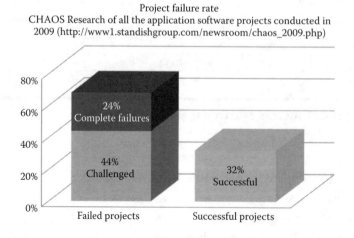

Figure I.2   IT project success and failure rates (2009).

weather forecasts are getting more accurate with the Doppler radar technology. Thus, the high failure rate of projects of 68% is a bitter pill to swallow of all project professionals. On the basis of your industry and company, you may be experiencing far better or even worse results than those reported by the Standish Group.

Thirty-two percent success rate on projects—you can get better probability of success just flipping a coin.

The KPMG study was published in the United Kingdom in 2002 and was based on a survey of 134 public companies. According to the report, 56% of the companies surveyed had to write off at least one IT project in the previous year, at an average cost of US$12.5M. The highest loss for a single project was placed at US$210 million. The total loss from just one failed IT project was around US$1.7 billion for these 134 companies alone. Can we even predict how much money is being wasted annually if we include failed projects from governments, private organizations, small businesses, and other international projects? A safe estimate will be several billions of dollars wasted every year due to failed projects.[7] Knowing these facts, would you like to open that bottle of champagne or prefer to leave it chilled for a day with better statistics on project success rate?

I.4 Do Failed Projects = Failed Project Managers?

A valid question to ask at this point is *"are project managers failing to manage projects or are projects failing for other reasons?"* To answer this question with adequate wisdom, we need to look at the project environment today. The conditions of the project landscape have changed drastically in the last few decades.

Project managers or the brave "project warriors" have to fight against the following factors, which have increased exponentially over the last few decades:

   i. Complexity of technology based projects
   ii. Speed to market requirements due to global competition and
   iii. Worldwide dispersion of project teams

In short, projects are significantly more complex and need to be completed at "blink" speeds and with resources that are completely diverse and dispersed. Project management technology has not advanced enough in last few decades to address the modern-day challenges of our project managers. Can we truly blame the project managers for the projects failing?

I.5 Criticality of 12 Pillars to Future of Project Leadership

I.5.1 The Plight of Project Managers Today

Have you ever had the experience when you are transparent to everyone, where nobody seems to even notice that you are around, until you have a failure and then everybody knows your name and points you out to others, when you walk by? Many project managers today feel their job is more like that of a night watch person—getting noticed only when there is a break-in (failure). We need to bring the "honor" of leading projects back into organizations immediately. Leading and managing critical projects should be one of the most exciting and challenging endeavors in the career of an individual. Leading a successful strategic project should propel the project leader and the team to the status of corporate superheroes who have powers to transform organizations.

> **Leading a successful strategic project should propel the project leader and the team to the status of corporate superheroes who have powers to transform organizations.**

I.5.2 Project Leaders as Corporate Superheroes

The primary goal of the 12 pillars in this book is to provide you with guidelines that will allow you to become "the best project leader" or a "corporate superhero" who cannot only be chosen for the "best of the best" projects every time but can also "hit them out of the ball park" without fail. This book does not come with a cape and lessons on "how to fly"; however, it will allow you to get practical advice and learn techniques for reaching the stars in the field of project leadership.

Neil Armstrong did not use a cape and superpowers to fly to the moon but with the help of his team, he did manage to step off the "Eagle" and walk on the moon, making him a superhero to the entire world. The entire world knows Armstrong's famous words, as he stepped on to the surface of the moon—*"One small step for man but a giant leap for mankind."* The words should inspire us project leaders to visualize the immense possibilities every project we undertake can have for our respective organizations. It should inspire us enough that at the end of each project, we can take a deep breath and resolutely say *"One small step for our project team, one giant leap for our corporation."*

Thus, in my opinion, not all superheroes fly in the sky, "leap tall buildings in a single bound" or climb up walls. I believe true superheroes are those who consistently "keep their feet on the ground, their eyes on the stars and their heart focused on bridging that gap (for the good of all stakeholders)." All project leaders can aspire to and actually become superheroes

> **All project leaders can aspire to and actually become superheroes if they follow a few simple ground rules that have been laid out in this book in the form of the 12 pillars.**

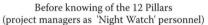

Before knowing of the 12 Pillars   After following the 12 pillars
(project managers as 'Night Watch' personnel)   (project managers as 'Super-Heroes')

Figure I.3   Difference between a project manager before and after following the principles detailed in the 12 pillars.

if they follow a few simple ground rules that have been laid out in this book in the form of the 12 pillars. Figure I.3 shows the difference between a project manager before and after following the principles detailed in the 12 pillars.

I.5.3 No False Claims

I do not claim to be the "world's greatest project leader" or even close. However, I do believe that the practical insight from "12 pillars" presented here are essential not only to the triumph of project managers and to successful completion of modern-day projects but they are also critical to the future of the field previously known as "project management," and for which the appropriate term, in future, will be "project leadership." Yes, it is a bold statement. I stand by it and hopefully you will too, once you read the 12 pillars and reach your own conclusions.

I.5.4 A Book about Mastering the Art of Project Leadership

A successful project leader is a project manager who not only knows how to manage the stakeholders of the project but is also proficient at the art of leading every project to a successful conclusion. Thus, *The 12 Pillars of Project Excellence* is primarily a book about leadership. Moreover, any project professional, who raise these 12 pillars over a strong foundation of the fundamentals of project management, will be able to continually scale new heights in project results and be transformed into a true master project leader. I also believe that organizations can use this book to understand the factors that can assist or harm the creation of an effective project culture within their organization. Another critical application of this book is for executives who wish you understand the techniques to maximize profits from strategic projects and also develop future leaders who can take their organization to new heights.

The 12 Pillars of Project Excellence is primarily a book about leadership.

Thus, this is a unique book that can be used to learn and enhance the following three critical skills, which are not addressed in the field of project management today:

i. Organizations will learn the art of assessing and improving their overall project culture.
ii. Executives will learn the art of maximizing profits by optimizing the talents of their project leaders.
iii. Project leader will learn the art of mastering the fundamentals of project leadership.

I.6 Use of Force Field Analysis in the 12 Pillars of Project Excellence

I.6.1 How Will Organizations Benefit from the 12 Pillars?

Organizations realize that they need to provide the right soil and adequate water (culture) and provide natural sunlight (executive support) so that the plants (project managers) within the organization can thrive to grow strong trees (master project leaders). However,

it is very difficult to gauge the project culture of an organization. This book provides a great quality tool called the force field analysis for conducting a thorough assessment of the organizational project culture. The same tool can also be used by projects leaders to assess their own strengths and weaknesses.

I.6.2 What Is a Force Field Analysis?

A Force Field Analysis is a practical technique created by the well-known social psychologist Kurt Lewin[11] (1890–1947) to look at all the balancing forces for and against a decision to be made. The analysis helps us in identifying which of the two opposing forces, the "driving forces" (DF) supporting the decision or the "resisting forces" (RF) opposing the decision, are more predominant based on the weighting factors. Once the analysis is complete, we need to create a plan to strengthen the DF supporting the decision to and reduce the impact of the RF opposing the decision. Figure I.4 shows a simple version of the force field analysis. The "12 pillars of project excellence" uses an advanced form of force field that is quantitative versus qualitative to assess the forces driving or resisting the principles of each of the 12 pillars.

I.6.3 Two Types of Force Field Analysis

Two force field assessments in each pillar are used to enhance the learning and conduct a practical assessment of existence of the principles of each pillar within

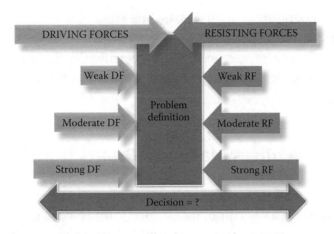

Figure I.4   A simple version of a force field analysis template.

your own organization, department, or team culture and also as a self-assessment tool of your own strengths.

I.6.3.1 Organizational Culture Assessment

The organizational assessment is conducted to assess the culture of the organization for the specific pillar. The results of the organizational force field analysis are used to create a detailed action plan to enhance the DF and reduce the RF to align the culture toward the principles of each pillar.

I.6.3.2 Self-Assessment

The self-assessment is conducted to assess your own strengths and opportunities for the specific pillar. You will use the results of the self-assessment force field analysis to create a detailed action plan to enhance the DF and reduce the RF to align your strengths toward the principles of each pillar.

I.6.4 Creating an Action Plan

After conducting each of the force field analysis, you will be guided, step by step, to create an action plan to continuously improve the alignment of the organizational culture and own strengths with the principles of each pillar by increasing the scores of the DF and by reducing the scores of the RF.

I.6.5 Continuous Improvement

The principles detailed in the 12 pillars need to be continuously enhanced to get optimal benefits. Thus, it is highly recommend that the action plan created on the basis of the results of each force field analysis be evaluated and updated at least every 3 months. It is also highly recommended to retake both the force field analysis assessment annually to rebaseline the culture and strengths and to update the action plans.

Thus, the "12 pillars of project excellence" is truly applicable throughout the organization as the culture of an organization is created by the cumulative behavior of all their employees.

I.7 How Can Executives Maximize Profits from Projects

Most executives may not understand the jargon of project management, but they know that successful projects can make a significant impact on the bottom line of the organization. They also know that project success primarily depends on the project manager's skills and talent. However, according to the OASIG Study (1995), "at best, 7 out of 10 projects 'fail' in some respect."[8] What can executives do to ensure that a majority of their projects are successful? Are there some simple tips that can be most beneficial?

At best, 7 out of 10 projects 'fail' in some respect.

Although we can easily write a 500-page book on this topic, here are four simple things executives can do to immediately increase the success rate on their organizational projects. They are as follows:

A. Understand the impact of organizational structure on the performance of project managers.
B. Develop project leaders not project managers.
C. Select project leaders as early in the project as possible and allow the same leaders to close out the projects.
D. Encourage use of "lean thinking" throughout the organization.

I.7.1 Understanding the Impact of Organizational Structure on the Performance of Project Managers

There are four basic types of organization structures:

I.7.1.1 Functional Structure

The functional organization has a traditional hierarchical structure with functional managers in charge of various departments.

The functional organization has a traditional hierarchical structure with functional managers in charge of various departments. Project managers report to respective functional managers. Functional organizational structure is not conducive for project success because of less authority to project managers and more barriers to project success like resource limitations, project budget, and other factors.

I.7.1.2 Weak Matrix Structure

The weak matrix organization has a blended structure with project managers reporting to both the functional managers and the program managers. Weak matrix organizational structure is better than functional but not completely conducive for project success because of having to report to two managers and some barriers to project success like resource limitations, project budget, and other factors. Weak matrix organizational structures are most common in organizations today.

The weak matrix organization has a blended structure with project managers reporting to both the functional managers and the program managers.

I.7.1.3 Strong Matrix Structure

The strong matrix organization has a blended structure with project managers reporting to both the functional managers and sponsoring executives (Directors, vice presidents, and above). Strong matrix organizational structure is much better than both functional and weak matrix structure and can be very conducive for project success as project managers will have support from the executive sponsors, reducing the barriers to project success significantly. This structure provides the best opportunities for project leaders to excel and have the most impact on the generating profits for an organization. However, the project managers in a strong matrix are required to have adequate proficiency to lead key strategic projects for executive sponsors.

The strong matrix organization has a blended structure with project managers reporting to both the functional managers and sponsoring executives.

I.7.1.4 Project Organization Structure

Project organizational structures have project managers reporting to program managers or to sponsoring executives (directors, vice presidents, and above). Project organizational structure is best for project success and has least amount of barriers to project success. Project organizational structures are not very common and mostly exist in consulting or project-oriented firms.

Figure I.5 clearly shows the influence of the four organization structure types on the authority of project managers and barriers to project success. It indicates that

a. The authority of project managers increases as the organization structure goes from "functional (low authority)" to "pure project" type (high authority).
b. The barriers to project success increase as the organization structure goes from "pure project" (least barriers) to "functional" type (most barriers).

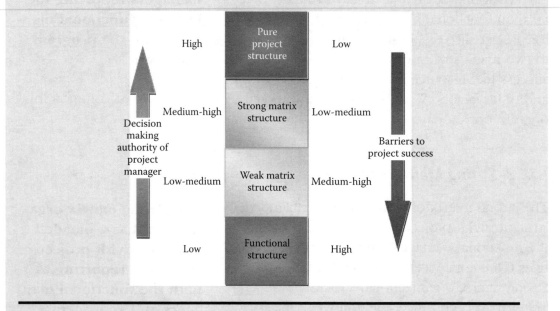

Figure I.5   Influence of organization structure on authority of project managers and barriers to project success.

I.7.2 Developing Project Leaders and Not Project Managers

Developing project leaders is the key theme of Pillar I. Strong project leaders know how to motivate teams to "get things done" with minimal resources, least budget, and within schedule and to generate maximum profits. Thus, executives, as a part of succession planning, can use the strong matrix structure and have project leaders report directly to them so they can develop strong project leaders and provide some additional business training and get future executives who can have a great impact on the growth of the organization.

I.7.3 Selecting Project Leaders as Early in the Project as Possible and Allowing the Same Leaders to Close Out the Projects

It is important to get the project leader involved as early as possible on any critical project. Some corporations wait till the "project planning or implementation" phase to instate the project manager, almost as an afterthought. This leads to many challenges and has a definite impact on the results of the project. On the other hand, some corporations tend to pullout the project managers at the end of the project implementation or the monitoring phase and leave the closeout phase to the team. This does significant harm to the career of a project manager as "project closeout" is where the actual impact of the project is realized and many lessons are learned during this critical phase.

I.7.4 Encouraging the Use of Lean Thinking throughout the Organization

Executives understand that it is not enough to "work hard" to be profitable. They know that to be truly successful, organizations must learn to "work smart" by eliminating waste that can have a major financial and intellectual impact on the organization. Lean is a method of continuously making conscious choices to radically redefine and dynamically optimize strategy, systems, pro-

> **Truly successful, organizations must learn to "work smart" by eliminating waste that can have a major financial and intellectual impact on the organization.**

cesses, and services to remove waste and add value for clients, employees, and shareholders.[9] Thus, executives must teach their project managers and everyone in the organization the art of "lean thinking" where waste or muda[10] (Japanese term for waste) can be reduced significantly or completely eliminated as shown in Pillar VI.

I.8 How Will Project Leaders Learn the Art of Mastering the Fundamentals of Project Leadership?

There are three general categories of project managers in an organization:

    A. Highly experienced project managers
    B. Project managers with some experience
    C. Project managers with no experience (in training)

Although the 12 pillars book is applicable to all the above three categories, the approach to using the book will be different for each category as shown below.

I.8.1 Highly Experienced Project Managers

Extremely experienced project managers can use the 12 pillars for "validation" of their strengths as project leaders and for finding the "gold nuggets" within the theory, case studies, assessments, and exercises to enhance their own strengths to a level of a master project leader.

I.8.2 Project Managers with Some Experience

Project managers with some experience can, at first, use the 12 pillars for "unlearning" some of the principles of project management that were damaging to their career. After the "unlearning" process is complete, they can use it for "learning" the principles of project leadership from the theory and case studies of the 12 pillars, use force field self-assessments for discovering their own strengths, and create action plans for enhancing their strengths and advancing from project managers to project leaders to master project leaders.

I.8.3 Project Managers with No Experience (in Training)

Project managers with no experience can use the 12 pillars for "learning" the principles of the project leadership from the theory and case studies of the 12 pillars, use force field self-assessments for discovering their own strengths, and create action plans for enhancing the strengths and advancing from project managers to master project leaders.

I.9 Twelve Simple Steps to Maximize Benefit from the 12 Pillars

Here are some tips and step-by-step approach for getting the best value out of this book. These steps are shown in Table I.1 for project teams in organizations and in Table I.2 for individuals.

I.10 Setting the Right Expectations for This Book

I.10.1 Not a Silver Bullet

The lessons in 12 pillars are not meant to be a silver bullet to cure all ills of the project world.

The lessons in 12 pillars are not meant to be a silver bullet to cure all ills of the project world. Along the journey to being a master project leader, you may still have your share of bloopers and missteps and may even get some well-deserved Razzie awards (the golden raspberry award for recognizing the worst in films) for projects. You may still walk into a "hornet's nest" by rubbing some stakeholders in the wrong way and make some faux pas in your career by taking on some projects with "dim-witted" objectives. However, it is certain that once you achieve mastery in the principles of the 12 pillars, you will learn to proactively minimize these to a level of nonexistence.

Table I.1 Step-by-Step Approach for Getting the Best Value Out of "12 Pillars" (for Groups)

Steps	Activity
Step 1	• Read each pillar carefully
Step 2	• Read the case study associated with each pillar • Reflect on your own experiences
Step 3	• Conduct the organization assessment force field analysis
Step 4	• Select nine or more executives, stakeholders, or project members • Ask them to conduct the organizational force field analysis survey • Calculate the first average score (without your score) • Compare the average score with your score • Calculate the second average score (with your score) • Reflect on your understanding of the organizational project culture
Step 5	• Create an action plan based on the second average result from step 4
Step 6	• Consciously practice the principles required to enhance organization culture • Update the results in the action plan every 3 months
Step 7	• Review and complete the organizational exercises for each pillar
Step 8	• Create an action plan based on the results from exercises
Step 9	• Consciously practice the principles required to enhance organization culture • Update the results in the action plan every 3 months
Step 10	• Repeat the process every year and re-baseline the action plans

I.10.2 The Pace of Progress

Please note that the case studies included in this book are authentic but the details of the individuals and corporations are omitted or changed for purpose of respecting the confidentiality of individuals and organizations.

Success in the application of these pillars will not "magically manifest" themselves at once. You will need to create a good action plan based on the results of the force field survey and actively focus on the action plan to increase the DF and reduce the RF. As you work on different projects, teams, and environments, you will gradually develop deeper insights into the existence and the importance of each pillar. It will be like playing a new video game where as you advance to a more advanced level, you will have a new superpower at your disposal. However, once the successes start, expect to be entrusted with major strategic corporate projects by your executives. Mother Theresa, once said, "In this life, we cannot do great things. We can only do small things with great love." Thus,

Table I.2 Step-by-Step Approach for Getting the Best Value Out of "12 Pillars" (for Individuals)

Steps	Activity
Step 1	• Read each pillar carefully
Step 2	• Read the case study associated with each pillar • Reflect on your own experiences
Step 3	• Take the self-assessment force field analysis survey
Step 4	• Reflect on your understanding of the self-assessment
Step 5	• Create an action plan based on the result from step 4
Step 6	• Consciously practice the principles required to enhance individual skills • Update the results in the action plan every 3 months
Step 7	• Review and complete the individual exercises for each pillar
Step 8	• Create an action plan based on the results from exercises
Step 9	• Consciously practice the principles required to enhance individual skills • Update the results in the action plan every 3 months
Step 10	• Repeat the process every year and re-baseline the action plans

use this book with patience as a guide to achieve small breakthroughs every day with passion—the final results will truly amaze you.

I.11 Transformative Power of the 12 Pillars

Applying the principles of the 12 pillars to yourself and to the organization will definitely be the turning point in your career. By reading this book, you will

1. Learn to be a leader of leaders by acquiring the five powers of leadership.
2. Understand the importance of having balanced organizational project structures.
3. Learn the art of creating powerful project vision statements.
4. Understand how to use charters as contracts.
5. Be the motivator-in-chief for your team.
6. Learn the critical aspects of lean thinking on projects.
7. Understand how to prevent Meeticide™ (death by meetings) on projects.
8. Acquire the ways to simplify risk assessments and take calculated project risks.

9. Learn the importance of decoding and shielding the project data.
10. Discover the art of celebrating failures and using them in creating a true learning project organization.
11. Recognize the ways to relieve project stress.
12. Realize how to appreciate your most valuable project assets and create a dynamic environment of optimal performance and results on all projects.
13. Learn the art of leading diverse, dispersed, and virtual teams.
14. Learn that it is critical to share your passion and make it your priority to ensure your team members believe in themselves and share your passion for the projects.
15. Learn to always set standards for project success, higher than those set by your project sponsors.

When you apply all the lessons learned from this book, you may consistently hear comments from experienced team members working on your most complex projects, such as "I did not think achieving this (objective) was ever possible, I still cannot believe we did it!"

Also, on the basis of the number of executive and upper management within your organization truly following the principles of the 12 pillars, you can expect to see a marked improvement in the culture of the organization toward projects and project leaders. You can expect to see more support for project leaders from the top levels of the organizations.

Please do not think these objectives as a "utopia" or as "mission impossible." Even if you do at this point, trust the advice of Walt Disney, who said *"It's kind of fun to do the impossible."*

I.12 Please Note: The 12 Pillars Follow The "Tao of Simplicity"

One thing you will observe throughout this book is the simplicity of the truths within each pillar. As a true believer in the simplicity of lean technology, I have come to adopt the "Tao of simplicity." Studying the Tao or "the way," I have learned

"Complexity and chaos" are two sides of the same coin as are "simplicity and sophistication"

that "complexity and chaos" are two sides of the same coin as are "simplicity and sophistication," as shown in Figure I.6. For those who are expecting "complex theories of quantum project mechanics," my candid advice to you is, "return the

Figure I.6   Two sides of a coin—complexity and chaos and simplicity and sophistication.

book immediately and get your money back." For others who take the first step on the journey, by going to Pillar I: Be a Project Leader, remember that "a project of a thousand activities starts with a single task." A powerful transformation awaits you—God speed ahead.

I.13 Tips for Using the CD Accompanying This Book

Appendix A explains some tips for making the best use of the attached CD.

Instructions for CD

Insert CD into the CD-ROM Drive and perform the following steps.

1. Open the Force Field Analysis Portfolio using Adobe Reader.
2. Double click to open the required file.
3. Enter your name (Self Assessment) or team name (Organizational Assessment) on top. right corner of the Force Field Analysis.
4. The current date will be automatically populated on top left corner of the Force Field Analysis.
5. Enter your score for each Self or Organizational Driving and Resisting Force using the pull-down menu in each field.
6. The valid scores are as given below.

   Never – 0   Rarely – 3   Sometimes – 5
   Mostly – 7   Always – 10

   Note: The Sum of Scores for Organizational Driving Force Field and Organizational Resisting Force Field must be less than or equal to Ten (10).
7. Make sure you enter valid scores for all Forces.
8. If you have entered wrong scores and like to reenter, click "RESET" to reset all your scores.
9. When you enter all your scores, click "SUBMIT" to submit the form and all scores.
10. Scroll down to see the Action Plan for both the Driving forces and Resisting forces.
11. Scroll further down to enter Target Scores (Goal), from the pull-down menu, for Driving Forces based on the action plan.
12. Scroll further down to enter Target Scores (Goal), from the pull-down menu, for Resisting Forces for your team based on the action plan.
13. Review all target scores for accuracy.
14. If target scores are acceptable, Save the Portfolio using File à Save as … Button.
15. Repeat the above steps for all Organizational Analysis files.
16. Repeat the above steps for all Self-Analysis files.
17. Save the Portfolio.
18. Repeat all the above steps every three months or as required.

Please Note: **That the CD has copyrighted material and cannot be shared or duplicated. Each individual within the team needs to have and utilize their own CD which is included with the book.**

References

1. Lombardi, V. T. (1913–1970). Leadership quotes, http://www.coach4growth.com/good-leadership-skills/leadershipquotes.html (accessed October 27, 2010).
2. Project Management Institute (PMI). 2008. *A Guide to the Project Management Body of Knowledge (PMBOK Guide)*, 4th Ed., p. 5. 14, Campus Blrd, Newtown Square, PA 19073.
3. Nzedge.com.Adventures, Sir Edmund Hillary King of the World. 1998–2010, http://www.nzedge.com/heroes/hillary.html (accessed October 27, 2010).
4. Dominguez, J. (July 2009). The Curious Case of the Chaos Report 2009, http://www.projectsmart.co.uk/the-curious-case-of-the-chaos-report-2009.html (accessed October 27, 2010).
5. Johnson, J. (2010).*The Standish Group Report*. Boston, MA: The Standish Group International Inc.
6. The Standish Group International Inc. CHAOS Summary 2009, http://www1.standishgroup.com /newsroom/chaos_2009.php (accessed October 27, 2010).
7. Bogorad, I. (October 2009). The Real Cost of Failed Projects, http://www.projectsmart.co.uk/the-real-costs-of-failed-projects.html (accessed October 27, 2010).
8. IT Cortex c.a. Failure rate, Statistics over IT Projects Failure Rate. (2005). The OASIG Study, http://www.it-cortex.com/Stat_Failure_Rate.htm (accessed October 27, 2010).
9. Dalal, A. (September 2010), "Keep it simple," *Quality Progress Magazine*, 43(9): p. 24.
10. Greg. (2009). Muda, What Is It, http://www.thetoyotasystem.com/lean_concepts/muda_what_is_it.php (accessed October 27, 2010).
11. Lewin, K. (1943). "Defining the field at a given time," *Psychological Review*, 50, 292–311. Republished in *Resolving Social Conflicts & Field Theory in Social Science*, Washington, DC: American Psychological Association, 1997.

Chapter 1

Pillar I: Be a Project Leader

> "Project Management" is a misnomer.
> "Project Leadership" is the right choice.

1.1 Introduction

On May 29, 1953, Edmund Hillary and his guide, Sherpa Tenzing Norgay, were the first ever human beings to scale the summit of Mount Everest, which was described in Sir Hillary's own words as "knock the bastard off." During the climb, do you think that Hillary would have been satisfied if Sherpa Tenzing had just "managed" the expedition? The answer is quite obvious. The climb was successful because Sherpa Tenzing carried the load and "led" the way through the treacherous terrain so both Hillary and Tenzing could reach the pinnacle of Mount Everest safely.

A project, by definition, is a "temporary" endeavor undertaken to create a "unique" product, service, or result.[1] Thus, every project is like an expedition through the unknown terrain to reach the summit of success. When something "unique" is being created, how can we expect to manage it? Are we not required to lead the "unique" transformation effort? Today, most project managers fail because there is too much "management" and too little "leadership" during the journey.

Only project managers who undergo a paradigm shift and transform themselves into project leaders by providing guidance and direction to their team can be truly successful in their expeditions every time. Attempting to manage a project is like trying to hang on to the tail of a wild tiger as illustrated in Figure 1.1. The focus is always on countering the tiger's every move to avoid the fatal jaws. Thus, a project manager is constantly in a reactive mode and there is no time for creativity. On the other hand, leading a project is like riding a tame tiger. Although there is a healthy level of anxiety and adventure, the focus is on guiding it in the right direction as illustrated in Figure 1.2. Thus, a project leader is always proactive.

"Project management" is a misnomer.
"Project leadership" is the right choice.

Figure 1.1 Project management: hanging on the tail of a wild tiger.

Figure 1.2   Project leadership: riding a tame tiger.

1.2 Project Leader versus Project Manager

Now, let us see the difference between a project leader and a project manager (Table 1.1). Please note that the term "project manager" or "manager" or "project leader" or "leader" do not refer to the title but to the skill-set and more importantly, the mind-set of the individual. Project leader should have variety of skills to achieve superior project results. The skill level of project leader is more advanced compared with that of a project manager. In many organizations, the role of the project leader and the competencies necessary to perform the role have not been defined correctly. Although project managers are sufficient to manage a complex, mission-critical projects, it is increasingly clear that project managers must possess an extensive array of leadership skills to contribute significantly to a project. It is widely believed that effective use of leadership skills leads to successful projects and to increased professionalism in the organization. Table 1.2 lists the differences between items leaders focus on versus items that managers focus on.[2] Using Six Sigma (Six Sigma refers to the statistical, data-driven approach to strive for near-perfect quality, usually 3.4 or less defects in a million in any process—from manufacturing to transactional and from product to service[3]) terminology, we can define project manager, project leader, and advanced project leader as follows:

Please note that the term "project manager" or "manager" or "project leader" or "leader" do not refer to the title but to the skill-set and more importantly, the mind-set of the individual.

> Project manager is similar to a "green belt" level.
> Project leader is similar to a "black belt" level.
> Advanced project leader is similar to a "master black belt" level.

Project leaders are more matured project managers who possess five magic powers. These five powers are described in the next section.

Table 1.1 Differences between a Project Leader and a Project Manager

Project Leader	Project Manager
• Leads and motivates the team • Leads project activities • Makes decisions regarding cost and schedule	• Manages project resources • Manages project activities • Manages cost and schedule
• Develops project team • Influences stakeholders • Influences project management team	• Retains project team • Manages stakeholders • Manages project management team
• Mostly develops own style of working	• Mostly follows other's style of working
• Always proactive and have adequate time and energy to focus on core vision	• Constantly in a reactive mode and focuses time and energy on tactical aspects of project objectives
• Focuses on people, relationships, their skills, and project culture	• Focuses on detailed project planning, execution, and monitoring

Table 1.2 Differences between Items Leaders and Managers Focus on

Leaders Focus on	Managers Focus on
• Vision	• Goals and objectives
• Selling what and why	• Telling how and when
• Longer range	• Shorter range
• People	• Organization and structure
• Democracy	• Autocracy
• Enabling	• Restraining
• Developing	• Maintaining
• Challenging	• Conforming
• Originating	• Imitating
• Innovating	• Administrating
• Inspiring trust	• Directing and controlling
• Policy	• Procedures
• Flexibility	• Consistency
• Risk opportunity	• Risk avoidance
• Top line	• Bottom line

Source: Verma, V. K., and Wideman, R. M. (2002). *Project Manager to Project Leader? And the Rocky Road Between …* , Revision 3, p. 3. With permission. This material is offered to individual readers who may use it freely in connection with their project work. It may not be used by commercial or noncommercial organizations without permission. http://www.maxwideman.com.

1.3 Five Powers of Project Leaders

Advanced project leaders possess five special or magical powers, which set them apart from project managers:

1. Power of delegation
2. Power of dynamic leadership
3. Power of visualization
4. Power of lean thinking
5. Power of humility

Figure 1.3 illustrates the five powers of a project leader. Let us see how these five powers transform a project manager into an effective project leader.

1.3.1 *Power of Delegation*

1.3.1.1 *Definition*

Delegation means abdicating of the decision-making authority on the project to the team but retaining the final responsibility for the success or the failure of the project by the leader.

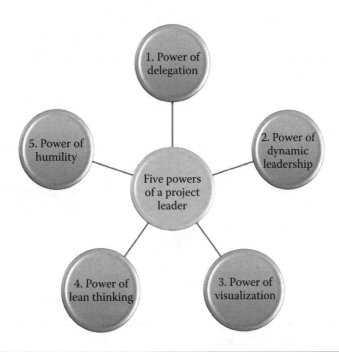

Figure 1.3 Five powers of a project leader.

1.3.1.2 Explanation

A project manager counts on "control," whereas a project leader depends on "trust." In President Theodore Roosevelt's (1858–1919) words,

"The best executive is one who has sense to pick good people to do what he wants done, and self-restraint enough from meddling with them while they do it"[4]

Because project managers depend on "control" to be successful, "letting go" and "delegating the project control" to the team members are the most difficult aspect for most project managers (it surely was for me, too). To most project managers, this is like putting their life and career in the hands of the team or experts and scares "the living hell" out of them.

A project leader needs to have dynamic and customized leadership and motivational style. Their style must be tailored to each of the individuals on their diverse team in order for them to give their very best effort for the project success. This is similar to the concept of situational leadership,[5] wherein the leaders use progressive styles from directing, coaching, supporting, and delegating for their personnel who range from low maturity to high maturity. Although the leaders can direct, coach, or support, they can develop team members even in these roles. Thus, as seen in Figure 1.4, the predominant style of leaders is delegation. A valid question you may ask is, "So what is the use of a project leader if all they do is delegate?" This is a fair question. The answer to the question is that "delegation is not easy." The leaders need to know when, how, and whom to delegate to. They use delegation not as a way to off-load their work but primarily as a way to develop other leaders. Leaders have enough confidence in their own abilities that have learned the fine art of firing themselves from their current position. They look at this as a growth strategy so that they can challenge their skills on bigger and more complex projects with a higher impact on the success of their organization than the last one they completed.

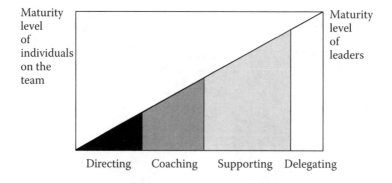

Figure 1.4   Maturity model of leaders.

Thus, successful project leaders know how to lead by example and to skill-fully lay down the "tracks" in the right direction. When they are sure that "the train" is moving along fine on the "right track," they then are willing to "hand over the controls" and "get out of the way." When they muster enough courage, learn this skill of "letting go of the controls," and trust their team enough to take over the controls, they undergo a transformation from a "project manager" to a successful "project leader" and progress from "green belt" and are eligible for "black belt" level education. In a project, there are number of tasks a project leader can delegate while planning for a project, executing the project, and controlling the project. Figure 1.5 shows some examples of task delegation in projects.

1.3.1.3 Performing Effective Delegation

Effective delegation allows a project leader to influence more important aspects of a project rather than just simple tasks. Many project managers try to micro-manage every aspect of a project. This results not only in over burdening the project manager but also in suppression of creative ideas and solutions from the team members. An effective project leader directs the team and influences the team members to reach their goals. Effective delegation is a technique used by project leaders not only to effectively manage their time on a project but also to develop and augment confidence and leadership skills among their team members. Effective delegation encompasses following activities:

- Selecting the best people for the delegation of tasks. Delegating right tasks to right people based on their skills, abilities, and performance.
- Getting buy-in from the team resources on the tasks to delegate.
- Providing adequate time to perform the activities. This is necessary for successful execution of tasks. Team members usually try to perform the tasks in their own way when delegated.
- Encouraging and accommodating team members. This process builds confidence in the team members and builds trust in the project leader.
- Checking the results and providing guidance to perform the tasks and not forcing a particular style of leadership on the team members.
- Rewarding the team members after successful execution of tasks. Building team member's self-confidence by rewarding is a real key for effective delegation.

Leadership and delegation should be balanced in a project. Excessive delegation leads to failure of projects because of lack of control, whereas excessive leadership leads to micromanagement. Figure 1.6 shows some differences between leading and delegating.

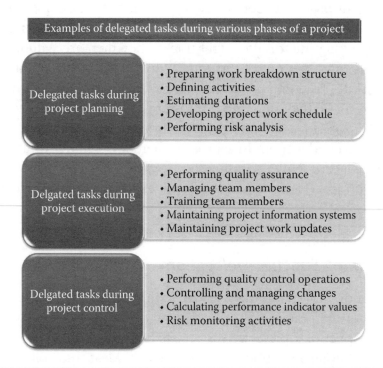

Figure 1.5   Examples of delegated tasks during various phases of a project.

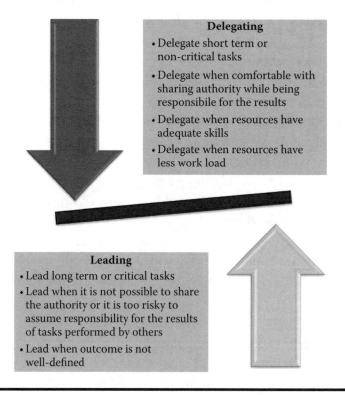

Figure 1.6   Differences between delegating and leading.

1.3.2 Power of Dynamic Leadership

1.3.2.1 Definition

Dynamic leadership is defined as adapting the leadership styles on the basis of the situations, places, and people.

1.3.2.2 Explanation

Upon further maturity, the project leaders acquire the power of "dynamic leadership," which gives them an ability to adjust their style on the basis of the following:

a. The situation at hand
b. The type and the quality of resources being led
c. The project life cycle phase

Project leaders need to know how to lead all levels and types of resources within the organization and beyond (consultants, contractors, etc.). Dynamic leadership also focuses on the leadership effort based on the phases of a project. There are typically five phases of a project life cycle depending on types and complexity of projects and most of these phases overlap. The *Guide to the Project management Body of Knowledge (PMBOK)*, Fourth Edition, discusses how the project phases interact with the five process groups, namely, initiating, planning, executing, monitoring, and controlling and closing. Figure 1.7 shows the phases of a project life cycle.[1]

The five phases can be defined as follows:

1. Start-up (initiating)
2. Preparation (planning)
3. Implementation (execution)
4. Check and update (monitoring and control)
5. Closure (closing)

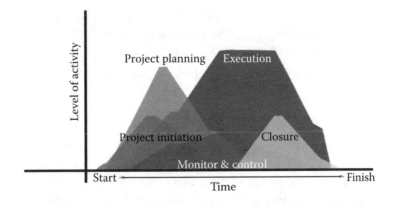

Figure 1.7 Phases of a project life cycle. (Adapted from Project Management Institute, *The Guide to the Project Management Body of Knowledge (PMBOK Guide),* **4th edn., p. 41, 2010.)**

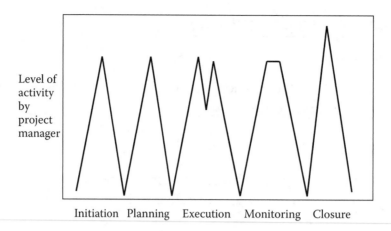

Level of activity by project manager

Initiation Planning Execution Monitoring Closure

Figure 1.8 Project manager effort curve.

As explained, the major issue with project management is the reactive or constant fire-fighting mode of operations throughout the project life cycle. The effort expended by a project manager is illustrated in Figure 1.8, which is called the *project manager effort curve*. This sawtooth activity graph is typical when the project manager is attempting to manage or control every aspect of the project like holding on to the tail of a tiger. Great project leaders use delegation in combination with dynamic leadership because that is the key strategy to allow them to have a smoother level of activity and also allow them to be the stewards of the project by safely and proactively guiding the project to a successful close.

1.3.2.3 Dynamic Leadership Model

The project leader must "lead" from the front lines, providing vision and direction to the project, when needed. At other times, the project leader must become a "servant leader." His task then changes to monitoring the progress of the project against the schedule and help make any required adjustments. Also, he assumes the role of a "lookout person" who is proactively looking ahead for any potential issues and removing obstacles from the path of the team. The project leader must also be an avid "learner" and learn from each success and every failure. Thus, there are three key styles in dynamic leadership model.

1. Leader
2. Servant leader/facilitator
3. Learner

When project managers transform into leaders, the effort expended during projects is significantly more stable with fundamentally less variation in level of effort and looks a double bathtub rather than a sawtooth. It is called the *project leader effort curve* and is shown in Figure 1.9.

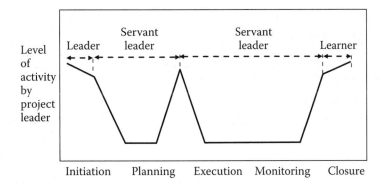

Figure 1.9   Project leader effort curve.

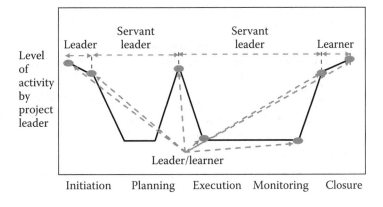

Figure 1.10   Complete project leader effort curve.

It is also important to understand that at the beginning of each phase, it is necessary to create detailed specifications that "chart the course" for the team. Once the experts are in place and the team is trained and ready to take charge during each phase, true leaders take on a role of managing the expectations of their team and eliminating potential roadblocks from each phase and ensure successful completion of the phases and the project. Similarly, at the end of each phase, it is critical to conduct detailed "tollgate" reviews that determine if all requirements are completed and signed off. Also, the ends of the phases are great opportunities to learn lessons, which may help during the remainder of the same project or on future projects. Thus, it is also critical that the project leader "lead from the front," during the beginning and end of each project phase and also "learn" during the tollgate reviews of each and every phase, as shown in Figure 1.10.

Project leadership role changes on the basis of the project phases. Table 1.3 shows a project leader's "leadership role" during each project phase. This will vary on the basis of the types of projects and experience of team leader and the team members. In short, project leaders with expertise in dynamic leadership wear the appropriate caps of "leader, servant leader, and facilitator and learner" as needed on the journey to ensure that the project reaches the final goal safely and on schedule. If they gain expertise in dynamic leadership style, they then

Table 1.3 Project Leader's "Leadership Role" during Each Project Phase

Phase	Leadership Role (Beginning of Phase)	Leadership Role (End of Phase)
Project start-up	• Conduct project feasibility study • Lead the effort to create a project charter, if the project is feasible	• Complete project charter and get it approved • Complete the effort to identify stakeholders for the project • Define the initial resource requirements and estimate a project budget
Project preparation	• Lead the effort to develop project management plans • Lead the process to collect requirements and develop the work breakdown structure • Work with experts to develop a project schedule, estimate project costs, create a quality management plan, and a communications strategy • Lead the effort to identify, collect, and communicate key project metrics • Lead the effort to select/hire resources • Lead the team to identify risks, complete risk analysis, and develop risk mitigation strategies • Lead the team to define vendor requirements	• Get a sign-off on project plan from the stakeholders • Get a sign-off on the risk mitigation plan from the stakeholders • Review project schedule and get stakeholders' approval • Complete tollgate review and lead the project team into the execution phase
Project implementation	• Lead all critical efforts related to successful execution of the project • Lead key project meetings and all communication efforts • Lead quality assurance activities and procurement efforts • Lead the team efficiently and help resolve conflicts • Lead the team to implement proactive strategies to avoid out-of-control situations, which may adversely impact success of the project when timeline, cost, quality, or other key metrics of the project are at risk of not meeting charter specifications • Provide training and guidance to team members	• Ensure that the project is meeting all charter specifications, including the criteria for budget, schedule, and quality • Ensure project is meeting all charter specifications and criteria • Complete tollgate review • Document all lessons learned during the phase

Project monitoring	• Lead vertical reporting effort • Lead when timeline, cost, quality or other key metrics of the project are not meeting specification in project management plans • Lead the change control activities and communicate any important changes to the stakeholders	• Ensure high-priority risks are mitigated • Ensure all stakeholders are aware of the project performance at the end of this phase • Ensure that all vendor issues are resolved • Complete the tollgate review • Document all lessons learned
Project closure	• Ensure that the project has met all the required project specifications • Ensure all obligations toward stakeholders and vendors are met • Lead the effort to document the completed project	• Update the risk analysis documents • Officially closeout all contracts • Hold lessons learned meetings and document all lessons learned during the project • Hold celebrations and appreciate all the team members, sponsors, stakeholders, vendors, and consultants for their efforts • Officially closeout the project

move up from "black belt" and are eligible for a "master black belt" level education, which includes learning about the power of visualization, the power of lean thinking, and the power of humility.

1.3.2.4 Qualities of a Dynamic Leader[6]

The following comprises of only few of many qualities that a dynamic leader should possess.

- Dynamic leaders refine their own leadership style and share it with other team members.
- Dynamic leaders know when to lead, when to manage, and when to stand down.
- Dynamic leaders possess vision and foresee problems. They convert challenges into opportunities for growth.

- Dynamic leaders influence others and take wise decisions on the basis of situation, people, and place.
- Dynamic leaders measure the effectiveness of their own leadership by their ability to empower others in any situation.
- Dynamic leaders empower others by engaging the innate hidden potential in them, more than by mere instruction.

1.3.2.5 Other Leadership Models

In analyzing the root causes of failed projects, it is learned that leadership plays an important role in leading the project in right direction. Project leaders can add value to organization by using their skills, talents, and styles. The roles of project leaders in a project vary from project to project. There are a variety of roles that a leader can play in an organization. There are traditional roles, situational roles, and shared roles.

Learning organizations require a new view of leadership. The traditional view of how leaders energize their troops is derived from a deeply individualistic and nonsystemic worldview. Traditional view of leadership "is based on assumptions of people's powerlessness, their lack of personal vision and inability to master the forces of change, deficits which can be remedied only by a few great leaders." Against this traditional view, there is a "new" view of leadership that centers on "subtler and more important tasks." In a learning organization, leaders are designers, stewards, and teachers. They are responsible for building organizations where people continually expand their capabilities to understand complexity, clarify vision, and improve shared mental models.[7]

According to shared model, leadership can be explored as a social process—something that happens between people. It is not so much what leaders do, as something that arises out of social relationships. As such, it does not depend on one person but on how people act together to make sense of the situations that face them. Table 1.4 explains the difference between classic leadership and shared leadership.[7] Situational leadership is another form of leadership model in which the leader takes decisions on the basis of situation in the organization or a project. In this model, the leader does not follow a single style of leadership. The leadership style depends on the team, tasks, and situations in which the leader is engaged in. Situational leadership theory[5] is proposed by Paul Hersey and Ken Blanchard, and this theory categorizes leadership styles into four behavioral types. Figure 1.11 explains these four models of leadership.

1. Directing (telling style)
2. Coaching (selling style)
3. Supporting (participative style)
4. Delegating (delegating style)

Table 1.4 Comparison between Classic Leadership and Shared Leadership

Classic Leadership	Shared Leadership
• Displayed by the leader's position in a group or hierarchy	• Identified by the quality of leader's interactions rather than their position
• Leadership is evaluated by whether the leader solves problems	• Leadership is evaluated by how people are working together
• Leaders provide solutions and answers	• Leaders work to enhance the process and to make it more fulfilling
• Distinct differences between leaders and followers: character, skill, etc.	• The leader and team members are interdependent and are active participants engaged in the process of leadership
• Communication is often passive and formal	• Communication is active and a mix of formal and social. Values democratic processes, honesty, and shared ethics
• Can often rely on secrecy, deception, and payoffs	

Source: Doyle, M. E., and Smith, M. K., Shared leadership, *Encyclopedia of Informal Education*, 2001. http://www.infed.org/leadership /shared_leadership.htm.

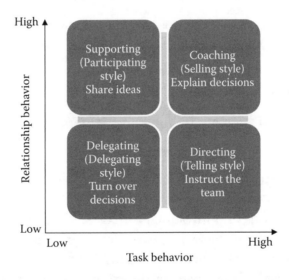

Figure 1.11 Situational leadership model. (Adapted from Hersey P. and Blanchard, K. H., *Management and Organizational Behavior*, Prentice-Hall, Englewood Clifts, NJ, 1988.)

1.3.2.6 Example of Dynamic Leadership

An example of using dynamic leadership was in a particular 1-week Kaizen[3] project (*Kaizen* is a Japanese word, which means Good (*Zen*) Change (*Kai*) and is a time-sensitive, focused event by some team members to complete a task swiftly and efficiently), in which my team consisted of the president of the company, his daughter (an employee), the vice president of the company, the plant manager, the supervisors, the facilities personnel, and several shop floor employees.

Every individual on the team not only had a different status but also had very different personalities, very different agendas, and obviously needed different styles of motivation. The vice president of the organization and the daughter of the president did not see eye to eye on this team, and I had to use significant tact to ensure both were equally motivated. There were some other issues too— throughout the week; I was dealing with difficult team dynamics, several confrontations between team members, and difficult personalities. However, once I was aware of these differences, I created adequate buffers between the identified team members, keeping the personnel-related distractions to a minimum and infused each individual with a sense of purpose for a common goal in a language that excited them so that they stay focused on their assigned tasks and did not impact the project. The team was able to completely relayout a significantly large assembly area and get increased efficiency within a week. Dynamic leadership was a key to the success of this project.

1.3.3 Power of Visualization

1.3.3.1 Definition

Visualization is the process of consciously previewing, understanding, and analyzing the data, images, and scenarios.

1.3.3.2 Explanation

Walt Disney (1901–1966), a great visionary and leader, once said,

"If you can dream it, you can do it!"[8]

Walt Disney is a fantastic example of one man with a great dream who influenced the entire planet. What did Walt Disney mean by a dream? By definition, a dream is a series of subconscious and involuntary images, ideas, and emotions present in our minds during various stages of sleep. However, what Disney is referring to is not an "unconscious and involuntary dream" but "conscious and voluntary vision" or "visualization" of your path or direction. Execution of the vision is also critical. Walt Disney not only knew how to dream but also knew how to execute. Several decades after Walt Disney's passing, Michael Eisner was the CEO of Disney, and the animation business, the cornerstone of Walt's vision, was in complete doldrums. Jeffrey Katzenberg, the current CEO of DreamWorks Animation and cofounder of Dream Works Studios, served as the chairman for board at Walt Disney (1984–1994). On his first day, Jeffrey was invited to Michael Eisner's office and asked to take care of the "problem" of animation. Jeffery turned the animation business around in a few years. When asked by Charlie Rose (May 17, 2010) how he was able to achieve the turnaround, he modestly answered, "Walt, the genius had left the road map detailing all the processes for making a successful animation film. All it needed was for someone to read it and implement his vision."[9]

1.3.3.3 Who Uses Visualization?

The U.S. military uses visualization extensively in the training protocol for command and control, intelligence, logistics, and information operations. Capt. Sully Sullen Berger when piloting U.S. Airways Flight 1549 encountered the sudden and catastrophic failure of both the engines during takeoff. Sully, a former Air Force pilot, may not have visualized the exact scenario of that day, but because of his Air Force training in visualization and resulting control over his emotional state, he was able to make an almost impossible landing in the Hudson River and saved 159 lives.

James Cameron's movie *Avatar* takes the audience on one of the most amazing 3-D visual and emotional journeys of our time. Cameron has taken the "Mickey and Minnie" concepts of Disney's animation characters to a whole new level with his 3-D CGI technology. But what both Walt Disney and James Cameron have in common are that they are great at visualization—how else could they create the fantasylands that have captured the hearts and minds of billions around the globe? *Unless they dreamt it first, they could not have done it!*

1.3.3.4 Why Is the Power of Visualization a Secret Power of Great Leaders?

Having the "power to visualize" is an innate strength for some visionaries like Walt Disney but is not necessarily an attribute that everyone possesses. This power is, however, the secret weapon of almost all great leaders—even if they are not aware that they possess it. Why is this power a secret weapon for leaders? The answer is simple—because leaders set the direction and path for the rest of the organization. "Mapping out" or "visualizing" the path and direction before embarking on a journey greatly increases your chances of getting there successfully.

1.3.3.5 Why Is the Power of Visualization Valuable for Project Leaders?

This is also an extremely valuable power to have for a project leader. Can project managers be trained to develop this amazing power? Yes. If the project managers train their minds to visualize, they surely can possess and master this secret weapon. It is all about learning the techniques and then practice, practice, and more practice until they learn how to visualize effectively, virtually "walking through" their projects and leading the team through the peaks and valleys of a project life cycle. Visualization also enables them to focus on value-added tasks and eliminate the non-value-added wastes. This is the key requirement of lean technology.

1.3.3.6 The Science of Visualization

The science behind the power of visualization clearly shows how and why visualization works to transform our visualized path into a reality. At the base of our brain exists what is called the "reticular activation system" (RAS). This small, thick cluster of neurons nestled within the brain stem controls the level of consciousness and other vital functions of the body. The RAS can be programmed to set goals and objectives similar to the way we program our computers. The only difference is that the programming language for RAS is not a software language. It can only be programmed using visual images. In fact, RAS cannot comprehend words at all. Thus, visualization is the only way to program our internal super computer. Visualization is the key to reach your goals faster with greater certainty.

1.3.3.7 Can We Teach Project Managers to Visualize?

The answer is "absolutely, positively, yes!" All it takes is a lit bit of guidance and a lot of practice. My company, Pinnacle Process Solutions, Intl., has developed a step-by-step process to help individuals understand themselves, develop focus and concentration necessary for visualization, trigger the right brain activity to "walk-through" projects, and translate the visuals into an actionable plan. It uses advanced technology and has been designed to transform individuals to master the art, science, and practice of visualization within a few days.

1.3.3.8 The Power of Visualization

Visualization is a power that all project leaders need to develop as professionals and leaders to achieve profession goals. We need to teach this technique to our coming generations.

Great project leaders or "master black belt" project leaders have a special ability to visualize every step of the project, including its failures and successes in their minds. They acquire this power through developing a combination of experiences, trusting their intuition and by significantly raising level of awareness. All they need to do is share this vision with all stakeholders and motivate them and proactively remove obstacles from their path during each phase of the project. Project leaders use their power of visualization to take their projects to ultimate success every time, no matter the type of projects, scope, or environment. This is their formula for success. The power of visualization of a leader and the success of a project are directly related, as shown in Figure 1.12. Project leader is responsible for achieving project objectives. The ability of a project leader to lead and guide various activities in a project decides the success of a project. There are different ways a project leader can visualize the success of a project in the early stages of a project depending on project parameters. Figure 1.13 lists the parameters that a project manager can visualize during initiating, planning, execution, monitoring, controlling, and even during the closeout phase of a project. These parameters will vary from project to project.

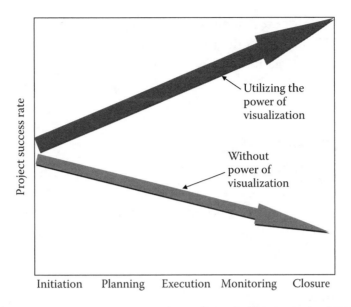

Figure 1.12   Power of visualization and success during project phases.

Figure 1.13   Example of visualization parameters for project success.

1.3.3.9 Impact of Using the Power of Visualization

Power of visualization has a significant positive impact on the project. It is through the power of visualization organizational leadership teams react to and plan for change in the goals and targets of an organization. Project leaders should identify all parameters for failure of the project and visualize the changing pattern for each parameter. Risk is an uncertain event that occurs in a project. A project leader should visualize the risk in advance and plan for it to prevent its impact on the project. In addition to risk, budget, schedule, resources, and quality are important parameters that have huge impact on the success of a project. The Standish

Group's 2009 CHAOS report reiterates the importance of power of visualization of a project leader. This report identifies that 44% of the projects were challenged, which are late, overbudget, and/or with less than the required features and functions, and 24% failed, which are cancelled before completion or delivered and never used.[10]

1.3.4 Power of Lean Thinking

1.3.4.1 Definition

Lean is a tool, which allows us to identify value-added tasks and eliminate the non-value-added elements. Value is always defined from the view-point of the customer.

1.3.4.2 Explanation

Value-added tasks have three basic characteristics:

1. The customer is willing to pay for the tasks.
2. There is a physical transformation of the product or service.
3. The tasks are performed right the first time (there is no rework).

The power of "lean thinking" requires the project leader to stand in the shoes of the customer, examine each and every task performed during the project from the customer's viewpoint, and have a mind-set of using the minimal time, money, and resources required to complete the tasks with optimal quality.

Thus, power of "lean thinking" will transform the project leaders into customer-centric, well-organized, efficient ambassadors of the customer. They will be able to provide what the customer needs, when the customer needs, and how the customer needs every time, thus learning the art of truly "delighting" the customers. Lean thinking truly shaped various industries into profitable organizations. Lean thinking tries to understand what is needed to enhance the quality of the product and what tasks and the resources add only value to the product. Any non-value-added tasks or resources are eliminated. Power of lean thinking is essential in a project's execution. If project managers develop power of lean thinking, it helps transform them into project leaders.

1.3.4.3 Principles of Lean Thinking

Lean thinking concentrates on the quality of the product and customer satisfaction.

Five lean principles are listed below.[11]

1. Specify what creates a *value* from the customer's perspective.
2. Identify all steps across the whole *value stream.*
3. Take actions that create *value flow.*
4. Only make what is *pulled* by the customer just in time.
5. Strive for *perfection* by continually removing successive layers of waste.

Here are some examples of how the principles of lean thinking can be applied to any project.

- Many project leaders tend to include stakeholders who may not contribute to the project. This does not add any value from the customer's perspective and in fact wastes productive time for stakeholder and for the project leader.
- During requirement collection phase, gathering unwarranted requirements for the project not only increases the schedule time but also reduces the availability of resources during execution of project.
- During execution of projects, if project leaders do not use the power of lean thinking, they tend to focus more on tasks rather than on developing the people. Hence, unqualified individuals are assigned to critical tasks, ultimately leading to the failure of the project.
- Reaching quality targets is also an important element of lean thinking. To reach the quality objectives set in a project, project leaders must focus on quality planning, quality assurance, and quality control processes.

Meeting quality requirements has three aspects such as satisfying the customer, preventing the defects instead of inspecting the failures, and continuous improvement. All of the above principles lay the foundation for a project leader to develop the power of lean thinking.

1.3.4.4 Example of Using Lean Thinking

How a project leader can use lean thinking in the implementation of a project is described in Figure 1.14.

1.3.5 Power of Humility

1.3.5.1 Definition

Power of humility focuses on unknown things in a project. A leader who can openly acknowledge that he or she does not know everything and one who sincerely respects the knowledge and experience of others is considered to possess the "power of humility."

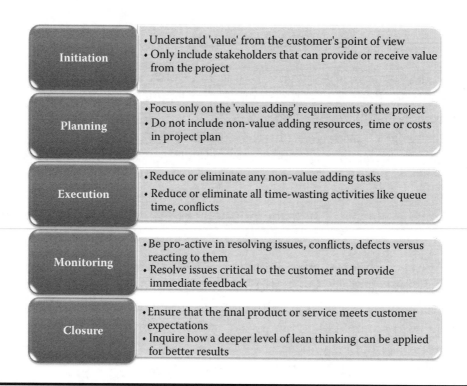

Figure 1.14   Examples of lean activities in various project phases.

1.3.5.2 Explanation

> *To be humble to superiors is duty, to equals courtesy, to inferiors nobleness*

(Benjamin Franklin, 1999–2010; Think Exists).[12]
The dilemma is as one climbs up the ladder of project leadership, it is very common to develop an ego, which actually destroys this power. The other dilemma is that you can only pursue this power but never attain it. As soon as you claim you are humble, you have just proven otherwise. Thus, to attempt to harness this power, the project leaders must remind themselves constantly that they are not an expert in any area of the project and that their primary role is to facilitate for others to provide their expertise openly to the project. To check if one truly is eligible to be on the path to the "power of humility," the project leader must be able to answer the following questions honestly:

1. If one of the team members has a better solution than I do for a problem, will I acknowledge it and provide support to implement their solution?
2. If I make a mistake in decision making, do I apologize to the team or do I make excuses for the failure?
3. Do I show respect not only to the superiors but also to each and every member on my team?

These three fundamental questions, if answered in affirmative, can help you understand if you are truly on the path to possessing this essential "power of humility." An open mind, which curiously seeks opportunities to learn new concepts and innovative ways, is the foundation of a humble behavior.

1.3.5.3 Situations Involving Power of Humility

1.3.5.3.1 Conflict Management

Conflicts are inevitable in an organization or in a project environment. Conflicts can arise because of individual work styles, lack of communication, and improper role definition. It is the responsibility of a project manager to resolve the conflict and control the team. Conflict resolution increases productivity and improves team relationships. Project leader should not shy away from a conflict. Sometimes, conflict management involves situations where project leader should listen to resources without any ego. The project leader should understand the situations causing conflicts from both resources involved in conflict.

1.3.5.3.2 Influencing the Team

Power of humility is very much useful in influencing the team or management. A project leader should listen to the team and gather relevant information. The project leader must not allow ego to prevent them from learning new concepts or new methods to enhance the working relationships of the team.

1.3.5.3.3 Decision Making

During decision making, project leaders need to focus on the goals of the project. They must study team environment, understand the consequences of their decision, and study various alternatives before making the decision. These tasks require power of humility for project leader as it is critical to understand the opinions of their team members before making decisions.

1.3.5.3.4 Team Meetings

During team meetings, project leaders need to take responsibility for any wrong decisions they make during project execution. Project leaders should not hesitate to take complete responsibility for the damage their decisions has caused. In case of successes, they should appreciate the team instead of taking the credit to themselves. The power of humiliation plays key role in both successes and failures of a project. Figure 1.15 lists the qualities of a project leader with power of humility.

1.3.5.3.5 Sharing the Glory

The practical application of the "power of humility" was evident when Sir Edmund Hillary and Sherpa Tenzing Norgay were involved in the international politics of "who reached the summit of Mount Everest first?" On April 25, 2003, in an interview with Charlie Rose, Peter Hillary, the son of Sir Edmund Hillary,

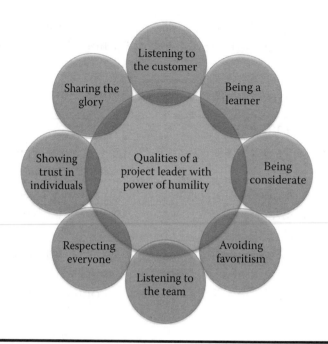

Figure 1.15   Qualities of a project leader with power of humility.

Figure 1.16   An artistic illustration of Sir Edmund Hillary and Sherpa Tenzing Norgay on the way to the summit of Mount Everest.

and Jamling Tenzing Norgay, the son of Tenzing Norgay, told Charlie in no uncertain terms that both their fathers were quite adamant in their claim that "we were tied together by a rope and we both reached the summit together." They also stressed that their fathers always gave importance to teamwork and said that the entire crew should equally share in the glory of the success of the expedition to the summit of Mount Everest.[13] Figure 1.16 shows an artistic illustration of Sir Edmund Hillary and Sherpa Tenzing Norgay on the way to the summit of Mount

Everest and the joint celebration on being the first mountain climbers to reach the highest peak on the earth on May 29, 1953.

Thus, Sir Edmund Hillary and Sherpa Tenzing left a great legacy for all project leaders to follow. As shown by them, it is not enough to be just successful in challenging undertakings, it is also critical to be humble about our achievements and share the glory with the entire team.

Pillar I Summary

Today, most project managers fail because there is too much "management" and too little "leadership" during the project life cycle. Only project managers who undergo a paradigm shift and transform themselves into project leaders by providing guidance and direction to their team can be truly successful in their projects every time.

Project leadership is the key to success. It is critical for successful project leaders to develop and use the following five powers in order for the project to have short-term and long-term successes:

1. Power of delegation
2. Power of dynamic leadership
3. Power of visualization
4. Power of lean thinking
5. Power of humility

It is vital for organizations to identify and develop exceptional project leaders from among the project managers and team leaders. These five powers reinforce the importance of project leaders to lead and succeed in an organization. Figure 1.17 lists the important points in each of the five powers.

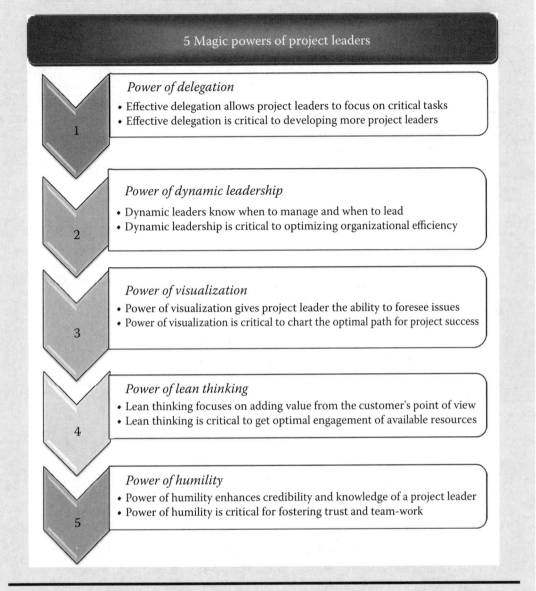

Figure 1.17 **Summary of five magic powers of project leaders.**

Pillar I Case Study

Be a Project Leader

INTRODUCTION

This case study is about implementation of specialized version of flow manufacturing in four business units.

CHALLENGE

In January 2000, while working with a company in North America, I was handpicked and almost forced by our vice presidents to forego my dream of being on our corporate acquisition team and lead one of the most adventurous and critical transformation projects in the history of my division. We were manufacturing high-quality surgical instruments but at a rate much slower than our customer needed them. Our division was growing so rapidly that our workforce had to work entire weekends for almost 6 months. Thus, we decided to implement a specialized version of flow manufacturing in four business units in 8 months to keep up with the demand. The project also included selection of a consulting firm, selection of the flow software, and implementation of a kanban system and hands-on training of all personnel.

SITUATION

My learning curve on this technology was quite steep. I knew I had to be on the "bleeding edge" as this was a new undertaking for the entire organization with no internal expertise. I formed a steering committee made up of executives and all business unit managers and managers from supporting departments, like IT, facilities, and so forth. My first order of business was to interview each stakeholder individually and have them share their greatest fear about this undertaking. For example, I interviewed the director of human resources, and he mentioned that his fear was that our culture of "recognition of individuals" would be adversely impacted because of the team approach of this technology. Thus, I included "preservation of corporate culture" a part of our mission statement. The director of sales does not want our sales team to even know we are making this significant change in operations. He told me to make sure that this transformation is transparent to our salespeople and to our customers. That too became the part of our mission statement.

SOLUTION

"The journey of a thousand miles, starts with one step," is a translation of one of the most famous quotes from *Tao Te Ching*, the wisest book ever written, according to some scholars. My version of this quote is, "Every macro problem can be solved, if approached from a micro level." At the start, this project truly seemed like hanging on to the tail of the tiger or like having a mammoth elephant on our plate. I advised my team to "tame the tiger" or to "eat the elephant one bite at a time." Thus, during the project with the first business unit, my leadership style was to be a microleader. I was involved in every little detail although we had external consultants. I personally interviewed all software firms and consulting firms and made recommendation to the steering committee and also selected project teams. We had to change more than 500 assembly documents to a different format and get authorization within less than a month. I hired a team of interns to work on this around the clock.

Implementation

When the time came to convert the business unit to flow manufacturing, it almost felt as though we were giving that business a heart transplant over the weekend. Every piece of furniture was moved out of a space of roughly 10,000 sq. ft. on Saturday morning with our president on the shop floor with his fingers crossed. By 6:00 a.m. Monday morning, one could not recognize the business unit at all—it was completely transformed and just perfect. The software had been implemented too and was live. I was as anxious and nervous as it was a make-or-break moment in my career as a project leader. But honestly, the heavier load on my shoulder was of impacting the patients in hospitals who depended on our products for their surgeries. A few of us had been at the site for more than 48 hours without sleep or shower—but even a bulldozer could not have moved me from that area until I was absolutely sure we were successful. Although, per Murphy's Law, we did face a major issue in the material kanban system, but nonetheless, on the very first day of production, we increased our productivity by more than 300%. Being a microleader had really paid off.

"Seeing is believing"—actually witnessing the enormous impact our effort had on the business and the employees made our team feel that all their hard work and sacrifice was well worth it. However, in all the celebration, I had to sadly remind the team that we had had four more battles to fight (four more business units to implement this technology in), and we were far from perfect. Once the team had gotten an opportunity to catch their breath, we had to regroup to understand what went right and what we could improve on in future. I had to initiate an autopsy of the first implementation by conducting a detailed and critical "lessons learned" meeting with the entire team including the consultants. The meeting was extremely productive, and we took several steps to overcome the issues we had encountered in the first implementation. We also realized that some of the steps taken by our consulting firm were not adding value. I took special permission from the CEO of the consulting firm to change their procedures and processes for our future implementations.

After 3 months, fast-forwarding to the second business unit, I ensured that all lessons learned were useful in creating systems and procedures to "take our game to the next level." We did have some new lessons learned this time around too, but the good news is that we did not repeat any mistakes from the previous implementation. None of the new lessons learned had any major impact on our project. We had to stay overnight during the weekend before "line live" on Monday, and we were there on all four's moving material and helping in any way we could for the 6:00 a.m. start. We had another great success and again saw some amazing results.

Six months after we started the project, we began the implementations in the third business unit. I could visualize the entire project in my mind—start to finish. I shared that vision with my consultants and team and almost played the role of an internal consultant at this time—letting the newly created "experts" make decisions and improve on the ideas I had previously implemented. This time, the "line live" preparations were complete on Friday evening itself, and the entire team was able to spend the weekend at home resting.

Results

The entire project was a tremendous success and saved the division several million dollars within the first year and also had a significant impact on product quality and employee morale. Although we conducted "open heart surgery" on five of our business units, we did not miss a single minute of production or a single shipment due to this project. However, the highlight was when one of the most respected assembler/team leader at our division said to me

"Adil, I am glad we did this—now I can spend my weekends at home in my pajamas playing with my grandkids."

We also won the *Industry Week's* "Top 10 Manufacturing Plants" award the same year we completed this project.

Lessons Learned

So what is the role of the leader when things are going well? Do we just put out feet on the desk and blow smoke rings from the "cigar of celebration" in the air. Negative. We give back and enhance the technology; we sharpen our saw and hone our skills to allow us lead our teams to the next level. Before I had started this project, I attended a conference in flow manufacturing as a participant and a student. Within next 6 months, I was selected as a speaker at the next flow manufacturing conference where I presented two papers. Shortly, after the conference, I got a letter inviting me to be the chairperson on the next flow manufacturing conference. Thus, within a year, I had gone from being a student of the technology to being invited as a chair at the conference. This was a good indicator of the steepness of my learning curve on this project. Shortly after, I was invited to co-chair another conference with the CEO of our consulting firm and also invited to speak at several conferences hosted by our consulting firm as I had used some innovative techniques for optimizing the implementations. After my presentations, executives of other companies came up to me and thanked me for sharing these with case studies with them—I was just happy I was giving back to the technology, which had helped my organization.

The fourth unit was a clean room implementation and was very unique from material handling point of view. I had to be back in the role of a microleader. Once we were sure that we had a detailed plan for the execution, I stepped back and let the resources I had trained take over completely. I ended up actually completing another implementation in the document control department during this same time period.

Could I have been successful if I had "managed" this project? There was absolutely no chance. If I had not pulled this mammoth by its nose and dragged it every inch of the way over the finish line, others, and I including our sponsors, would have been surely trampled under it. The tombstone on the grave of my project management career would have read, "Here lies the Project Manager (me), he tried his best to 'manage' the project's thunder; but, now, sadly rests six feet under."

Pillar I   Force Field Analysis

PILLAR I: FORCE FIELD ANALYSIS OF ORGANIZATIONAL ASSESSMENT

Table 1.5 shows force field analysis of organizational assessment. The Organizational assessment is conducted to assess if the culture of the organization is in alignment with the principles of Pillar I. Tables 1.6 through 1.8 are used to develop and implement an action plan to increase the impact of the organizational driving forces and decrease the impact of the organizational resisting forces.

PILLAR I: FORCE FIELD ANALYSIS OF SELF-ASSESSMENT

Table 1.9 shows force field analysis of self-assessment. The self-assessment is conducted to assess if your own strengths are in alignment with the principles of Pillar I. Tables 1.10 through 1.12 are used to develop and implement an action plan to increase the impact of the self-driving forces and decrease the impact of the self-resisting forces.

PILLAR I: RECOMMENDATIONS FOR OPTIMAL RESULTS FROM FORCE FIELD ANALYSIS

For optimal results and actual transformation of culture and strengths conducive to the creation of advanced master project leaders, the following three steps are necessary:

1. Both the organizational and self-evaluation assessments must be completed.
2. A well-designed action plan must be created and implemented to increase the driving forces and decrease the resisting forces.
3. The principles of each pillar must be constantly practiced and improved.

It is highly recommended that both the organization assessments and self-assessments be conducted *every year* and the action plan be updated at least every 3 months.

Note: The sum of scores for Organizational Driving Force and Organizational Resisting Force for each point must be less than or equal to TEN.

The sum of scores for Self Driving Force and Self Resisting Force for each point must be less than or equal to TEN.

Table 1.5   Pillar I: Force Field Organizational Analysis

Team Name: _____   Date: _____

Does My Organization Drive or Resist the Culture of Project Leadership?				
0 Never		5 Sometimes		7 Mostly
3 Rarely		OEF + ORF ≤ 10		10 Always
No. Driving Forces	Score Organizational Driving Force (ODF)	Score Organizational Resisting Force (ORF)		Resisting Forces
1 My organizational culture promotes the key leadership principle of "trust."				My organizational culture uses the key management principle of "control."
2 My organizational culture encourages and rewards leaders who "go the extra mile" to get exceptional results.				My organizational culture encourages managers to use blame and retribution as tools to address project failures.
3 My organization has a risk-taking, optimistic attitude.				My organization has a risk-averse, pessimistic attitude.
4 My project sponsors and others have a hands-off approach.				My project sponsors and others micromanage.
5 My organization provides leadership opportunities based on talent and passion.				My organization provides management opportunities based on seniority and rank.
6 The executives and leaders within my organization use delegation as a way to develop talent and grow the confidence.				The executives and managers within my organization do not usually delegate important tasks to others on the team.
7 My organization encourages project leaders to explore techniques that are beyond the boundaries of traditional project management methodology.				Project managers are prevented from deviating from the fixed organizational project management methodology and culture that resists change.

8	My organization culture judges "value and success" from the perspective of satisfaction of the end customer.			My organization culture judges "value and success" from the perspective of profit and loss statements of the project.
9	My organization has a culture of continuous improvement and is always receptive to change.			My organization culture resists change and does not like to make any updates to existing systems.
10	In my organization, the leaders are generally humble and open to new ideas.			In my organization, the leaders display arrogance and prefer "status quo."
	Total ODF Score			*Total ORF Score*

Result	Conclusion	Recommended Action Review and Update Every Quarter (3 months)
ODF >> ORF	My company culture strongly drives the culture of project leadership.	Use Tables 1.6 through 1.8 to set goals and create an action plan to preserve or continuously improve the culture.
ODF > ORF	My company culture drives the culture of project leadership.	Use Tables 1.6 through 1.8 to set goals and create an action plan to increase ODF to create a stronger culture of project leadership.
ORF >> ODF	My company culture strongly resists the culture of project leadership.	Use Tables 1.6 through 1.8 to set goals and create an action plan to increase the ODF and reduce the ORF to create a stronger culture of project leadership.
ORF > ODF	My company culture resists the culture of project leadership.	Use Tables 1.6 through 1.8 to set goals and create an action plan to reduce the ORF to create a stronger culture of project leadership.
ODF = ORF	My company culture does not drive or resist the culture of project leadership.	Use Tables 1.6 through 1.8 to set goals and create an action plan to increase the ODF to create a stronger culture of project leadership.

Table 1.6   Pillar I: Analysis of ODF and ORF Results

Result	Existing Organizational Culture	If Goal Is to Create a Moderately Strong Project Leadership Culture	If Goal Is to Create a Very Strong Project Leadership Culture
ODF			
ODF ≤ 25	No or minimal project leadership	Focus on improving scores in at least 5 DF	Focus on improving scores in at least 7 DF
25 < ODF ≤ 50	Weak project leadership	Focus on improving scores in at least 3 DF	Focus on improving scores in at least 5 DF
50 < ODF ≤ 75	Moderate project leadership	Focus on improving scores in at least 1 DF	Focus on improving scores in at least 3 DF
ODF > 75	Strong project leadership	N/A	Preserve or continuously improve the culture
ORF			
ORF > 75	No or minimal project leadership	Focus on decreasing scores in at least 5 RF	Focus on decreasing scores in at least 7 RF
50 < ORF ≤ 75	Weak project leadership	Focus on decreasing scores in at least 3 RF	Focus on decreasing scores in at least 5 RF
25 < ORF ≤ 50	Moderate project leadership	Focus on decreasing scores in at least 1 RF	Focus on decreasing scores in at least 3 RF
ORF ≤ 25	Strong project leadership	N/A	Preserve or continuously improve the culture

Note: ODF indicates organizational driving forces; ORF indicates organizational resisting forces; DF indicates driving forces; RF indicates resisting forces.

Table 1.7   Pillar I: Action Plan to Increase Organizational Driving Forces (ODF)

Team Name: _____   Date: _____

No.	Driving Force	Current Score	Goal (Target Score) ⬆	Action Plan to Increase DF Score	Complete by (Date)	Assigned to (Department Name or Initials of Person)
1	My organizational culture promotes the key leadership principle of "trust."					
2	My organizational culture encourages and rewards leaders who "go the extra mile" to get exceptional results.					
3	My organization has a risk-taking, optimistic attitude.					
4	My project sponsors and others have a hands-off approach.					
5	My organization provides leadership opportunities based on talent and passion.					
6	The executives and leaders within my organization use delegation as a way to develop talent and grow the confidence.					
7	My organization encourages project leaders to explore techniques that are beyond the boundaries of traditional project management methodology.					
8	My organization culture judges "value and success" from the perspective of satisfaction of the end customer.					
9	My organization has a culture of continuous improvement and is always receptive to change.					
10	In my organization, the leaders are generally humble and open to new ideas.					
	Total ODF					

Table 1.8 Pillar I: Action Plan to Decrease Organization Resisting Forces (ORF)

No.	Resisting Force	Current Score	Goal (Target Score) ⬇	Action Plan to Decrease RF Score	Complete by (Date)	Assigned to (Department Name or Initials of Person)
1	My organizational culture uses the key management principle of "control."					
2	My organizational culture encourages managers to use blame and retribution as tools to address project failures.					
3	My organization has a risk-averse, pessimistic attitude.					
4	My project sponsors and others micromanage.					
5	My organization provides management opportunities based on seniority and rank.					
6	The executives and managers within my organization do not usually delegate important tasks to others on the team.					
7	Project managers are prevented from deviating from the fixed organizational project management methodology and culture that resists change.					
8	My organization culture judges "value and success" from the perspective of profit and loss statements of the project.					
9	My organization culture resists change and does not like to make any updates to existing systems.					
10	In my organization, the leaders display arrogance and prefer "status quo."					
	Total ORF					

Table 1.9   Pillar I: Force Field Self-analysis

Name: _____   Date: _____

	Do My Strengths Drive or Resist the Principles of Project Leadership?				
	0 Never		5 Sometimes	7 Mostly	
	3 Rarely		SDF + SRF ≤ 10	10 Always	
No.	Driving Forces	Score Self–Driving Force (SDF)	Score Self–Resisting Force (SRF)	Resisting Forces	
1	I "lead" the project or my portion of the project rather than "manage" it.			I "manage" the project or my portion of the project rather than "lead" it.	
2	I proactively manage the expectations of my resources and do not interfere with experts and trained personnel.			I am reactive in managing the expectations of my resources and prefer to actively manage all resources.	
3	I lead during the beginning of each project phase and use lessons learned from previous phases for improvement.			I manage the team during the entire project and focus on project completion versus learning form the phases.	
4	I always use team building, training, and skill-enhancing activities for my project teams.			I rarely engage my team in team building, training, or skill-enhancing activities.	
5	I always delegate important tasks to capable members of my project team.			I never delegate important tasks to members of my project team.	
6	I always recognize and reward my team immediately after their achievement.			I reward my team members after the end of the project for their achievement.	
7	I am open to using nontraditional project management techniques.			I do not deviate from the traditional project management methodology.	
8	I equate the project success to the delighting of my end customer.			I believe that project success is based solely on the project profit and loss statement.	
9	I am always receptive to change and continuous enhancement of personal and team member skills.			I am not always open to change and do not like to make any adjustments to existing systems or processes.	
10	I consider myself as a servant leader to my team and proactively remove roadblocks from their path.			I consider myself as the manager in charge of the team and address the issues and roadblocks as they arise.	
	Total SDF score			*Total SRF score*	

Result	Conclusion	Recommended Action *Review and Update Every Quarter (3 months)*
SDF >> SRF	My strengths strongly support the principles of project leadership.	Use Tables 1.10 through 1.12 to set goals and create an action plan to continuously improve the strengths.
SDF > SRF	My strengths support the principles of project leadership.	Use Tables 1.10 through 1.12 to set goals and create an action plan to increase SDF to allow a stronger drive toward the principles of project leadership.
SRF >> SDF	My strengths strongly resist the principles of project leadership.	Use Tables 1.10 through 1.12 to set goals and create an action plan to increase SDF and reduce SRF to allow a stronger drive toward the principles of project leadership.
SRF > SDF	My strengths resist the principles of project leadership.	Use Tables 1.10 through 1.12 to set goals and create an action plan to reduce SRF to allow a stronger drive toward the principles of project leadership.
SDF = SRF	My strengths do not drive or resist the culture of project leadership.	Use Tables 1.10 through 1.12 to set goals and create an action plan to increase the SDF to allow a stronger drive toward the principles of project leadership.

Table 1.10   Pillar I: Analysis of SDF and SRF Results

Result	Existing Strengths	If Goal Is to Create a Moderately Strong Culture Toward the Principles of Project Leadership	If Goal Is to Create a Very Strong Culture Toward the Principles of Project Leadership
SDF			
SDF ≤ 25	No or minimal project leadership	Focus on improving scores in at least 5 DF	Focus on improving scores in at least 7 DF
25 < SDF ≤ 50	Weak project leadership	Focus on improving scores in at least 3 DF	Focus on improving scores in at least 5 DF
50 < SDF ≤ 75	Moderate project leadership	Focus on improving scores in at least 1 DF	Focus on improving scores in at least 3 DF
SDF > 75	Strong project leadership	N/A	Preserve or continuously improve the strengths
SRF			
SRF > 75	No or minimal project leadership	Focus on decreasing scores in at least 5 RF	Focus on decreasing scores in at least 7 RF
50 < SRF ≤ 75	Weak project leadership	Focus on decreasing scores in at least 3 RF	Focus on decreasing scores in at least 5 RF
25 < SRF ≤ 50	Moderate project leadership	Focus on decreasing scores in at least 1 RF	Focus on decreasing scores in at least 3 RF
SRF ≤ 25	Strong project leadership	N/A	Preserve or continuously improve the strengths

Note: SDF, self-driving forces; SRF, self-resisting forces.

Table 1.11   Pillar I: Action Plan to Increase Self-Driving Forces (SDF)

Name: _____   Date: _____

No.	Driving Force	Current Score	Goal (Target Score) ⬆	Action Plan to Increase DF Score	Complete by (Date)	Required Resources
1	I "lead" the project or my portion of the project rather than "manage" it.					
2	I proactively manage the expectations of my resources and do not interfere with experts and trained personnel.					
3	I lead during the beginning of each project phase and use lessons learned from previous phases for improvement.					
4	I always use team building, training, and skill-enhancing activities for my project teams.					
5	I always delegate important tasks to capable members of my project team.					
6	I always recognize and reward my team immediately after their achievement.					
7	I am open to using nontraditional project management techniques.					
8	I equate the project success to delighting my end customer.					
9	I am always receptive to change and continuous enhancement of personal and team member skills.					
10	I consider myself as a servant leader to my team and proactively remove roadblocks from their path					
	Total SDF					

Table 1.12   Pillar I: Action Plan to Decrease Self-Resisting Forces (SRF)

Name: _____   Date: _____

No.	Resisting Force	Current Score	Goal (Target Score) ⬇	Action Plan to Decrease RF Score	Complete by (Date)	Required Resources
1	I "manage" the project or my portion of the project rather than "lead" it.					
2	I am reactive in managing the expectations of my resources and prefer to actively manage all resources.					
3	I manage the team during the entire project and focus on project completion versus learning form the phases.					
4	I rarely engage my team in team building, training, or skill-enhancing activities.					
5	I never delegate important tasks to members of my project team.					
6	I reward my team members after the end of the project for their achievement.					
7	I do not deviate from the traditional project management methodology.					
8	I believe that a project's success is based solely on the project profit and loss statement.					
9	I am not always open to change and do not like to make any adjustments to existing systems or processes.					
10	I consider myself as the manager in charge of the team and address the issues and roadblocks as they arise.					
	Total SRF					

Pillar I   Exercises

PILLAR I: ORGANIZATIONAL-LEVEL SKILL SET–ENHANCEMENT EXERCISES

GROUP EXERCISES

These exercises are best completed within a group of project managers, project leaders, executives, and stakeholders from within a department or an organization.

1. Using Table 1.13, identify at least five advantages to your organization in creating a culture of project leadership described in Pillar I and rate them from 1 to 5 (1 = least important, 5 = most important) to enhancing your organization culture from that of project management to project leadership.
2. Using Table 1.14, identify at least five roadblocks within your organization in creating a culture of project leadership described in Pillar I and rate them from 1 to 5 (1 = least difficult to overcome, 5 = most difficult to overcome).
3. Using Table 1.15, identify individuals within your organization or any external resource who excel at the following and can help lead the organization toward developing the five powers described in Pillar I.

Table 1.13   Pillar I: Advantages of Applying Principles of Pillar I to Your Organization

No.	Advantages of Applying Principles of Pillar I to Enhancing Your Organization Culture	Rating (1 = Least Important) (5 = Most Important)	Explain the Rating
1			
2			
3			
4			
5			

Table 1.14   Pillar I: Five Roadblocks to Creating a Culture of Project Leadership Using Pillar I

No.	Roadblocks to Applying Principles of Project Leadership Described in Pillar I to Your Organization	Rating (1 = Least Difficult to Overcome) (5 = Most Difficult to Overcome)	Explain the Rating
1			
2			
3			
4			
5			

Table 1.15   Pillar I: Identify Individuals Who Can Help Lead the Organization

No.	Powers of Project Leaders	Internal Resources	External Resources
1	Power of delegation		
2	Power of dynamic leadership		
3	Power of visualization		
4	Power of lean thinking		
5	Power of humility		

Table 1.16   Pillar I: Record Percentage of Time Spent in Each Activity

Phase	% Time Spent				
	Delegation	*Dynamic Leadership*	*Visualization*	*Lean Thinking*	*Rewarding/ Sharing the Glory*
1. Project start-up					
2. Project preparation					
3. Project implementation					
4. Project monitoring					
5. Project closure					

4. Using Table 1.16, pick at least three of the most experienced individuals from among the project managers within your organization and have them honestly create a baseline for a typical project within your organization that they are managing from start to finish.

5. *Scenario analysis*: SUNSOFT is an IT organization that makes top-of-the-line software for server security and user authentication. It employs 20 program managers in the United States and 15 program managers and 220 project managers in India. One of the most critical issues with this organization, both in the United States and in India, is the high turnover rate of 25% among the project managers. The exit interviews from the last 36 project managers, who left the organization, tend to suggest the following five as the main reasons for leaving:

   i. No scope for growth within the organization

   ii. Excessive micromanagement by the program managers both in the United States and in India

     iii. No scope to use the creativity and innovation for the project managers

     iv. Too much effort required in reprogramming and defect correction

     v. Program managers receive the rewards (bonuses, incentives) for successes, and project managers are forced to share the blame (reprimand, demotions) for errors.

On the basis of the scenario and data from the exit interviews, use Table 1.5 to create a force field analysis with driving forces and resisting forces to answer the following two questions:

a) Does SUNSOFT drive or resist the culture of project leadership?
b) What changes does SUNSOFT need to make to change the organizational culture?

PILLAR I: PERSONAL-LEVEL SKILL SET–ENHANCEMENT EXERCISES

INDIVIDUAL EXERCISES

These exercises are to be completed individually after reviewing Pillar I in detail.

1. Using Table 1.17, reflect on a recently completed project spanning at least 3 or more months. Draw a typical level of activity curve during various stages of projects you have managed or lead. On the basis of the project effort curve, are you a manager or a leader?

Table 1.17 Pillar I: Level of Activity Curve

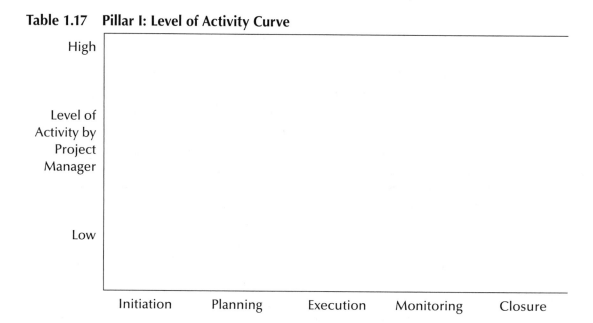

2. Using Table 1.18, reflect on last 2 weeks of ongoing projects. Complete the task delegation worksheet and answer the following questions:
   a. How comfortable were you to delegate the tasks?
   b. Would you feel comfortable in increasing the frequency of delegations?
   c. What lessons did you learn from delegating these tasks?
3. Using Table 1.19, reflect on a recently completed project spanning at least 3 months. In the worksheet, identify the activities or tasks you lead during the course of the project or your portion of the project.
4. Using Table 1.20, reflect on a recently completed project spanning at least 3 months. In the worksheet, identify any instances of visualizing any activities or tasks before completing them. Answer the following questions:
   a. What are the advantages of visualization based on your experience?
   b. What additional visualization activities can you use to lead projects in future?

Table 1.18 Pillar I: Task Delegation Worksheet

Task	To Whom Did You Delegate? (e.g., Team Member, Project Leader, etc.)	Result of Delegation (Successful, Failed, or Any Other Comments)

Table 1.19   Pillar I: Leadership Roles during Recently Completed Project

Project Phase	Leadership Roles
1. Project start-up	
2. Project preparation	
3. Project implementation	
4. Project monitoring	
5. Project closure	

Table 1.20   Pillar I: Visualization Worksheet

Name of the Project	Project Phase	Visualization Parameters (Task Parameters, Cost Parameters, Schedule Parameters, etc.)

5. *Scenario analysis*: SUNSOFT is an IT organization that makes top-of-the-line software for server security and user authentication. It employs 20 program managers in the United States and 15 program managers and 220 project managers in India. One of the most critical issues with this organization, both in the United States and in India, is

the high turnover rate of 25% among the project managers. The exit interviews from the last 36 project managers, who left the organization, tend to suggest the following five as the main causes for their resignations:

i. No scope for growth within organization
ii. Excessive micromanagement by the program managers both in the United States and in India
iii. No scope to use the creativity and innovation for the project managers
iv. Too much effort required in reprogramming and defect correction
v. Program managers receive the rewards (bonuses, incentives) for successes, and project managers are forced to share the blame (reprimand, demotions) for errors

Imagine that you are director of programs at SUNSOFT and have been entrusted by the boss, the vice president of programs, to reverse the trend of turnover within your organization. On the basis of the data from the exit interviews and the learning from Pillar I of the book on *12 Pillars of Project Excellence*, answer the following:

a) Which key principles from Pillar I will you use to help the organization retain and develop a majority of project managers in the United States and in India?
b) Using Table 1.21, explain in detail, how you will deploy the plan within your organization and the other benefits to your organization by deploying the principles of Pillar I.

Table 1.21   Pillar I: List Benefits of Deploying Key Leadership Principles

Key Leadership Principle	Details of Deployment Plan	Benefits

Pillar I   References

1. Project Management Institute. (2008). *A Guide to the Project Management Body of Knowledge (PMBOK Guide)*, 4th Ed., pp. 5 and 41, 14, Campus Blrd, Newton Square, PA 19073.
2. Verma, V. K., and Wideman, R. M. (2002). *Project Manager to Project Leader? And the Rocky Road Between …* , Revision 3, p. 3.
3. Dalal, A. F. (May 2009). "Go lean, save green," *Six Sigma Forum Magazine*, 8(3):34.
4. http://quotationsbook.com/quote/22933/, (accessed July 8, 2010; http://creativecommons.org/licenses/by/2.0/uk/).
5. Hersey, P., and Blanchard, K. H. (1988). *Management and Organizational Behavior.* Englewood Cliffs, NJ: Prentice-Hall.
6. Runion, M. (2009). *Dynamic Leadership: A Measure of Your Leadership Effectiveness*, http://www.speakstrong.com/articles/leadership/dynamicleadership.html (accessed July 19, 2010).
7. Doyle, M. E., and Smith, M. K. (2001) "Shared leadership," *Encyclopedia of Informal Education*, http://www.infed.org/leadership/shared_leadership.htm (accessed July 21, 2010).
8. http://quotationsbook.com/quote/11435/, (accessed July 8, 2010).
9. Charlie Rose Interview with Jeffrey Katzenberg, CEO, Dream Works Animation, May 17, 2010, http://www.charlierose.com/view/interview/11015 (accessed October 27, 2010).
10. The Standish Group International Inc. (2010). *CHAOS Summary 2009*, http://www1.standishgroup.com/newsroom/chaos_2009.php (accessed October 27, 2010).
11. The Chartered Institute of Purchasing & Supply. (2010). *Lean Constructions—A Contractor's Perspective*, http://www.cips.org (accessed October 27, 2010).
12. http://thinkexist.com/quotes/benjamin_franklin/, (accessed October 27, 2010).
13. Charlie Rose Interview with Jamling Tenzing Norgay and Peter Hillary, April 25, 2003, http://www.charlierose.com/view/interview/2005 (accessed October 27, 2010).

Chapter 2

Pillar II: Create a Balanced Project Organization Structure

A project without a well-balanced organization structure is like a high-rise building without a stable foundation—both will eventually fail.

2.1 Introduction

On complex project assignments, the absence of second pillar can lead to the failure of an entire project. Thus, the importance of this pillar cannot be ignored in any complex project.

2.1.1 Factors for Project Failure

What are the major reasons for project failures? Experts have been looking for answers to this question for long time. The failure of projects is not due to unknown reasons. Thorough analysis of failed projects reveals some truths about project failures.

Figure 2.1 provides a snapshot of the top factors responsible for project failure on the basis of my experience. Although these factors will vary depending on your corporate culture, maturing in project management, and on the type of industry, in general, approximately 80% of the issues can be attributed to the following two factors:

1. Poor communications
2. Ambiguous requirements

Communication plays a critical role in the successful execution of a project. During project execution, project leaders spend majority of their time in communicating. The communication can be verbal, nonverbal, written, formal, or informal. It is essential for a project manager to analyze effective communication strategies during a project. We will take a deeper dive into the critical subject of "communications" in Pillar V.

2.1.1.1 Lack of Communications—A Leading Cause of Project Failures

In recent history, one of the most high-profile examples of a failed project due to communication problem is the loss of Mars climate orbiter from the National

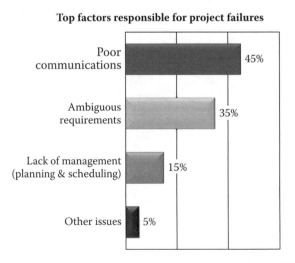

Figure 2.1   Top factors responsible for project failures.

Aeronautics and Space Administration (NASA). This was caused by an error in the formal communication between two geographically separated teams. While navigating spacecraft close to the mars surface, one team used metric units and other team used English units. Both teams communicated only numbers without formally communicating the units associated with those numbers. This caused the spacecraft to go below the minimum distance collapsing on Mar's surface (NASA, 1999). A detailed case study of the root cause analysis of this failure will be shown in Pillar IX, which deals primarily with project failures.

Another study by Oz and Sosik (2000) revealed the best reason for IT projects failure as lack of communication or poor communication.[1] Most of the IT projects have shown repeated pattern of communication failure.

2.1.1.2 Ambiguous Understanding of Customer Requirements

A customer's or a stakeholder's role in defining or refining customer requirements is also an important element in project success. A stakeholder is a person, group of people, or an organization that has positive or negative influence on the project. Defining the scope of the project requires clear-cut requirement gathering from the customer. Gathering valid requirements is critical to create an accurate baseline for the project. It helps the project manager in reducing not only the project schedule time but also the rework during the execution phase. Proper requirement collection ties back to effective communication with the customer. If adequate effort is not spent in gathering accurate requirements from the customer, the estimation of project scope, timeline, budget, and quality will be poor and can lead to project failure.

2.1.1.3 Other Data on Project Failures

According to Mr. Jim Johnson, President of the Standish Group, which has been involved with collecting project-failure-related data for over a decade for the CHAOS report, whom I had discussions on the data about project failures, the following are the five most common yet ignored reasons of project failure:

1. Unhealthy project ecosystems including poor execution of the 10 CHAOS factors of success, lack of or poor user involvement, little to no executive support, unclear business objectives, weak organizational emotional maturity, and so forth
2. Poor organizational communication and collaboration
3. Poor project estimating skills
4. Poor balance between autonomy and governance
5. Overreliance on tools, process, and governance

According to Mr. Johnson, over half the projects, although completed, will usually be overbudget, late, and will have missing features. The leading cause of most challenged projects is poor estimating skills.

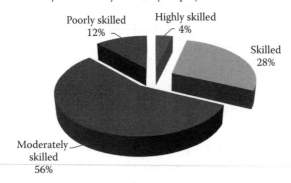

Figure 2.2 Top factors responsible for project failures. (Courtesy of Jim Johnson, Standish Group International, 2010.)

To get a deeper insight into poor estimation skills, the Standish Group posed the following question to numerous IT Executives:

"How would you rate your organization's ability to accurately estimately your project's time and cost?"

Figure 2.2 shows the responses collected to this question.[2] On the basis of the responses, it is quite clear that the executives are astute and are quite aware of the lack of organizational skill-set to accurately conduct "project estimations." However, "poor estimation" is a result of poor communications between the client, the project managers, and the stakeholders.

Thus, poor communication is clearly the leading cause of poor estimation and project failures. Poor communication sometimes is due to unclear channels of communications, which in turn is due to poor project organization structures. Thus, one of the primary ways to improve communications is to have a well-defined project organization structure that will allow project teams to be able to communicate efficiently to achieve success in projects of any size, duration, or complexity.

2.2 Project Organization Structure

2.2.1 Definition

A project organization structure helps facilitate, coordinate, share, and implement activities in a project.

2.2.2 Explanation

Both poor communications and ambiguous requirements can be directly attributed to the absence of a robust and balanced project organization structure. The project communication methods and the number of communication channels depend on the project organization structure. The project organization structure forms a basis for communication planning strategy to keep stakeholders in the loop and to keep information flowing in the right directions. For a complex project, creating an effective organization structure for the cross-functional teams is necessary to gather project requirements and execute the project successfully.

Both poor communications and ambiguous requirements can be directly attributed to the absence of a robust and balanced project organization structure.

This chapter focuses on various organization structures and use of those structures in managing a successful project. Figure 2.3 shows a typical organization structure for projects. This type of project organization structure works great for small, low-impact, and low-risk projects and reduces uncertainty in small projects as the communication flows from both top-down and bottom-up channels. However, the project manager is completely responsible for the success or failure of these projects. The project manager has no cover and is fully exposed from the top. This may not be an issue at times, but if the project is not progressing well, the entire responsibility of failure falls completely on the project manager. However, in complex projects, this structure has many disadvantages. Let me explain this with an analogy.

2.2.3 Analogy

If you are a squad leader in the Army and you have been tasked with capturing a group of what are believed to be unarmed civilians for questioning, the orders will be given from above, and your squad of soldiers under your command as the squad leader will undertake the completion of the task. First of all, if you are an intelligent squad leader, you will send out one or more scouts to determine whether or not the situation is as expected. On confirming that the situation is as expected, you will lead your squad to the completion of the task. However, the situation is very different and the group to be captured is very strong, well armed, and has a potential to resist capture, to fight back, and possibly to defeat you. Once the scouts have determined that the situation is not as expected and that there is risk involved in the task that was not anticipated, you will probably pursue

Figure 2.3   Typical organization structure for simple projects.

a different strategy. You, as squad leader, will communicate with those above you in the chain of command and request assistance. It does not matter how intelligent you are, you need help in decisions, resources, technology, and expertise in this situation. That assistance may take the form of aerial reconnaissance to provide additional intelligence about the situation and to better assess the strength of the threat, potentially followed by air support to augment the capabilities of your squad and/or the provision of additional ground troops to assure the success of the mission. The decisions are not directly coming from a project leader, instead coming from other elements that are involved in the project organization structure.

Thus, the project organization structure is very important in improving efficiency and effectiveness of the delivery of a project and to facilitate points of contact for a large and highly complex project that cross multiple agencies and organizations. As the number of stakeholders increase, the complexity of project administration increases, and as the components of a project increase, the ability to lead and manage a project becomes exceedingly difficult and thus the need for effective project organization structure becomes vital.

2.3 Project Types

Projects can be divided into four different categories: simple, medium, complex, and highly complex on the basis of the objective, scope, estimates on budget and

Table 2.1   Difference between Simple, Medium, Complex, and Highly Complex Projects

Project Element	Simple Project	Medium Project	Complex Project	Highly Complex Project
Objective	Immediate	Immediate	Long term	Very long term
Scope	Clearly defined	Clearly defined	Not clearly defined	Ambiguous
Budget	Usually low	Medium	High	Very high
Risks	Known	Known	Somewhat known	Mostly unknown
Resources	Few	High	High	Very high
Requirements	Clearly defined	Clearly defined	Keep changing	Highly volatile
Activities	Very well defined	Well defined	Not clearly defined	Keep changing
Contracts	Very few	Few	High	Very high
Project leader's authority	Full	Full	Partial	Partial
Degree of uncertainty	Very less	Less	High	Very high
Time frame	Short	Short	Long	Very long
Stakeholders	Few	Few	Many	Numerous

time, resources, and risks. Each of these project types uses different project structure. Table 2.1 lists some of the differences between simple, medium, complex, and highly complex projects. The following examples provide an insight into how each type of project can be categorized.

2.3.1 Examples

- A university wants to start a new project to set up "Instructional Technology Center." This center is designed for students to take 15 different courses online. This is a simple project as it requires a project manager along with a group of technical team members to implement the system. There is no ambiguity in requirements and the communication channels are correctly defined in this type of project. The project organization structure is simple with a project manager at the top of the organization with everybody below him. The project manager is responsible for all the decisions and reports to only one sponsor. This is an example of a simple project.

- A state government wants to upgrade its network infrastructure across three different state buildings in the city. The project manager is required to report to stakeholders from three different agencies. In this project, the requirements are clear and the objective of the project is clearly defined with communication across multiple agencies. However, the project leader is required to consult different stakeholders before making a decision. The organization structure for this type of project is slightly bigger than the one described previously. This is an example of a medium complexity project.

- A project initiated by a drug manufacturer to conduct research and to develop a new drug to add to its existing product line is an example of a complex project. This project involves stakeholders from within the organization and multiple agencies like the government, the Food and Drug Administration, the clinical patients, and the insurance industry. Project leader should have good understanding of the nature of project activities, tasks, resources, and goals. Project leaders cannot make decisions on their own but is instead required to escalate complex decisions to a team of experts or executives who can make a collective safety, efficacy, and other business decisions. Hence, this type of projects need more complex project structure compared with the examples shown above and represents an example of a complex project.

- NASA developed "spirit" and "opportunity" rovers to find out the deep secrets of Mars. This was an entirely unique and complex project that no one had ever attempted. There were several unknown risks involved in the project. Many agencies and group of experts were involved in this project, and the decision was often taken by group of people as a team, not by a single individual. The nature of uncertainty in this project caused requirements to change quite often. This type of highly complex projects takes significantly long time and a huge number of resources, expertise, contractors, and new technologies. The costs involved in this project were also very high. The project organization structure for this project was very complex involving various government agencies and private agencies. Thus, this represents an example of a highly complex project.

2.4 Elements of the Project Organization Structure

The characteristics of project vary on the basis of the complexity of the project. Figure 2.4 demonstrates how different characteristics of a complex project necessitate various elements in the project organization structure. It is possible quite often that requirement gathering cannot be clearly defined in complex projects. In such cases, the customer should be part of the project team to help the team understand the requirements, the objectives, and the scope of the project. It takes significant analysis and discussions before making any decision on some critical

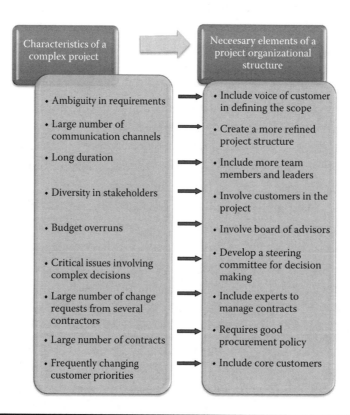

Figure 2.4 Characteristics of a complex project and impact on project organizational structure.

issues. This requires a steering committee along with board of advisors to foresee the impact of the decisions. Figure 2.5 shows an example of a recommended organization structure for medium complexity to complex projects. Figure 2.6 shows an example of a recommended organization structure for projects ranging from "complex" to "highly complex" projects that can have a major impact on the success of the project.

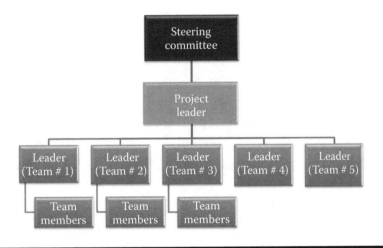

Figure 2.5   Recommended organizational structure for medium complexity to complex projects.

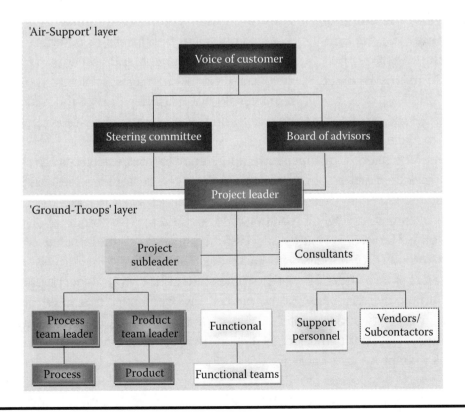

Figure 2.6   Recommended organizational structure for complex to highly complex projects.

The following are the elements of the proposed project structure for complex to high-complexity projects:

A. Voice of customer
B. Steering committee
C. Board of advisors
D. Project leader
E. Project subleader
F. Consultants (if needed)
G. Team leaders and teams
  - Functional team leaders and teams
  - Process team leaders and teams
  - Product team leaders and teams
  - Support team leaders and teams
  - Vendors/subcontractors

We need to review each of the elements in detail to understand the impact it can have on the success of complex or very complex projects.

2.4.1 Voice of Customer

In general, a project cannot exist without a customer. Thus, the voice of the customer can be considered the most important guide to any project.

In general, a project cannot exist without a customer. Thus, the voice of the customer can be considered the most important guide to any project. The customer can be internal or external, a single person or a department, and accessible or inaccessible to the project manager. Typically, the project manager do not hear the voice of the real customer but usually get the project specifications through the several layers of corporate filters likes sales manager, sales team members, customer service representatives, and some stakeholders. The filters sometimes have a tendency to completely change the message as each of the parties convey what they think the customer asked for, just like in the game the kids play called "telephone." Sometimes what reaches the project manager is altered completely in content, facts, and theme. Customer involvement in all phases of the projects is vital for successful completion of the projects. Table 2.2 gives list of various project phases and activities that need customer involvement.[3] From Table 2.2, it is understood that customers are critical from concept phase of the project to the delivery phase of the project. Involvement of customers allows them a better visibility and a greater understanding of impact of their product or service requirements during project execution. In a complex project, there are two approaches to improve customer's participation.

1. The ideal solution is to have a customer representative dynamically involved with the project. The scope of involvement of the representative should be agreed

Table 2.2   Project Activities Involving Customer Participation

Project Phase	Project Processes[2]	Involvement of Customer
Initiation	Develop business case	Business case is developed on the basis of the customer's needs
	Develop project charter	Project charter lists the needs of the customer
	Identify stakeholders	Including customers in the team prevents any future scope changes
Planning	Collect requirements	Customer's needs are collected, prioritized, and sorted
	Define activities	Customer imposed dates are used for creating project plan
	Determine budget	Expenditure of funds should be reconciled with the funding limits set by customer
	Plan quality	Customer sets the quality approval limits for accepting products
	Plan communications	Customer needs to be informed on the progress of the project and progress of various activities
Execution	Perform quality assurance	Customer's quality standards are measured by auditing the products
	Distribute information	Customers should be informed of delays in the project
	Manage stakeholder expectations	Customer expectations should be managed and their issues should be addressed
Monitor and control	Verify scope	Customer accepts deliverables that meets the requirements specifications
	Control scope	Customer proposed change requests should be processed
	Perform quality control	Keeping errors out of the hands of customer is very important

Source: Project Management Institute, *A guide to the Project management Body of Knowledge (PMBOK Guide)*, 4th Edn., pp. 43, 2008.

upon at the onset so the only true function of the representative is to help create the project requirements and provide ongoing guidance to the project. This has to be approached very carefully to ensure that the involvement does not intentionally or unintentionally lead to any significant scope creep on that project.

2. When it is not possible to have the customer representative dynamically involved, create a voice of customer committee whose primary responsibility is to interface with the customer at least during the requirements gathering phase and on an ongoing basis for any clarifications and adjustments.

The responsibilities of voice of customer committee include defining project specifications, input, and feedback from end customers or internal resources closest to customer (sales and customer service).

The less the filters between the project leader and the customer, the better the chances for project success because it helps to address both the primary factors for project failures, namely, poor communications and ambiguous requirements.

2.4.2 Steering Committee

Appointing a steering committee on complex projects can be one of the smartest moves of your project career. The steering committee consists of the following at a minimum:

Appointing a steering committee on complex projects can be one of the smartest moves of your project career.

- Sponsor
- Key stakeholders
- Project leader
- Team leaders

A customer representative, if available, can also be included as a part of the steering committee. The purpose of the steering committee is threefold:

1. Creating a formal two-way communication channel between project leader and key stakeholders
2. Providing "air cover" or "executive guidance" throughout the course of the project.
3. Facilitating swift decision making and resolution of key issues

Responsibilities of the steering committee are as follows:

- Provide leadership and direction in complex projects
- Evaluate high-risk items and advocate risk mitigation techniques to the project team
- Act on issues escalated from the project leader and provide solutions in a timely manner
- Ensure that the project objectives are met at the high level and the direction of the project aligns with the long-term goal of the organization
- Provide assistance for cross-functional teams of the project and make decisions on resource assignments and releases
- Authorize and approve high-level scope change requests that influence the objective of the project
- Analyze frequent updates on the project and coordinate different agencies for success of the project

The steering committee must be kept up to date on the high-level progress of the project. Depending on the criticality and requirements of the project, the steering committee should meet at least for any critical and urgent decision making and also during phase-gate reviews.

2.4.3 Board of Advisors

Creating a board of advisors is not mandatory but can be very helpful on complex projects. The board of advisors consists of key influential personnel who do not have time to provide support to the project but their periodic guidance can potentially benefit the project. It may consist of executives and other experts, internal or external to the project and to the organization. These experts may or may not be the stakeholders on the project. Assistance from an individual advisor or from the board of advisors can be requested on an as-needed basis.

Responsibilities of the board of advisors are as follows:

- Provide guidance, expertise, and support to the project leader and team members when required
- Provide unbiased and effective decisions on technical aspects of the product
- Provide guidance regarding other business opportunities related to the projects
- Suggest ideas on emerging trends and techniques in the product development

Figure 2.7 gives the advantages of using elements of air-support-like voice of customer, steering committee, and board of advisors in the project organization structure of a complex project.

2.4.4 Project Leader

As seen from Figures 2.5 and 2.6, the project leader acts as the pivot point of the project, balancing the project demands from the ranks above with the practical execution of the project tasks by the teams, consultants, and vendors below. Thus, the project leader needs to act as a liaison between the two layers—the layer above called the "air-support" layer, providing the project guidance support, and the layer below called the "ground-troops" layer, providing the project execution support. Traditional project managers do not usually create a top layer or sometimes create a thin version of the top layer on complex projects. This can lead to several complications on the projects and also to complete project failures. If possible, the project leader in association with the sponsor must be involved in selecting the steering committee members, the board of advisors, and the team leaders.

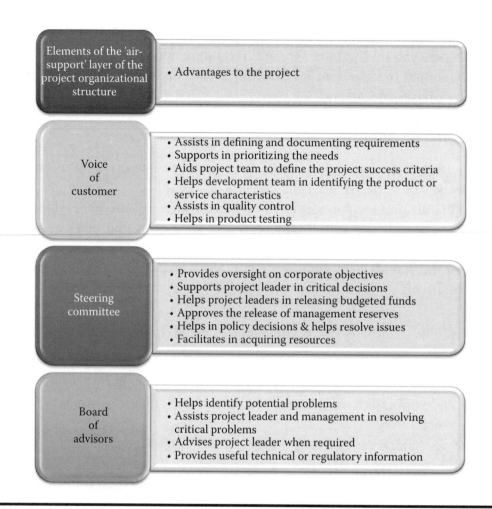

Figure 2.7 **Advantages of using "air-support" layer in organizational structure for complex projects.**

Some of the responsibilities of project leaders are as follows:

- Responsible for a project from its inception till final delivery
- Lead and direct resources, resolve conflicts, and delegate tasks
- Manage and influence stakeholders, customers, vendors, and project teams
- Delegate tasks to control scope, schedule, quality, and costs to keep the project along the path of success
- Plan various communication methods and distribute information
- Work with multiple functional managers and influence them in managing resources
- Responsible for balancing the interests of stakeholders
- Perform active role in resolving issues in their control and escalate issues that are beyond their control to the steering committee and/or to the board of advisors

The project leader and the steering committee, the board of advisors, and the customer representatives form the air-support layer of the project team and can play a critical role in steering the project toward success in achieving all the objectives identified by the customer.

2.4.5 Project Subleader

Appointing a project subleader is a wise move for most complex projects. The project leader's responsibilities can be overwhelming at times and having a backup person can be beneficial to the project. The subleaders also have a chance to work with a "mentor" and can use this opportunity to hone their own style of project leadership while providing invaluable support to the project leader and the team.

The primary responsibilities of the project subleaders are as follows:

* Help the project leader to maintain the project within budget, schedule, and scope
* Manage different teams under their direction and report any issues to the project leader
* Facilitate conflict resolution and problem solving
* Recognize and reward the teams for their accomplishments
* Support and help team leaders align their goals with the project goals
* Manage stakeholders and distribute information after approval from project leader
* Lead schedule development, quality control operations, and testing activities

2.4.6 Consultants (if Needed)

Sometimes, in complex projects, there may be a need of having both internal and external consultants. If the project involves new technologies and new directions, consultants can provide significant expertise and depth of knowledge to the project team. The consultant must then be integrated into the project team. Depending on the criticality of the need of the consultant to the project and the nature of the services they are rendering, the consultant can report to a project leader, a subleader, or a team leader.

The consultant usually has a particular "formula" or methodology, and the project leader needs to clearly understand the approach, solutions, and technology of the consultants before selecting them. Most of the time, the consultant's services must be customized to fit the culture and the requirements of the project and the organization. The project leader is responsible for ensuring that the consultants approach and technology will not disrupt the daily operations of the organizations or the progress of the teams working on the project. The project leader should also ensure that the consultant's time is completely used for the benefit of the project.

The primary responsibilities of consultants are as follows:

- Work with the project team to attain the deliverables of the project
- Focus time on the expertise or services they are consulting for to benefit the project and the project team
- Share and educate team members on the services they are rendering

2.4.7 Team Leaders and Teams

Team leaders and teams are part of the ground troops of the project organization structure. One of the approaches is to design the team on the basis of process focus and product or service focus. The process team will ensure that all the processes required to complete the project per customer requirements are well designed, accurate, based on lean thinking, and correctly followed. The product or service team will ensure that the actual product or service required by the customer meets all the criteria agreed to in the project charter including quality, scope, cost, resources, risk, and schedule. An alternative approach is to create the teams required to execute the project on the basis of functional departments within the organization. The teams can be identified as marketing team, research and development team, advanced manufacturing team, information technology team, or others as required. The decision between creating a functional team or a process–product/service team can be made on the basis of the requirements of the project. Other teams to be considered can be support teams like facilities, special functions, and others. It is also important to consider that the project leaders or the team leaders are also responsible for performance of vendors/subcontractors, and they need to integrate into the team, as required, at the appropriate level and with appropriate reporting relationship.

The core responsibilities of teams are as follows:

- Perform different project activities but not limited to requirement collection, activity definition, costs estimation, risk identification, risk analysis, work breakdown structure development, and project schedule preparation.
- Perform all project activities in project execution phase
- Perform and maintain all quality control activities
- Provide task status and escalate issues to the project leader or subleader
- Participate in project progress discussions, meetings, and team-building activities

Figure 2.8 shows a clear difference between an unbalanced project structure and a balanced project structure when working on complex projects. Once a balanced

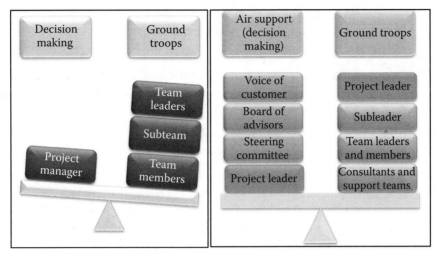

Figure 2.8   Unbalanced and balanced organization structures for complex projects.

structure is created, it is critical to clarify the roles and the responsibilities of various individuals and teams and the required level of communications in the project.

2.5 Responsibility Assignment Matrix

Responsibility assignment matrix (RAM) is used to define the responsibilities of each individual in the project to the tasks in a project. RASCI chart is one form of RAM. For every step of planning a project, the following is defined.[4]

R = Responsible: The personnel who are responsible for delivering the project and/or task successfully. If too many people are responsible for a given task, it will result in out-of-control situation. Same way, if a person is responsible for too many tasks, they might have been overallocated. Thus, a balanced project structure needs to be designed to avoid these imbalances in task assignments.

A = Accountable: The personnel who have accountability and authority of the task or project. The personnel responsible for a task are accountable to personnel indicated as "accountable" in the RASCI matrix for their assigned work. In a risk assignment process, one person or group may take risk ownership responsibility and other person or group will assume the risk response accountability. Thus, this element in a RASCI matrix is assigned to the list of personnel or groups who are controlling various tasks.

S = Supportive: The personnel or team of individuals who provide resources, tools, or services to the team without which the project cannot continue as planned. Project leader should have an eye on these tasks because projects can be delayed if supporting tasks are not performed as planned.

C = Consulted: Someone whose input adds value and/or buy-in is essential for ultimate implementation. Too many consultations during a project can delay tasks and too little consultations for a critical task could result in the failure of the project. Thus, a balanced project structure provides equal importance to this element along with other elements of the RASCI matrix.

I = Informed: The personnel or groups of individuals who need to be notified of results or actions taken but do not need to be involved in the decision-making process. During project execution, stakeholders should be informed of project progress. Failure to distribute information to the appropriate personnel or groups in a timely manner can lead to conflicts.

This chart is very important to avoid ambiguity in work assignments when many external and internal agencies are involved in the project. Table 2.3 shows the RASCI chart for a balanced organization structure.

Table 2.3 An Example of a RASCI Chart for a Balanced Organization Structure

Elements of the Project Organization Structure	Project Phases				
	Initiation	Planning	Execution	Monitoring	Closeout
Voice of customer	A	C/I	C/I	I	A
Board of advisors	S	S	S	S	S
Steering committee	S/R	S/R	A/I	A/I	S/R
Project leader	R/A	R/A	R/A	R/A	R/A
Project subleader	S/R	S/R	S/R	S/R	S/R
Consultants	C	C	R	R/S	S
Vendors/subcontractors	C	C	R	R	S
Teams	R	R	R	R	R
Support teams	R	R	R	R	S

Note: R, responsible; A, accountable; S, supportive; C, consulted; I, informed.

Pillar II   Summary

Poor communication is clearly the leading cause of project failures. Poor communication sometimes is due to unclear channels of communications, which in turn is due to poor project organization structures. Thus, one of the primary ways to improve communications is to have a well-defined project organization structure that will allow project teams to be able to communicate efficiently to achieve success in projects of any size, duration, or complexity.

One of the first orders of business for successful project leaders on complex projects is to create a stable and balanced project structure consisting of a voice of customer committee, steering committee, board of advisors, project leader, project subleader, team leaders, support team leaders, team members, and consultants/vendors or subcontractors.

The major benefits of this project organization structure are as follows:

1. The structure allows for formal communication channel to and from the customer.
2. Project structure creates a formal communication chain so issues can be communicated in real times to the stakeholders and experts and feedback received immediately to take approved corrective action.
3. Project structure is more balanced with adequate cover for the project from above and support from below.

Figure 2.9 lists the important elements discussed in this chapter regarding the benefits of creating a stable organization structure for the projects.

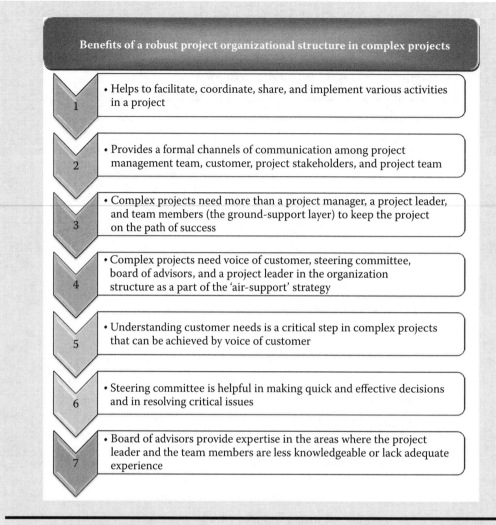

Figure 2.9 Summary of benefits of a robust organizational structure in complex projects.

Pillar II   Case Study
Develop a Balanced Project Organization Structure

INTRODUCTION

This case study is about the positive effects of using balanced project structure in a health care industry project.

CHALLENGE

A multibillion dollar organization in the health care industry had a program for developing a suite of software products for their various product lines as a growth strategy and to set themselves apart from their competitors. Their sales team had already sold one of the products in the suite to an existing customer for a few million dollars. The crisis was that they had missed several key deadlines to demonstrate the software to the client because they had not even created specifications for the "vapor-ware" the sales team had already sold. An experienced program manager, who was a director within the organization, was assigned to the complex program. The program manager had assigned several project managers to each of the product lines. He was very confident in his own abilities and the abilities of the team to execute this project. However, he had no results to show after 3 months of significant effort. His superiors were getting worried, and there were several heated exchanges between the program manger and his superiors. He finally agreed to allow them to get him some external resources to support him and his project managers. The superiors invited me to come for an initial visit as a consultant on the program.

SITUATION

During our initial meeting, the first order of business was to ask three questions to the program manager.

1. Who is the sponsor of the program and how is his relationship with the sponsor?
2. Is he directly in contact with the end customer?
3. What is the current program organization structure?

The program manager replied to the above questions as follows:

1. There was no defined sponsor for the program. However, he knew that some of his reports were being reviewed by the vice presidents and even the CEO.
2. He had no direct contact with the end customer but was communicating through some sales and marketing personnel with the client.
3. The following was the program reporting structure he had created as shown in Figure 2.10.

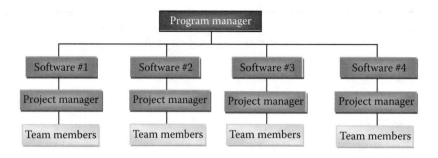

Figure 2.10   Initial program structure for the software development project.

SOLUTION

On the basis of the issues they were having getting the program off the ground, the answers were not surprising. The recommendation to him was that he had some fundamental issues that if not addressed immediately would prevent the program from progress. Initially, he thought that he was following the fundamentals of project management and he did not think any changes were needed in the program structure. After some discussions, he embraced the changes we discussed to the structure. The following were the key elements of the new structure:

i. Program office (accountability): Consisted of the executive board, the new product development committee, the project sponsors, and the program manager. The key responsibilities were creating project charter, staffing the project office, providing a voice of customer to project office via the project sponsors, strategic decision making, and resolving conflicts in using resources between various projects.
ii. Project office (responsibility): The project sponsors, the program manager, the steering committees, the project managers, and the project leads were part of this team. The key responsibilities were creation of project plans, communication strategy, and dashboard to show the project progress.
iii. Time commitment (availability): This element was built on the basis of the percentage of time required by the members of the program and project office for each project phase.

The new organization structure was defined as shown in Figure 2.11.

IMPLEMENTATION

The new structure was proposed to the executive committee, and it was approved and embraced immediately. It was decided that the recruitment of key players will be limited to the two most critical projects, and as they get experience, they will move the remaining two projects slated to start within 2 years after launch of the initial two pilots.

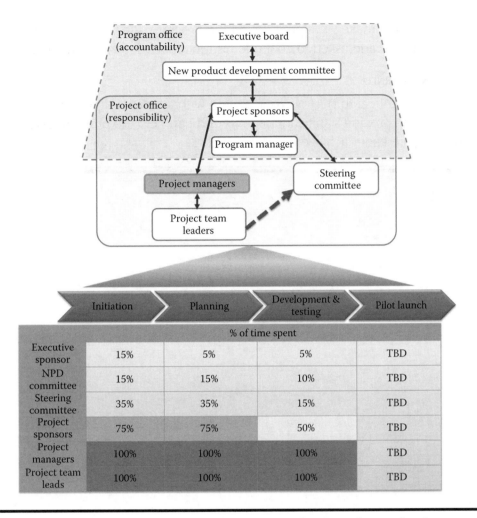

Figure 2.11 New program and project office structure for the software development project.

Results

The positive impact on the project was immediately visible. The executive committee members were engaged in the process and provided adequate guidance to the project sponsors and program manger on the basis of feedback from the clients. In turn, the project sponsors were able to provide more guidance to the program manager and the project managers. When you looked at the program manager, he looked much more relieved and focused as compared with when he was operating under the old structure. He had formal communication channels to the sponsors and the executives, and it helped him significantly to get much needed clarifications on requirements and resources needed to execute. Although the project structure was very effective and the program manger's performance had improved tremendously, there was significant political upheaval created because of the old program structure as the program manager had ruffled a few feathers at the executive level. As a result, during the annual review, approximately 3 months after he had begun to make great progress on the program, the program manger was replaced and asked to continue his functional duties as a director.

LESSONS LEARNED

Thus, it is critical to start off your project with a balanced project structure. It can provide significant benefits and can help the program and the project leader achieve long-term success.

Pillar II   Force Field Analysis

PILLAR II: FORCE FIELD ANALYSIS OF ORGANIZATIONAL ASSESSMENT

Table 2.4 shows force field analysis of organizational assessment. The organizational assessment is conducted to assess if the culture of the organization is in alignment with the principles of Pillar II. Tables 2.5 through 2.7 are used to develop and implement an action plan to increase the impact of the organizational driving forces and decrease the impact of the organizational resisting forces.

PILLAR II: FORCE FIELD ANALYSIS OF SELF-ASSESSMENT

Table 2.8 shows force field analysis of self-assessment. The self-assessment is conducted to assess if your own strengths are in alignment with the principles of Pillar II. Tables 2.9 through 2.11 are used to develop and implement an action plan to increase the impact of the self-driving forces and decrease the impact of the self-resisting forces.

PILLAR II: RECOMMENDATIONS FOR OPTIMAL RESULTS FROM FORCE FIELD ANALYSIS

For optimal results and actual transformation of culture and strengths conducive to the creation of advanced master project leaders, the following three steps are necessary:

1. Both the organizational and self-evaluation assessments must be completed.
2. A well-designed action plan must be created and implemented to increase the driving forces (DF) and decrease the resisting forces (RF).
3. The principles of each pillar must be constantly practiced and improved.

It is highly recommended that both the organizational assessments and the self-assessments be conducted every year and the action plan be updated at least every 3 months.

Note: The sum of scores for Organizational Driving Force and Organizational Resisting Force for each point must be less than or equal to TEN.

The sum of scores for Self Driving Force and Self Resisting Force for each point must be less than or equal to TEN.

Table 2.4 Pillar II: Force Field Organizational Analysis

Team Name: _____   Date: _____

Does My Organization Drive or Resist a Balanced Project Organizational Structure?				
0 Never		5 Sometimes	7 Mostly	
3 Rarely		ODF + ORF ≤ 10	10 Always	
No.	Driving Forces	Score Organizational Driving Force (ODF)	Score Organizational Resisting Force (ORF)	Resisting Forces
1	My organization understands the importance of a balanced project organizational structure for effective communications and providing structured executive support to project leaders for success in complex projects.			My organization does not consider project organizational structure as an important aspect of team communications and project management is the sole responsibility of project managers, who report project metrics to executives.
2	My organization uses different project organizational structures on the basis of the type of project.			My organization always uses the same kind of project structure irrespective of the type of project.
3	Customer voice is critical to our project success, and we include the customer as an integral part of our project organizational structure in complex projects.			Customer voice is initially heard in my organization, but the customer is not as an integral part of our project organizational structure in any projects.
4	During every major project, a steering committee is appointed, and it plays an important role in the decision-making process.			During every project, the project manager takes the prime responsibility of the project and makes all key decisions.
5	For complex projects, we create a board of advisors, which provides guidance and support to the project leaders, when needed.			In a complex project, my organization builds strategies and goals for the whole project but not for individual components.

6	Task delegations are done in a structured way from the steering committee to the project leader and from project leaders to team leaders and members.			Task delegations are usually done from project managers to team members.
7	Issue escalations are done from team member to the team leader, then to project leader (when needed), and from the project leader to the steering committee (when needed).			Issue escalations are usually done from team members to project managers.
8	Experts, consultants, contractors, and vendors are included as a part of the project organization structure in complex projects.			Expert's opinions are heard as and when required. Vendors and contractors are not part of the project organization structure.
9	The entire steering committee including the project leader and the entire team takes complete responsibility for the success or failure of a project.			Project manager and the core team take complete responsibility for success or failure of the project.
10	Project leaders use the RASCI chart as a Responsibility Assignment Matrix (RAM) to clarify the roles and responsibilities of various individuals and teams and the required level of communications in the project.			Project managers usually do not create a document to clarify the roles and responsibilities of various individuals and teams and the required level of communications in the project.
	Total ODF score			*Total ORF score*

Result	Conclusion	Recommended Action Review and Update Every Quarter (3 months)
ODF >> ORF	My company culture strongly drives a culture of a balanced project organizational structure.	Use Tables 2.5 through 2.7 to set goals and create an action plan to preserve or continuously improve the culture of a balanced project organizational structure.
ODF > ORF	My company culture drives the culture of a balanced project organizational structure.	Use Tables 2.5 through 2.7 to set goals and create an action plan to increase ODF to create a more balanced project organizational structure.
ORF >> ODF	My company culture strongly resists the culture of a balanced project organizational structure.	Use Tables 2.5 through 2.7 to set goals and create an action plan to increase the ODF and reduce the ORF to create a more balanced project organizational structure.
ORF > ODF	My company culture resists the culture of a balanced project organizational structure.	Use Tables 2.5 through 2.7 to set goals and create an action plan to reduce the ORF to create a more balanced project organizational structure.
ODF = ORF	My company culture does not drive or resist the culture of a balanced project organizational structure.	Use Tables 2.5 through 2.7 to set goals and create an action plan to increase the ODF to create a more balanced project organizational structure.

Table 2.5 Pillar II: Analysis of ODF and ORF Results

Result	Existing Organizational Culture	If the Goal Is to Create a Moderately Strong Culture of a Balanced Project Organization Structure	If the Goal Is to Create a Very Strong Culture of a Balanced Project Organization Structure
ODF			
ODF ≤ 25	No or minimal culture of creating a balanced project organization structure	Focus on improving scores in at least 5 DF	Focus on improving scores in at least 7 DF
25 < ODF ≤ 50	Weak culture of creating a balanced project organization structure	Focus on improving scores in at least 3 DF	Focus on improving scores in at least 5 DF
50 < ODF ≤ 75	Moderate culture of creating a balanced project organization structure	Focus on improving scores in at least 1 DF	Focus on improving scores in at least 3 DF
ODF > 75	Strong culture of creating a balanced project organization structure	N/A	Preserve or continuously improve the culture
ORF			
ORF > 75	No or minimal culture of creating a balanced project organization structure	Focus on decreasing scores in at least 5 RF	Focus on decreasing scores in at least 7 RF
50 < ORF ≤ 75	Weak culture of creating a balanced project organization structure	Focus on decreasing scores in at least 3 RF	Focus on decreasing scores in at least 5 RF
25 < ORF ≤ 50	Moderate culture of creating a balanced project organization structure	Focus on decreasing scores in at least 1 RF	Focus on decreasing scores in at least 3 RF
ORF ≤ 25	Strong culture of creating a balanced project organization structure	N/A	Preserve or continuously improve the culture

Table 2.6 Pillar II: Action Plan to Increase Organizational Driving Forces (ODFs)

Name: _____   Date: _____

No.	Driving Force	Current Score	Goal (Target Score) ⬆	Action Plan to Increase DF Score	Complete by (Date)	Assigned to (Department Name or Initials of Person)
1	My organization understands the importance of a balanced project organizational structure for effective communications and providing structured executive support to project leaders for success in complex projects.					
2	My organization uses different project organizational structures on the basis of the type of project.					
3	Customer voice is critical to our project success, and we include the customer as an integral part of our project organizational structure in complex projects.					
4	During every major project, a steering committee is appointed, and it plays an important role in the decision-making process.					
5	For complex projects, we create a board of advisors, which provides guidance and support to the project leaders, when needed.					

6	Task delegations are done in a structured way from the steering committee to the project leader and from project leaders to team leaders and members.					
7	Issue escalations are done from team member to the team leader, then to project leader (when needed), and from the project leader to the steering committee (when needed).					
8	Experts, consultants, contractors, and vendors are included as a part of the project organization structure in complex projects.					
9	The entire steering committee, including the project leader, and the entire team take complete responsibility for the success or failure of a project.					
10	Project leaders use the RASCI chart as a Responsibility Assignment Matrix (RAM) to clarify the roles and responsibilities of various individuals and teams and the required level of communications in the project.					
	Total ODF					

Table 2.7 Pillar II: Action Plan to Decrease Organizational Resisting Forces (ORFs)

No.	Resisting Force	Current Score	Goal (Target Score) ⬇	Action Plan to Decrease RF Score	Complete by (Date)	Assigned to (Department Name or Initials of Person)
1	My organization does not consider project organizational structure important aspect of team communications, and project management is the sole responsibility of project managers, who report project metrics to executives.					
2	My organization always uses the same kind of project structure irrespective of the type of project.					
3	Customer's voice is initially heard in my organization, but the customer is not as an integral part of our project organizational structure in any projects.					
4	During every project, the project manager takes the prime responsibility of the project and makes all key decisions.					
5	In a complex project, my organization builds strategies and goals for the whole project but not for individual components.					
6	Task delegations are usually done from project managers to team members.					
7	Issue escalations are usually done from team members to project managers.					

8	Expert's opinions are heard as and when required. Vendors and contractors are not part of the project organization structure.					
9	The project manager and the core team take complete responsibility for success or failure of the project.					
10	Project managers usually do not create a document to clarify the roles and responsibilities of various individuals and teams and the required level of communications in the project.					
	Total ORF					

Table 2.8   Pillar II: Force Field Self-analysis

Name: _____   Date: _____

Does My Behavior Drive or Resist a Balanced Project Organizational Structure?				
0 Never		5 Sometimes		7 Mostly
3 Rarely		SDF + SRF ≤ 10		10 Always
No.	Driving Forces	Score Self-Driving Force	Score Self-Resisting Force	Resisting Forces
1	I prefer to use different organization structure on the basis of the complexity of the project.			I prefer to use a similar organizational structure on all my projects.
2	I usually use a RASCI chart to clarify the required level of communications on the basis of the roles and responsibilities of various individuals, teams, and departments in the projects.			I do not clearly define the communication channels on my projects by using a responsibility assignment matrix (RAM).
3	As a project leader, I improve communications in my projects by first focusing on designing an appropriate organizational structure for the project.			As a project manager, I try to improve communications in my projects by ensuring that almost all communications are directed through me.
4	I always involve customers and make them an integral part of the project organizational structure on complex projects.			I get input from customers during the project but do not include them in project organizational structure.
5	Although I am a project leader, I appoint a steering committee and request them to take collective decisions in complex projects, when necessary.			Being a project manager, I take complete responsibility for project's decisions.

6	I attempt to create a balanced project structure, with air support, consisting of a customer representative, steering committee, and/or board of advisors on complex projects.			I usually manage a team but do not create air support consisting of a customer representative, steering committee, and/or board of advisors.
7	I include a team of advisors, consultants, and experts in the project team to make more accurate and timely decisions in a complex projects.			I use the expertise of consultants and advisors but do not include them in the project team as it complicates the decision-making process in a complex project.
8	I include functional managers as part of project team to prevent delays in resource acquisition.			I acquire resources as and when required to complete tasks but do not include functional managers in the project team.
9	I include vendors or subcontractors in my team to reduce delays in product delivery.			I strive to keep the project team as small as possible by not including vendors or subcontractors.
10	When I have to make tough decisions on a project, I immediately reach out to the steering committee and to the board of advisors and consider their advice before making any decisions.			When I have to make tough decisions on a project, I trust my knowledge as a project manager and make the decision quickly.
	Total SDF score			*Total SRF score*

Result	Conclusion	Recommended Action Review and Update Every Quarter (3 months)
SDF >> SRF	My behavior strongly supports the culture of creating a balanced project organization structure.	Use Tables 2.9 through 2.11 to set goals and create an action plan to continuously enhance the behavior to create a balanced project organization structure.
SDF > SRF	My behavior supports the culture of creating a balanced project organization structure.	Use Tables 2.9 through 2.11 to set goals and create an action plan to increase SDF to allow a stronger behavior toward creating a balanced project organization structure.
SRF >> SDF	My behavior strongly resists the culture of creating a balanced project organization structure.	Use Tables 2.9 through 2.11 to set goals and create an action plan to increase SDF and reduce SRF to allow a stronger behavior toward creating a balanced project organization structure.
SRF > SDF	My behavior resists the culture of creating a balanced project organization structure.	Use Tables 2.9 through 2.11 to set goals and create an action plan to reduce SRF to allow a stronger behavior toward creating a balanced project organization structure.
SDF = SRF	My behavior does not drive or resist the culture of creating a balanced project organization structure.	Use Tables 2.9 through 2.11 to set goals and create an action plan to increase the SDF to allow a stronger behavior toward creating a balanced project organization structure.

Table 2.9 Pillar II: Analysis of SDF and SRF Results

Result	Existing Behavior	If the Goal Is to Create a Moderately Strong Behavior Toward Principles of Project Organization	If the Goal Is to Create a Very Strong Behavior Toward Principles of Project Organization
SDF			
SDF ≤ 25	No or minimal activities in creating a balanced project organization structure	Focus on improving scores in at least 5 DF	Focus on improving scores in at least 7 DF
25 < SDF ≤ 50	Weak activities in creating a balanced project organization structure	Focus on improving scores in at least 3 DF	Focus on improving scores in at least 5 DF
50 < SDF ≤ 75	Moderate activities in creating a balanced project organization structure	Focus on improving scores in at least 1 DF	Focus on improving scores in at least 3 DF
SDF > 75	Strong activities in creating a balanced project organization structure	N/A	Preserve or continuously improve the behavior
SRF			
SRF > 75	No or minimal activities in creating a balanced project organization structure	Focus on decreasing scores in at least 5 RF	Focus on decreasing scores in at least 7 RF
50 < SRF ≤ 75	Weak activities in creating a balanced project organization structure	Focus on decreasing scores in at least 3 RF	Focus on decreasing scores in at least 5 RF
25 < SRF ≤ 50	Moderate activities in creating a balanced project organization structure	Focus on decreasing scores in at least 1 RF	Focus on decreasing scores in at least 3 RF
SRF ≤ 25	Strong activities in creating a balanced project organization structure	N/A	Preserve or continuously improve the behavior

Table 2.10   Pillar II: Action Plan to Increase Self-Driving Forces (SDFs)

Name: _____   Date: _____

No.	Driving Force	Current Score	Goal (Target Score) ⬆	Action Plan to Increase DF Score	Complete by (Date)	Required Resources
1	I prefer to use different organization structure on the basis of the complexity of the project.					
2	I usually use a RASCI chart to clarify the required level of communications on the basis of the roles and responsibilities of various individuals, teams, and departments in the projects.					
3	As a project leader, I improve communications in my projects by first focusing on designing an appropriate organizational structure for the project.					
4	I always involve customers and make them an integral part of the project organizational structure on complex projects.					
5	Although I am a project leader, I appoint a steering committee and request them to take collective decisions in complex projects, when necessary.					

6	I attempt to create a balanced project structure, with air support, consisting of a customer representative, steering committee, and/or board of advisors, on complex projects.					
7	I include a team of advisors, consultants, and experts in the project team to make more accurate and timely decisions in a complex projects.					
8	I include functional managers as part of project team to prevent delays in resource acquisition.					
9	I include vendors or subcontractors in my team to reduce delays in product delivery.					
10	When I have to make tough decisions on a project, I immediately reach out to the steering committee and to the board of advisors and consider their advice before making any decisions.					
	Total SDF					

Table 2.11 Pillar II: Action Plan to Decrease Self-Resisting Forces (SRFs)

Name: _____   Date: _____

No.	Resisting Force	Current Score	Goal (Target Score) ⬇	Action Plan to Decrease DR Score	Complete by (Date)	Required Resources
1	I prefer to use a similar organizational structure on all my projects.					
2	I do not clearly define the communication channels on my projects by using a RAM.					
3	As a project manager, I try to improve communications in my projects by ensuring that almost all communications is directed through me.					
4	I get input from customers during the project but do not include them in project organizational structure.					
5	Being a project manager, I take complete responsibility of project's decisions.					
6	I usually manage a team but do not create air support consisting of a customer representative, steering committee, and/or board of advisors.					

7	I use the expertise of consultants and advisors but do not include them in the project team as it complicates the decision-making process in a complex project.					
8	I acquire resources as and when required to complete tasks but do not include functional managers in the project team.					
9	I strive to keep the project team as small as possible by not including vendors or subcontractors.					
10	When I have to make tough decisions on a project, I trust my knowledge as a project manager and make the decision quickly.					
	Total SRF					

Pillar II   Exercises

PILLAR II: ORGANIZATIONAL-LEVEL SKILL SET–ENHANCEMENT EXERCISES

Group Exercises

These exercises are best completed within a group of project managers, project leaders, executives, and stakeholders from within a department or an organization.

1. Using Table 2.12, identify at least five advantages to your organization in creating a culture of designing a balanced project organization structure for your complex projects and rate them from 1 to 5 (1 = least important, 5 = most important).
2. Using Table 2.13, identify at least five roadblocks within your organization in creating a culture of designing a balanced project organization structure for your complex projects leadership and rate them from 1 to 5 (1 = least difficult to overcome, 5 = most difficult to overcome).
3. Using Table 2.14, identify a recent complex project completed by one of the experienced project managers in your organization. Draw the project organization structure used to accomplish the project. Draw a new project structure for the project on the basis of the principles of Pillar II. What benefits can you expect from the new structure?

Hint:

Identify the problems in defining the requirements, communications, and project planning faced by the project manager during the project and design the project structure to address the issues, if possible.

Table 2.12   Pillar II: Five Advantages of Applying Principles of Pillar II to Your Organization

No.	Advantages of Applying Principles of Pillar II to Enhancing Your Organization Culture	Rating (1 = Least Important) (5 = Most Important)	Explain the Rating
1			
2			
3			
4			
5			

Table 2.13   Pillar II: Five Roadblocks to Creating a Culture of a Balanced Project Organizational Structure Using Pillar II

No.	Roadblocks to Applying Principles of Pillar II to Your Organization Culture	Rating (1 = Least Difficult to Overcome, 5 = Most Difficult to Overcome)	Explain the Rating
1			
2			
3			
4			
5			

Table 2.14   Pillar II: Old and New Project Organization Structure

Project	Old Project Organization Structure	New Project Organization Structure
Identify problems in the old structure and benefits of the new structure		

Table 2.15   Pillar II: An Example of Air Support

An Example of a Project That Required an Air Support	Was the "Air Support" Provided Proactively? (Explain)	Was the "Air Support" Provided after the Project Was at a Risk of Falling? (Explain)

4. Using Table 2.15, identify and explain an example from your organization of a project that required air support. Was the air support provided proactively or was it provided after the project was at risk of failing?

5. Scenario analysis: THREE-D is a multinational video game software development organization that has clients in the United States and in Canada. Mii is one of the primary customers of THREE-D, and their business accounts for 40% of revenue for THREE-D. Mii was launching a new video game in China and contracted THREE-D to create a video game in partnership with their distributor for the Chinese market. THREE-D started the project and put their most experienced project manager on the project. During the course of

the project of approximately 8 months, there were many issues, and the project failed miserably to deliver on schedule, cost, or within budget, resulting in a loss of $1.9 million dollars to Mii. This created a major rift in the relationship with Mii. However, because the president of THREE-D knew his counterpart at Mii personally, they were able to come to an agreement for future projects. The president of Mii requested a detailed report on the failures and wanted a detailed action plan to address these on future projects. A lesson-learned meeting between all the parties involved identified the following three key reasons for the failure of the project:

1. THREE-D did not completely understand the product specifications and the requirements of the product launch in the Chinese market.
2. Poor communications between the three parties, Mii, THREE-D, and the Chinese distributor.
3. Poor project estimates on budget, schedule, and resources were submitted to Mii by the project manager at THREE-D.

You are the director of programs at THREE-D and are entrusted by your president to use the findings from the lessons-learned meeting and create a plan of action to avoid similar modes of failure on future projects. The president has asked you to use the principles of Pillar II from the book *12 Pillars of Project Excellence*.

Using Table 2.16, create an action plan on the basis of the principles of Pillar II of the *12 Pillars of Project Excellence* to be presented to the presidents of THREE-D and Mii for future success on projects.

Table 2.16 Pillar II: Action Plan for Scenario Analysis Based on the Organizational Skill-enhancement Principles of Pillar II

No.	Finding from Lessons Learned Meeting	Which Principles from Pillar II Can Be Applied to Address This Failure Mode	Action Plan to Avoid Similar Failure Mode on Future Projects
a.	THREE-D did not completely understand the product specifications and the requirements of the product launch in the Chinese market		
b.	Poor communications between the three parties, Mii, THREE-D, and the Chinese distributor		
c.	Poor project estimates on budget, schedule, and resources were submitted to Mii by the project manager at THREE-D		

Hints: Ask the following questions:
  a. Can creating a balanced project structure help improve the results?
  b. Who else can be added in the project organization structure above the project manager?
  c. Who else can be added in the project organization structure below the project manager?
  d. Can consultants or industry experts be included on the project team?
  e. What would be some examples of balanced organization structures for similar projects and what benefits can they provide?

PILLAR II: PERSONAL-LEVEL SKILL SET–ENHANCEMENT EXERCISES

INDIVIDUAL EXERCISES

These exercises are to be completed individually after reviewing Pillar II in detail.

1. Using Table 2.17, list last three projects you worked on as a project manager/leader, identifying the situations in which customer was dissatisfied with the progress of the project and answer following questions:
   a. List the reasons for customer dissatisfaction.
   b. Which principles of Pillar II could have been applied to reduce or eliminate the reasons for the dissatisfaction?
2. Using Table 2.18, identify three situations on a project in which it was very difficult for you to make a quick decision on your own on a critical matter and answer following questions:
   a. List the reasons for your inability to make a quick decision.
   b. Which principles of Pillar II could have been applied to enhance your ability to make a decision with confidence?

Table 2.17   Pillar II: List of Three Projects—Customer Focus

No.	Name of the Project	Describe the Situation That Caused Customer Dissatisfaction	Reasons for Customer Dissatisfaction	Which Principles of Pillar II Could Have Been Applied to Reduce or Eliminate the Reasons for the Customer Dissatisfaction
1				
2				
3				

Table 2.18   Pillar II: List of Three Projects—Decision Focus

No.	Name of the Project	Describe the Situation That It Was Difficult to Make Quick Decision on Your Own	Reasons for Your Inability to Make a Quick Decision	Which Principles of Pillar II Could Have Been Applied to Enhance Your Ability to Make a Decision with Confidence?
1				
2				
3				

Table 2.19   Pillar II: Project Organization Structure

Name of the Project	Additional Positions Above You (e.g., Sponsor, Lead, etc.)	Responsibilities (e.g., Approve Financial Decisions, Advise the Team, etc.)	Which Results Would Have Been Impacted?	How Would They Have Helped Improve the Results?

Table 2.20   Pillar II: Project Organization Structure

Name of the Project	Additional Positions Below You (e.g., Team Lead, etc.)	Responsibilities (e.g., Resource Planning, Task Execution, etc.)	Which Results Would Have Been Impacted?	How Would They Have Helped Improve the Results?

3. Using Table 2.19, reflect on a recently completed complex project and list the responsibilities of various people in your project organizational above your position. Answer following questions:
   a. Do you feel creating a balanced project structure on the basis of the principles of Pillar II would have helped improve the results?
   b. Who else can be added in your project organization structure above you to improve the results?
   c. Which results would have been impacted by adding the identified positions?
   d. How would they have helped improve the project results?
4. Using Table 2.20, reflect on a recently completed complex project and list the responsibilities of various people in your project organizational below your position. Answer following questions:
   a. Do you feel creating a balanced project structure on the basis of the principles of Pillar II would have helped improve the results?

    b. Who else can be added in your project organization structure below you to improve the results?

    c. Which results would have been impacted by adding the identified positions?

    d. How would they have helped improve the project results?

5. Scenario analysis: THREE-D is a multinational video game software development organization, which has clients in the United States and in Canada. Mii is one of the primary customers of THREE-D, and their business accounts for 40% of revenue for THREE-D. Mii was launching a new video game in China and contracted THREE-D to create a video game in partnership with their distributor for the Chinese market. THREE-D started the project and put their most experienced project manager on the project. During the course of the project of approximately 8 months, the project manager faced the following issues:

    a. The project manager was asked to use the same requirements used for launch in the U.S. and Canadian market, and there was no information provided about the requirements of the Chinese market.

    b. On several occasions during the project, the project manager did not know who needed to be contacted for particular issues. The project manager became the sole decision maker and had to make several assumptions to provide quick decisions on behalf of the customer, Mii, and on behalf of their own organization, THREE-D, on tough issues facing the project.

    c. The project manager used a traditional project structure without use of consultants or experts and was unable to make accurate estimations of project schedule, budget, and resource requirements.

As a result of the above issues, the project failed miserably to deliver on scope, schedule, or within budget resulting in a loss of $1.9 million dollars to Mii. This created a major rift in the relationship with Mii. However, because the president of THREE-D knew his counterpart at Mii personally, they were able to come to an agreement for future projects. The project manager's superior had a high level of respect for the abilities of the project manager and recommended that the project manager be given another chance to salvage the reputation of THREE-D. The presidents of both the companies took his recommendation seriously and agreed to let the project manager stay on and work on the upcoming project of launching a new game in the European market. However, they requested the superior that the project manager needs to provide them with a detailed report on the reason the project failed and the changes the project manager will make in his approach on the upcoming project to ensure that it is successful.

Table 2.21 Pillar II: Action Plan for Scenario Analysis Based on the Self-Enhancement Principles of Pillar II

No.	Top 5 Errors Made during the Handling of the Project for the Chinese Market Launch	Which Principles from Pillar II Should Be Used for Success in the Future Project?	Requests for the Superiors of THREE-D and Mii for Support in Applying These Principles?	Major Benefits of Applying the Principles from Pillar II to You Personally and to Your Career as a Project Manager?
1.				
2.				
3.				
4.				
5.				

Imagine that you are the project manager in the above scenario. Your superior has requested a detailed report and a very detailed plan of action from you so that he can take the necessary steps to provide you with the support you require. On the basis of the learning from Pillar II of the book on *12 Pillars of Project Excellence,* answer the following using Table 2.21:

a. What were the top five errors you made during the handling of the project for the Chinese market launch?

b. Which key principles from Pillar II will you use to address these errors to ensure success in the project involving the launch of the new game in the European market?

c. What requests will you have for the superiors of THREE-D and Mii for supporting you in applying the principles identified in Pillar II to make this launch successful?

d. What will be some major benefits to you personally and to your career as a project manager by applying the principles of Pillar II?

Pillar II   References

1. Muller, R. (2003). *Communication of Information Technology Project Sponsors and Managers in Buyer–Seller Relationships,* http://www.dissertation.com/book.php?book=1581121989 &method=ISBN (accessed October 27, 2010).
2. Johnson, J. (2010). *The Standish Group Report.* Boston, MA: The Standish Group International Inc.
3. Project Management Institute. (2008). *A Guide to the Project Management Body of Knowledge (PMBOK Guide),* 4th Ed., p. 43, Table 3-1. 14, Campus Blrd, Newtown Square, PA 19073.
4. Kosmala, M. (2009). *Project Management: 6 Steps to Creating a Successful RASCI Chart.* The Canoe group Inc., http://www.thecanoegroup.com/470/project-management-6-steps-to-creating-a-successful-rasci-chart (accessed October 27, 2010).

Chapter 3

Pillar III: Delight the Customers with Project Vision Statement

A powerful "project vision statement" to the project is like an "altimeter" to an aircraft. Both help determine the altitude.

3.1 Introduction

3.1.1 Delight the Customers

Successful project leaders are a special breed of individuals for whom mediocrity is not an option. For them, "just satisfying" customers is not enough; they only aim "to delight" their customers. They are not satisfied until they hear a "WOW!" from their stakeholders and customers at the completion of every project. These project leaders all have one thing in common—they set their project vision higher than others even dare to dream. **Their motto is "aim for the stars; if we fall short, we will at least land on the moon."** These are the project leaders who reach the status of superheroes in any corporation. They become legends, and their superiors and project teams believe in their "magical" powers to extract water from a stone.

3.1.2 How Can a Project Vision Statement Be Used to Delight Your Customer?

Similar to an altimeter that determines the altitude of an aircraft, a project vision statement sets the "altitude" of the project.

Similar to an altimeter that determines the altitude of an aircraft, a project vision statement sets the "altitude" of the project. The project leader must create a common project vision of high standards at the very start of the journey. They must motivate their team to "dream big" and "go the extra mile," so at the end of the project, the customer can react with "Wow—this is awesome!"

3.2 Project Vision Statement

3.2.1 Definition

Project vision statement for a project provides a high-level purpose, defines a crystal clear objective, and sets the tone for the execution of the project. It lays the foundation for the ultimate success of the project.

3.2.2 Explanation

The "project vision statement" is one of the tools used by successful project leaders to motivate and to set the soaring standards for the team to achieve.

The "project vision statement" is one of the tools used by successful project leaders to motivate and to set the soaring standards for the team to achieve. The project vision statement is analogous to an aircraft altimeter that helps determine

Figure 3.1   A project vision acts as an aircraft altimeter.

the altitude of the aircraft as shown in Figure 3.1. The pilot and the cockpit crew navigate on the basis of the planned altitude, but in case the aircraft deviates from the planned elevation, they need to react immediately and reset the aircraft to the planned altitude.

A project vision statement is created in consensus with the team and must include the following:

1. Commitment to higher standards
2. Precise objectives from customer's point of view
3. Clear and measurable criteria for success
4. Guidelines for teamwork
5. Culture change goals

3.2.3 Example

An example of a project vision statement used by one of my teams is as follows:

> **"To inspire teamwork and successfully implement Pinnacle flow technology at ABC Corporation to increase material velocity and throughput, improve product quality and process documentation, reduce inventory and related costs while sustaining current growth and preserving the corporate culture."**

3.2.4 Why Is a Project Vision Statement Important?

Here are some comments made by Sam Walton,[1] one of the founders of Wal-Mart:

> **Capital isn't scarce; Vision is.**
> **High expectations are the key to everything.**[1]

A complex project is bound by scope, budget, and schedule constraints. A project leader and a project team should identify the needs of the customer and balance competing demands from scope, schedule, quality, and budget. Changing requirements during execution of the project can create additional risks leading to confusion among team members. The project team must thus identify what is and what is not covered within the project. They should assess the situation for successful execution of the project. A project vision statement provides high-level scope of the project so that the team can focus on the project's objectives instead of the individual stakeholder's objective. Project vision statement along with project scope defines a clear boundary for the project. Figure 3.2 gives illustrates some of the advantages of creating a project vision statement in a project.

3.2.5 How Is a Project Vision Statement Created?

A project vision statement must be created by the team with guidance from the project leader. It is created using a few brainstorming sessions where the charter requirements are distilled with carefully selected words and is combined with

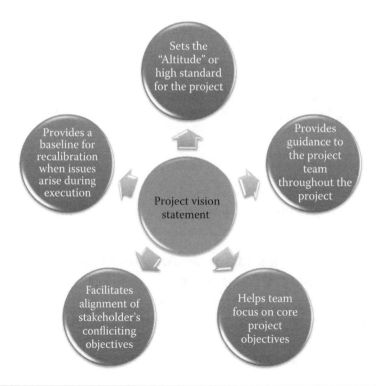

Figure 3.2 Advantages of a project vision statement.

words that define the mind-set of the team toward carrying out plans to completion and includes any constraints defined by the stakeholders.

3.3 Steps to Create a Project Vision Statement

The following sequence of steps are used to create a project vision statement.

3.3.1 Create a Project Vision Committee

Creating a project vision committee is the first step in creating a project vision statement. Core members of the project should be involved in this committee. A committee with too many members may not end up in consensus. Hence, the committee should have few (five to seven) core members who can create realistic project vision statement. Too much time should not be taken in creating a project vision statement because it will reduce the enthusiasm of the committee.

3.3.2 Review the Charter

The charter is created to formally to approve a project and document initial requirements for the project. Charter is the bridge between the project and the strategy of the organization. It also links project to the operations happening in the organization. Project statement of work and business case is used to prepare a charter, and it contains information about the services or products delivered by project. The characteristics of a product are described very well in the project charter. High-level milestones and high-level requirements are also mentioned in the project charter. Because project charter contains such important documented information regarding a project, it should be reviewed by the project vision committee thoroughly to create a project vision statement.

3.3.3 Interview Key Stakeholders

This is a critical step in creating a project vision statement that is often missed. If the project is critical to the organization and will result in substantial changes in processes, systems, personnel, or culture of the organization, it is imperative for the project leader and subleader to spend some face time with key stakeholders that may be impacted by the project. There are two key advantages for the project leader and for the stakeholder when this activity is done. The first advantage is that by initiating a face-to-face meeting with the stakeholders, the project leader demonstrates the stakeholder that their opinion and issues are important and will be considered proactively. This allows an immediate rapport to be formed with the stakeholder, which can be very helpful during the project execution. The second advantage is that the project leader is not blindsided by making any false assumptions about the impact of the project on the stakeholder but captures their concerns and proactively addresses those by including it in the project vision statement. For example, if the project requires a new advanced server to be installed by the research and development (R&D) team on the premises and if the director of information technology is impacted, they should be interviewed for any major concerns. If the concern is energy usage, then that requirement regarding energy consumption such as "ensuring minimal energy consumption" should be captured and included as a part of the project vision statement.

3.3.4 Identify the Priority Areas of Focus

Once project charter is reviewed, choosing high-priority areas is the next step in writing a project vision statement. The priority areas must be established to represent the objectives of the project. These areas represent the action items that the project is intended for and lays the foundation for creating a powerful project vision statement. The priority areas are chosen to meet customer's objective with utmost quality.

3.3.5 Create Initial Project Vision Statement

The priority areas are then converted into effective phrases to create an initial project vision statement. The central idea of the project vision statement gives a clear direction to the team in the project; project vision motivates and encourages project team members during project execution. Project vision statement facilitates the activities in a project, and it embodies the objectives of the organization. All these elements are taken into account while writing an initial project vision statement. Care must be taken to target the audience it is intended for.

3.3.6 Brainstorm for the Final Project Vision Statement

After creating the initial project vision statement, brainstorm the statement to see any new values or phrases can be added to the statement. Adding more phrases to make it a good statement undermines the very essential purpose of project vision statement. Project vision statement should be precise and short. Remember, the project vision statement should align with organization goals and should be realistic. The project vision statement should be focused and short with about one to three sentences.

3.3.7 Create a Final Powerful Project Vision Statement

This is the final step in creating the project vision statement. As project vision statement forms the core of the project objectives, powerful phrases need to be used in creating a final project vision statement, and all committee members should approve it before finalizing it. Once the project vision statement is finalized, it can be used on all project documents. Figure 3.3 gives different steps involved in creating a project vision statement.

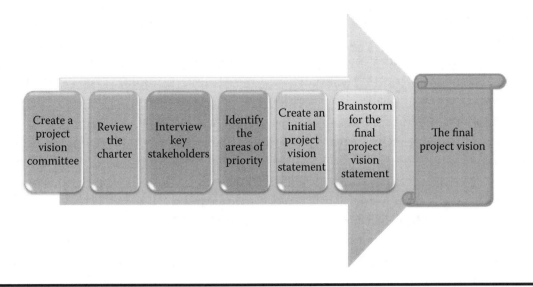

Figure 3.3   Steps to create a project vision statement.

3.4 The Goal of Creating a Project Vision Statement

The goal of creating a project vision statement should be well understood by a project leader. Project vision statement forms the boundary for the project life cycle, which contains various elements in a project. The project vision statement once built lasts for the entire life cycle of the project and acts as a catalyst for whole life of the project, thus forming an important pillar for project excellence.

Thus, it is very clear that the first step to delighting the customer is to create a powerful project vision statement. But why should the project leader take their valuable time to do so? Why not just provide the minimal possible project performance if the customer has no choice but to accept it? This is the question that differentiates a project leader from a project manager. The project leaders understand the tremendous benefit that can bring in their own career and in the careers of the team members by creating a powerful project vision statement.

3.4.1 Setting Higher Standards versus "Gold Plating"

An important point of clarification is that setting higher standards is not the same as "gold plating," which has a negative connotation as it refers to adding features that are not required by the customer. Project leaders with an experience in the power of lean thinking understand what adds value from the point of view of a customer. They set higher standards on value-added items and discard or minimize the focus on the non-value-added items.

3.5 A Permanent Project Vision Statement of Project Leaders

Getting a customer takes months or years of dedicated effort, but losing one takes less than a minute. Project leaders need to follow this same principle if they are serious about their careers. I will now share with you one of the best piece of advice I ever got from one of my managers. I was working as a manufacturing engineer and kept pestering him for more and more challenging assignments/projects. He finally told me "I have no control over corporate projects. If you want to lead corporate projects, all you need to do is create your own 'fan club' within this organization. Have a fan in every department at every level of the organization. Your fan club will always pull for you whenever a new and challenging project opens up." I owe a lot to his advice as I took it to heart and changed my entire paradigm. It even helped me change my perception and thought process from "What is my corporation doing for me?" to a very powerful realization of **"What can I do for my corporation?"**

It is important to talk about a personal vision statement at this point. In addition to a project vision statement, every project leader must create a vision statement in their work life. Project leader should dream of leading high-profile corporate projects in their life and enjoy the success from such projects. Creating a personal vision statement and corporate vision statement can help create a "corporate fan club" for a project leader. Figure 3.4 lists the impact of a personal vision statement on project leaders. I created my personal vision statement "delight every customer, every time" and stayed focused on delighting my internal customers with every interaction, with every small task I performed, and generated fans at all levels. A great example of this was when a manager in the R&D department once during an off-hand conversation mentioned that he was having significant losses and impact on customer satisfaction because of obsolescence of our manuals and literature and long lead times for reprinting. He asked for my help. I investigated alternatives to printing the literature at a print shop, found a great on-demand printing system, and worked with the R&D team to create a justification for the investment. I presented the capital expenditure request to the president of the company. When he saw that not only are we saving a significant revenue annually by eliminating obsolescence but can

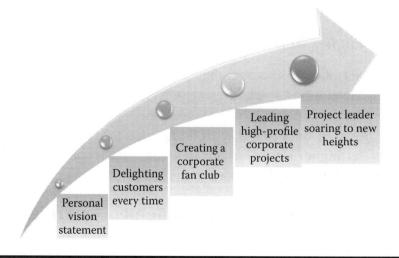

Figure 3.4 Impact of a personal vision statement on project leaders.

actually save another $800,000 annually, he was delighted and signed it immediately. The budget was approved, and I purchased, installed, and validated the system into production, almost a year from my conversation with the director of R&D, who was now the vice president of R&D. I worked closely with the R&D team and the new director to ensure all their requirements were met. I did all this while I was holding a full-time job as a manufacturing engineer in operations. At the end of the project, I got this note from the director of R&D: "Adil, if you hadn't joined the team, we'd be still wandering aimlessly. You did a SPECTACULAR job of assigning tasks, clearing up confusion, ironing out details and making decisions. On behalf on my R&D team—we are grateful for your superb effort." This director had a great informal network within the organization. Subsequently, I kept being nominated to lead strategic and corporate-critical projects. I continued collecting more fans throughout the organization.

I also helped department managers by undertaking projects within their department to improve their processes. For example, I was approached by our new document control manager to apply the principles of flow in his department. This department was a huge bottleneck for our division, and it was slowing down the releases of Engineering Change Notifications (ECNs) for new and existing products considerably with average throughput times for completion being over 90 days and in cases exceeding a year. The on-time percentage for ECNs was about 6%. I agreed to help him overhaul the document control unit in our division. None of our executives were even aware that we were working on this effort. After some simulation modeling, layout changes, and implementation of some innovative technology, the throughput times for ECNs and prints reduced to 2 days (1.87 to be exact—approximately 90% improvement), and on-time percentage was more than 90% (more than 85% improvement). The turnaround of this department had an amazing impact on our entire division, and the results of this "below the radar" project were so surprising to the executives that my mailbox was inundated with kudos from the president and other executives.

Here are just a few comments from my fans, which I created at various levels in the organization, which I share with utmost humility, to make the point of "how will you know you have a fan within the organization":

> *Adil has set the standard for other project managers to emulate.... He brought this project in ahead of schedule and under budget!*
>
> —Manufacturing Manager

> *Adil, well-done—I'm hearing a lot of good things about the impact you're having on this division!*
>
> —General Manager and President

> *True Leadership can be measured by the impact that ideas have on others—you are impacting this facility but others as well. Great job!!!*
>
> —Director, Human Resources

These comments from my fans not only motivated me to continue making more fans but were also catalysts for getting decisions in my favor when executives were deciding on the project leader for their next strategic project. Thus, each success led to a bigger and more critical project, and I ended up creating a niche for myself in the organization as an internal consultant and a corporate program leader.

The work performed on the projects also helped several of my team members to start a "corporate fan club" of their own and rise to new heights in their career. An intern who was selected to work on one of my projects with me impressed one of the managers significantly with his work. Upon graduation, he was offered a full-time position within the company on the basis of positive feedback from the manager and myself.

Thus, successful project leaders never have to wait for "the big one" to show up. Their delighted customers are a like a "corporate fan club" that influence the superiors to "give the right of first refusal" of any strategic or corporate-critical projects to these project leaders. They are sought after and courted by every department including the "C" level executives. They are truly valued as "project leaders *par excellence*" or "corporate superheroes."

Pillar III   Summary

Every successful project leader must use a project vision statement that sets soaring standards and results in delighting the customers on each project. This also helps to create a "corporate fan club" throughout the organization. Project vision statement for any project gives the definitive state that a project is going to achieve. Project vision statement lays the foundation for ultimate success of the project. Project vision statement creates a boundary for various elements in a project.

1. A project vision statement provides high-level scope of the project so that team can focus on the project's objectives instead of individual stakeholder's objectives.
2. Project vision statement is created using a structured methodology. The steps followed in creating a project vision statement are forming a committee, reviewing the charter, interviewing the stakeholders, identifying initial priority areas, preparing an initial project vision statement, brainstorming for the final vision statement, and creating a powerful final project vision statement.
3. Preparing a project vision statement provides not only a path for successful project but also a path for career development for individuals in the team.

Figure 3.5 gives the summary of important points in developing a project vision statement.

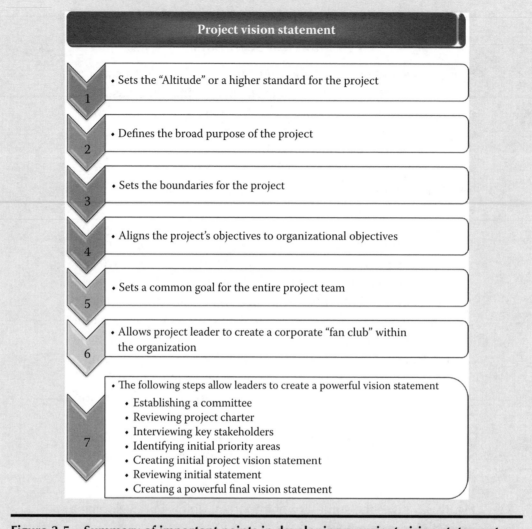

Project vision statement

1. • Sets the "Altitude" or a higher standard for the project

2. • Defines the broad purpose of the project

3. • Sets the boundaries for the project

4. • Aligns the project's objectives to organizational objectives

5. • Sets a common goal for the entire project team

6. • Allows project leader to create a corporate "fan club" within the organization

7. • The following steps allow leaders to create a powerful vision statement
   - Establishing a committee
   - Reviewing project charter
   - Interviewing key stakeholders
   - Identifying initial priority areas
   - Creating initial project vision statement
   - Reviewing initial statement
   - Creating a powerful final vision statement

Figure 3.5 Summary of important points in developing a project vision statement.

Pillar III   Case Study

DEVELOP A PROJECT VISION STATEMENT WITH HIGH STANDARDS

INTRODUCTION

This case study is about using a project vision statement to set high standards for two different highly complex acquisition projects with numerous problems.

CHALLENGE

While working as a manufacturing engineer in a clean room operations, I was also filling the role of a clean-room packaging engineer. Our corporation had acquired a $1 billion corporation, almost equal to us in revenue but double in size (resources, inventory, etc.). The role of my division was to consolidate some product lines, eliminate some, and market others with our label on it. Initially, I was given a minor sidekick role of conducting packaging validations; however, one day, I was summoned to the office of our vice president. He wanted me to take over the entire project.

SITUATION

When he explained to me the dire state of the project, I was quite amazed. Most of the staff and some entire departments at the acquired facility in New Jersey had been laid off. Their subcontractors were shut down because of existing inventory on some products exceeding 20 years of sales and the union at the facility was chanting slogans against our firm and CEO during work hours. I did not know whether to thank him for this opportunity or to escape from his office as soon as he broke eye contact with me.

However, I accepted on one condition—he will stand by my decisions 100% of the time. He was true to his word. I spent 2 weeks at the acquired plant in New Jersey, fearful every time I entered or exited the facility through a crowd of animated union workers. One of their subcontracting packaging house was owned by a 60-year-old lady and her son. She was almost in tears when I went there at the end of my visit and told me that in the last 20 years this was the first time she had to shut down operations and lay off her workers, who, to her, were no less than close family members.

IMPLEMENTATION

This situation had a deep emotional impact on me and my team, and getting her "packaging house fully operational within 1 month" became part of my team's project vision statement. We made a promise to her that we would get the operations up and running within the next 4 weeks. Within 6 weeks of taking over this project (4 weeks after making the promise) and going through a tangled mess and "a spaghetti-bowl" of issues—technical, human, and logistical—the project was back on track and the integration was completed successfully. We were shipping product both from the acquired location in New Jersey and from our facility in Michigan without any further issues.

I had made quite a few fans inside and outside our organization. Here is an unsolicited note sent to my functional manager by one of the team members who left the team as she was taking over new duties after being promoted to manager of human resources. "I just wanted to praise Adil for his focus on the acquisition project. It is a huge project with many 'opportunities' and could be quite overwhelming for a quite a few people. Adil has done an unbelievable job organizing everyone and breaking it down into pieces that are manageable. He is also ensuring support to everyone involved. That helps a lot. Adil is definitely a role model for me as far as project planning and execution goes."

RESULTS

No good deed goes unpunished—the day before I was set to close out the this project, my vice president again summoned me to his office and was almost laughing when he told me that he had signed me up to lead another critical acquisition project—this time I would be leading the effort from the very start. That was a dream come true for me. I had been waiting for a project like this one for a very long time. It was not an easy project but it was one of my favorites—one which I could take from project vision statement to completion.

The organization I was working for was acquiring a product line that was developed for cauterizing the area after removal of tumors or to cauterize microscopic blood vessels. This product was developed by a metallurgist as a last resort to saving his young daughter's life. The daughter had a brain tumor, and after the removal of tumor, the shunts placed in the brain to divert the blood flow was not working, but there was no device fine enough to cauterize the damaged blood vessel. The father literally walked into the surgery with this product (this was many years before the current Food and Drug Administration regulations requiring clinical trials) and had the surgeon successfully operate on the daughter using this product, thus giving her a new life. This product was patented, and the father formed a company. After several years of growth, he and his son, who also joined the family business, could not keep up with the legal fees of fighting infringements on the patent. Thus, after significant due diligence, our company decided to acquire the product line. Throughout the acquisition, our team had to be very sensitive, as if we were acquiring a beloved baby from the family. The importance of the sensitivity on this acquisition was an integral piece of our project vision statement for this project.

Once the project vision statement was created, I dove deep into this project and savored every moment like a child would an ice cream on a hot, sunny day. Because of the efforts of my fantastic team and the strong relationship we forged with the owners of the acquired company, we were ready to ship their products from our facility with our logo and labels even before the contract was fully signed off by the executives. At the project closing celebrations, the corporate vice president of acquisitions, Matt, congratulated the team and commented that "This has never been done in the history of our corporation—we usually have to wait for at least six months after the contract is signed before the acquired product is ready to be shipped."

My vice president sent me the following note, "You have put your heart and soul into this project and as a result it has been a huge success already. You are very talented and highly skilled person who couples these talents with strong interpersonal skills which is a formula for success every time. Thanks."

LESSONS LEARNED

Learning the subtle art of using the project vision statement for every project to integrate project objectives with a passion to set higher standards and delight internal and external customers propelled me from being an obscure manufacturing engineer in the clean room to leading two major acquisition projects for the corporation and then onto other critical projects for other divisions of the corporation. Thus, the biggest lesson learned was that customers you delight using a project vision statement become members of your "corporate fan club." These fans may have connections within your organization, and they will be glad to use it when you delight them every time. Figure 3.6 shows the illustration on corporate fan club.

Figure 3.6   A corporate fan club.

Pillar III   Force Field Analysis

PILLAR III: FORCE FIELD ANALYSIS OF ORGANIZATIONAL ASSESSMENT

Table 3.1 shows force field analysis of organizational assessment. The organizational assessment is conducted to assess if the culture of the organization is in alignment with the principles of Pillar III. Tables 3.2 through 3.4 are used to develop and implement an action plan to increase the impact of the organizational driving forces and decrease the impact of the organizational resisting forces.

PILLAR III: FORCE FIELD ANALYSIS OF SELF-ASSESSMENT

Table 3.5 shows force field analysis of self-assessment. The self-assessment is conducted to assess if your own strengths are in alignment with the principles of Pillar III. Tables 3.6 through 3.8 are used to develop and implement an action plan to increase the impact of the self-driving forces and decrease the impact of the self-resisting forces.

PILLAR III: RECOMMENDATIONS FOR OPTIMAL RESULTS FROM FORCE FIELD ANALYSIS

For optimal results and actual transformation of culture and strengths conducive to the creation of advanced master project leaders, the following three steps are necessary:

1. Both the organizational and the self-evaluation assessments must be completed.
2. A well-designed action plan must be created and implemented to increase the driving forces and decrease the resisting forces.
3. The principles of each pillar must be constantly practiced and improved.

It is highly recommended that both the organization assessments and the self-assessments be conducted every year and the action plan be updated at least every 3 months.

Note: The sum of scores for Organizational Driving Force and Organizational Resisting Force for each point must be less than or equal to TEN.

The sum of scores for Self Driving Force and Self Resisting Force for each point must be less than or equal to TEN.

Table 3.1   Pillar III: Force Field Organizational Analysis

Team Name: _____   Date: _____

Does My Organization Drive or Resist a Culture of Setting Higher Standards using a Project Vision Statement?				
0 Never		5 Sometimes	7 Mostly	
3 Rarely		ODF + ORF ≤ 10	10 Always	
No.	Driving Forces →	*Score Organizational Driving Force (ODF)*	*Score Organizational Resisting Force (ORF)*	← Resisting Forces
1	My organization understands the importance of creating a project vision statement at the start of every critical project.			My organization does not create a project vision statement for any project.
2	My organization stresses the importance of setting higher standards and superior results on projects to "delight" our customers.			My organization focuses on the criticality of completing the project with minimal importance given to final project metrics.
3	"Going the extra mile" or "going beyond the call of duty" to delight the customer is appreciated and rewarded.			Organizational culture discourages personnel from "going out on a limb" or to exceed normal standards of customer satisfaction.
4	Project leaders in our organization use the project vision statement as a tool to set the standards (altitude) of their projects.			Project managers use the project metrics to set the standards on their project.
5	The executives listen to the voice of the internal "fan club" during the selection process of project leaders.			Seniority or rank is the major factors in selecting project managers for critical projects.
6	Project leaders are assigned to projects as early as possible in the project life cycle.			Project managers are generally assigned to projects during the mature stages of the project life cycle.

7	Project leaders have full access to the end customers or their representatives to acquire and clarify all the project requirements accurately.			Project managers gather project requirements from sales, marketing, sponsors, or other sources as access to the end customers or their representatives is restricted.
8	Project leaders, core team members, and stakeholders participate in brainstorming sessions to create a powerful project vision statement.			Project managers usually do not create project vision statements or sometimes use one or two individuals to create a vision statement.
9	My organization culture encourages the project leaders to create their personal project vision statement that allows them to set a higher standard in any activity they undertake.			Our project managers never create a personal project vision statement to set standards of performance.
10	In my organization, project leaders who put every effort to excel at every activity they undertake usually have an informal network of supporters or a "fan club."			In my organization, our project managers do not create an informal network of supporters or a "fan club."
	Total ODF score			*Total ORF score*

Result	Conclusion	Recommended Action Review and Update Every Quarter (3 months)
ODF >> ORF	My company culture strongly drives a culture of creation of a project vision statement.	Use Tables 3.2 through 3.4 to set goals and create an action plan to preserve or continuously improve the culture of higher standards using a project vision statement.
ODF > ORF	My company culture drives the culture of creation of a project vision statement.	Use Tables 3.2 through 3.4 to set goals and create an action plan to increase ODF to create a culture of higher standards using a project vision statement.
ORF >> ODF	My company culture strongly resists the culture of creation of a project vision statement.	Use Tables 3.2 through 3.4 to set goals and create an action plan to increase the ODF and reduce the ORF to create a culture of higher standards using a project vision statement.
ORF > ODF	My company culture resists the culture of creation of a project vision statement.	Use Tables 3.2 through 3.4 to set goals and create an action plan to reduce the ORF to create a culture of higher standards using a project vision statement.
ODF = ORF	My company culture does not drive or resist the culture of creation of a project vision statement.	Use Tables 3.2 through 3.4 to set goals and create an action plan to increase the ODF to create a culture of higher standards using a project vision statement.

Table 3.2   Pillar III: Analysis of ODF and ORF Results

Result	Existing Organizational Culture	If the Goal Is to Create a Moderately Strong Culture of Setting Higher Standards Using a Project Vision Statement	If the Goal Is to Create a Very Strong Culture of Setting Higher Standards Using a Project Vision Statement
ODF			
ODF ≤ 25	No or minimal culture of setting higher standards using a project vision statement	Focus on improving scores in at least 5 DF	Focus on improving scores in at least 7 DF
25 < ODF ≤ 50	Weak culture of setting higher standards using a project vision statement	Focus on improving scores in at least 3 DF	Focus on improving scores in at least 5 DF
50 < ODF ≤ 75	Moderate culture of setting higher standards using a project vision statement	Focus on improving scores in at least 1 DF	Focus on improving scores in at least 3 DF
ODF > 75	Strong culture of setting higher standards using a project vision statement	N/A	Preserve or continuously improve the culture
ORF			
ORF > 75	No or minimal culture of setting higher standards using a project vision statement	Focus on decreasing scores in at least 5 RF	Focus on decreasing scores in at least 7 RF
50 < ORF ≤ 75	Weak culture of setting higher standards using a project vision statement	Focus on decreasing scores in at least 3 RF	Focus on decreasing scores in at least 5 RF
25 < ORF ≤ 50	Moderate culture of setting higher standards using a project vision statement	Focus on decreasing scores in at least 1 RF	Focus on decreasing scores in at least 3 RF
ORF ≤ 25	Strong culture of setting higher standards using a project vision statement	N/A	Preserve or continuously improve the culture

Table 3.3 Pillar III: Action Plan to Increase Organizational Driving Forces (ODFs)

Team Name: _____   Date: _____

No.	Driving Force	Current Score	Goal (Target Score) ⬆	Action Plan to Increase DF Score	Complete by (Date)	Assigned to (Department Name or Initials of the Person)
1	My organization understands the importance of creating a project vision statement at the start of every critical project.					
2	My organization stresses the importance of setting higher standards and superior results on projects to "delight" our customers.					
3	"Going the extra mile" or "going beyond the call of duty" to delight the customer is appreciated and rewarded.					
4	Project leaders in our organization use the project vision statement as a tool to set the standards (altitude) of their projects.					
5	The executives listen to the voice of the internal "fan club" during the selection process of project leaders.					
6	Project leaders are assigned to projects as early as possible in the project life cycle.					

7	Project leaders have full access to the end customers or their representatives to acquire and clarify all the project requirements accurately.					
8	Project leaders, core team members, and stakeholders participate in brainstorming sessions to create a powerful project vision statement.					
9	My organization culture encourages the project leaders to create their personal project vision statement that allows them to set a higher standard in any activity they undertake.					
10	In my organization, project leaders who put every effort to excel at every activity they undertake usually have an informal network of supporters or a "fan club."					
	Total ODF					

Table 3.4 Pillar III: Action Plan to Decrease Organization Resisting Forces (ORF)

Name: _____   Date: _____

No.	Resisting Force	Current Score	Goal (Target Score) ⬇	Action Plan to Decrease RF Score	Complete by (Date)	Assigned to (Department Name or Initials of the Person)
1	My organization does not create a project vision statement for any project.					
2	My organization focuses on the criticality of completing the project with minimal importance given to final project metrics.					
3	Organizational culture discourages personnel from "going out on a limb" or to exceed normal standards of customer satisfaction.					
4	Project managers use the project metrics to set the standards on their project.					
5	Seniority or rank is the major factor in selecting project managers for critical projects.					
6	Project managers are generally assigned to projects during the mature stages of the project life cycle.					
7	Project managers gather project requirements from sales, marketing, sponsors, or other sources as access to the end customers or their representatives is restricted.					
8	Project managers usually do not create project vision statements or sometimes use one or two individuals to create a vision statement.					

9	Our project managers never create a personal project vision statement to set standards of performance.					
10	In my organization, our project managers do not create an informal network of supporters or a "fan club."					
	Total ORF					

Table 3.5 Pillar III: Force Field Self-Analysis

Team Name: _____   Date: _____

	Does My Behavior Drive or Resist a Culture of Setting Higher Standards using a Project Vision Statement?				
	0 Never		5 Sometimes		7 Mostly
	3 Rarely		SDF + SRF ≤ 10		10 Always
No.	Driving Forces	Score Self-Driving Force (SDF)	Score Self-Resisting Force (SRF)		Resisting Forces
1	I always go "the extra mile" to delight my clients (internal and external).				I only focus on achieving the project metrics and do not try to "delight" the customers.
2	I set high standards for myself and my team members on all projects.				I never set higher standards for myself and my team members than those defined by the final project metrics.
3	As a first step of setting high standards for all my projects, I create a project vision statement.				I never create project vision statement for any of my projects.
4	I always have a "fan club" of supporters within my organization who recommend me for projects.				I never have any supporters within my organization who recommend me for projects.
5	I always prepare the project vision statement by conducting brainstorming session with the key members of the project team.				I never involve all the key team members when I prepare a vision statement.
6	I interview important stakeholders in my project before preparing the project vision statement.				I always inform the stakeholders about the vision statement after it has been finalized.
7	I acquire the project requirements directly from the end customers or their representatives.				I gather the project requirements from sales, marketing, sponsors, or other sources as I do not have to the end customers.

8	I prepare vision statement based on systematic structured approach starting with reviewing the project objectives and charter.			I prepare vision statement based on traditional unstructured approach.
9	I create my personal project vision statement with high standards in any activity I undertake.			I never create a personal project vision statement with high standards of performance.
10	I allocate time to develop informal relationships within and outside of my organization.			I do not spend any time in developing informal relationships within and outside of my organization.
	Total SDF score			*Total SRF score*

Result	Conclusion	Recommended Action Review and Update Every Quarter (3 months)
SDF >> SRF	My behavior strongly supports a culture of setting higher standards using a project vision statement.	Use Tables 3.6 through 3.8 to set goals and create an action plan to continuously enhance the behavior to set high standards using a project vision statement.
SDF > SRF	My behavior supports a culture of setting higher standards using a project vision statement.	Use Tables 3.6 through 3.8 to set goals and create an action plan to increase SDF to allow a stronger behavior toward setting high standards using a project vision statement.
SRF >> SDF	My behavior strongly resists a culture of setting higher standards using a project vision statement.	Use Tables 3.6 through 3.8 to set goals and create an action plan to increase SDF and reduce SRF to allow a stronger behavior toward setting high standards using a project vision statement.
SRF > SDF	My behavior resists a culture of setting higher standards using a project vision statement.	Use Tables 3.6 through 3.8 to set goals and create an action plan to reduce SRF to allow a stronger behavior toward setting high standards using a project vision statement.
SDF = SRF	My behavior does not drive or resist a culture of setting higher standards using a project vision statement.	Use Tables 3.6 through 3.8 to set goals and create an action plan to increase the SDF to allow a stronger behavior toward setting high standards using a project vision statement.

Table 3.6   Pillar III: Analysis of SDF and SRF Results

Result	Existing Behavior	If the Goal Is to Create a Moderately Strong Behavior Toward the Principle of Setting Higher Standards Using Vision Statement	If the Goal Is to Create a Very Strong Behavior Toward the Principle of Setting Higher Standards Using Vision Statement
SDF			
SDF ≤ 25	No or minimal activities in creating a project vision statement	Focus on improving scores in at least 5 DF	Focus on improving scores in at least 7 DF
25 < SDF ≤ 50	Weak activities in creating a project vision statement	Focus on improving scores in at least 3 DF	Focus on improving scores in at least 5 DF
50 < SDF ≤ 75	Moderate activities in creating a project vision statement	Focus on improving scores in at least 1 DF	Focus on improving scores in at least 3 DF
SDF > 75	Strong activities in creating a project vision statement	N/A	Preserve or continuously improve the behavior
SRF			
SRF > 75	No or minimal activities in creating a project vision statement	Focus on decreasing scores in at least 5 RF	Focus on decreasing scores in at least 7 RF
50 < SRF ≤ 75	Weak activities in creating a project vision statement structure	Focus on decreasing scores in at least 3 RF	Focus on decreasing scores in at least 5 RF
25 < SRF ≤ 50	Moderate activities in creating a balanced project vision statement	Focus on decreasing scores in at least 1 RF	Focus on decreasing scores in at least 3 RF
SRF ≤ 25	Strong activities in creating a project vision statement	N/A	Preserve or continuously improve the behavior

Table 3.7   Pillar III: Action Plan to Increase Self-Driving Forces (SDFs)

Name: _____   Date: _____

No.	Driving Force	Current Score	Goal (Target Score) ⬆	Action Plan to Increase DF Score	Complete by (Date)	Required Resources
1	I always go "the extra mile" to delight my clients (internal and external).					
2	I set high standards for myself and my team members on all projects.					
3	As a first step of setting high standards for all my projects, I create a project vision statement.					
4	I always have a "fan club" of supporters within my organization who recommend me for projects.					
5	I always prepare the project vision statement by conducting brainstorming session with the key members of the project team.					
6	I interview important stakeholders in my project before preparing the project vision statement.					
7	I acquire the project requirements directly from the end customers or their representatives.					
8	I prepare vision statement based on systematic structured approach starting with reviewing the project objectives and charter.					
9	I create my personal project vision statement with high standards in any activity I undertake.					
10	I allocate time to develop informal relationships within and outside of my organization.					
	Total SDF					

Table 3.8 Pillar III: Action Plan to Decrease Self-Resisting Forces (SRFs)

Name: _____   Date: _____

No.	Resisting Force	Current Score	Goal (Target Score) ↓	Action Plan to Decrease RF Score	Complete by (Date)	Required Resources
1	I only focus on achieving the project metrics and do not try to "delight" the customers.					
2	I never set higher standards for myself and my team members than those defined by the final project metrics.					
3	I never create a project vision statement for any of my projects.					
4	I never have any supporters within my organization who recommend me for projects.					
5	I never involve all the key team members when I prepare a vision statement.					
6	I always inform the stakeholders about the vision statement after it has been finalized.					
7	I gather the project requirements from sales, marketing, sponsors, or other sources as I do not have access to the end customers.					
8	I prepare vision statement based on traditional unstructured approach.					
9	I never create a personal project vision statement with high standards of performance.					
10	I do not spend any time in developing informal relationships within and outside of my organization.					
	Total SRF					

Pillar III   Exercises

PILLAR III: ORGANIZATIONAL-LEVEL SKILL SET–ENHANCEMENT EXERCISES

GROUP EXERCISES

These exercises are best completed within a group of project managers, project leaders, executives, and stakeholders from within a department or an organization.

1. Using Table 3.9, identify at least five advantages to your organization in applying the principles of Pillar III by creating a culture of setting higher standards for "delighting customers" by creating project vision statements on all major projects. Rate the advantages from 1 (least important) to 5 (most important).
2. Answer the questions in the brainstorming aid to creating a project vision statement as shown in Table 3.10. Discuss the answers with key stakeholders of a selected project and examine if this can be helpful in creating a powerful vision statement for a project.
3. Identify one successful completed project in your organization. Use all the steps of creating a project vision statement using brainstorming techniques with the project team of the completed project. Prepare the final powerful project vision statement with the group. Using Table 3.11 (row 1), document the final vision statement and identify and list at least three ways the project vision statement would have benefited in improving the project results if it had been created at the beginning of the project.

Table 3.9   Pillar III: Five Advantages of Applying Principles of Pillar III to Your Organization

No.	Advantages of Applying Principles of Pillar III for Setting Higher Standards for "Delighting Customers" by Creating Project Vision Statements on All Major Projects	Rating (from 1 = Least Important to 5 = Most Important)	Explain the Rating
1			
2			
3			
4			
5			

Table 3.10 Pillar III: Brainstorming Aid to Creating a Vision Statement

Question	Answer in Brief
What are the strengths and special characteristics of your organization?	
What are the primary objectives of your organization?	
What are the very key objectives of a selected project?	
Are the objectives of the selected project aligned with the objectives of the organization?	
What characteristics and strengths of the organization culture can be used to help set higher standards on the selected project?	

Table 3.11 Pillar III: List Projects, Vision Statement, and Benefits

Projects	Project Vision Statement	Three Ways the Project Vision Statement Would Have Benefited in Improving the Project Results if It Had Been Created at the Beginning of the Project
1. Successful project		a. b. c.
2. Failed project		a. b. c.

4. Identify one failed project in your organization. Use all the steps of creating a project vision statement using brainstorming techniques with the project team of the completed project. Prepare the final powerful project vision statement with the group. Using Table 3.11 (row 2), document the final vision statement and identify and list at least three ways the project vision statement would have benefited in improving the project results if it had been created at the beginning of the project.

5. Scenario analysis: Rockheed Corporation is a new defense contractor working with various government agencies for the last 3 years. The corporation is currently in the probationary period of 5 years but already has had a history of poor results and a series of projects that delivered the products but did not completely satisfy the customers. The following are the major themes that come up during customer acceptance reviews:

   a. The product barely meets specifications.

   b. The product performance is not reliable.

c. The project is overbudget and has missed the scheduled delivery dates several times.

d. The aesthetics appeal of the product is low.

Rockheed has just won a bid for the sophisticated HHUD-NV military project worth 100 million dollars. Rockheed will be designing and manufacturing a sophisticated heads-up display (HUD) unit with night vision (HV) capabilities for the next generation of helicopter pilots to be used by the Navy. The CEO of Rockheed is extremely concerned about the standards the project managers are delivering to and fears that they will no longer be eligible to bid on government contracts if the issues are not addressed. They have called just an executive board meeting to come up with a project vision statement to set extremely high standards for upcoming Helicopter HUD with Night Vision (HHUD-NV) project, which can generate profits of over 30 million dollars for Rockheed. The CEO has suggested the assembled executives that they follow the principles and the steps provided in Pillar III of the *12 Pillars of Project Excellence* to come up with a powerful vision statement for the entire project team.

Table 3.12   Pillar III: Vision Statement for Scenario Analysis Based on Principles of Pillar III

No.	*Steps to Creating the Vision Statement for Rockheed's Upcoming HHUD-NV Project*	*Hint*	*Describe Final Deliverable (Make All Necessary Assumptions)*
1.	Create a project vision committee	Focus on • Who is needed? • Why are they needed?	
2.	Review the project charter	Document necessary assumptions made	
3.	Interview key stakeholders	Focus on who are the key stakeholders and list all questions	
4.	Create initial project vision statement	Ensure all concerns of the CEO are addressed Focus on who should participate	
5.	Create final project vision statement	Focus on • Is it powerful? • Does it set higher standards? • Is it aligned with all project and organizational objectives?	

Imagine that you and your group are the executives of Rockheed Corporation. Using Table 3.12, create a powerful vision statement to be presented to the CEO.

PILLAR III: PERSONAL-LEVEL SKILL SET– ENHANCEMENT EXERCISES

INDIVIDUAL EXERCISES

These exercises are to be completed individually after reviewing Pillar III in detail.

1. Using Table 3.13, identify at least five advantages to your career as a project manager of applying the principles of Pillar III by creating a powerful vision statement to set higher standards for "delighting customers" on all future major projects. Rate the advantages from 1 (least important) to 5 (most important).
2. Using Table 3.14, identify at least five roadblocks to applying the principles of Pillar III and creating a powerful vision statement to set higher standards for "delighting customers" on all your future major projects. Rate the identified roadblocks from 1 (least difficult to overcome) to 5 (most difficult to overcome).
3. a. Identify two successful projects you have led or have recently completed. Prepare the final powerful project vision statement for each project. Using Table 3.15, document the final vision statements and identify and list at least three ways the project vision statements would have benefited you in leading the projects if it had been created at the beginning of the project.
   b. Identify two failed projects you have managed or have recently completed. Prepare the final powerful project vision statements for each project. Using Table 3.16, document the final vision

Table 3.13   Pillar III: Five Advantages of Applying Principles of Pillar III to Your Career

No.	Advantages of Applying Principles of Pillar III by Creating a Powerful Vision Statement to Set Higher Standards for "Delighting Customers" on All Future Major Projects	Rating (from 1 = Least Important to 5 = Most Important)	Explain the Rating
1			
2			
3			
4			
5			

Table 3.14   Pillar III: Five Roadblocks to Applying Principles of Pillar III

No.	Roadblocks to Applying Principles of Pillar III to Creating Powerful Vision Statements on Future Major Projects	Rating (from 1 = Least Difficult to Overcome to 5 = Most Difficult to Overcome)	Explain the Rating
1			
2			
3			
4			
5			

Table 3.15   Pillar III: List Successful Projects, Vision Statements, and Benefits

Projects	Project Vision Statement	Three Ways the Project Vision Statement Would Have Benefited You in Leading the Project if It Had Been Created at the Beginning of the Project
Successful Project 1		a. b. c.
Successful Project 2		a. b. c.

statements and identify and list at least three ways the project vision statements would have benefited you in leading the projects to success if it had been created at the beginning of the project.

4. Use Table 3.17 and select an upcoming major project you are leading or going to be a part of. Create a personal vision statement for setting the highest personal standards of performance on that project. Review and explain how you applied the personal vision statement throughout the life cycle of the project and the results achieved as a result of applying the personal vision statement during that project phase.

Table 3.16   Pillar III: List Failed Projects, Vision Statement, and Benefits

Projects	*Project Vision Statement*	*Three Ways the Project Vision Statement Would Have Benefited You in Leading the Project to Success if It Had Been Created at the Beginning of the Project*
Failed Project 1		a. b. c.
Failed Project 2		a. b. c.

Table 3.17   Pillar III: Applying a Personal Vision Statement to an Upcoming Project

Name of upcoming project		
Your role in the project		
Personal vision statement for setting highest standards on the project		
Phase	*Explain how the personal vision statement was applied during the phase*	*Explain results achieved by applying the personal vision statement*
1. Project start-up		
2. Project preparation		
3. Project implementation		
4. Project monitoring		
5. Project closure		

5. Scenario analysis: Rockheed Corporation is a new defense contractor working with various government agencies for the last 3 years. The corporation is currently in the probationary period of 5 years but already has had a history of poor results and a series of projects that delivered the products but did not completely satisfy the customers. The following are the major themes that come up during customer acceptance reviews:

    a. The product barely meets specifications.
    b. The product performance is not reliable.
    c. The project is overbudget and has missed the scheduled delivery dates several times.
    d. The aesthetics appeal of the product is low.

Rockheed has just won a bid for the sophisticated HHUD-NV military project worth 100 million dollars. Rockheed will be designing and manufacturing a sophisticated HUD unit with night vision (HV) capabilities for the next generation of helicopter pilots to be used by the Navy. The CEO of Rockheed is extremely concerned about the standards the project managers are delivering to and fears that they will no longer be eligible to bid on government contracts if the issues are not addressed. Imagine that you have been selected to lead the HHUD-NV project for Rockheed. Your superior has suggested that you create a powerful personal vision statement using the principles of Pillar III of the *12 Pillars of Project Excellence* to raise your standard of project management and set goals and objectives that will be used to set the highest altitude for the HHUD-NV and motivate your project team during the entire life cycle of the project.

Using Table 3.18, create a powerful personal vision statement to be presented to your superior at Rockheed Corporation. Explain how the personal vision statement was applied to set higher standards compared with previous projects during each project phase. Explain how you used the personal vision statement to motivate the project team to achieve outstanding results during each phase of the life cycle of project HHUD-NV? Document all necessary assumptions.

Table 3.18 Pillar III: Applying a Personal Vision Statement to Scenario Analysis

Name of upcoming project	HHUD-NV	
Your role in the project	Project leader	
Personal vision statement for setting highest standards on the project		
Phase	*Explain how the personal vision statement will be applied to set highest standards*	*How will you use the personal vision statement to motivate the project team to achieve outstanding results?*
1. Project start-up		
2. Project preparation		
3. Project implementation		
4. Project monitoring		
5. Project closure		

Pillar III   Reference

1. Sam Walton, 1918–1992, http://quotationsbook.com/quote/40852/ (accessed September 27, 2010).

Chapter 4

Pillar IV: Sign the Charter

A "charter" to a project is like a "constitution" to a great country. Both establish a solid framework for success.

4.1 Introduction

4.1.1 Why Projects Fail?

If you have practiced the power of visualization explained in Pillar I, this will be a good time to put it into practice. Get ready for a small exercise.

This year, you determined and set your goal to lose your weight. Visualize that your birthday celebrations are few days ahead and your family wants to support your goal of weight loss. They have all chipped in for your gift, which is a state-of-the-art, ten-speed mountain bike. However, because of a tight budget, the family had to get you an "assembly-required" bicycle. For the next 5 minutes, visualize yourself assembling your new mountain bike. Visualize every major task you will complete to assemble your ten-speed mountain bike.

After the visualization exercise, answer the following questions:

1. Did you open the box and immediately begin the assembly process?
2. Did you prefer to use the trial-and-error approach to assembly rather than reviewing the assembly instructions?

If you answered "yes" to both of the questions above, you are "normal." This is a common approach used by most. We carry the same mind-set on corporate projects. We usually tend to leap off the starter block into the race before the starter gun has gone off, as illustrated in Figure 4.1. In other words, we jump right on to the problem instead of understanding, analyzing, and reviewing it. In project terms, we tend to start the projects before understanding the complete customer requirements. One of the leading reasons for project failures is ambiguous requirements.[1] If the requirements are not clearly understood and not defined

One of the leading reasons for project failures is ambiguous requirements.

and documented correctly by the project leader and the team, the customer's expectations are not met, resulting in project failure.

Figure 4.1   A false start.

4.2 Ambiguous Requirements

Ambiguous requirements are the result of unclear or missing critical information. This leads to confusion and rework. For example, in an information technology project, the team spends too much time trying to get clarification so they can design, code, and test. It is very difficult for architects to develop relevant models, for developers to write defect-free code, and for testers to develop the right test cases without clear requirements. Unfortunately, reworking requirements is so common that it can become an accepted practice. Rework is just built into the schedule and budget (reprint courtesy of the International Business Machines Corporation ©, 2009).

4.2.1 Importance of Gathering Accurate Requirements

Many projects with no initial planning tend to suffer from the same fate as the race with a false start. Similar to a race where some athletes can get disqualified due to a false start resulting from confusion, project teams can fail and project careers can end because of confusion created by poorly planned projects. As all the remaining athletes have to get back to the starter block for starting the race again after initial disqualification, the project team has to start again at the initiation phase after the preliminary failure.

Many projects with no initial planning tend to suffer from the same fate as the race with a false start.

This type of poorly planned projects follows seven different phases, which are defined as follows[2]:

1. Project initiation without defined requirements
2. Wild enthusiasm
3. Disillusionment
4. Chaos
5. Search for the guilty
6. Punishment of the innocent
7. Definition of the requirements

In a poorly planned project, the project sponsor and the project leader initiate the project without defined requirements. Like any other new project, initially there is a great deal of enthusiasm, and the team is fired up about the unlimited potential of success in the project. After a while, usually reality sets in when mostly everyone is trying to figure out "what are we trying to achieve." Disillusionment sets in over most of the team. When disillusionment persists for some period of time, the team gets frustrated with the confusion and chaos sets in. This chaos is finally visible to the sponsors and stakeholders when it finally impacts the milestones and budget. They then demand to confront the "guilty." Usually, someone who

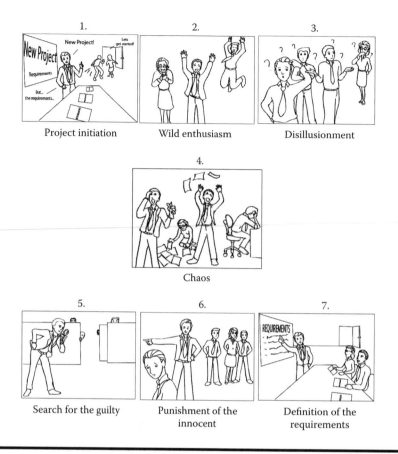

Figure 4.2   Illustration on "how projects fail."

is the weakest or slowest, a rookie, or the politically unsavvy is blamed for the mess. They get punished for taking the project to the brink of failure. The rest of the team springs into action and arranges a project crisis meeting to clearly define the requirements, roles, and responsibilities. This phenomenon has been observed personally numerous times during my consulting career, in several corporations including some Fortune 500 companies. Figure 4.2 illustrates the seven phases involved in project failures related to poor planning.

The major reason for failure is that we do not follow the fundamentals. Edward Deming created the Deming cycle or the plan, do, check, and act (PDCA) cycle[3] for a process or a project as shown in Figure 4.3.

The Deming cycle clearly distinguishes the planning from other process. Initial planning is required to define the overall parameters of the project and establish complete requirements of the project, as explained in the following:

Plan: Design or revise a plan for a process or a project.
Do: Implement the plan and measure the results.
Check: Compare results to customer requirements.
Act: Update to improve the process or project.

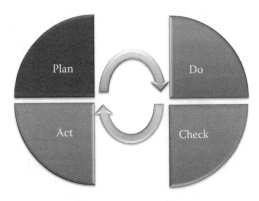

Figure 4.3   Deming cycle (Plan, Do, Check, Act).

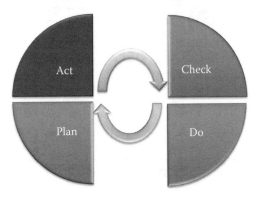

Figure 4.4   Reverse Deming cycle (Act, Check, Do, Plan).

However, projects fail because they follow the reverse Deming cycle or the act, check, do, and plan cycle, as shown in Figure 4.4.

In the Reverse Deming cycle, the requirements are defined after the entire project team emerges from being immersed in total chaos and as a means to conduct damage control and revive the project and redeem their own careers, as explained in the following:

Act: Act before understanding customer requirements.
Check: Check why the project is in utter chaos.
Do: Do damage control.
Plan: Finally, plan to correctly identify customer requirements.

4.2.2 Avoiding the Pitfalls of Ambiguous Requirements

How does a project leader avoid the pitfalls of ambiguous requirements? How does the project leader make sure that all detail requirements are bound by high-level project requirements? The answer is well defined in project management methodology, and it is the creation of a project charter.

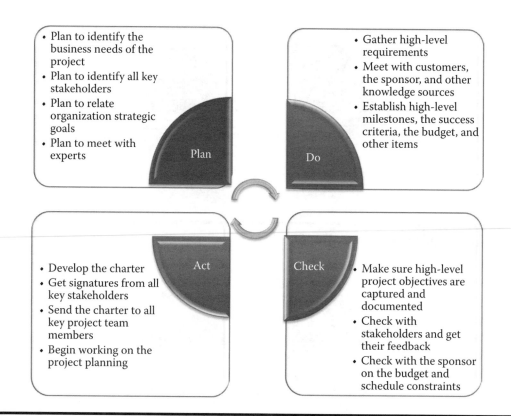

Figure 4.5   Tasks in plan, do, check, and act cycle.

As per the *PMBOK*, a project charter is a document issued by the project initiator or sponsor that formally authorizes the existence of a project and provides the project manager with the authority to apply organizational resources to project activities.[4] Although every project usually starts with a charter, why are only 32% of projects (average from years 2000 to 2008)[5] deemed successful? The answer to this question is critical and will be explained in this pillar. If project leaders follow the Deming cycle in a systematic approach and gather requirements with a high level of accuracy and create a charter with precision, they will have a higher probability of completing the project that will be considered successful. Figure 4.5 explains the importance of PDCA cycle in preparing a charter.

4.3 Project Charter: Setting the Longitude and Latitude for a Project

Just like it would be extremely challenging to be a captain of a ship that leaves the harbor without knowing the precise purpose and destination of the voyage, it would be quite challenging to lead a project with ambiguous requirements.

If we do not know where we are going, we will definitely get there, but we may not be as lucky as Christopher Columbus when he accidently discovered America on October 12, 1492.

4.3.1 Definition

A charter is a document defined at the initial stages of a project that "charts" the course of the project and provides direction to the team members. Project requirements are detailed in a project charter.

4.3.2 Explanation

Every country that has a great constitution can become great. Every team in sports who has a winning game plan can win. That means the first step to win a game is to prepare a plan. Thus, every project that has a well-defined project charter stands a significantly better chance of being successful. Thus, it is absolutely critical to have a project charter at the beginning of every project. The development of a charter is the starting point for the project. Project charter contains names of individual team members needed to complete initiation phase of the project. Project charter can be developed on the basis of a number of documents within and outside the organization. Table 4.1 lists some sample documents required for development of a charter.

Table 4.1 Sample Example of Documents/Elements Required for Developing a Charter

Document/Element	Purpose
Organizational strategic plan	This document lists the goals and strategies of an organization. This document represents a road map for the organization to reach its goals. Project charter should be aligned with the organization goals.
Project statement of work	Project statement of work describes the product, service, or results of a project and is used to prepare a charter. Some projects are developed on the basis of the business needs of the organization. Project statement of work should align with organizational strategy.
Business case	Business case identifies if the project is worthwhile to take up. Business case contains the business need of the project and cost benefit analysis.
Project selection criteria document	Project selection criteria give the parameters needed to justify the selection of a particular project.
Historical knowledge	Historical knowledge contains valuable information from previous similar successful projects. All internal project standards are also part of this information.

Figure 4.6   Charter sets the longitude and latitude for a project.

4.4 Difference between a Charter and a Vision Statement

It is worthwhile to discuss the difference between a vision statement and a charter at this point. The project leader should understand that there is a clearly defined difference between a vision statement and project charter.

> **The charter sets "the latitude and the longitude" of the project,** as shown in Figure 4.6, whereas **the vision statement sets its "altitude." A charter is similar to our "body and mind," providing some structure and logic; a vision statement is similar to our "spirit," defining our attitude toward life. A charter defines the "what", and a vision statement defines the "how" for a team.**

However, they must work in unison and adhere to the laws and regulations in order for us to be successful. Thus, both the charter and the vision statement must be aligned not only to each other but also to the short- and long-term business plan of the organization. Figure 4.7 gives the importance of a vision statement and a project charter to the project.

4.5 Does Creating a Vision Statement and a Charter Guarantee Project Success?

Many project leaders are under the false impression that creating a vision statement or a charter will automatically lead to success in projects.

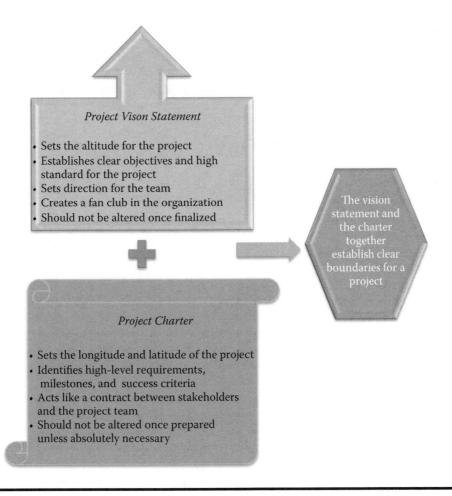

Project Vison Statement

- Sets the altitude for the project
- Establishes clear objectives and high standard for the project
- Sets direction for the team
- Creates a fan club in the organization
- Should not be altered once finalized

Project Charter

- Sets the longitude and latitude of the project
- Identifies high-level requirements, milestones, and success criteria
- Acts like a contract between stakeholders and the project team
- Should not be altered once prepared unless absolutely necessary

The vision statement and the charter together establish clear boundaries for a project

Figure 4.7   Importance of a project vision statement and project charter to the project.

However, that is not the case in most situations. It is important for project leaders to understand that the vision statement and the charter allow the project leader to begin the project on the right trajectory. However, it is up to the project leader and the team to maintain and close the project at the trajectory where the project meets all customer and stakeholder requirements as defined in the vision statement, charter, quality plan, schedule, and budget and all other documents for the project to be considered successful.

4.6 Developing a Project Charter

The importance of project charter development is to document the high-level needs of the customer to define critical success factors and to identify the resources required to complete the project. The charter also describes the business requirements that the project is intended to attain and the major advantages of successfully executing the project to the organization. A project manager is usually selected before or during preparation of the project charter and is required to work closely with project sponsor and core stakeholders to create an effective project charter.

Although it is not a common practice, the project leader also needs to work closely with the end customer while defining the charter. Because project charter defines high-level requirements of the project, it is critical that the project leader get an agreement between the stakeholders and the sponsor on the scope of the project.

4.6.1 Contents in the Project Charter

- Goals and objectives of the project
- Name of the project manager
- High-level requirements
- Required resources
- Deliverables
- High-level milestones
- Budgetary requirements
- Project success criteria
- High-level constraints and assumptions

Because the charter forms the longitude and the latitude for the entire project, the contents in the project charter should be written after thorough discussion with the stakeholders, the sponsor, and also the end customer. Project goals and objectives describe the target for the project, which are part of project vision statement, whereas the scope identifies the boundaries of that target. Project success criteria describe the factors or characteristics that are deemed critical to the success of the project, without which the project is most likely to fail. High-level assumptions and constraints are related to scope, budget, schedules, business requirements, and technology. The milestones, which are planned completion dates for project deliverables, must also be recorded in the project charter to ensure the project schedule is initiated during the planning stages. Most project managers consider the charter as a checklist item to be completed as part of their responsibilities. Once complete, it is filed away and referred to only when chaos or disagreement breaks out. However, even when referred to, the charter may still be unable to resolve the conflict because the stakeholders can use their own interpretation due to the ambiguity of the requirements. A good charter if defined well and used along with a powerful vision statement can lay the foundation of a successful project. The characteristics of a good charter are listed below:

- **Clearly written in business terms**
  The charter should be clearly written in business terms. The information should be organized and detailed enough for all the team members to understand. Each section should contain brief summary of the information. Detailed documents can also be added if the summary information is not sufficient to clarify the details. Figure 4.8 lists part of the sample charter document.

Project Charter

1. Executive Summary	
* Project Name:	
* Sponsor:	
* Project Manager:	Date:

2. Stakeholders

	Name	Department	Telephone	E-mail
(Persons or groups with a significant interest in this project)				
Stakeholder 1				
Stakeholder 2				
Stakeholder 3				

3. Project/Service Description

* Project Purpose/Business Justification

* Objectives (in business terms)

Business need A	Project objective A
Business need B	Project objective B

* Deliverables (list high-level deliverables)

Deliverable 1
Deliverable 2

* This Project Does Not Include (list the specific items not included in this project)

1.
2.

Figure 4.8   Sample project charter.

- **Specific and measurable**

  Because the charter is a living document that the project team will refer to throughout the lifetime of the project, the information in the charter should not be vague. A good charter incorporates specific, measurable, and quantifiable information. Some organization-specific or industry-specific buzzwords or acronyms can be used as long as all the stakeholders and the team members can clearly understand the contents.

- **Linked to business benefits**

  The charter should link the objectives of the project to the business benefits. The business benefits should be quantifiable and measurable. It is advisable

Detailed business benefits				
List all business benefits in specific, measurable terms.				
Benefit no.	**Cost savings**	**Time savings**	**Quality improvement**	**Other savings**
Benefit 1	Saves $200,000 in next 2 years	No savings	No improvement	
Benefit 2	No significant savings	Product delivery time reduces by 3 days	Rejection rate reduces by 15 percent	
Benefit 3	$10,000-$12,000 savings per month	Reduces down time by 3 hours	No significant improvement	Man hours per product will be reduced from 15 to 13
Totals				

Figure 4.9 Sample project business benefit document.

to write business benefits in a tabular form to detail each benefit using cost, time, and quality terms. Figure 4.9 lists sample project business benefit document.

4.7 Good Charter versus Great Charter

Only one or two key attributes set the great athletes apart from good athletes. Similarly, there are two more elements that great project leaders have the foresight to add to create a great project charter and to significantly increase the chances of success in any project.

The elements that separate a good charter from a great charter are as follows.

4.7.1 Complete Buy-in from All Stakeholders

Getting buy-in from the key stakeholders is an essential element to finalize the charter. The key to getting complete buy-in from the stakeholders is for the project leader to take time to understand the "stake" in the project for key stakeholders. They need to understand the issues, the positive or the negative impact of the project, and the motivation factors of the key stakeholders. The best strategy to get buy-in from the key stakeholders is to explain each section of the project charter and help them understand how each of them can impact their business benefit. When the project leader gets buy-in from the key stakeholders, they form a team of allies that will support the project objectives against all odds.

4.7.2 Signature from Key Stakeholders on the Charter

Once the charter is approved by key stakeholders, getting their signatures on the charter completes the process of charter development. Very complex projects take years to complete, and getting signed approved charter ensures the commitment of stakeholders and averts the risk of project leader being the victim of project failure due to changes in project objectives, goals, and requirements.

The two elements described above are not done with the intention to cover our behinds. To the contrary, **this document becomes a symbol that embodies "oneness of purpose" or "the constitution" or the "common war cry" for all involved.** Also, during the course of the project when there are factions formed and sides taken and decisions are to be made, the charter becomes the "lighthouse" and shows the path to safety and success.

Let's look at the U.S. Constitution, one of the world's oldest surviving constitutions, created almost 200 years ago by the founding fathers. It is still considered the most influential legal document in existence. The constitution is a living document, and although it has several amendments and continually needs to be interpreted by the Supreme Court, its basic tenets have remained virtually unchanged and unchallenged since its inception. Apart from the underlying wisdom, what is the major reason for the success of this document? The key reason for the success is that the forefathers had the wisdom to make it a "legal" agreement and had representatives from 13 original colonies, namely, Connecticut, Delaware, Georgia, Maryland, Massachusetts, New Hampshire, New Jersey, New York, North Carolina, South Carolina, Pennsylvania, Rhode Island, and Virginia, all sign the document.[6] When we follow the constitution, we not only implicitly trust the wisdom of the forefathers but also respect the document as a guiding light steering the country in times of prosperity and a recession. We only amend the constitution when it is absolutely necessary. Similarly, the charter is meant to be adhered to without making any major changes, trusting the wisdom of the stakeholders. Thus, a signed charter becomes a contract between the project team and the key stakeholders.

> Just like a contract cannot be altered without adequate investigation of the impact of changes, renegotiation of terms between and countermeasures implemented, a signed charter requires an assessment of the impact of the changes in project scope, an update to budget and resource requirements presented for approval to the stakeholders, and an agreement on the new baseline of the project.

Table 4.2 shows the similarities between a charter and a legal contract. For long-term (3–5 years) projects, is advisable to use a "phased charter" approach. With this approach, the charter provides an overview of the plan and details are agreed upon for only one year at a time.

One of the major reasons for failure of projects is "scope creep," that is, adding elements to project which were not agreed upon initially. Scope creep

Table 4.2 Similarities between a Contract and a Charter

Contract	Charter
• A contract contains the services, products, or results that will be accomplished by the contracting party.	• A charter contains project objectives and high-level requirements that will be accomplished by the project team.
• A contract document establishes risks involved and uses some risk mitigation techniques.	• A charter establishes high-level constraints and assumptions and some risk mitigation techniques.
• Enterprise information and historical organizational knowledge are considered while preparing a contract.	• Enterprise information and historical organizational knowledge are considered while preparing a charter.
• Business need, life cycle, cost, schedule, and resources are taken into account while preparing a contract.	• Business need of the organization, budget, milestones, and resources are taken into account during charter preparation.
• In complex procurement process, contract negotiations are carried out before signing the contract to reach prior agreement on the contract terms.	• In complex projects, mutual agreement should be reached between all parties involved on the high-level requirements of the project before signing the final charter.
• Signatures of parties involved are taken while a making a final contract document.	• Stakeholders, sponsor and project manager's signatures are taken while making a final charter document.
• A contract is a legal agreement. Once it is finalized, changes must be done with mutual consent of parties involved.	• A charter is an agreement between stakeholders and project team. Changes must be made with mutual consent only when it is absolutely necessary and only after thoroughly evaluating the impact of the changes.
• A contract forms the basis for performance reporting, quality control, scope control, and change control.	• A charter also forms the basis for performance reporting, quality control, scope control, and change control.
• A contract documentation is a live document and is vital throughout the life cycle of the contract and the information in the contract document needs to be managed and controlled.	• A charter is a live document and is very important throughout project life cycle. This document should be frequently referred, managed, and controlled.

mostly occurs when the voice of the customer and all key stakeholders is not taken into account during high-level requirement gathering, or during the creation of project charter. Sometimes there are business reasons for scope creep too. Scope creep needs to be avoided at all costs unless it impacts safety or the survival of the corporation. If it cannot be avoided, a thorough assessment of budget and resources must be conducted and presented to the key stakeholders for approval.

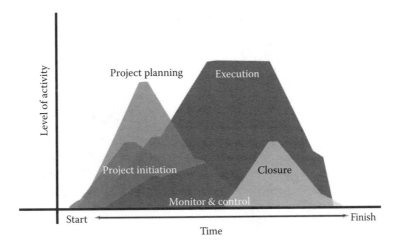

Figure 4.10   Project phases.

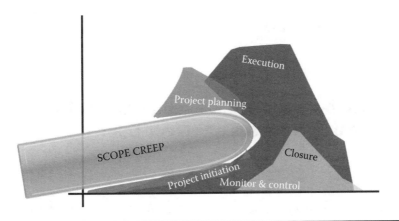

Figure 4.11   Bullet of scope creep.

The phases of a project without any scope changes are shown in Figure 4.10. Scope creep has a major impact on cost, quality, timeline, availability, and morale of the resources. The impact is less during the initial stages and increases exponentially as the project gets more mature (represented by the "bullet" in Figure 4.11). The deeper the bullet of "scope creep" penetrates the project phases, the more damage it will produce and more significant negative impact it will have on the overall success. **Thus, a signed charter acts as a shield for deflecting the deadly bullet of scope creep, preventing severe damage to the project results and the profit margins** as shown Figure 4.12.

The deeper the bullet of "scope creep" penetrates the project phases, the more damage it will produce and more significant negative impact it will have on the overall success.

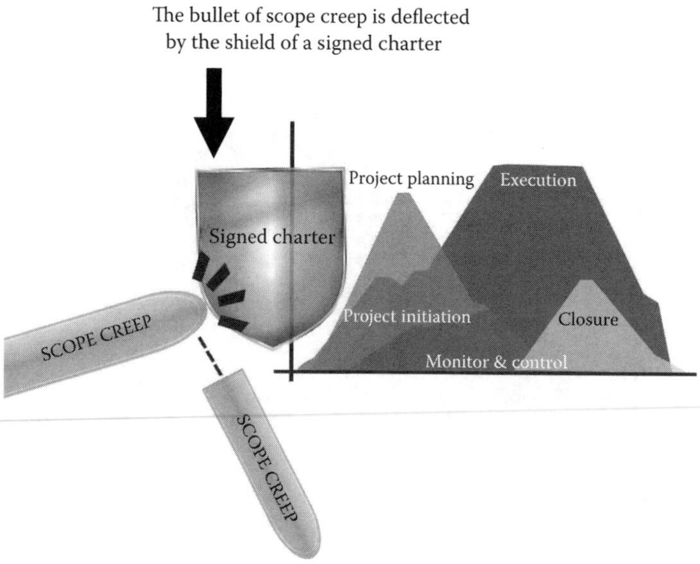

The bullet of scope creep is deflected
by the shield of a signed charter

Figure 4.12   Signed charter as a shield.

4.8 Difference between the Use of a Charter by a Project Manager versus a Project Leader

There is a major difference between how a project manager uses the charter versus how a project leader uses it. In many projects, the charter is used by project managers as an initial document to start a project. Once the project starts, they rarely use charter in remaining project phases. The importance of charter is ignored by the sponsor and the project manager over the course of the project. In contrast, a project leader understands how valuable it is to refer back to charter in each phase of the project. Thus, it is important not only to prepare a great charter but also to use the charter throughout the life cycle of the project. Table 4.3 shows the major differences in the design, implementation, and enforcement of a charter by a project manager and a project leader.

Table 4.3   Charter as Viewed by a Project Manager and by a Project Leader

Project Manager	Project Leader
Uses charter to initiate a project	Uses charter to initiate, plan, execute, monitor, control, and close a project
Lists the objective of the project, budget, and resources in the charter and uses other documents to list risks, assumptions, and constraints	Lists not only the objective of the project but also the high-level requirements, constraints, milestones, resources, risks, assumptions, and project success criteria in the charter
Works with sponsor to prepare the project charter	Works with sponsor, key stakeholders, and customers to prepare the project charter
Does not require signatures from stakeholders	Requires signatures from sponsor, key stakeholders, and customers
Uses charter as a reference document for the initial phase of the project	Uses charter as a key document and a communications tool between stakeholders, team, and project manager
Amends the charter as and when required, like any other project document	Uses the charter as a legal contract between all the key stakeholders of the project and amend it only when it is absolutely necessary

Pillar IV   Summary

Ambiguous requirements are the result of unclear or missing critical information, and this leads to confusion and rework, failed projects, and even failed project careers. It is important for project leaders to understand that the charter allows the project leader to begin the project on the right trajectory.

Every successful project requires a completed and signed charter that acts as a shield against scope creep. The charter needs to be adhered to by all stakeholders, without major changes, until the completion of that project. The contents of the project charter should be written after thorough discussions with the customers, the key stakeholders, and the sponsor. A charter is a critical artifact to document all the key requirements of the project with clarity and without ambiguity.

1. A charter sets the longitude and the latitude of a project. A well-designed charter should list all pertinent information for a project and should be agreed upon by the sponsor, the stakeholders, and the project managers.
2. The charter should contain information that is measurable and quantifiable.
3. There is a major difference between the design, the implementation, and the enforcement of a charter by a project manager and a project leader. Project leaders use the charter as a legal contract between all the key stakeholders of the project and amend it only when it is absolutely necessary, thus proactively avoiding any damage to the project results due to the scope creep.

Figure 4.13 describes the key aspects of a project charter.

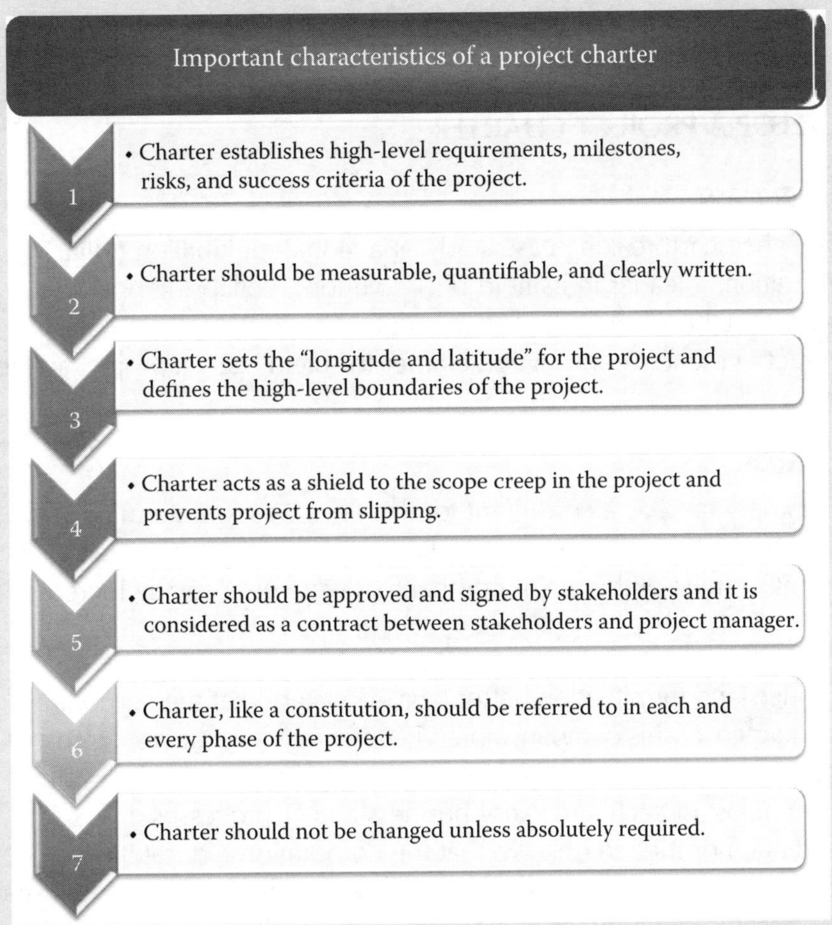

Important characteristics of a project charter

1. • Charter establishes high-level requirements, milestones, risks, and success criteria of the project.

2. • Charter should be measurable, quantifiable, and clearly written.

3. • Charter sets the "longitude and latitude" for the project and defines the high-level boundaries of the project.

4. • Charter acts as a shield to the scope creep in the project and prevents project from slipping.

5. • Charter should be approved and signed by stakeholders and it is considered as a contract between stakeholders and project manager.

6. • Charter, like a constitution, should be referred to in each and every phase of the project.

7. • Charter should not be changed unless absolutely required.

Figure 4.13   Important characteristics of a project charter.

Pillar IV Case Study

DEVELOP A PROJECT CHARTER

INTRODUCTION

This is the heartbreaking case study of a global multibillion dollar corporation, a leader in its field of IT solutions, collapsing primarily, in my opinion, because of the lack of adherence to Pillar IV of having a contract in the form of a signed charter to shield against project scope creep.

CHALLENGE

My primary task, as a consultant for this firm, was to determine why the company profit margins were shrinking considerably while the profit margins of most of the major competitors were on a steady increase.

SITUATION

To understand the situation better, our team started at the corporate headquarters of this company, interviewed many executives, almost all department managers and key personnel, and created detailed value stream maps[7] of each and every business and IT processes. I was surprised and horrified to observe that the corporation did not have a well-defined charter for most of their projects, and they allowed customers to make changes to the project scope and to the technical specifications without any penalties to the client, even after the project was 75% to 90% complete. It all started when the technical sales team would promise the customer products that were not even conceived by the research and development department and by the operations teams. A "specifications" document was created by the sales team and the project was "live." A project manager was assigned sometime during the project planning phase on the basis of availability and entrusted with delivery of the product to the customer within the required timeline. It was chaos from thereon. The timelines slipped, and the changes to the specifications were so frequent that their rework was almost certain at several key assembly steps. After numerous missed deadlines spanning over a year, the customer would completely change the specifications and even add features (scope creep) on the basis of the latest technological updates.

Everyone in operations blamed the project managers for all the issues within the corporation and hated them. Project managers were considered the "Darth Vader clan," the "dark side" of the corporation. However, when we did the value stream maps exercise with the project management group, it was fairly clear that the project managers were merely messengers and they were being shot for delivering the unpleasant messages of specification changes and scope creep. Project managers had absolutely no control over the dealings with the end customer specifications—they were just updating the "charter" as requested by the client liaisons. Thus, in my opinion, they might as well let go all the project managers and just hire one highly skilled magician to make the products appear as needed (luckily, I kept this opinion to myself).

ROOT CAUSE

Because of the nonexistence of a good charter and allowing scope creep during mature stages of project completion, there were significant delays in delivering the final product to the customers. The customers were then appeased by making allowances in several million dollars in favor of the customer, even without a thorough review of the agreed upon terms in the contract. This was identified as the root cause of the loss in profit margins.

SOLUTION

On the basis of this finding, I tried to warn the executives of the seriousness of not having a signed-off charter for their new product deployments. I also discussed the importance of a thorough review of existing client contracts before permitting an overhaul of the specifications at a mature stage in the project. The solution proposed was to appoint the project managers at the inception stage of the project and to allow them to create a specification documents along with the technical sales team, which could be converted into a project charter. The proposed solution also stressed the importance of having the charter agreed upon and signed off by all the key stakeholders. We also recommended the charter not be allowed to fall victim to the scope creep. In cases where there was no choice but to consider amending the charter due to customer request, a thorough review of the contract terms was required, and the costs involved to allow the scope creep had to be calculated. The project steering committee was then required to provide an addendum to the client agreement, requiring additional budget to cover the costs for the additional time and resources and other items related to the scope creep. By rough estimates, this solution would allow the company regain its profit margins and solidify its position once again as a leader in the competitive market.

IMPLEMENTATION AND RESULTS

Just like the *Titanic* could not react quickly enough to avoid the iceberg on that fateful day of April 14, 1912,[8] in spite of several warnings, the gigantic IT organization was not calibrated to react swiftly to our recommended solutions. As a result, just like the *Titanic* sank shortly after the damage caused by the iceberg, taking almost 2200 people with it to the bottom of the ocean, the IT firm was sold to one of its competitors along with its global employees and project managers, resulting in the end of a legacy.

LESSONS LEARNED

As described in this pillar, do not underestimate the importance of having a signed off charter as a shield against scope creep. Absence of a signed off charter on large projects can easily topple powerful organizations and ruin numerous careers and lives.

Pillar IV   Force Field Analysis

PILLAR IV: FORCE FIELD ANALYSIS OF ORGANIZATIONAL ASSESSMENT

Table 4.4 shows force field analysis of organizational assessment. The organizational assessment is conducted to assess if the culture of the organization is in alignment with the principles of Pillar IV. Tables 4.5 through 4.7 are used to develop and implement an action plan to increase the impact of the organizational driving forces and decrease the impact of the organizational resisting forces.

PILLAR IV: FORCE FIELD ANALYSIS OF SELF-ASSESSMENT

Table 4.8 shows force field analysis of self-assessment. The self-assessment is conducted to assess if your own strengths are in alignment with the principles of Pillar IV. Tables 4.9 through 4.11 are used to develop and implement an action plan to increase the impact of the self-driving forces and decrease the impact of the self-resisting forces.

PILLAR IV: RECOMMENDATIONS FOR OPTIMAL RESULTS FROM FORCE FIELD ANALYSIS

For optimal results and actual transformation of culture and strengths conducive to the creation of advanced master project leaders, the following three steps are necessary:

1. Both the organizational and the self-evaluation assessments must be completed.
2. A well-designed action plan must be created and implemented to increase the driving forces and decrease the resisting forces.
3. The principles of each pillar must be constantly practiced and improved.

It is highly recommended that both the organization assessments and self-assessments be conducted every year and the action plan be updated at least every 3 months.

Note: The sum of scores for Organizational Driving Force and Organizational Resisting Force for each point must be less than or equal to TEN.

  The sum of scores for Self Driving Force and Self Resisting Force for each point must be less than or equal to TEN.

Table 4.4   Pillar IV: Force Field Organizational Analysis

Team Name: _____   Date: _____

	Does My Organization Drive or Resist a Culture of Setting Higher Standards by Creating a Signed Charter?				
	0 Never		5 Sometimes		7 Mostly
	3 Rarely		ODF + ORF ≤ 10		10 Always
No.	Driving Forces →	*Score Organizational Driving Force (ODF)*	*Score Organizational Resisting Force (ORF)*		← Resisting Forces
1	My organization promotes *PMBOK* project principles and phased approach to managing projects and gives high importance to the charter.				My organization rarely follows *PMBOK* project principles and phased approach to managing projects and gives minimal importance to the charter.
2	My organization has a strong culture of gathering high-level requirements of the project before starting it.				My organization encourages starting a project first and collecting the requirements as we progress.
3	My organization encourages project managers to get buy-in on the requirements from the stakeholders before beginning a project.				My organization encourages a "cowboy" culture of getting started on projects without getting buy-in from key stakeholders on the requirements.
4	Our organizational culture promotes following PDCA cycle.				My organization culture promotes following the act, check, do, and plan cycle.
5	There is a thorough understanding within the organization regarding the impact of scope creep on projects and conscious avoidance of any scope creep on projects.				There is a lack of understanding within the organization regarding the impact of scope creep on projects and a culture of permitting scope creep on most projects.
6	Our project leaders possess skills to evaluate, quantify, and explain the impact of potential scope creep to executives in terms of dollars, time, and quality.				Our project managers lack the skills to evaluate, quantify, and explain the impact of potential scope creep to executives in terms of dollars, time, and quality.

7	My organization focuses on the historical knowledge base and project success criteria while preparing the charter.			My organization does not focus on the historical knowledge base and project success criteria while preparing the charter.
8	The project leaders in my organization create a specific, measurable, and clearly written charter that is linked to business benefits.			The project managers in my organization create a charter with a checklist of items to be completed in the initial phase of the project.
9	My organization always supports our project leaders in creating an excellent charter that helps the stakeholders understand how each element impacts their business results.			My organization requires that our project manger create a charter and notify the stakeholders to review it when it is ready.
10	Project leaders in my organization refer to the project charter during each phase of the project.			Project managers in my organization use the charter only to initiate the project.
	Total ODF score			*Total ORF score*

Result	Conclusion	*Recommended Action* *Review and Update Every Quarter (3 months)*
ODF >> ORF	My company culture strongly drives a culture of creation of a signed project charter.	Use Tables 4.5 through 4.7 to set goals and to create an action plan to preserve or continuously improve the culture of setting higher standards using a signed project charter.
ODF > ORF	My company culture drives the culture of creation of a signed project charter.	Use Tables 4.5 through 4.7 to set goals and to create an action plan to increase ODF to create a culture of setting higher standards using a signed project charter.
ORF >> ODF	My company culture strongly resists the culture of creation of a signed project charter.	Use Tables 4.5 through 4.7 to set goals and create an action plan to increase the ODF and reduce the ORF to create a culture of setting higher standards using a signed project charter.
ORF > ODF	My company culture resists the culture of creation of a signed project charter.	Use Tables 4.5 through 4.7 to set goals and create an action plan to reduce the ORF to create a culture of setting higher standards using a signed project charter.
ODF = ORF	My company culture does not drive or resist the culture of creation of a signed project charter.	Use Tables 4.5 through 4.7 to set goals and create an action plan to increase the ODF to create a culture of setting higher standards using a signed project charter.

Table 4.5   Pillar IV: Analysis of ODF and ORF Results

Result	Existing Organizational Culture	If the Goal Is to Create a Moderately Strong Culture of Setting Higher Standards Using a Signed Project Charter	If the Goal Is to Create a Very Strong Culture of Setting Higher Standards Using a Signed Project Charter
ODF			
ODF ≤ 25	No or minimal culture of setting higher standards using a signed project charter	Focus on improving scores in at least 5 DF	Focus on improving scores in at least 7 DF
25 < ODF ≤ 50	Weak culture of setting higher standards using a signed project charter	Focus on improving scores in at least 3 DF	Focus on improving scores in at least 5 DF
50 < ODF ≤ 75	Moderate culture of setting higher standards using a signed project charter	Focus on improving scores in at least 1 DF	Focus on improving scores in at least 3 DF
ODF > 75	Strong culture of setting higher standards using a signed project charter	N/A	Preserve or continuously improve the culture
ORF			
ORF > 75	No or minimal culture of setting higher standards using a signed project charter	Focus on decreasing scores in at least 5 RF	Focus on decreasing scores in at least 7 RF
50 < ORF ≤ 75	Weak culture of setting higher standards using a signed project charter	Focus on decreasing scores in at least 3 RF	Focus on decreasing scores in at least 5 RF
25 < ORF ≤ 50	Moderate culture of setting higher standards using a signed project charter	Focus on decreasing scores in at least 1 RF	Focus on decreasing scores in at least 3 RF
ORF ≤ 25	Strong culture of setting higher standards using a signed project charter.	N/A	Preserve or continuously improve the culture

Table 4.6   Pillar IV: Action Plan to Increase Organizational Driving Force (ODF)

Team Name: _____   Date: _____

No.	Driving Force	Current Score	Goal (Target Score) ⬆	Action Plan to Increase DF Score	Complete by (Date)	Assigned To (Department Name or Initials of the Person)
1	My organization promotes *PMBOK* project principles and phased approach to managing projects and gives high importance to the charter.					
2	My organization has a strong culture of gathering high-level requirements of the project before starting it.					
3	My organization encourages project managers to get buy-in on the requirements from the stakeholders before beginning a project.					
4	Our organizational culture promotes following PDCA cycle.					
5	There is a thorough understanding within the organization regarding the impact of scope creep on projects and conscious avoidance of any scope creep on projects.					

6	Our project leaders possess skills to evaluate, quantify, and explain the impact of potential scope creep to executives in terms of dollars, time, and quality.					
7	My organization focuses on the historical knowledge base and project success criteria while preparing the charter.					
8	The project leaders in my organization create a specific, measurable, and clearly written charter that is linked to business benefits.					
9	My organization always supports our project leaders in creating an excellent charter that helps the stakeholders understand how each element impacts their business results.					
10	Project leaders in my organization refer to the project charter during each phase of the project.					
	Total ODF					

Table 4.7 Pillar IV: Action Plan to Decrease Organizational Resisting Force (ORF)

Name: _____   Date: _____

No.	Resisting Force	Current Score	Goal (Target Score) ⬆	Action Plan to Decrease RF Score	Complete by (Date)	Assigned to (Department Name or Initials of the Person)
1	My organization rarely follows *PMBOK* project principles and phased approach to managing projects and gives minimal importance to the charter.					
2	My organization encourages starting a project first and collecting the requirements as we progress.					
3	My organization encourages a "cowboy" culture of getting started on projects without getting buy-in from key stakeholders on the requirements.					
4	My organization culture promotes following the act, check, do, and plan cycle.					
5	There is a lack of understanding within the organization regarding the impact of scope creep on projects and a culture of permitting scope creep on most projects.					

6	Our project managers lack the skills to evaluate, quantify, and explain the impact of potential scope creep to executives in terms of dollars, time, and quality.					
7	My organization does not focus on the historical knowledge base and project success criteria while preparing the charter.					
8	The project managers in my organization create a charter with a checklist of items to be completed in the initial phase of the project.					
9	My organization requires that our project manger create a charter and notify the stakeholders to review it when it is ready.					
10	Project managers in my organization use the charter only to initiate the project.					
	Total ORF					

Table 4.8   Pillar IV: Force Field Self-Analysis

Name: _____   Date: _____

Does My Behavior Drive or Resist a Culture of Setting Higher Standards by Creating a Signed Charter?				
0 Never		5 Sometimes		7 Mostly
3 Rarely		SDF + SRF ≤ 10		10 Always
No.	Driving Forces	*Score Self-Driving Force (SDF)*	*Score Self-Resisting Force (SRF)*	Resisting Forces
1	I always give importance to gathering the detailed project requirements before starting the project.			I am always eager to start the project first and collect the project requirements later.
2	I always use PDCA cycle to gather project requirements.			I always use the act, check, do, and plan cycle to gather project requirements.
3	I check the project charter to make sure it is concise, specific, measurable, and linked to business objectives.			I develop the project charter just like a simple checklist to be completed as a formality at the beginning of the project.
4	I do my best to prevent scope creep on my projects and do not change the project charter unless absolutely necessary.			I make changes to the project charter when scope creep occurs during the project life cycle.
5	If scope creep is unavoidable, I evaluate and explain its potential adverse impact on the project results to all stakeholders and team members.			I do not have time on projects to evaluate potential adverse impact of scope creep on the project results and deal with the impact when it happens.
6	Along with project objectives, I always include high-level milestones, risks, and constraints in the charter.			I only include the high-level objectives in the project charter.
7	I ensure that adequate time has been spent on developing the project charter, and finalize it after getting complete buy-in from all stakeholders.			I spend some time to prepare the charter, and always inform the stakeholders about the finalized project charter.

8	I treat the project charter as a constitution of the project.			I treat the project charter as a document required to initiate the project.
9	I always ensure that the charter aligns with short- and long-term organizational goals.			I do not think that a charter needs to be aligned with organizational goals.
10	I get the project charter signed by all stakeholders like a contract and use it as a dynamic document throughout the life cycle of the project.			I use project charter to kick off the project and do not see the need to refer to it during the rest of the project.
	Total SDF score			*Total SRF score*

Result	Conclusion	Recommended Action Review and Update Every Quarter (3 months)
SDF ≫ SRF	My behavior strongly supports a culture of setting higher standards using a signed project charter.	Use Tables 4.9 through 4.11 to set goals and to create an action plan to continuously enhance the behavior to set high standards using a signed project charter.
SDF > SRF	My behavior supports a culture of setting higher standards using a signed project charter.	Use Tables 4.9 through 4.11 to set goals and to create an action plan to increase SDF to allow a stronger behavior toward setting high standards using a signed project charter.
SRF ≫ SDF	My behavior strongly resists a culture of setting higher standards using a signed project charter.	Use Tables 4.9 through 4.11 to set goals and to create an action plan to increase SDF and reduce SRF to allow a stronger behavior toward setting high standards using a signed project charter.
SRF > SDF	My behavior resists a culture of setting higher standards using a signed project charter.	Use Tables 4.9 through 4.11 to set goals and to create an action plan to reduce SRF to allow a stronger behavior toward setting high standards using a signed project charter.
SDF = SRF	My behavior does not drive or resist a culture of setting higher standards using a signed project charter.	Use Tables 4.9 through 4.11 to set goals and to create an action plan to increase the SDF to allow a stronger behavior toward setting high standards using a signed project charter.

Table 4.9 Pillar IV: Analysis of SDF and SRF Results

Result	Existing Behavior	*If the Goal Is to Create a Moderately Strong Behavior Toward the Principle of Setting Higher Standards Using a Signed Project Charter*	*If the Goal Is to Create a Very Strong Behavior Toward the Principle of Setting Higher Standards Using a Signed Project Charter*
SDF			
SDF ≤ 25	No or minimal activities in creating a signed project charter	Focus on improving scores in at least 5 DF	Focus on improving scores in at least 7 DF
25 < SDF ≤ 50	Weak activities in creating a signed project charter	Focus on improving scores in at least 3 DF	Focus on improving scores in at least 5 DF
50 < SDF ≤ 75	Moderate activities in creating a signed project charter	Focus on improving scores in at least 1 DF	Focus on improving scores in at least 3 DF
SDF > 75	Strong activities in creating a signed project charter	N/A	Preserve or continuously improve the behavior
SRF			
SRF > 75	No or minimal activities in creating a signed project charter	Focus on decreasing scores in at least 5 RF	Focus on decreasing scores in at least 7 RF
50 < SRF ≤ 75	Weak activities in creating a signed project charter	Focus on decreasing scores in at least 3 RF	Focus on decreasing scores in at least 5 RF
25 < SRF ≤ 50	Moderate activities in creating a signed project charter	Focus on decreasing scores in at least 1 RF	Focus on decreasing scores in at least 3 RF
SRF ≤ 25	Strong activities in creating a signed project charter	N/A	Preserve or continuously improve the behavior

Table 4.10   Pillar IV: Action Plan to Increase Self-Driving Force (SDF)

Name: _____   Date: _____

No.	Driving Force	Current Score	Goal (Target Score) ⬆	Action Plan to Increase DF Score	Complete by (Date)	Required Resources
1	I always give importance to gathering the detailed project requirements before starting the project.					
2	I always use PDCA cycle to gather project requirements.					
3	I check the project charter to make sure it is concise, specific, measurable, and linked to business objectives.					
4	I do my best to prevent scope creep on my projects and do not change the project charter unless absolutely necessary.					
5	If scope creep is unavoidable, I evaluate and explain its potential adverse impact on the project results to all stakeholders and team members.					

6	Along with project objectives, I always include high-level milestones, risks, and constraints in the charter.					
7	I ensure that adequate time has been spent on developing the project charter and finalize it after getting complete buy-in from all stakeholders.					
8	I treat the project charter as a constitution of the project.					
9	I always ensure that the charter aligns with short- and long-term organizational goals.					
10	I get the project charter signed by all stakeholders like a contract and use it as a dynamic document throughout the life cycle of the project.					
	Total SDF					

Table 4.11   Pillar IV: Action Plan to Decrease Self-Resisting Force (SRF)

Name: _____   Date: _____

No.	Resisting Force	Current Score	Goal (Target Score) ⬇	Action Plan to Decrease RF Score	Complete by (Date)	Required Resources
1	I always start the project first and collect the project requirements later.					
2	I always use the act, check, do, and plan cycle to gather project requirements.					
3	I develop the project charter just like a simple checklist to be completed as a formality at the beginning of the project.					
4	I make changes to the project charter when scope creep occurs during the project life cycle.					
5	I do not have time on projects to evaluate potential adverse impact of scope creep on the project results and deal with the impact when it happens.					
6	I only include the high-level objectives in the project charter.					
7	I spend some time to prepare the charter and always inform the stakeholders about the finalized project charter.					

8	I treat the project charter as a document required to initiate the project.					
9	I do not think that a charter needs to be aligned with organizational goals.					
10	I use project charter to kick off the project and do not see the need to refer to it during the rest of the project.					
	Total SRF					

Pillar IV   Exercises

PILLAR IV: ORGANIZATIONAL-LEVEL SKILL SET–ENHANCEMENT EXERCISES

GROUP EXERCISES

These exercises are best completed within a group of project managers, project leaders, executives, and stakeholders from within a department or an organization.

1. Using Table 4.12, identify at least five advantages to your organization in applying the principles of Pillar IV for setting higher standards and establish a contract by using a signed project charter on all major projects. Rate the advantages from 1 (least important) to 5 (most important).
2. Using Table 4.13, prepare a project charter using the checklist for a recently completed project. Identify each element of the charter

Table 4.12   Pillar IV: Five Advantages of Applying Principles of Pillar IV to Your Organization

No.	Advantages of Applying Principles of Pillar IV for Setting Higher Standards to Establish a Contract by Creating Signed Project Charters on All Major Projects	Rating (from 1 = Least Important to 5 = Most Important)	Explain the Rating
1			
2			
3			
4			
5			

Table 4.13   Pillar IV: Checklist of Elements for a Project Charter

Elements of a Charter	Describe Each element for a Recently Completed Project (If Any Element Is Not Used, Explain "Why")
Name of the project	
Name of the project manager	
High-level project objectives	
High-level scope	
Organizational strategies	
Key stakeholders	
Constraints	
Assumptions	
High-level risks	
High-level milestones	
Project success criteria	
Items project does not include	
Deliverables	
Budgetary requirements	
Resource requirements	
Business needs	
High-level organizational structure	
Project approval requirements	

that you used in the project. If any of the elements are not used, explain why it is not used.

3. Identify one successful project in your organization. Identify all the elements of the charter marked using the checklist in the Table 4.13. Prepare the project charter, and using Table 4.14 (row 1), identify and list at least three ways the project charter would have benefited in improving the project results if it had included all these elements in it and had been approved by the project stakeholders.

4. Identify one failed project in your organization. Identify all the elements of the charter using the checklist in the Table 4.13. Prepare the project charter, and using Table 4.14 (row 2), identify and list at least three ways the project charter would have benefited in improving the project results if it had included all these elements in it and had been approved by the project stakeholders.

5. Scenario analysis: A Government agency contracted Novansoft to rewrite their legacy medical system into a latest Web-based user-friendly system to process Medicaid claims. Novansoft started this project with greatest enthusiasm, and stakeholders in this project were excited to be part of this massive project. Novansoft planned to follow project management methodology throughout the life cycle of the project. However, during the project execution, few newly identified key stakeholders suggested major scope changes to the system to accommodate new patient services. Because of the pressure from the sponsor, Novansoft accommodated those scope changes. Although Novansoft documented initial milestone dates for this project, delays in the work schedule caused the project end dates to move. Because new risks were created from the scope changes, project team had to accommodate few software adjustments to carry out the project. After multiple delays in the deadline, the project finally completed a year after inception. However, software problems started within a week after the system went live. Hundreds of Medicaid claims were not processed, and health care practitioners were unable to get

Table 4.14   Pillar IV: List Projects, Project Charter, and Benefits

Projects	Three Ways the Signed Project Charter Would Have Benefited in Improving the Project Results if It Had Been Created with All the Elements and Accepted by All Stakeholders
1. Successful project	a. b. c.
2. Failed project	a. b. c.

Table 4.15   Pillar IV: Investigate the Reasons for Failure Based on Principles of Pillar IV

No.	Elements of the Charter	Explain the Failure Reasons Behind Each Element	Recommendations for Future Projects
1.	Identification of stakeholders		
2.	Identification of high-level scope		
3.	Identification of high-level milestones		
4.	Identification of high-level risks		
5.	Development of charter		
6.	Stakeholders' signatures		
7.	Project success criteria		

Medicaid information on time. Many patients' services were turned down by hospitals due to inconsistent information. Comprehensive analysis was carried out by the steering committee over the failure of the project to determine what went wrong. Imagine you are part of the steering committee to investigate the failure. Using Table 4.15, list each element of failure and the reasons behind each element on the basis of the principles described in Pillar IV. Also, make recommendations for future projects.

PILLAR IV: PERSONAL-LEVEL SKILL SET– ENHANCEMENT EXERCISES

INDIVIDUAL EXERCISES

These exercises are to be completed individually after reviewing Pillar IV in detail.

1. Using Table 4.16, identify at least five advantages to your career as a project manager of applying the principles of Pillar IV by establishing a signed project charter on all future major projects. Rate the advantages from 1 (least important) to 5 (most important).
2. Using Table 4.17, identify at least five roadblocks to applying the principles of Pillar IV by establishing a signed project charter on all future major projects. Rate the identified roadblocks from 1 (least difficult to overcome) to 5 (most difficult to overcome).
3. (a) Identify two successful projects you have led or have recently completed. Prepare the charter for each project. Using Table 4.18, identify and list at least three ways the signed project charter would have benefited you in leading the projects

Table 4.16 Pillar IV: Five Advantages of Applying Principles of Pillar IV to Your Career

No.	Advantages to Your Career of Applying Principles of Pillar IV for Setting Higher Standards to Establish a Contract by Creating Signed Project Charters on All Major Projects	Rating (from 1 = Least Important to 5 = Most Important)	Explain the Rating
1			
2			
3			
4			
5			

Table 4.17 Pillar IV: Five Roadblocks to Applying Principles of Pillar IV

No.	Roadblocks to Applying Principles of Pillar IV by Establishing a Signed Project Charter on Future Major Projects	Rating (from 1 = Least Difficult to Overcome to 5 = Most Difficult to Overcome)	Explain the Rating
1			
2			
3			
4			
5			

Table 4.18 Pillar IV: List Successful Projects, Vision Statements, and Benefits

Projects	Signed Project Charter	Three Ways the Signed Project Charter Would Have Benefited You in Leading the Projects if It Had Been Created with All the Elements and Accepted by All Stakeholders
Successful Project 1		a. b. c.
Successful Project 2		a. b. c.

if it had been created with all the elements and signed by
stakeholders.

(b) Identify two failed projects you have managed or have recently
completed. Prepare the charter for each project. Using
Table 4.19, identify and list at least three ways the project charter would have benefited you in leading the projects to success if it had been created with all the elements and signed by
stakeholders.

4. Use Table 4.20 and select an upcoming major project you are
leading or going to be a part of. List different activities involved in
PDCA in creating a project charter.

Table 4.19   Pillar IV: List Failed Projects, Vision Statement, and Benefits

Projects	Three Ways the Signed Project Charter Would Have Benefited You in Leading the Projects if It Had Been Created with All the Elements and Accepted by All Stakeholders
Failed Project 1	a. b. c.
Failed Project 2	a. b. c.

Table 4.20   Pillar IV: List Activities Involved in PDCA Cycle

	List Activities Involved in Preparing the Project Charter
1. Plan	1. 2. 3.
2. Do	1. 2. 3.
3. Check	1. 2. 3.
4. Act	1. 2. 3.

5. Scenario analysis: A government agency contracted Novansoft to rewrite their legacy medical system into a latest Web-based user-friendly system to process Medicaid claims. Novansoft started this project with greatest enthusiasm, and stakeholders in this project were excited to be part of this huge project. Novansoft planned to follow project management methodology throughout the life cycle of the project. However, during the project execution, few newly identified key stakeholders suggested major scope changes to the system to accommodate new patient services. Because of the pressure from the sponsor, Novansoft accommodated those scope changes. Although Novansoft documented initial milestone dates for this project, delays in the work schedule caused the project end dates to move. Because new risks were created from the scope changes, the project team had to accommodate few software adjustments to carry out the project. After multiple delays in the deadline, the project finally completed a year after inception. However, software problems started within a week after the system went live. Hundreds of Medicaid claims were not processed, and health care practitioners were unable to get Medicaid information on time. Many patients' services were turned down by hospitals because of inconsistent information. Comprehensive analysis was carried out by the steering committee over the failure of the project to determine what went wrong.

Imagine you are working for Novansoft as a project manager. Using Table 4.21, list various measures you would have taken in preparing the project charter to prevent scope creep and project failure.

Table 4.21 Pillar IV: Measures Taken to Prevent Project Failure in Scenario Analysis

Activities in the Initiation Phase	*List Various Measures Taken to Prevent Project Failure*
1. Develop high-level scope	
2. Identify stakeholders	
3. Develop clearly written project charter	
4. Prevent future scope creep	
5. Gather acceptance from stakeholders	

Pillar IV   References

1. Bishop, M. (2009). *2009 Standish Group CHAOS Report: Worst Failure Rate in a Decade*, http://www.irise.com/blog/index.php/2009/06/08/2009-standish-group-chaos-report-worst-project-failure-rate-in-a-decade/ (accessed October 27, 2010).

2. Kerzner, H. (2003). *Project Management: A Systems Approach to Planning, Scheduling, and Controlling*. Hoboken, NJ: John Wiley & Sons Inc.

3. Arveson, P. (1998). *The Deming Cycle*, http://www.balancedscorecard.org/thedemingcycle /tabid/112/default.aspx.

4. Project Management Institute. (2008). *A Guide to the Project Body of Knowledge (PMBOK Guide)*, 4th Ed., p. 75, 14 Campus Boulevard Newtown Square, PA 19073-3299 USA.

5. The Standish Group International, Inc. (2010). *CHAOS Summary 2009*, http://www1.standishgroup.com/newsroom/chaos_2009.php (accessed October 27, 2010).

6. U.S. Constitution & Amendments. (2010). Naperville, IL: Oak Hill Publishing Company, http://www.constitutionfacts.com/?section=constitution&page=intro.cfm (accessed August 27, 2010).

7. Rother, M., and Shook, J. (2008). *Learning to See: Value Stream Mapping to Add Value and Eliminate MUDA*. Cambridge, MA: Lean Enterprise Institute Inc.

8. Committee of Commerce United States Senate. (1912). *Titanic Disaster Report: Investigations into Loss of S.S .Titanic*. Report No. 806, pp. 7–8, http://www. senate.gov/reference/reference_item// titanic.htm (accessed October 27, 2010).

Chapter 5

Pillar V: Diffuse Your Passion

Communication Confuses; Passion Diffuses

5.1 Introduction

5.1.1 Why Is Communication So Important?

Lack of effective communication or poor communication is the leading cause of failures in projects.[1] Even when the common language is English, the message tends to get "lost in translation." The widespread existence of virtual teams speaking different languages, and spread across numerous time zones around the globe, makes the importance of this Pillar extremely critical to the future success of project leaders.

A single speech by Martin Luther King, delivered to more than 200,000 civil rights supporters on August 28, 1963, from the steps of the Lincoln Memorial, is considered to be one of the greatest and most notable speeches in human history. The 16-minute "I Have a Dream" speech helped define the history of the United States of America by giving birth to the American Civil Rights Movement. According to U.S. Representative, John Lewis, *"Dr. King had the power, the ability, and the capacity to transform those steps on the Lincoln Memorial into a monumental area that will forever be recognized. By speaking the way he did, he educated, he inspired, and he informed not just the people there, but people throughout America and unborn generations."*[2]

How can someone inspire the entire nation and change the course of history by communicating for just 16 minutes, whereas some others cannot even get their message through after speaking for months or even years?

This question will be answered in this chapter with a detailed analysis on communication techniques, modes, and methods, and the answer has the ability to take project leadership to an entirely new level of sophistication.

5.1.2 Why Is Being an Excellent Communicator Critical?

It does not matter where we are in the world and what profession we are in, communication is very important to convey feelings, thoughts, and emotions to one person or group of others. Effective communication can create new links between people hundreds of miles away, and ineffective communication can break the understanding between people in the same room. Communication is vital in every instance of our daily life. We need to look at the qualities that make a person a powerful communicator who can win the hearts of millions with a few minutes of a heartfelt speech. What are the qualities that great leaders possess that allow them to not only effectively communicate their ideas but also inspire others to take action?

Let's explore these critical questions together. Let's take a journey back in time by using our power of visualization. I want you to close your eyes and envision a battleground. Visualize two massive armies facing each other, separated by a few hundred yards. Visualize yourself as a small bird with an ability to hover around and observe and listen in on both sides. Although neither army can see where the other army ends, but from your point in the sky, you can see that one of the army is almost twice the size of the other army and have a significantly larger infantry, cannons, and ammunition. As both sides are preparing for battle, the general of the bigger and stronger army can be observed slowly making his way to the front on his horse. You observe that he faces his army with some apprehension and raises his sword slightly to shoulder height. Visualize that you quickly move to a spot where you can hear the speech of the general. You notice his voice is little shaky as he utters the following words, *"My troops—although, I think that we are fighting for a just cause, and we have a good enough strategy, I am unsure of the outcome of this battle. I fear that this battlefield will be the final resting place for many of us. I hope that some of us can survive to take care of the young and weak on our land. All I ask of you today is to take care of yourselves and do not take unnecessary risks. May the best army win today."* You observe that the confidence radiating from the faces of the general's army quickly disappearing. You see that the faces are now tensed and depressed. As they look at each other and their faces are beginning to get grimmer and they seem to be very anxious. This uneasiness is sensed by the horses and they too seem to be restless and are quickly getting out of formation making the army look very weak and disorganized.

Now, you observe that the general from the other side is coming forward on his horse in full stride. The horse runs to the front of the line and takes a sharp U-turn as the general faces his army with the horses' front hoofs slashing the air as it raises itself to full height on its hind legs. As you are making your way to the other side, you can already hear the loud boom of the general's voice on the other side requesting full attention from his troops. You can see that he has his sword drawn and confidently raised fully above his head and is waving it as if slicing the air. He then addresses his army with an inspiring tone of voice **"Today, I do not just see just 10,000 ordinary warriors; I see 10,000 heroic generals standing before me. Each one of you is a force far mightier than any force our enemy has ever faced. We have waited for this day for many years—this is YOUR day, this is YOUR time now. I do not say that the battle ahead of us will be easy—but I know each of you will fight till your last breath for our cause, which is near and dear to each one of our hearts. Surrender is not an option. Today is one of the greatest days of our lives—the only option we have today is to be victorious! Which of you lions are going to be with me till the end?"** You suddenly hear a thunderous roar of the entire army saying in one voice ***"I WILL!"*** The entire army, including the horses, seems to be suddenly energized and it is as if the general has replicated his confidence and attitude into each one of them, transforming them from within and giving them a purpose to seize the day!

Let's end the visualization session and come back to the present day.

Answer these three questions.

1. Which general inspired you the most to take action?
2. Which army do you think won the battle?
3. If you had to pick a side, which general would you serve with in battle and why?

If you are like most people I know, the answer to these three questions are quite obvious. The general who spoke with confidence and gusto was definitely more inspirational, and his army stands a much better chance of winning the battle. If you like winning, it is obvious which generals' side you will want to serve on.

5.1.3 Why Is Being an Excellent Communicator Critical to a Project Leader?

Although the objectives of winning a battle are very different from successfully completing a project, it is important to understand that battles are not won by cannons, and projects are not completed by software, but by the determination of men and women who wisely use the weapons or tools available to them to successfully achieve the goals and objectives set forth by the leader with complete conviction. Just as a general communicates the importance of winning a battle and inspires the army to go forward without fear, it is critical for project leaders to inspire the team to undertake and successfully complete all the project objectives without the slightest amount of hesitation.

Just as a general communicates the importance of winning a battle and inspires the army to go forward without fear, it is critical for project leaders to inspire the team to undertake and successfully complete all the project objectives without the slightest amount of hesitation.

5.2 Mastering the Art of Excellent Communications

The project leader should be a conduit for the information flowing downward from the corporate hierarchy and rising upward from individual teams, moving laterally across all departments and teams, and corporation or 360 degrees communication. Project leaders must make best use of all methods of communication at their disposal—staff meetings, one-on-one meetings, steering committee meetings, e-mails, project repository, project Web sites, bulletin boards, flyers, weekly newsletters, corporate magazine articles, etc.

Although being an excellent communicator is a critical requirement for being a project leader, communication is a learned skill and can be mastered once we understand the common key ingredients required in becoming an excellent communicator. The following seven ingredients are absolutely necessary to master the art of excellent communications.

5.2.1 Seven Ingredients to Mastering the Art of Communication

1. Believing in the project's goals and objectives
2. Exuding self-confidence and determination
3. Conveying a clear "common goal"
4. Declaring the challenges ahead
5. Breaking down all barriers
6. Selecting the "right" communication strategy
7. Inspiring the "right" action

5.2.1.1 Believing in the Project's Goals and Objectives

Unless the project leader is able to absorb the fundamental directives set forth by the customer and the sponsor, and believe in the importance of achieving them, how can they convincingly communicate its importance to the team and to all other stakeholders? Thus, a project leader needs to truly understand and believe in the project's goals and objectives before effectively communicating it to others. It is absolutely acceptable to doubt some elements of the objectives at first. But it is up to the project leader to gather the required information and work with the customer and sponsor until the project leader clearly understands the objectives without any ambiguity and is convinced of the benefits that the successful completion of the project can bring to the customer and to the sponsor. The items in a project that form a baseline for the project's goals and objectives are discussed in Figure 5.1.

5.2.1.2 Exuding Self-Confidence and Determination

Have you ever lead a complex, long-term project in which you were 100% sure that the team would achieve every objective they set out to achieve at the onset of the project? It is quite normal not only to be unsure of the final outcomes but also to sometimes doubt your own abilities to successfully complete any complex long-term project. However, the major difference between project managers and project leaders with excellent communication skills is, although the project leaders may have butterflies flying in their stomach, they will exude utmost confidence while communicating with the team members and with the sponsors.

Successful project leaders need to convey their determination by their actions. Consider a complex project involving hundreds of team members

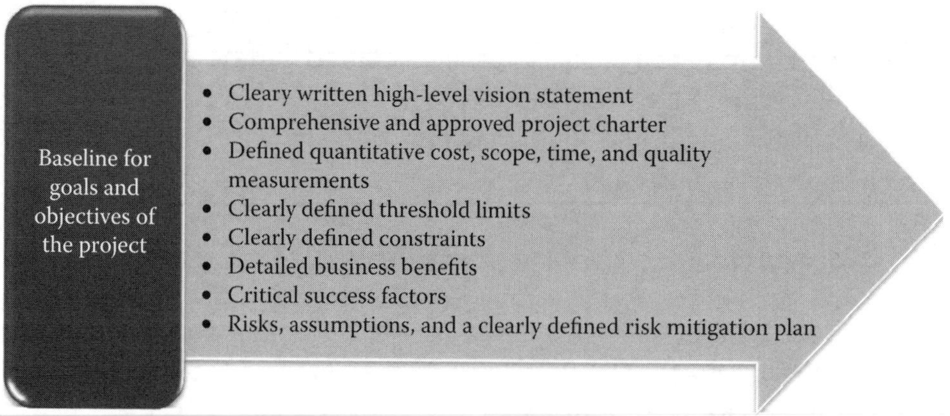

Figure 5.1 is represented by an arrow diagram with the following content:

Baseline for goals and objectives of the project

- Cleary written high-level vision statement
- Comprehensive and approved project charter
- Defined quantitative cost, scope, time, and quality measurements
- Clearly defined threshold limits
- Clearly defined constraints
- Detailed business benefits
- Critical success factors
- Risks, assumptions, and a clearly defined risk mitigation plan

Figure 5.1 Baseline for goals and objectives of the project.

spread globally. This type of project has a general tendency of going off-track several times during project execution. Project team members tend to get disappointed and lose focus if the project is not brought back on track immediately. When the project goes off-track, many project managers try to use routine communication methods such as team meetings, e-mail updates, reports, and presentations in an attempt to resolve problems. Does this type of communication really bring energy back into team members and make them active? Not sure? Then, how should a project leader communicate to their project team when a project goes off-track? Project leaders need to immediately communicate their utmost determination to find and eliminate the root cause of the problems responsible for getting the project off-track. They need to use project charter and vision statements to motivate the team and involve them in root cause analysis of why the project parameters are deviating from the charter and vision statement. They need to identify the constraints and prepare a plan based on the facts to eliminate the constraints. The project leader should strongly commit to specific measurable steps to execute this plan with an accelerated time frame and communicate this plan to all the project stakeholders.

Self-confidence and determination are key ingredients in making a project leader an excellent communicator.

Thus, self-confidence and determination are key ingredients in making a project leader an excellent communicator. This is extremely necessary during the course of complex projects because several issues may arise which may shake the confidence of the sponsor, executives, and the customer. Also, the project leader can effectively manage bad situations from getting worse by showing determination in taking the appropriate action necessary to correct the situation and get the project back on track. Executives are wise enough to know that, no matter how detailed the planning, unknown variables will always create roadblocks and impede the progress of any complex project.

The project leaders who have the ability to blast through the roadblocks created by known and unknown variables, and show confidence and determination under fire, are the ones who ultimately earn the respect of executives and sponsors. Their self-confidence and determination to overcome roadblocks will raise their credibility as a successful project leader to a much higher level.

5.2.1.3 Conveying a Clear Common Goal

In order for a project leader to be an excellent communicator, he or she needs to be able to clearly define and communicate a "common goal" to the team. A project leader needs to use the project vision statement and charter to set a well-defined goal for the entire project. The common mistake many project managers make is allowing the teams to interpret these documents differently while setting their team goals. By doing so, the communication between the team breaks down, as sometimes seen during requirement-gathering sessions, design meetings, and change management meetings. The reason for this breakdown in communications is simple. Because both the charter and vision statement can be interpreted by different teams from their own points of view, a common goal is not set for the meetings. Because of false interpretation of important documents, the communication between various individuals and groups tends to go in different directions, not resulting in an agreement. This is similar to blind men around an elephant trying to distinguish various parts of the elephant based on their own understanding. For consensus to be reached, the blind men need to be informed that it is just one object that they are all touching and trying to interpret. It creates a deeper level of understanding and allows them to reach consensus.

Thus, the project leader must integrate all the project documents to synthesize and create a common goal for the project, which can be communicated to all stakeholders.

5.2.1.4 Declaring the Potential Challenges Ahead

A project leader must be honest and talk in plain and simple terms about the potential challenges and constraints ahead of the project with the team members, the stakeholders, and even the customers. When I was entrusted with projects that were sure to have problems, I always worked upfront with the team and even with the customers. I always used the analogy of a bronco, and informed my team and my clients that at times, during the initial phases of the project implementation, they may feel that they are riding a bucking bronco and warn them to be prepared for a rough ride. But I also assured them that I had the skills necessary to tame the bronco quickly and bring it under control so that there will be smooth riding after that.

Thus, straight talk, regarding the potential challenges ahead on a project, is very critical to building credibility with the team members, sponsors, stakeholders, and even the customers.

5.2.1.5 Breaking Down All Barriers

The biggest barrier to communication is not being able to listen effectively to receive feedback. The project leaders not only need to convey their thoughts to the project team and stakeholders but also need to get feedback from them to ensure that their message was received accurately. The project leader also needs to constantly gather information from them to keep the project on track. Thus, a project leader must be an excellent speaker and an excellent listener.

To be an excellent listener, the project leader must

- Listen effectively and actively
- Ask questions when appropriate
- Respond appropriately
- Stay focused on the topic of the conversation
- Convey empathy

To be an excellent communicator, in addition to being an excellent speaker and an excellent listener, the project leader requires additional skills to organize, manage, and distribute the information gathered, as required. The project leaders also need to use their general leadership skills such as coordinating skills, negotiating skills, and conflict-resolution skills, and their technical abilities.

Although a project leader is not expected to be a master of all subject areas of a project, general knowledge and some basic concepts and lingo about quality, reliability, programming, testing, finance, and other aspects related to projects can help them better understand the challenges facing the team members and thus make them superior leaders and communicators.

Therefore, to become an excellent communicator, project leaders need to develop important skills necessary to break communication barriers. Figure 5.2 gives communication barriers in a project.

5.2.1.6 Selecting the Right Communication Strategy

As discussed earlier, successful project leaders need to possess a variety of skills to become excellent communicators. However, possessing excellent communication skills does not guarantee success in projects. There are a few things that are critical for a project leader to standardize in order to communicate more effectively during the course of the project. The project leader must learn the art of selecting the right communication strategy, which includes communicating the right information, to the right audience, at the right time, using the right mode of communications.

5.2.1.6.1 Communicating the Right Information

Communicating the right information is challenging in the current business environment and in the age of information overload. Accurate, consistent, and valid data are essential for individuals or groups to take the most appropriate

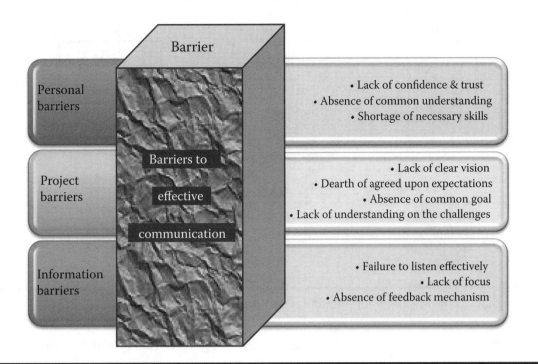

Figure 5.2   Barriers to effective communication in a project.

action during project execution. Communicating out-of-date or inappropriate information severely impedes the decision-making process. For example, change management activities and procedures to carry out that change should be published to the entire project team, well in advance before the project goes to the execution phase. If the project team is not aware of such information, it will result in unwanted changes and in scope creep. Another example of communicating the right information can be that the project management team and key stakeholders should be notified of budget shortfalls and schedule problems in order to make effective decisions. Also, when using vendors in the project, it is critical to inform the vendor regarding any defects in the supplied products. This information may not be important to some project stakeholders but it is vital for the timely execution of any project.

The most important requirement for providing the right information is the ability of project leaders to take the immense quantity of information thrown at them and be able to successfully separate the "signal" from the "noise." Successful project leaders master the art of identifying and filtering the signal from the noise and transfer the right quality and quantity of information to positively affect the project. If the signal-to-noise ratio of this communication is too low, the communication will be tuned off as it will be considered "static noise" or nuisance, as seen in Figure 5.3. Also, if the frequency of communication is too low, the project may be adversely affected. Listening to feedback is critical! A good example of a low signal to noise is when

Successful project leaders master the art of identifying and filtering the signal from the noise and transfer the right quality and quantity of information to positively affect the project.

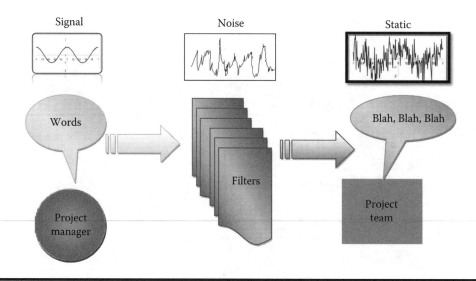

Figure 5.3   Transmission of information with filters.

you get one important e-mail for every hundred spam e-mails (noise) in your box. It is very easy to miss that critical e-mail (signal) because of the high "noise" level.

5.2.1.6.2 Communicating to the Right Audience

A simple approach needs to be designed to communicate information to the right audience during the course of a project. For example, sending budgetary information to a team member does not make any financial impact on the project or sending detailed task-related information to the sponsor can be a waste of the sponsor's valuable time and may be counterproductive to the relationship with the sponsor. How many times have we sent out an e-mail to a big list and then realize that it was not necessary to inundate some key people on the list with the details? Thus, when you follow the golden rule of counting to 10 before sending out an e-mail, make sure you also follow another golden rule of checking your e-mail list twice before sending it out.

Communication sent to the right audience can lead to increased efficiency, improved decision making, accurate judgment, and correct feedback. Table 5.1 provides an example of types of project information and intended audience.

Thus, to convey the right information, it is critical for project leaders to create communication strategies for appropriate levels within the organization. There are three key communication strategies to be considered for optimal communications within a project and within the organization:

1. Vertical communication strategy
2. Lateral communication strategy
3. Corporate communication strategy.

5.2.1.6.2.1 **Vertical Communication Strategy**—Vertical communication strategy is created to communicate information between individuals and groups in

Table 5.1 Example of Types of Project Information and the Intended Recipients

Recipient	Types of Project Information
• Customers/key stakeholders	• Project progress information • Budget, schedule, risk, quality, procurement, and resource-related information
• Sponsor	• Project progress information • Budget, schedule, risk, quality, procurement, and resource-related information
• Project subleaders	• Project progress information • Team performance information • Change request and risk-related information
• Team leaders/ members	• Individual task information • Change request information • Defect and performance information • Team information • Risk-related information

a hierarchical organization. This strategy involves both upward and downward communications. This type of communication is more prevalent in a project within a projectized organization. The project leader communicates with project subleaders and team members below them and with core stakeholders and sponsors above them. As discussed in Pillar II, in a project organization structure, vertical communication plays key role in complex projects. Figure 5.4 represents vertical communication strategy in a complex project.

5.2.1.6.2.2 **Lateral Communication Strategy**—Lateral communication strategy involves communication between people of the same level in an organizational structure. This communication strategy involves sharing knowledge and expertise across different team members and project subleaders. Sharing team members across subteams and sharing project knowledge across project subleaders is also a part of lateral communication. One big advantage of lateral communication is that it improves the cohesiveness among team members and teams across geographically dispersed workers. Figure 5.5 represents the lateral communication strategy in a complex project.

5.2.1.6.2.3 **Corporate Communication Strategy**—Corporate communication strategy is a completely new concept in project communication. In a climate of economic uncertainty, executives look for every indication and assurance to make sure that their investment results in profits. In some companies, if the perception is that a certain project is not progressing well, the project manager is put under intense scrutiny and pressure. If the project manager is unable to change the perceptions, the executives may take drastic steps to cancel the project. Smart

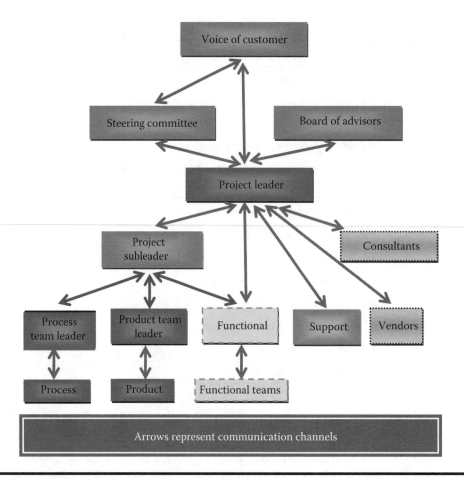

Figure 5.4   Vertical communications in complex projects.

project leaders anticipate the possibility of a project being "torpedoed" and use a proactive strategy to prevent this from happening in any of their projects. The strategy is to proactively communicate the successes, challenges facing the project, and any major milestones of the project corporate-wide and prevent any false rumors about the project from starting or spreading. This strategy, if implemented correctly, can also be a great motivator for the project team as they get recognized corporate-wide for their accomplishments and successes. To implement this strategy, the project leader needs to select the right approach and technology to disseminate the information, and needs to tailor it to the corporate culture. Figure 5.6 represents the corporate communication strategy in complex projects.

All three strategies, vertical, lateral, and corporate communication strategies, described above are required in a project to communicate the right information across all stakeholders within a project team and also beyond the corporate teams. Figure 5.7 represents the information flow in all three types of communication in a project.

5.2.1.6.3 Communicating at the Right Time

Time is of the essence when making important project decisions. One rule of thumb to always keep in mind is to "never surprise the sponsor or other executives on the project team." Sponsors like to be informed as soon as possible

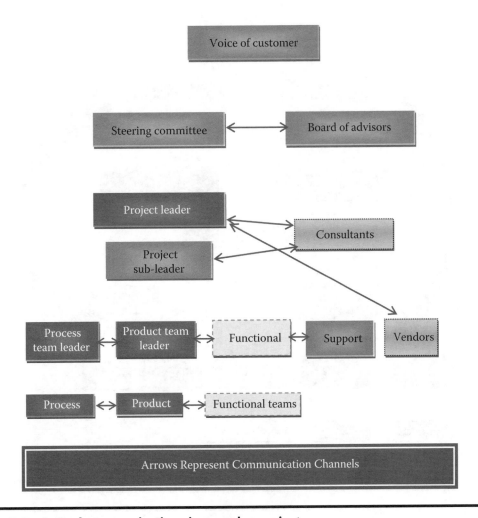

Figure 5.5   Lateral communications in complex projects.

about any major events on a project so that they can always be current in case they need to report information to their superiors. Reporting stale or incorrect information to their superiors can affect the sponsor's credibility and can, in turn, weaken or break the relationship of trust between the sponsor and the project leader. Also, if a project leader fails to respond to a risk in a timely manner, it may result in wastage of valuable budget and project time. Project leaders also need to apply the "never surprise" rule throughout the project ranks; they must require that the team members immediately disseminate any positive or negative information that may affect the project in a major way and never to surprise anyone by neglecting to report critical information. The time criticality of risk-related actions may magnify the importance of a risk. Thus, it is a good practice to include an expected response time from the owner of the task in a project risk register. Quantitative risk analysis tools can be used to evaluate the effect of each risk and the time frame for the response.[3]

5.2.1.6.4 Communicating Using the Right Mode

The mode of communication plays a crucial role in a project communication. Advances on the Internet, instant messaging, Voice Over Internet Protocol

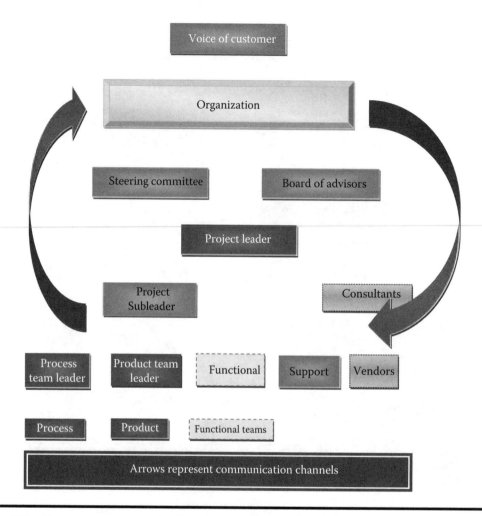

Figure 5.6 Corporate communications in complex projects.

(VOIP), live chat, and Twitter, have provided significant options regarding modes of communications available to globally dispersed teams. In spite of these modes, projects are still failing because of communication problems. Projects are failing because of communication problems not only between geographically separated team members but also between team members operating from a single location. The main reason is that there is still an element of "inspiring the right action" missing from the project managers. A significant percentage of IT and other projects today are run by virtual teams spread globally. The lack of "inspiration" is causing more problems in global teams. Thus, at this point, it is important to discuss effective communication between virtual teams.

5.2.1.6.4.1 The Right Mode of Communication for Virtual Teams—Virtual team communication strategy is critical to the success of current projects. A variety of Internet tools are available to plan, monitor, and execute projects in the virtual world. Virtual workspaces are available to handle global projects. Many Internet-based tools provide facilities to store the task list and online communication with team members. In spite of these tools, communications in virtual teams become complicated and projects are still failing. Creating

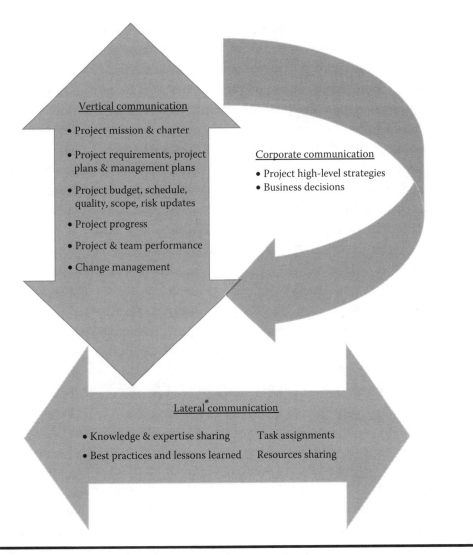

Figure 5.7 Information flow in three types of communications.

successful communication strategy for virtual needs focuses on three essential elements:

a. **Accountability:** Virtual teamwork starts with a high emphasis on individual responsibility, rather than group thinking. The project leaders need to take extra care to ensure that the team members are very clear about what their individual jobs are and what metrics they need to report to determine if the project is progressing well. They also need to clearly identify an escalation plan, in case there are any problems encountered by the virtual team members. The culture of the team members is also a vital element to consider in designing the communication strategy. I was consulting for a multibillion dollar United States–based IT firm that had some project managers in Asia. Although they had communicated the escalation plan clearly, they were not reporting the problems until it was too late. Their actions affected the critical path of the project several times and significantly delayed several system launches. I discussed with the vice president of the project group based in the United States that in some parts of Asia, admitting a problem can be considered a sign of weakness or ineptitude, and the offenders can face some form of reprimand or punishment. Thus, the team members tried their best to work through the problems without reporting them, hoping that the issue would be somehow resolved before it was too late. I explained to the vice president that the area manager of the Asia operations needs to clearly communicate that the escalation plan is merely put in place to get support from experts at the U.S. headquarters, so they can take immediate action and keep the project on track. This communication made a big difference, and as the fear of reprimand was gone, the team members started implementing the escalation plan as designed.

b. **Trust:** Without the establishment of a solid trusting relationship, it is impossible for virtual work to succeed. The project leader needs to establish a strong foundation of contractual trust, communication trust, and competence trust. The project leader must manage expectations, establish clear boundaries, and delegate appropriately. Project leaders should share the project challenges, risks, and other difficulties with the team members, admit their mistakes, when required, and provide honest feedback to the teams. A key element of establishing lasting trust is a mutual respect for the virtual team members and their respective habits and culture. The project leader must have a working knowledge of some customs that may be considered offensive in other cultures and avoid any words or slang during communications that may hurt the sentiments of the virtual team members.

c. **Creating a learning environment:** Most project team members sincerely try their best to meet all the project requirements and correct any errors immediately so as not to affect the project in any way. However, they may not possess all the skills necessary to complete the tasks themselves. It is important for the project leaders to keep the tasks simple, communicate key goals to everyone, incorporate values in everything they do, and provide individual and team learning opportunities while creating and encouraging an atmosphere of openness.[4]

Effective communications and project success rate will definitely increase by focusing on these three areas when deploying projects using virtual teams. Figure 5.8 lists the information shared in an open communication environment with trust.

5.2.1.7 Inspiring the Right Action

The six ingredients of excellent communications discussed in the previous section are of absolutely no use if the project leader fails to inspire the team to take the right action. Even if the communication strategy is designed perfectly and all the technical aspects of communication are considered, if the project leader cannot inspire the team to take the right or desirable action, the communication

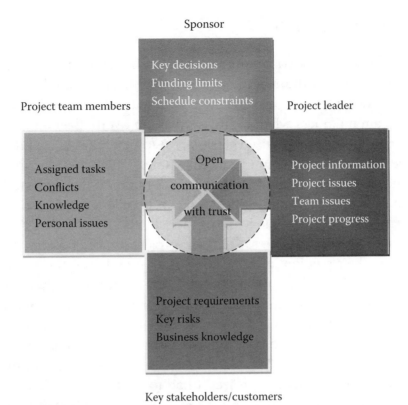

Figure 5.8 **Information shared in an open communication environment with trust.**

strategy is of absolutely no use and projects are bound to fail. Thus, this is the most critical but most difficult characteristic required to master the art of excellent communications. This is the primary reason the success rate of projects is fairly low, especially in IT projects.

What should a project leader do to inspire the team? The answer can be found by turning our attention to sports. What makes ordinary teams transform themselves into champions under a great coach? The transformation happens only when the coach can sell his players his own "dream" and ignite a passion within each and every player on the team to win the trophy. Victory or failure depends more on a state of mind of individuals or teams rather than on their athletic abilities. Each member needs to completely believe in his/her own abilities and in the abilities of the entire team to win. Even when an individual fails, the coach keeps inspiring them to overcome the failures and be the champion they truly are. Without that unwavering belief in their abilities, an undying passion to win, and a sense of higher purpose, it is difficult for individuals or teams to be champions no matter how skilled they are.

Thus far, we have discussed the seven key ingredients to master the art of communication. However, all these seven ingredients are not effective if the project leader does not possess the quality to diffuse the passion, which will be discussed in the next section.

5.3 Diffuse the Passion

A great project leader must communicate with his/her team members just like a coach communicates with the athletes on his/her team. What distinguishes a great project leader from a project manager is how they react and communicate with project team members when a project is going overbudget and beyond the schedule. Great project leaders use the situation to instill more confidence in the team members to carry out the project deliverables. This type of inspiration and communication is critical to allow projects to continue on the right track.

They also need to possess an ability to be an excellent salesperson, when required. Successful project leaders are passionate about their views, ideas, and goals, and will go the extra mile to sell their project to stakeholders. They tend to communicate their passion in every conversation and correspondence with their project teams. The Chaos report from Standish Group clearly indicates that many projects die during the initiation and planning stages. A key reason for the project termination is that project leaders are not able to sell the importance and benefits of these projects to the chief financial officers and other decision makers to get the support for funding. There have been several instances in my career that even before undertaking the project, I had to "sell" the idea and benefits to the chief financial officer and to other key executives. Although they played "hardball" with me on several occasions and insisted that I prove that the estimated return on investment was achievable "beyond a reasonable doubt," I heard from several sources that they were just testing my mettle and they had already made a decision to go ahead based on my passion for the project. Project leaders need to learn not to give up when pressed for more information but allow their energy and their passion for the project outcome overcome all the hurdles in the way of getting the "green" signal for undertaking challenging projects for the organization.

Great project leaders also recognize that the foremost reason communication fails is that people truly are under the wrong impression that others are interested in listening to them. As seen in Figure 5.3, they understand the mechanics that our words are created using the raw materials of our own perceptions, viewpoints, and judgments. These words, when communicated, go through the filters of perceptions and judgments which exist on the other side. When there is excessive filtering, the message the other side gets is just "blah! blah! blah!"

Great project leaders also understand that unless the entire team shares the same vision and mission of the project as they do, trying to communicate is as futile as trying to catch an "AM" signal on an "FM" radio. They know that this results not only in lack of communication but can also lead to significant confusion within the team, as seen in Figure 5.9. True success is achieved when the team completely believes in the goal they are trying to achieve—they are tuned in at the right frequency with the leader. Thus, true leaders do not attempt to

Figure 5.9 Confusion among project team due to lack of communication during vision or mission sharing.

merely communicate with words, but they bring the team to the same level of higher frequency. The higher frequency is nothing but their passion. When the project leaders share their passion with the team, the team members make it their own passion and run with it! True communication follows the laws of thermodynamics. The team leader's exothermic reaction (giving out energy in the form of his passion) generates an endothermic reaction within team members (internal release of that passion among team members), resulting in a blast of exothermic effort (passion is multiplied by many factors and released as the common energy of the team). It is like putting a match to some fireworks; the energy released is enormous, as seen in Figure 5.10. When project leaders clearly communicate the project's vision and mission and share their passion with the team members, the team members make it their own passion, as shown in Figure 5.11, and align the project in the path of success.

When project leaders clearly communicate the project's vision and mission and share their passion with the team members, the team members make it their own passion, as shown in Figure 5.11, and align the project in the path of success.

Thus, for true and effective communication to take place between the project leaders and the project teams, the main questions to be answered are

i. How much passion do the project leaders have for the project's goals and objectives?

ii. Can they effectively share that passion with the project's team members?

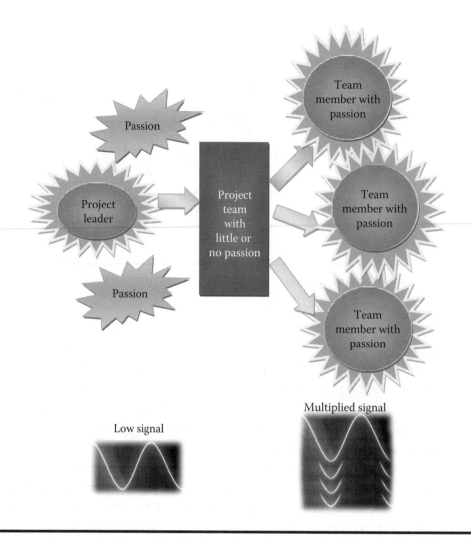

Figure 5.10 Communication with diffusion of passion.

Figure 5.11 Project leaders sharing their passion with the project team.

Pillar V   Summary

Communication is vital in every instance of our daily life. In spite of the vast variety of communication methods in today's hi-tech world, projects are still failing, primarily because of failure to communicate. The basic reason for this failure is because the project leaders are not following the right approach and not inspiring the right action by diffusing their passion to team members.

To determine the qualities that great leaders possess that allow them to not only effectively communicate their ideas but also to inspire others to take action, it is important to look at the qualities of powerful communicators who can win the hearts of millions with a few minutes of a heartfelt speech.

Project leaders need to master the art of excellent communications and be a coach, salesperson, and motivator-in-chief to diffuse their passion across the project organization and lead their team to a successful finish on every project. A successful project leader needs to master effective communication skills throughout his/her career. True leaders use their own passion to tune their team members to their own frequency, creating a common mission for the project. Figure 5.12 lists the seven important points in project communication.

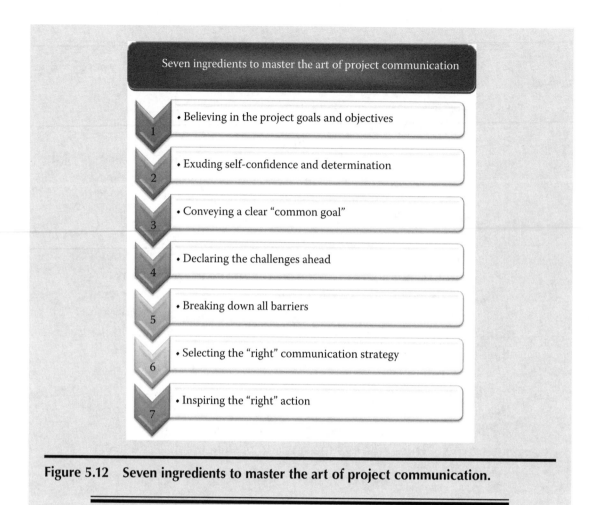

Figure 5.12   Seven ingredients to master the art of project communication.

Pillar V   Case Study

DIFFUSE YOUR PASSION

INTRODUCTION

This case study is about the implementation of a specialized version of flow manufacturing in four business units.

CHALLENGE

When I was entrusted with the leadership of transforming an entire division of a Fortune 500 company from batch manufacturing to flow manufacturing, it became quite apparent to me, to be successful, I would need to communicate effectively at all levels of the organization.

SITUATION

Apart from my own career, I knew that my stakeholders and some of my fans had invested their own careers in this project. We were the first division in the entire corporation to embark on this transformation. They had trusted our team to chart new territory not only for our division but for our corporation, and had given me the responsibility to lead the team and make it happen. I was aware that any negativity toward the project could end the journey in its tracks—the Christopher Columbus of flow transformations may never find the Promised Land, or may never even leave the shore. That was a little too much weight on our shoulders, but I had complete confidence in our abilities to be successful.

SOLUTION

To us, "success was the only option." We had to innovate and create a communication strategy to match the existing culture of my division. Thus, we devised "three laws of communication":

1. Let it flow
2. Avert a blow
3. Have your passion show.

LET IT FLOW

The ecstasy of leading such a critical project subsided very quickly when I visualized myself as an "ant" trying to communicate with the "elephant" (the organization), as shown in Figure 5.13. This project required some very fundamental changes to our systems—manufacturing, IT, materials, supplier strategy, documentation, etc. How can we communicate this change to the entire organization? Why would they listen to us? It was clear that we needed support—we needed to project my words through the mouth of an elephant to make the

Figure 5.13   An ant (a project manager) attempting to communicate with the elephants (organization).

Figure 5.14   An ant (project leader) successfully communicating with the elephants (organization) via the chief elephant (the president).

playing field even. Our president was due to speak at our quarterly luncheon for all 600 of our employees. There is usually plenty of good food, which always gets employees in a cheerful mood. I asked our vice president to request our president (the highest ranked "elephant" in-house) to talk briefly during the luncheon about

a. The criticality of this project to our division's success
b. The need for employees to fully support our team
c. An unequivocal assurance to all employees that efficiency improvements in the organization because of the project would not result in any layoffs.

The president graciously agreed to convey the message. The words of the "ant" coming out of the "elephant's" mouth were quite powerful and were received well as shown in Figure 5.14. All the employees now knew that we were planning some major changes, we needed their support, and most importantly, there was no cause for *fear*—the sky would not fall on their head. I could not have asked for a better kick-off to this project. The communication train had left the station in style.

AVERT A BLOW

Winston Churchill once said, "A lie travels halfway around the world before the truth has a chance to puts its pants on."[5] Thus, our biggest fear was not "how will we manage the communications?" but "how will we prevent miscommunication." Our leadership was well known for "management by walking around." They would walk among the ranks and get "the good, the bad, and the ugly" from the ranks. One of the great things about this kind of culture was that "opinions did count and influence decisions."

The project we were undertaking involved significant changes that would directly affect the ranks and we were well aware that not all these changes would be perceived as positive initially. We knew there was significant FEAR (false expectation appearing real) syndrome among some. Our first order of business was to conduct our own investigation and find those who had negativity toward this project. Not surprisingly, we found a handful of people who were still negative. The ones who had genuine concerns were invited to be a part of the team. We embraced the "enemy" and the "enmity" disappeared. Others were categorized by one of our investigators as "compulsive complainers." She explained "if they were to win a million dollar lottery today, they would immediately complain about having to pay the taxes." We knew that they were not a serious threat to the project success.

Another key ingredient that we added to our communicating strategy was "positivity." During our first team meeting, we warned the team, including our interns and consultants, that being on this project may feel like "hanging on to a wild bronco while being kicked in the face." We asked them to promise that all their concerns were to be only discussed within the team and they would not only always have their "game face" on but "exude positivity" when they were interacting with the rest of our organization. I was convinced that I could not afford the organization to sense our stress easily as they may equate it to our failure. The strategy worked quite well at times. Sometimes, the team members were always zipping by so fast, you never got a chance to observe their "game faces."

> ### HAVE YOUR PASSION SHOW
> "Communicate with your mouth and they may listen,
> Communicate with your pen and they may read,
> Communicate with your might and they may comply, but
> Communicate with true passion in your heart and they will
> follow you anywhere."

IMPLEMENTATION

We were extremely passionate about this project. We knew that for this project to succeed, we needed to "infect" our team with the same passion and diffuse it throughout the team so all members exhibited the same intensity of passion.

As part of another project I had just completed for the research and development department, we had capabilities in-house to print on-demand and customize our print jobs at the touch of a button. I designed a neat format for my project updates in the style of a booklet. Apart from a mission statement, project plans, upcoming trainings, and other project-related details, I included a section called Excellence Awards or "Go Baby Go!" (stolen from my vice president); this included the names of team members and others in the organization who went the extra mile to help the team. These booklets were distributed throughout the organization and were placed strategically throughout our building complex. An example of this booklet can be seen in Figure 5.15. If anyone on the team did something extraordinary, everyone in the organization knew about it, including the president, and stopped them in the halls and congratulated them. This helped boost the passion for the project and motivation level was quite high among the team members and other support teams. Everyone wanted to genuinely bring their "A game" to the table. Even our interns became ambassadors of our passion for this project, and although they put in gruelling hours, they felt passionate about making a difference and getting recognition from the topmost levels of the organization.

During the course of the project, we also published articles on our successes and challenges for the division-wide periodicals.

RESULTS

At the completion of the project, we published an article in the corporate magazine to showcase, for other divisions, the amazing transformation and outstanding results we achieved from implementing this technology.

LESSONS LEARNED

This article actually led another division of the corporation to embrace this technology and embark on their own internal journey, which I was also invited to lead and which helped me in further refining the strategy of diffusing the passion.

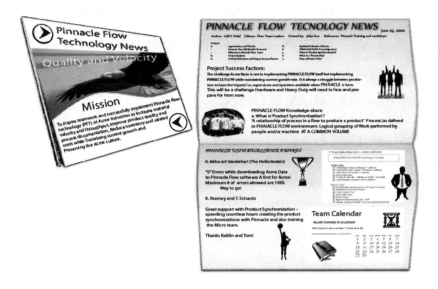

Figure 5.15   An example of a project communication booklet distributed corporate-wide.

Pillar V   Force Field Analysis

PILLAR V: FORCE FIELD ANALYSIS OF ORGANIZATIONAL ASSESSMENT

Table 5.2 shows force field analysis of organizational assessment. The organizational assessment is conducted to assess if the culture of the organization is in alignment with the principles of Pillar V. Tables 5.3 through 5.5 are used to develop and implement an action plan to increase the effect of the organizational driving forces and decrease the effect of the organizational resisting forces.

PILLAR V: FORCE FIELD ANALYSIS OF SELF-ASSESSMENT

Table 5.6 shows force field analysis of self-assessment. The self-assessment is conducted to assess if your own strengths are in alignment with the principles of Pillar V. Tables 5.7 through 5.9 are used to develop and implement an action plan to increase the effect of the self-driving forces and decrease the effect of the self-resisting forces.

PILLAR V: RECOMMENDATIONS FOR OPTIMAL RESULTS FROM FORCE FIELD ANALYSIS

For optimal results and actual transformation of culture and strengths conducive to the creation of advanced master project leaders, the following three steps are necessary:

1. Both the organizational and self-evaluation assessments must be completed.
2. A well-designed action plan must be created and implemented to increase the driving forces and decrease the resisting forces.
3. The principles of each pillar must be constantly practiced and improved.

It is highly recommended that both the organization assessments and self-assessments be conducted every year and the action plan be updated at least every 3 months.

Note: The sum of scores for Organizational Driving Force and Organizational Resisting Force for each point must be less than or equal to TEN.

The sum of scores for Self Driving Force and Self Resisting Force for each point must be less than or equal to TEN.

Table 5.2 Pillar V: Force Field Organizational Analysis

Team Name: _____   Date: _____

No.	Driving Forces	Score Organizational Driving Force (ODF)	Score Organizational Resisting Force (ORF)	Resisting Forces
Does My Organization Drive or Resist the Culture of Effective Communications?				
0 Never		5 Sometimes		7 Mostly
3 Rarely		ODF + ORF ≤ 10		10 Always
1	Communication at all levels within my organization is excellent and does not result in any inefficiency.			Communication is not managed very effectively within my organization.
2	The leaders within my organization stress the importance of being effective communicators.			The managers within my organization do not communicate effectively.
3	My organizational culture promotes the key communication principle of "passion" for the mission and vision.			My organizational culture uses the traditional principles of communications.
4	The organization establishes a formal communication strategy between key stakeholders—project sponsor, steering committee, project leaders, and team on complex projects.			There is no formal communication strategy between key stakeholders of projects.
5	Regular feedback from project teams is used to gauge the effectiveness of the communication style of their leaders.			No feedback regarding communication effectiveness is requested from the project teams.
6	There is a formal reward and recognition for leaders who are able to tune their teams to a common mission and motivate them to "go the extra mile."			There is no formal system of reward and recognition for managers for being effective communicators.
7	Organization structure for simple projects has well-defined lateral and vertical channels of communication.			Organization structure for simple projects does not clearly define the channels of communication.

8	The organization understands the importance of the channel of overall corporate communications on complex projects.			The organization does not use the channel of corporate communications on complex projects.
9	Damaging rumors and gossips related to organizational changes and personnel are addressed efficiently and with care and sophistication.			There is no formal attempt to address or confront any damaging rumors and gossips.
10	Organization promotes trust, respect, open communications, and critical information travels rapidly throughout the organization.			There is a lack of trust and respect, and informal rumors spread faster in my organization than formal critical information.
	Total ODF score			*Total ORF score*

Result	Conclusion	Recommended Action Review and Update Every Quarter (3 months)
ODF >> ORF	My company culture strongly drives the culture of effective communications.	Use Tables 5.3 through 5.5 to set goals and create an action plan to preserve or continuously improve the culture.
ODF > ORF	My company culture drives the culture of effective communications.	Use Tables 5.3 through 5.5 to set goals and create an action plan to increase ODF to create a stronger culture of effective communications.
ORF >> ODF	My company culture strongly resists the culture of effective communications.	Use Tables 5.3 through 5.5 to set goals and create an action plan to increase the ODF and reduce the ORF to create a stronger culture of effective communications.
ORF > ODF	My company culture resists the culture of effective communications.	Use Tables 5.3 through 5.5 to set goals and create an action plan to reduce the ORF to create a stronger culture of effective communications.
ODF = ORF	My company culture does not drive or resist the culture of effective communications.	Use Tables 5.3 through 5.5 to set goals and create an action plan to increase the ODF to create a stronger culture of effective communications.

Table 5.3   Pillar V: Analysis of ODF and ORF Results

Result	Existing Organizational Culture	If the Goal Is to Create a Moderately Strong Culture of Effective Communications	If the Goal Is to Create a Very Strong Culture of Effective Communications
ODF			
ODF ≤ 25	No or minimal culture of effective communications	Focus on improving scores in at least 5 DF	Focus on improving scores in at least 7 DF
25 < ODF ≤ 50	Weak culture of effective communications	Focus on improving scores in at least 3 DF	Focus on improving scores in at least 5 DF
50 < ODF ≤ 75	Moderate culture of effective communications	Focus on improving scores in at least 1 DF	Focus on improving scores in at least 3 DF
ODF > 75	Strong culture of effective communications	N/A	Preserve or continuously improve the culture
ORF			
ORF > 75	No or minimal culture of effective communications	Focus on decreasing scores in at least 5 RF	Focus on decreasing scores in at least 7 RF
50 < ORF ≤ 75	Weak culture of effective communications	Focus on decreasing scores in at least 3 RF	Focus on decreasing scores in at least 5 RF
25 < ORF ≤ 50	Moderate culture of effective communications	Focus on decreasing scores in at least 1 RF	Focus on decreasing scores in at least 3 RF
ORF ≤ 25	Strong culture of effective communications	N/A	Preserve or continuously improve the culture

Table 5.4   Pillar V: Action Plan to Increase Organizational Driving Force (ODF)

Team Name: _____   Date: _____

No.	Driving Force	Current Score	Goal (Target Score) ⬆	Action Plan to Increase DF Score	Complete by (Date)	Assigned to (Department Name or Initials of Person)
1	Communication at all levels within my organization is excellent and does not result in any inefficiency.					
2	The leaders within my organization stress the importance of being effective communicators.					
3	My organizational culture promotes the key communication principle of "passion" for the mission and vision.					
4	The organization establishes a formal communication strategy between key stakeholders—project sponsor, steering committee, project leaders, and team on complex projects.					
5	Regular feedback from project teams is used to gauge the effectiveness of the communication style of their leaders.					
6	There is a formal reward and recognition for leaders who are able to tune their teams to a common mission and motivate them to "go the extra mile."					
7	Organization structure for simple projects has well-defined lateral and vertical channels of communication.					

8	The organization understands the importance of the channel of overall corporate communications in complex projects.					
9	Damaging rumors and gossips related to organizational changes and personnel are addressed efficiently and with care and sophistication.					
10	Organization promotes trust, respect, open communications, and critical information travels rapidly throughout the organization.					
	Total ODF					

Table 5.5 Pillar V: Action Plan to Decrease Organizational Resisting Force (ORF)

Team Name: _____   Date: _____

No.	Resisting Force	Current Score	Goal (Target Score) ⬇	Action Plan to Decrease RF Score	Complete by (Date)	Assigned to (Department Name or Initials of Person)
1	Communication is not managed very effectively within my organization.					
2	The managers within my organization do not communicate effectively.					
3	My organizational culture uses the traditional principles of communications.					
4	There is no formal communication strategy between key stakeholders of projects.					
5	No feedback regarding communication effectiveness is requested from the project teams.					
6	There is no formal system of reward and recognition for managers for being effective communicators.					
7	Organization structure for simple projects does not clearly define the channels of communications.					
8	The organization does not use the channel of corporate communications on complex projects.					

9	There is no formal attempt to address or confront any damaging rumors and gossips.					
10	There is a lack of trust and respect, and informal rumors spread faster in my organization than formal critical information.					
	Total ORF					

Table 5.6   Pillar V: Force Field Self-Analysis

Name: _____   Date: _____

	Do My Strengths Drive or Resist the Principles of Effective Communications?				
	0 Never		5 Sometimes		7 Mostly
	3 Rarely		SDF + SRF ≤ 10		10 Always
No.	Driving Forces	Score Self-Driving Force (SDF)	Score Self-Resisting Force (SRF)		Resisting Forces
1	I strongly believe that being an excellent communicator is critical to being an excellent leader.				I strongly believe that managers can be very effective without being effective communicators.
2	I ensure that I completely understand and believe in the importance of the project objectives before convincing my team members of their benefits.				I depend on my sponsors and other superiors to understand the full benefits of the project objectives.
3	When discussing projects with my team members and sponsors, I exude total confidence with my communications and actions, even if there are some minor doubts in my mind.				I never openly and candidly communicate all the doubts, confusions, and misgivings I have in my mind about the project with my team and sponsors.
4	I am always upfront and provide a heads-up to all the stakeholders about the challenges the project team may face in the project ahead.				I allow the team to focus on the tasks at hand and rarely discuss the challenges the team may face in the project ahead.
5	I always proactively break down the barriers to effective communications by using the art of active listening, asking questions, and conveying empathy or by other means.				I am usually not aware of any barriers to communications and do not take any proactive steps to prevent them.
6	I use various modes of communication and the three channels of communications (vertical, lateral, and corporate) to communicate effectively on all my projects.				I just use traditional communication methods like e-mails, meetings, and reports to communicate in my projects.

7	I proactively try to filter out the noise within the communication so that the signal (key information) is not lost.			My role is to communicate; it is the other party's responsibility to interpret the signal and eliminate the noise.
8	I use my positivity and passion to communicate to my team members rather than just words.			I communicate the goals and objectives in plain words to the teams.
9	I proactively address any false information or gossip from affecting my project.			I do not care about people gossiping or spreading damaging rumors regarding my projects.
10	I always inspire the team to take the right or desirable action.			I do not consider it part of my role to inspire my team to take the desirable action.
	Total SDF Score			*Total SRF Score*

Results	Conclusions	Recommended Action Review and Update Every Quarter (3 months)
SDF >> SRF	My strengths strongly support the principles of effective communications.	Use Tables 5.7 through 5.9 to set goals and create an action plan to continuously improve the strengths.
SDF > SRF	My strengths support the principles of effective communications.	Use Tables 5.7 through 5.9 to set goals and create an action plan to increase SDF to allow a stronger drive toward the principles of effective communications.
SRF >> SDF	My strengths strongly resist the principles of effective communications.	Use Tables 5.7 through 5.9 to set goals and create an action plan to increase SDF and reduce SRF to allow a stronger drive toward the principles of effective communications.
SRF > SDF	My strengths resist the principles of effective communications.	Use Tables 5.7 through 5.9 to set goals and create an action plan to reduce SRF to allow a stronger drive toward the principles of effective communications.
SDF = SRF	My strengths do not drive or resist the culture of effective communications.	Use Tables 5.7 through 5.9 to set goals and create an action plan to increase the SDF to allow a stronger drive toward the principles effective communications.

Table 5.7   Pillar V: Analysis of SDF and SRF Results

Results	Existing Strengths	If the Goal is to Create Moderate Strengths Toward Principles of Effective Communications	If the Goal is to Create Very High Strengths Toward Principles of Effective Communications
SDF			
SDF ≤ 25	No or minimal culture of effective communications	Focus on improving scores in at least 5 DF	Focus on improving scores in at least 7 DF
25 < SDF ≤ 50	Weak culture of effective communications	Focus on improving scores in at least 3 DF	Focus on improving scores in at least 5 DF
50 < SDF ≤ 75	Moderate culture of effective communications	Focus on improving scores in at least 1 DF	Focus on improving scores in at least 3 DF
SDF > 75	Strong culture of effective communications	N/A	Preserve or continuously improve the strengths
SRF			
SRF > 75	No or minimal culture of effective communications	Focus on decreasing scores in at least 5 RF	Focus on decreasing scores in at least 7 RF
50 < SRF ≤ 75	Weak culture of effective communications	Focus on decreasing scores in at least 3 RF	Focus on decreasing scores in at least 5 RF
25 < SRF ≤ 50	Moderate culture of effective communications	Focus on decreasing scores in at least 1 RF	Focus on decreasing scores in at least 3 RF
SRF ≤ 25	Strong culture of effective communications	N/A	Preserve or continuously improve the strengths

Table 5.8   Action Plan to Increase Self-Driving Force (SDF)

Name: _____   Date: _____

No.	Driving Force	Current Score	Goal (Target Score) ⬆	Action Plan to Increase DF Score	Complete by (Date)	Required Resources
1	I strongly believe that being an excellent communicator is critical to being an excellent leader.					
2	I ensure that I completely understand and believe in the importance of the project objectives before convincing my team members of their benefits.					
3	When discussing projects with my team members and sponsors, I exude total confidence with my communications and actions, even if there are some minor doubts in my mind.					
4	I am always upfront and provide a heads-up to all the stakeholders about the challenges the project team may face in the project ahead.					
5	I always proactively break down the barriers to effective communications by using the art of active listening, asking questions, and conveying empathy or by other means.					
6	I use various modes of communication and the three channels of communications (vertical, lateral, and corporate) to communicate effectively on all my projects.					
7	I proactively try to filter out the noise within the communication so that the signal (key information) is not lost.					

8	I use my positivity and passion to communicate to my team members rather than just words.					
9	I proactively address any false information or gossip from affecting my project.					
10	I always inspire the team to take the right or desirable action.					
	Total ODF					

Table 5.9   Pillar V: Action Plan to Decrease Self-Resisting Force (SRF)

Name: _____   Date: _____

No.	Resisting Force	Current Score	Goal (Target Score) ⬇	Action Plan to Decrease RF Score	Complete by (Date)	Required Resources
1	I strongly believe that managers can be very effective without being effective communicators.					
2	I depend on my sponsors and other superiors to understand the full benefits of the project objectives.					
3	I never openly and candidly communicate all the doubts, confusions, and misgivings I have in my mind about the project with my team and sponsors.					
4	I allow the team to focus on the tasks at hand and rarely discuss the challenges the team may face in the project ahead.					
5	I am usually not aware of any barriers to communications and do not take any proactive steps to prevent them.					
6	I just use traditional communication methods like e-mails, meetings, and reports to communicate in my projects.					
7	My role is to communicate; it is the other party's responsibility to interpret the signal and eliminate the noise.					
8	I communicate the goals and objectives in plain words to the teams.					
9	I do not care about people gossiping or spreading damaging rumors regarding my projects.					
10	I do not consider it part of my role to inspire my team to take the desirable action.					
	Total SRF					

Pillar V   Exercises

PILLAR V: ORGANIZATIONAL-LEVEL SKILL SET–ENHANCEMENT EXERCISES

GROUP EXERCISES

These exercises are best completed within a group of project managers, project leaders, executives, and stakeholders from within a department or an organization.

1. Using Table 5.10, identify at least five advantages of applying the principles described in Pillar V regarding effective communication, within your organization, for complex projects and rate them from 1 (least important) to 5 (most important).
2. Using Table 5.11, identify at least five barriers to the principles described in Pillar V regarding effective communication, within your organization, for complex projects and rate them from 1 (least difficult to overcome) to 5 (most difficult to overcome).
3. Using Table 5.12, identify a recent complex project completed by one of the experienced project managers in your organization. Draw the project organization structure used to accomplish the

Table 5.10   Pillar V: Five Advantages of Applying the Principles of Pillar V to Your Organization

No.	Advantages of Applying the Principles of Pillar V Within Your Organizational Culture	Rating (from 1 = Least Important to 5 = Most Important)	Explain the Rating
1			
2			
3			
4			
5			

Table 5.11   Pillar V: Five Roadblocks to Applying the Principles of Project Leadership Described in Pillar V

No.	Roadblocks to Applying the Principles of Project Leadership Described in Pillar V to Your Organization	Rating (from 1 = Least Difficult to Overcome to 5 = Most Difficult to Overcome)	Explain the Rating
1			
2			
3			
4			
5			

Table 5.12   Pillar V: Lateral, Vertical, and Corporate Communications Within the Organization

project.
    a. Draw clearly defined lateral communication channels on the organizational structure.
    b. Draw clearly defined vertical communication channels on the organizational structure.
    c. Identify key individual or departments to be included in corporate communications.
4. Identify a recently completed complex project within your organization. Assemble the core team and ask them to candidly fill in the details of Table 5.13 regarding the art of selecting the right communication strategy. Estimate the percentage of time the project team communicated the right information, to the right audience, at the right time, using the right mode of communications. Provide at least two significant examples in each case.
Average the scores from all responses.

Table 5.13   Pillar V: the Art of Selecting the Right Communication Strategy Within the Organization

No.	The Right Communication Strategy	Roughly Estimate Percentage of Time Accomplished on the Project (1—0%, 2—25%, 3—50%, 4—75%, 5—100%)	Give at Least Two Critical Examples of How Each Was Accomplished during the Project
1	The Right Information		
2	To the Right Audience		
3	At the Right Time		
4	Using the Right Mode of Communications		
	Total		
	Average		

5. Scenario analysis: RELI-ON-US is a major shipping courier shipping packages all over the world. They are looking at installing an entirely new enterprise resource planning (ERP) system, which will link their internal systems to their customers and to their suppliers of packaging materials. The president of RELI-ON-US is extremely worried about the effect this complex project may have on their customers. Although the ERP company will have consultants who will help with the implementation, the president wants a comprehensive communications plan for this project as he has been informed that these types of project fail mostly because of poor planning and communications. The following are the key players for this implementation:

  i RELI-ON-US
  ii SAF (ERP vendor)
  iii Steering committee—all functional managers, HR, IT
  iv Senior project manager
  v Junior project manager
  vi IT department
  vii Operations and shipping
  viii Facilities
  ix Purchasing
  x BOX, TAPE, and BEYOND (supplier)

Using Table 5.14, identify all the players for the lateral, vertical, and critical points of the corporate communication channels. For each player, enter other player number(s), which are connected at the lateral level, the vertical level, or the corporate level. Using Table 5.15, visually represent the organizational chart with the interdependencies and clearly show the lateral, vertical, and corporate communication channels.

Hint

  a. Use a different color to indicate each of the lateral and vertical channels.
  b. Use a star symbol to indicate the corporate channels.
  c. Validate each channel to ensure communication will not breakdown.

PILLAR V: PERSONAL-LEVEL SKILL SET–ENHANCEMENT EXERCISES

INDIVIDUAL EXERCISES

These exercises are to be completed individually after reviewing Pillar V in detail.

1. Using Table 5.16, list the last three projects you worked on as a project manager/leader, identifying the situations in

Table 5.14   Pillar V: Scenario Analysis Defining Lateral, Vertical, and Corporate Communications Links Within the Organization

Player No.	The Key Players In ERP Implementation Project	Lateral Communication Link [Enter Player Number(s)]	Vertical Communication Link [Enter Player Number(s)]	Critical Corporate Communication Link [Enter Player Number(s)]
1	RELI-ON-US			
2	RAP (ERP Vendor)			
3	Steering committee—all functional managers, HR, IT			
4	Senior project manager			
5	Junior project manager			
6	IT department			
7	Operations and shipping			
8	Facilities			
9	Purchasing			
10	BOX, TAPE, and BEYOND (supplier)			

which the project failed or was affected negatively because of communication failure.

   a. List the reasons for the communication failure.

   b. Which principles of Pillar V could have been applied to reduce or eliminate the reasons for the dissatisfaction.

2. Identify a recently completed complex project you participated in as a manager or team member. Fill in the details of Table 5.17 regarding the percentage of time each of the seven critical ingredients of mastering effective communications were used during the course of the project. Provide at least two significant examples in each case.

3. Identify a recently completed complex project you participated in as a manager or team member. Fill in the details of Table 5.18 regarding the art of selecting the right communication strategy. Estimate the percentage of time you communicated the right information, to the right audience, at the right time, using the right mode of communications. Provide at least two significant examples in each case.

Table 5.15   Pillar V: Scenario Analysis—Visual Representation of the Lateral, Vertical, and Corporate Communications Within the Organization

Table 5.16   Pillar V: List of Three Projects—Customer Focus

No.	Name of the Project	Describe the Situation in Which Communication Failure Occurred	Reasons for Communication Failure	Which Principles of Pillar V Could Have Been Applied to Reduce or Eliminate the Reasons for the Communications Failure
1				
2				
3				

4. Using Table 5.19, identify situations on your projects where using more self-confidence and determination or more passion during your communications would have helped you significantly. How each situation would have helped the project be more successful?

Table 5.17 Pillar V: Mastering the Basics of Effective Communications

No.	The Seven Critical Ingredients to Master the Art of Excellent Communications	Roughly Estimate Percentage of Time Accomplished on the Project (1—0%, 2—25%, 3—50%, 4—75%, 5—100%)	Give at Least Two Critical Examples of How Each Was Accomplished during the Project
1	Believing in the project's goals and objectives		
2	Exuding self-confidence and determination		
3	Conveying a clear "common goal"		
4	Declaring the challenges ahead		
5	Breaking down all barriers		
6	Selecting the right communication strategy		
7	Inspiring the right action		
	Total		

Table 5.18 Pillar V: The Art of Selecting the Right Communication Strategy

No.	The Right Communication Strategy	Roughly Estimate Percentage of Time Accomplished on the Project (1—0%, 2—25%, 3—50%, 4—75%, 5—100%)	Give at Least Two Critical Examples of How Each Was Accomplished during the Project
1	The right information		
2	To the right audience		
3	At the right time		
4	Using the right mode of communications		
	Total		
	Average		

Table 5.19 Pillar V: Identify Situations for Self-Confidence or Determination

No.	Project	Situations That Needed More Self-Confidence and Determination or Passion	Explain How Each Situation Would Have Helped the Project
1.			
2.			
3.			
4.			
6.			

5. Scenario analysis: RELI-ON-US is a major shipping courier shipping packages all over the world. They are looking at installing an entirely new ERP system, which will link their internal systems to their customers and to their suppliers of packaging materials. The president of RELI-ON-US is extremely worried about the effect this complex project may have on their customers. You have been identified as the senior project manager on this project. The president wants a comprehensive communications plan from you on how you plan to use the principles of Pillar V to communicate with consultants from the ERP company, SAF, and the following key players of the organization. The following are the key players for this implementation:
   - i RELI-ON-US
   - ii SAF (ERP vendor)
   - iii Steering committee—all functional managers, HR, IT
   - iv Senior project manager (you)
   - v Junior project manager
   - vi IT department
   - vii Operations and shipping

      viii Facilities

      ix Purchasing

      x BOX, TAPE, and BEYOND (supplier)

Imagine that you are the project manager in the previous scenario. Based on the learning from Pillar V of the book *12 Pillars of Project Excellence*, answer the following using Table 5.20:

a. What are the top five errors of traditional communications will you avoid during this project?

b. Which key principles from Pillar V will you use to ensure success in the project involving the implementation of ERP at RELI-ON-US?

c. What will be some major benefits to you personally and to your career as a senior project manager at RELI-ON-US by applying the principles of Pillar V?

Table 5.20 Pillar V: Action Plan for Scenario Analysis Based on Effective Communication

No.	Top Five Errors to Avoid	Which Principles from Pillar V Should be Utilized for Success on this Project?	Major Benefits of Applying the Principles from Pillar V to You Personally as a Senior Project Manager?
1.			
2.			
3.			
4.			
6.			

Pillar V   References

1. Rosencrance, L. (2007). *Survey: Poor Communication Causes Most IT Project Failures*, http://www.computerworld.com/s/article/9012758/Survey_Poor_communication_causes_most_IT_project_failures (accessed October 27, 2010).
2. Lectura Montessori School Newsletter. (January 2010 Edition). p. 2. 6907 W. Roosevelt Road, Berwyn, IL 60402, United States.
3. Project Management Institute. (2008). *A Guide to the Project Management Body of Knowledge (PMBOK Guide)*, 4th Ed., p. 294. 14, Campus Blrd, Newtown Square, PA 19073.
4. *Communicating with Virtual Project Teams, Harvard Management Communication Letter*. (December 2000). http://hbswk.hbs.edu/archive/2122.html (accessed October 27, 2010).
5. Winston Churchill, 1874–1966. http://www.workinghumor.com/quotes/winston_churchill.shtml (accessed October 27, 2010).

Chapter 6

Pillar VI: Simplify Projects
Eliminate All Non-Value-Added Items from Projects

Make everything as simple as possible, but not simpler.[1]

Albert Einstein

6.1 Introduction

6.1.1 Lean Technology—Simplifying the Project

"Simplicity is the ultimate sophistication"[2] is one of the famous quotes attributed to Leonardo da Vinci, the legendary artist. His views are reflected in the world's most famous painting, the *Mona Lisa*. The simplicity of the drawing and the subtle nature of the smile have made it the highest valued art in the world today. Figure 6.1 shows the art of simplicity as seen in Leonardo da Vinci's *Mona Lisa*.

Almost anyone can complicate matters, but only the smart leaders can drill down to the core and excavate the required nuggets of knowledge. Simplicity to me is taking the most commonsense approach and the most practical path to completing a task. A powerful tool available to project leaders today to simplify projects is "lean technology," or as I call it, "the Science of Simplicity™."

A powerful tool available to project leaders today to simplify projects is "lean technology," or as I call it, "the Science of Simplicity™."

6.1.2 What Is a Lean Technology?

Lean technology is a philosophy of making a conscious choice to radically redefine and dynamically optimize strategy, systems, processes, and services that adds value to clients, employees, and shareholders. It is a powerful

Figure 6.1 The art of simplicity as seen in Leonardo da Vinci's, *Mona Lisa*. (Sketch based on Leonardo da Vinci's Mona Lisa, located in the Louvre Museum in France.)

commonsense tool used globally to eliminate waste from organizations, processes, and systems. The focus is on creating value for the client and eliminating anything that is non-value-added (NVA). Lean technology can be applied to eliminate waste in corporate offices, government, manufacturing, software development, energy utilization, or any processes that are used by any industry, organization, or entity. It can also be applied to projects to reduce project timeline and cost and improve quality.

There are several companies globally who have benefited from lean technology not only by leveraging millions of dollars in cost savings but also in superior client retention, gaining a competitive advantage, and developing a strong and lasting culture of continuous improvement.

Lean technology is now universal term for a compilation of core operation and improvement tools and services that can help any organization continuously and rapidly improve to deliver products or services of the highest quality, at the lowest cost, and in the shortest amount of time.[3]

6.2 Fundamental Principles of Lean

The fundamental principle of lean is to identify waste (*muda*) and separate it from value-added (VA) activities (VA from the point of view of the end customer) and necessary non-VA (NNVA) activities. *Muda* usually accounts for the greatest percentage of the three categories and can be of several types as shown in Figure 6.2. It is critical to identify the *muda* to eliminate it. Figure 6.3 shows eight types of *muda*, namely, transport, information (excess), motion, energy, waiting, overprocessing, overproduction, and defects. **The acronym "TIM E. WOOD"** shown in Figure 6.4 **is used to define the eight types of wastes.**

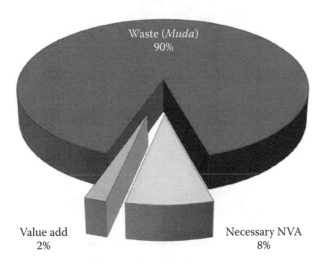

Figure 6.2   Value-added, necessary non-value-added, and waste (*muda*) activities in projects.

1.	T	TRAVEL
2.	I	INFORMATION
3.	M	MOTION
4.	E.	ENERGY
5.	W	WAITING
6.	O	OVERDOCUMENTATION
7.	O	OVERPROCESSING
8.	D	DEFECTS, REWORK

Figure 6.3 Eight types of *muda*.

Figure 6.4 TIM E. WOOD (acronym for eight types of *muda*).

The other category is called NNVA, which may include steps to be taken to satisfy some regulatory or other requirements but may not add any value to the project. When this awareness is used in conjunction with another tool called "value stream mapping"[4] (mapping the entire process from supplier to customer and identifying, demonstrating, and decreasing waste in the process), it becomes very clear what the ratio of VA to non-VA (NVA) activities is. A lower result of VA to NVA ratio indicates that there is considerable waste, and the team/division is not prioritizing VA activities and lacks customer focus. A higher result of VA to NVA ratio indicates that the team is focused on accomplishing VA activities from a customer's point of view. Successful project leaders learn the secret of eliminating the NVA activities so that their invaluable resources can focus only on what is critical to the success of the projects. This can have a major impact on time, quality, and cost aspects of projects. Anything that is a hindrance to the completion of a successful project (including the project leaders themselves) needs to be identified and/or eliminated.

We follow lean thinking in our daily lives without even realizing it as lean thinking. Imagine that you wanted to sell your home and you met with a realtor to start the process. The first suggestion that you would hear from the realtor is "to remove clutter" from your home. Realtor would say too much stuff makes room look smaller and "eats up" your space, and to get increased value for your home, it is critical for you to eliminate waste wherever possible. The next action item you would have from the realtor is to complete minor repairs like fixing the screens, painting the doors, cleaning the backyard, and so forth. These activities take less time and less money but add tremendous value to the home from customer's point of view and increase the visual appeal for the potential home buyers. This type of thinking is lean thinking. Lean thinking might create a smaller impact in your home but becomes invaluable when applying to different projects, which will allow the team to demonstrate significant savings in time and money.

6.3 Lean Thinking in Projects

The fundamental concepts of lean thinking are similar whether you follow them in your home or in the projects. These principles involve improving all processes in each phase of the project to gain incremental improvement, thereby resulting in a significant overall improvement for the entire project.

Advanced project leaders are lean thinkers, and they believe in applying the Science of Simplicity™ to every project they undertake. They are not limited by the eight wastes but look at all wastes that prevent them from creating value for their customer, within the legal and moral boundaries. Advanced project leaders understand that if they do not eliminate the waste from their projects, they face a far greater waste—**the ninth waste is intellectual waste of their resources in trying to complete the project while trying to chase down TIM E. WOOD and trying to deal with the other eight wastes** as shown in Figure 6.5. They understand that to eliminate the ninth waste, they have to wage

Figure 6.5   Intellectual waste (ninth waste) as a result of chasing TIM E. WOOD (eight wastes).

a war on the first eight wastes. Thus, project leaders are those who have undergone a paradigm shift from wanting their resources to work faster to leaders who want their resources to work smarter—to focus on eliminating the waste and thus use their time to focus on adding value to the customers. The principles of lean thinking applied to projects are shown in Figure 6.6 and described below.

A. Identify and improve value added (VA) activities.
B. Identify and reduce necessary non-value added (NNVA) activities.
C. Eliminate or reduce nonvalue added (NVA) activities and eliminate waste.

6.3.1 Identify and Improve VA Activities

Identifying all VA activities is the first and most critical step in lean thinking. What is a VA activity in a project? VA activities change the form, fit, or function of a product or service.[5]

> A VA activity is any activity that is important for the project to move toward completion per customer requirements. Any activity necessary to solve a problem, to add the information, to create a physical transformation, to gather requirements, to control quality, or even to brainstorm ideas are VA activities.

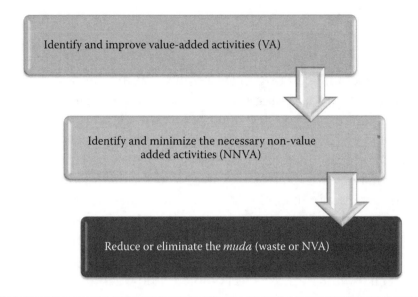

Figure 6.6 Principles of lean thinking in projects.

In other words, a VA activity if removed from a project can harm the objectives of the project. The best way to determine VA activities in a project is by focusing on two areas:

1. The customer
2. The product or service

6.3.1.1 VA Activity Related to the Customer

Lean principles focus on the customer and define value from the customer's point of view. Many project managers attempt to complete projects by focusing on completion of the project without even fully understanding the needs of the customer. However, lean thinking revolutionizes the mind-set about a customer in a project. Project leaders with lean thinking develop methods to focus on value from customer's point of view, considering not only the end product but also every aspect of the project. That means efforts should be made from initiation through closing of the project to identify value from the customer's point of view. Project leader can achieve this by conducting customer focus meetings.

Customer focus meetings are arranged to provide unique environment for customers to openly present their ideas and discuss about various possibilities in a structured way. Let us look at the quality control process of a project. Project managers consider quality control process as an important task for the project team and forget about customers. However, advanced project leaders think differently. They consider customer's ideas in quality control operations by preparing cause and effect diagrams and Pareto charts. By conducting customer focus meetings in quality control process, VA elements can be added in the process, thereby reducing defects. Project leaders can see significant difference in the customer's attitude toward the project after these meetings. Customer focus meetings can be conducted as frequently as possible if the meeting adds value to the project. Many techniques such as brainstorming, focus groups, or Delphi technique can be used to organize such meetings. Another example of involving customer is by developing a customized product on the basis of the customer's repeated needs without increasing the costs. A good example for defining value from customer point of view is described below. In a land management agency, customers wanted to have reports generated from a total of 60 different attributes of a land and lease management system. Every time they needed a report, they would submit a service request to an IT agency that manages the database. After the request was submitted, it was routed to a supervisor for approval. After the necessary approvals, the request was assigned to a developer or a team of developers, depending on the request. The developer then prepares the code, and after thorough testing, the report would be moved into production. The entire process takes at least 3 days to complete. Although the team justified this lead time based on the fact that the code was prepared on the basis of 60 different attributes, it was frustrating for the customers to wait for 3 days for a simple report.

After several complaints by unhappy customers, the project leader decided to look the problem from the customer's point of view. After thorough analysis of the customer's requirements, a project leader came up with an excellent solution for recurring requests from customers. As customers usually required a report from only a few of the attributes of the total 60 that were available, developers were requested by the project leader to develop a comprehensive online application for the customers to choose any field from 60 different attributes on the basis of their requirements and generate a report. This report provided a comprehensive solution for the customers. Although it took 10 days for developers to develop this solution, the customers were delighted to have this type of application. Now, customers could generate their report with any number of attributes within seconds, with a click of a button. This solution not only saved lot of time for both the customer and the developer but also delighted the customer. Figure 6.7 shows the complete cycle of a report before and after applying lean principles to the project. Thus, it can be seen how working with customers and involving them in VA activities can make a significant difference in the project. Now let us look at the VA activities from product point of view.

6.3.1.2 VA Activity Related to the Product or Service

VA activities can also be identified by focusing on the product and its characteristics. The project leader or the team should identify all activities without which the value of the product is diminished. Reducing product defects or service-related defects is a VA activity. In a construction project, identifying quality of the products like concrete, paints, and hardware is a VA activity because it increases the quality of the final product. In software development project, creating data flow diagrams and writing user stories are considered VA activities without which the

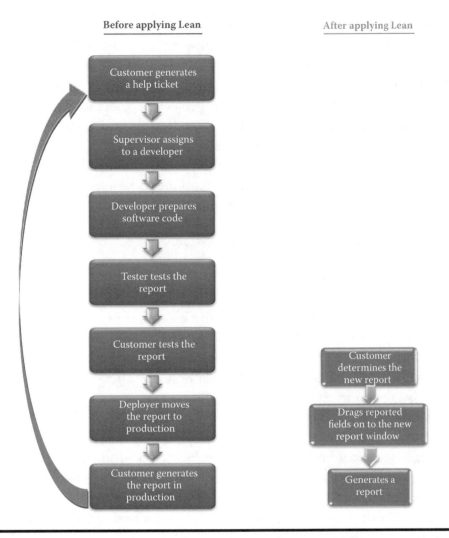

Before applying Lean

After applying Lean

Figure 6.7 The cycle of the report generation before and after implementing lean principles.

design of the product will be difficult. In a call center, monitoring the number of critical issues missed or the number of issues escalated unnecessarily is a VA activity as it provides an indication of major performance and system problems. A project leader with the help of the project team can create a value stream map and identify VA activities from the point of view of a product or service.

6.3.2 Identify and Reduce Necessary Non-Value-Added (NNVA) Activities

After identifying VA activities in a project, the next step is to identify and elimi-nate NVA activities in a project. However, all NVA activities cannot be eliminated as some of those activities are the NNVA activities, which are needed for vari-ous reasons in the project. Project leaders should follow a methodical approach while identifying NNVA activities in each phase of the project. An example of NNVA activity is the documentation of the software code. From customer's point of view, creating software documentation is an NVA activity, whereas creating user documentation is a VA activity. But from product perspective, the documentation is needed. This is an NVA activity but necessary to maintain the code. Let us look at another example in a construction project. Several regulations need to be adhered to in residential construction projects. Project leader should make sure that resources are assigned and tasks are allocated to handle these regulations. Although these regulations do not add to the quality of construction either from the customer point of view or from the product or service point of view, they are necessary to meet the government stipulated requirements. Project leaders can identify NNVA activities by performing two actions:

1. *Analyze the value of the activity on the customer's needs or on the characteristics of the product or service.*
2. *Analyze the impact of the activity on the process.*

If the activity does not add value to either the customer or the product or service but the lack of such activity delays the process or impacts the process, then it is considered as an NNVA activity. Another example of an NNVA activity is sending weekly project status reports to stakeholders. The product or the customer's needs are not impacted by not sending those reports. However, knowing the progress of the project is essential for all customers and stakeholders to continue the project. Another best example of NNVA activity is inspection. Although quality cannot be inspected into a project, a product, a service, or a process and it does not increase the value, it is sometimes necessary to perform one or several inspections, which are NVA, to ensure that the customer receives a good quality product or service. Thus, project leaders should carefully identify the NNVA activities and isolate them from the NVA activities or *muda*. The next section details some methods to classify NVA activities in a project.

6.3.3 Eliminate or Reduce NVA Activities and Eliminate Waste

After identifying VA activities and NNVA activities, eliminating waste or *muda* is the third and most important aspect of lean thinking as it sometimes accounts for more than 90% of project time. In a project, eliminating waste can remove unwanted processes from each phase and unwanted tasks from a process. In a software development project, eliminating waste can be achieved by removing unwanted databases, modules, lines of code, and applications. The project leader or project team can identify waste or reduce NVA activities in a project by asking the following question on the remaining activities.

Does this activity add value to the customer, the product, or the service?

If the answer to the question is "no," those activities, requirements, and resources are considered as NVA. Figure 6.8 identifies few VA, NNVA, and NVA activities in a project.

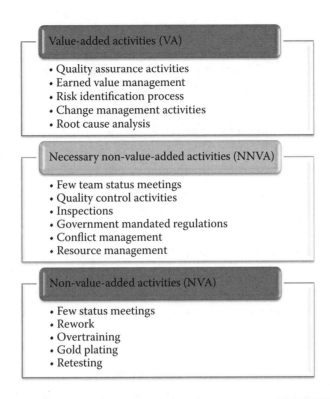

Figure 6.8 Example's of value-added, necessary non-value-added, and non-value-added activities in a project.

NVA activities are those activities that:

- Customer will be unwilling to pay for
- Do not help create conformance to the customer's specifications
- Do not impact the process

NVA activities can be eliminated, reduced, or simplified.[5] Project leaders should identify NVA activities or waste from initiation through closing and try to reduce the effect of those activities or eliminate those activities to provide value to the customers and increase the performance of the project. This will lead to breakthrough results in any type of project. An example of *muda* is waiting waste, which I have seen quite often when a project is on hold for the "expert" resource to become available. My advice—do not get hung up on getting only the best resources for your project. Their time is always very scarce as experts are always in demand. You have two options, you can either take someone who is not at that level of expertise yet, that is, "the expert's apprentice," or use whatever time the experts can spare to have someone on your team trained to keep the project moving. Thus, either your team has a resource who can always reach out to expert when needed or your team member gets a chance to learn something new and grow. Either way, the expert gets a chance to mentor and be a part of the project without spending too much time on it. Thus, you get the best of both worlds—a win–win situation.

Once the project leader learns the art of identifying *muda*, the added benefit will be that both the leader and the project team will have more time to focus on what is really critical to providing value to the customers.

"Gold plating" in a project is considered as one of the activities that a project leader needs to eliminate. Gold plating means providing extra features in the project not asked by customers. This should not be confused with delighting customers. Customers are delighted by meeting their requirements, involving them in every process of a project and informing them of the project progress. Gold plating can have serious consequences on the success of the project as it takes excess amount of time or resources to provide the features not asked by customers, thereby endangering the project objectives and vision. Scope creep can also occur as a result of gold plating. Every project leader should attempt to eliminate gold plating from the project and eliminate NVA activities without impacting their satisfaction.

Nonapplicable training is another waste that is quite prevalent in projects. Training is conducted for all resources with an aim to use everybody in the project, but in reality only 10% of the resources use their training skills or get an opportunity to use their training skills. Project leaders can eliminate such training waste by providing training to the individuals who can apply it on projects immediately. If project leaders analyze all activities in a project, many such NVA activities can be eliminated. We must admit that we are all predisposed to unnecessary complexity, greed, and waste. We must wage an immediate war on unnecessary complexity and on waste in our processes, projects, systems, governments, and lives. When we eliminate the eight wastes and capture TIM E. WOOD, we free our intellect capacity for other VA activities like problem solving, creativity, innovation, and growth. Figure 6.9 shows an increase in intellect capacity because of the TIM E. WOOD (eight wastes) being overcome. Keeping these in mind, let us see a classic example on lean.

> **We must wage an immediate war on unnecessary complexity and on waste in our processes, projects, systems, governments, and lives.**

6.4 A Classic Example of Lean

A classic example of using power of lean thinking, as described in Pillar I, is using lean thinking to solve one of the biggest problems facing our world today—poverty. One man, Muhammad Yunus, understood the problem of poverty from the point of view of the poor. He realized that in poor countries, the only hope for escaping poverty and starvation is through self-employment. The microentrepreneurs needed loans to start their microbusinesses, which range

Figure 6.9   Increase in intellect capacity due to TIM E. WOOD (eight wastes) being overcome.

from raising livestock to making handicrafts. However, they were dragged deeper into the abyss of debt by falling victims to high-interest-rate loans offered by the loan sharks and commercial banks. Mohammad Yunus created a solution for the microentrepreneurs that can be easy applied to the slums of Bangladesh and to the poorest housing developments of Chicago. He discovered that the poor needed very small capital investments to start their business. Yunus founded the Grameen Bank and used the strategy of microfinancing to fight the global war on poverty by providing the microbusinesses small loans at low interest rates. This strategy has helped several million people, and their families escape the clutches of poverty, starvation, and certain death. The goal is that by 2015, 100 million families will be free of poverty.[6,7]

Yunus's brilliance was identifying the *muda*, which in this case was the involvement of the loan sharks and commercial institutions who were doing more harm than good to the poor, and providing value to his customers by eliminating the need for it. In 2006, Yunus and the Grameen Bank were jointly awarded the Nobel Peace Prize "for their efforts to create economic and social development from below."

Pillar VI   Summary

Simplicity is taking the most commonsense approach and the most practical path to completing a task. A powerful tool available to project leaders today to simplify projects is "lean technology" or the Science of Simplicity™. Every successful project leader must practice the Science of Simplicity™ while leading projects. A powerful, commonsense, and practical tool available to simplify projects is "lean." Every project leader needs to be a lean thinker. The fundamental principle of lean is to identify waste (*muda*) or non-value-added (NVA) activities and separate them from value added (VA) and necessary non-value-added (NNVA) activities. The three principles of lean thinking that are applied to projects are as follows:

1. Identify and improve VA activities.
2. Identify and reduce NNVA activities.
3. Eliminate or reduce NVA activities and eliminate waste.

Muda usually accounts for the greatest percentage of the three categories and can be of several types. There are eight types of *muda*, namely, transport, information (excess), motion, energy, waiting, overprocessing, overproduction, and defects. Project leaders should make efforts to eliminate or reduce these eight types of wastes to avert intellectual waste. Figure 6.10 shows essential principles of lean thinking.

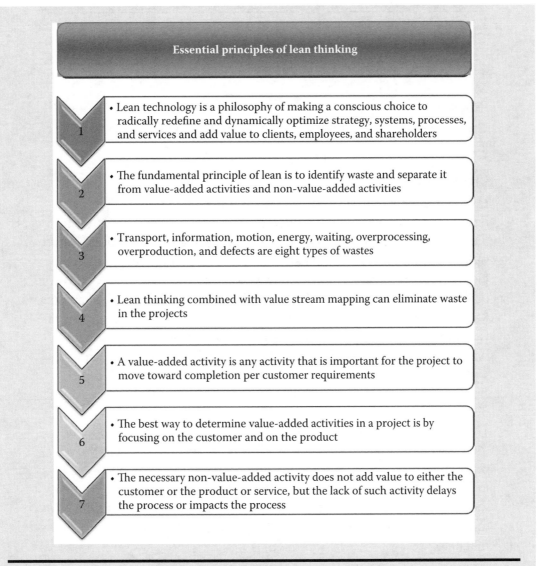

Figure 6.10 Essential principles of lean thinking.

Pillar VI   Case Study
Think Lean

INTRODUCTION

This case study is about the impact of lean thinking in a manufacturing industry.

CHALLENGE

I was consulting with a major corporation in Canada, making household items. Lean implementation was a corporate-driven initiative, and the plant manager of the division I was consulting with was quite proud of their lean improvement initiative conducted during the last 2 years. He mentioned to me, "Adil, I honestly don't know what more can you do to improve our processes." I told him that we would conduct some Kaizen[8] events and he will see the results for himself. A "Kaizen" event is a miniproject that involves a small team of individuals of diverse backgrounds coming together for about a week to identify and solve a specific issue.

SITUATION

The first Kaizen event was targeted for two of their highest production thermoforming machines. The objective of the event was to improve productivity by 20% and get some ergonomic improvements using 12 individuals from various departments of the organization. After training the team on lean basics, we identified some major improvement opportunities to increase productivity in the packaging area, at the front of the machine.

SOLUTION

As a part of my exercise of identification of opportunities for efficiency improvements, I was observing the loading and unloading of raw materials at the back of the thermoforming machine. It was a complicated four-step process:

1. The raw materials were large extruded rolls, each approximately 500 lb. and coming on a two-tier trolley, as seen in Figure 6.11, on wheels and were delivered to the machine by forklifts.
2. They were then unloaded on the floor using overhead hoists.
3. Then they were loaded on an unwind stand.
4. They were fed through the machine by in-feed operators.

We had good solutions to improve efficiency on the front end. I was positive that the team would beat their goal of 20% improvement in productivity by the end of the week. However, the back-end process

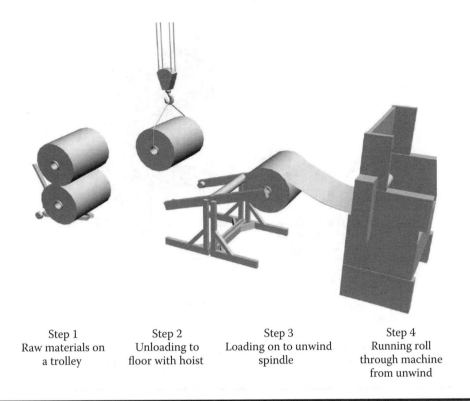

Step 1
Raw materials on
a trolley

Step 2
Unloading to
floor with hoist

Step 3
Loading on to unwind
spindle

Step 4
Running roll
through machine
from unwind

Figure 6.11   Before Kaizen: four-step process to move and process raw material through the thermoforming machine.

was not only inefficient but also potentially unsafe and resulted in considerable damage to the rolls. Because of the potential safety issues and significant NVA activity and confidence in the team's ability, I invoked the scope creep exception law: "addressing safety concerns should never be considered as scope creep." Although it was not in the charter, I challenged the team to think outside the box to eliminate the waste of unloading the roll onto the floor and then loading it onto the machine stand. I asked them, "Why can't we run both the rolls off the trolley itself?" They initially thought I was joking. When they figured that I was dead serious, they looked at me as if I was completely nuts or on some medications causing hallucinations.

IMPLEMENTATION

After the initial shock wore off, they decided to do a trial run, as if just to amuse me. We cordoned off the area for safety and tried feeding the rolls directly from the trolley.

To our amazement and surprise, both the top and the bottom rolls fed without any issues. They could not believe it. They had approximately 50 similar machines plant-wide, which were fed by more than 32 personnel in this manner for over a decade and now they saw that it was not needed. This is shown in Figure 6.12.

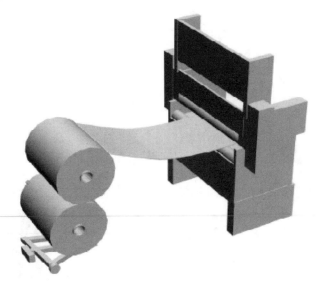

(T =top roll; B = bottom roll)

Step 1
Raw materials on a
trolley

Step 2
Running roll through machine
from unwind spindle

Figure 6.12   After Kaizen: two-step process to move and process raw materials through a thermoforming machine.

RESULTS

With some modifications to the trolleys, this solution could save the division $600,000 and make the operation ergonomic and safe for the operators while reducing scrap. Regarding the original scope of packaging improvements, the team identified and eliminated motion waste (131 trips to make one pallet versus 1 trip) eliminated transport waste (removed a conveyor), and designed a "customized roller-cum-palletizing system" for palletizing and transferring pallet to the automated transport-line cart more efficiently. The improvement from this week-long effort resulted in at least 52% improvement in productivity (pallets/man-hour), not to mention reduced stress on the operators because of the elimination of NVA moving. The cost savings on the front end were approximately $100,000.

The projected savings after all the elements of the improvements were installed from this week-long effort were at least $700,000. Agreed, there would be some costs and effort involved in modifying the trolleys. However, apart from the cost savings, we also made the operations easier, safer, more ergonomic, and much more user-friendly for the packers and in-feed operators for many future years. It was a win–win–win for the customers, the employees, and the company.

That's not all. The same solution could be applicable across the corporation in other divisions. The savings could be in several million of dollars—just by elimination of NVA items in their existing process.

LESSONS LEARNED

The plant manager and the other executives had now seen the power of lean tools they had not even imagined could be possible before. More than $700,000 of savings with just 1 week of effort was a dream come true for them. They were, thus, now completely converted to the using the power of "true lean tools" during their Kaizen projects.

Pillar VI   Force Field Analysis

PILLAR VI: FORCE FIELD ANALYSIS OF ORGANIZATIONAL ASSESSMENT

Table 6.1 shows force field analysis of organizational assessment. The organizational assessment is conducted to assess if the culture of the organization is in alignment with the principles of Pillar VI. Tables 6.2 through 6.4 are used to develop and implement an action plan to increase the impact of the organizational driving forces and decrease the impact of the organizational resisting forces.

PILLAR VI: FORCE FIELD ANALYSIS OF SELF-ASSESSMENT

Table 6.5 shows force field analysis of self-assessment. The self-assessment is conducted to assess if your own strengths are in alignment with the principles of Pillar VI. Tables 6.5 through 6.7 are used to develop and implement an action plan to increase the impact of the self-driving forces and decrease the impact of the self-resisting forces (Table 6.8).

PILLAR VI: RECOMMENDATIONS FOR OPTIMAL RESULTS FROM FORCE FIELD ANALYSIS

For optimal results and actual transformation of culture and strengths conducive to the creation of advanced master project leaders, the following three steps are necessary:

1. Both the organizational and self-evaluation assessments must be completed.
2. A well-designed action plan must be created and implemented to increase the driving forces and decrease the resisting forces.
3. The principles of each pillar must be constantly practiced and improved.

It is highly recommended that both the organization assessments and the self-assessments be conducted every year and the action plan be updated at least every 3 months.

Note: The sum of scores for Organizational Driving Force and Organizational Resisting Force for each point must be less than or equal to TEN.

The sum of scores for Self Driving Force and Self Resisting Force for each point must be less than or equal to TEN.

Table 6.1   Pillar VI: Force Field Organizational Analysis

Team Name: _____   Date: _____

	Does My Organization Drive or Resist a Culture of Lean Thinking?			
	0 Never	5 Sometimes		7 Mostly
	3 Rarely	ODF + ORF ≤ 10		10 Always
No.	Driving Forces	*Score Organizational Driving Force (ODF)*	*Score Organizational Resisting Force (ORF)*	Resisting Forces
1	My organization understands that lean is the application of common sense to creating an environment where employees can work smarter.			My organization has a negative view of lean and thinks that it is used primarily to eliminate jobs or make people work faster.
2	We understand that lean is not a complicated set of tools and techniques but it is the application of the Science of Simplicity™ to all areas of our organization.			We think that lean is philosophy that includes some tools and techniques but is not applicable to our organization.
3	My organization integrates the principles of lean thinking in all aspects of the business.			My organization does not understand or follow the principles of lean thinking.
4	My organization uses lean principles effectively and is fully aware of the *muda* or wastes described as TIM E. WOOD.			My organization does not focus on any activities related to identification and elimination of waste.
5	All the activities within our organization are aligned with providing value to our customers.			The activities within our organization are not aligned with adding value to customers but with profit and growth for the organization.
6	All the products, processes, and systems are designed from the point of view of our customers, and care is taken to eliminate or reduce all NVA activities.			All the products, processes, and systems are not designed from the viewpoint of our customers but with focus on maximizing profits.

7	We understand that gold plating or providing more to the customer than they are willing to pay for is a form of a waste and scope creep.			We tend to provide more features, functionality, and services to the customers than they require but do not consider it an example of waste or scope creep.
8	We understand that if we eliminate the eight wastes, we can allow our employees to focus on using their intellectual capacity to add value to our customers.			We do not think that the eight wastes are tied to using the intellect of our employees.
9	We regularly use lean tools like 5S,[a] kaizen events, and value stream mapping in our organizations.			We do not use any lean tools like 5S,[a] kaizen events, and value stream mapping in our organizations.
10	We believe that lean thinking is applicable to eliminating waste from any project.			We believe that lean thinking is applicable only to manufacturing processes.
	Total ODF score			*Total ORF score*

[a] 5S is a methodology for organizing, cleaning, developing, and sustaining a productive work environment. The methodology originates from a Japanese housekeeping idea named because of the five Japanese words each beginning with the letter "Se" or "Shi." They are *seiri* (sort), *seiton* (straighten), *seiso* (scrub), *seiketsu* (standardize), and *shitsuke* (sustain).

Result	Conclusion	Recommended Action Review and Update Every Quarter (3 months)
ODF >> ORF	My company culture strongly drives a culture of lean thinking.	Use Tables 6.2 through 6.4 to set goals and to create an action plan to preserve or continuously improve the culture of lean thinking.
ODF > ORF	My company culture drives the culture of lean thinking.	Use Tables 6.2 through 6.4 to set goals and to create an action plan to increase ODF to create a culture of lean thinking.
ORF >> ODF	My company culture strongly resists the culture of lean thinking.	Use Tables 6.2 through 6.4 to set goals and to create an action plan to increase the ODF and reduce the ORF to create a culture of lean thinking.
ORF > ODF	My company culture resists the culture of lean thinking.	Use Tables 6.2 through 6.4 to set goals and to create an action plan to reduce the ORF to create a culture of lean thinking.
ODF = ORF	My company culture does not drive or resist the culture of culture of lean thinking.	Use Tables 6.2 through 6.4 to set goals and to create an action plan to increase the ODF to create a culture of lean thinking.

Source: International Labor Organization. *Good Practice Guide, Factory Improvement Programme, What is 5S?*, (accessed Nov 11, 2010, www.ilofip.org/GPGs/What%20is%205S.pdf.)

Table 6.2   Pillar VI: Analysis of ODF and ORF Results

Result	Existing Organizational Culture	If the Goal Is to Create a Moderately Strong Culture of Lean Thinking	If the Goal Is to Create a Very Strong Culture of Lean Thinking
ODF			
ODF ≤ 25	No or minimal culture of lean thinking	Focus on improving scores in at least 5 DF	Focus on improving scores in at least 7 DF
25 < ODF ≤ 50	Weak culture of lean thinking	Focus on improving scores in at least 3 DF	Focus on improving scores in at least 5 DF
50 < ODF ≤ 75	Moderate culture of lean thinking	Focus on improving scores in at least 1 DF	Focus on improving scores in at least 3 DF
ODF > 75	Strong culture of lean thinking	N/A	Preserve or improve the culture
ORF			
ORF > 75	No or minimal culture of lean thinking	Focus on decreasing scores in at least 5 RF	Focus on decreasing scores in at least 7 RF
50 < ORF ≤ 75	Weak culture of lean thinking	Focus on decreasing scores in at least 3 RF	Focus on decreasing scores in at least 5 RF
25 < ORF ≤ 50	Moderate culture of lean thinking	Focus on decreasing scores in at least 1 RF	Focus on decreasing scores in at least 3 RF
ORF ≤ 25	Strong culture of lean thinking	N/A	Preserve or improve the culture

Table 6.3 Pillar VI: Action Plan to Increase Organizational Driving Force (ODF)

Team Name: _____   Date: _____

No.	Driving Force	Current Score	Goal (Target Score) ⬆	Action Plan to Increase DF Score	Complete by (Date)	Assigned to (Department Name or Initials of the Person)
1	My organization understands that lean is the application of common sense to creating an environment where employees can work smarter.					
2	We understand that lean is not a complicated set of tools and techniques but it is the application of the Science of Simplicity™ to all areas of our organization.					
3	My organization integrates the principles of lean thinking in all aspects of the business.					
4	My organization uses lean principles effectively and is fully aware of the *muda* or wastes described as TIM E. WOOD.					
5	All the activities within our organization are aligned with providing value to our customers.					

6	All the products, processes, and systems are designed from the point of view of our customers and care is taken to eliminate or reduce all NVA activities.					
7	We understand that gold plating or providing more to the customer than they are willing to pay for is a form of a waste and scope creep.					
8	We understand that if we eliminate the eight wastes, we can allow our employees to focus on using their intellectual capacity to add value to our customers.					
9	We regularly use lean tools like 5S, kaizen events, and value stream mapping in our organizations.					
10	We believe that lean thinking is applicable to eliminating waste from projects.					
	Total ODF					

Table 6.4   Pillar VI: Action Plan to Decrease Organizational Resisting Force (ORF)

No.	Resisting Force	Current Score	Goal (Target Score)	Action Plan to Decrease RF Score	Complete by (Date)	Assigned to (Department Name or Initials of the Person)
1	My organization has a negative view of lean and thinks that it is used primarily to eliminate jobs or make people work faster.					
2	We think that lean is a philosophy that includes some tools and techniques but is not applicable to our organization.					
3	My organization does not understand or follow the principles of lean thinking.					
4	My organization does not focus on any activities related to identification and elimination of waste.					
5	The activities within our organization are not aligned with adding value to customers but with profit and growth for the organization.					
6	All the products, processes, and systems are not designed from the viewpoint of our customers but with focus on maximizing profits.					

7	We tend to provide more features, functionality, and services to the customers than they require but do not consider it an example of waste or scope creep.					
8	We do not think that the eight wastes are tied to using the intellect of our employees.					
9	We do not use any lean tools like 5S, kaizen events, and value stream mapping in our organizations.					
10	We believe that lean thinking is applicable only to manufacturing processes.					
	Total ORF					

Table 6.5 Pillar VI: Force Field Self-Analysis

Name: _____   Date: _____

Does My Behavior Drive or Resist the Principles of Lean Thinking?				
0 Never		5 Sometimes	7 Mostly	
3 Rarely		SDF + SRF ≤ 10	10 Always	
No.	Driving Forces	*Score Self-Driving Force (SDF)*	*Score Self-Resisting Force (SRF)*	Resisting Forces
1	I have significant expertise in lean, and I truly believe in lean thinking and in making things simple.			I think that lean is used primarily to eliminate jobs or make people work faster.
2	I have implemented lean in manufacturing and business processes.			I have not formally used lean in any aspects of my work.
3	I always focus on activities that add value to customers while trying to eliminate all activities that are NVA.			I focus on results, and I do not try to analyze the activities as VA or NVA.
4	My teams and I focus on identifying and eliminating or reducing all NVA activities.			My teams and I focus on all activities irrespective of their classification.
5	I regularly use lean tools like 5S, kaizen events, and value stream mapping.			I have not used any lean tools like 5S, kaizen events, and value stream mapping.
6	I take care not to gold plate or provide more to the customer than they are willing to pay for, as it is a form of a waste and scope creep.			I tend to provide more features, functionality, and services to the customers than they require but do not consider it an example of waste or scope creep.
7	I proactively eliminate the eight wastes identified by TIM E. WOOD so that I can focus on using my intellect, creativity, and talent on more things.			I do not focus on eliminating any wastes as I do not believe that it has any impact on me using my intellectual capability.
8	I believe that a major portion of the total time of the project is NVA time (waiting, motion) and should be reduced or eliminated.			I believe that there is not a significant amount of waste in most projects and even if it is identified, there is not much that can be done about it.

9	To eliminate the *muda* of "waiting" for an expert resource, I gladly use the help from a capable "expert's apprentice" to keep the project moving.			I prefer to wait for the expert resources even if it significantly delays my projects.
10	I strongly believe that lean thinking is applicable to eliminating waste from all projects.			I do not believe in applying lean principles to all of my projects.
	Total SDF score			*Total SRF score*

Result	Conclusion	Recommended Action Review and Update Every Quarter (3 months)
SDF >> SRF	My behavior strongly supports the culture of lean thinking	Use Tables 6.6 through 6.8 to set goals and to create an action plan to continuously enhance the behavior to create a mind-set of lean thinking
SDF > SRF	My behavior supports the culture of lean thinking	Use Tables 6.6 through 6.8 to set goals and to create an action plan to increase SDF to allow a stronger behavior to create a mind-set of lean thinking
SRF >> SDF	My behavior strongly resists the culture of lean thinking	Use Tables 6.6 through 6.8 to set goals and to create an action plan to increase SDF and reduce SRF to allow a stronger behavior to create a mind-set of lean thinking
SRF > SDF	My behavior resists the culture of lean thinking	Use Tables 6.6 through 6.8 to set goals and to create an action plan to reduce SRF to allow a stronger behavior to create a mind-set of lean thinking
SDF = SRF	My behavior does not drive or resist the culture of lean thinking	Use Tables 6.6 through 6.8 to set goals and to create an action plan to increase the SDF to allow a stronger behavior to create a mind-set of lean thinking

Table 6.6 Pillar VI: Analysis of SDF and SRF Results

Result	Existing Behavior	If the Goal Is to Create a Moderately Strong Behavior Toward Principles of Lean Thinking	If the Goal Is to Create a Very Strong Behavior Toward Principles of Lean Thinking
SDF			
SDF ≤ 25	No or minimal activities in creating a mind-set of lean thinking	Focus on improving scores in at least 5 DF	Focus on improving scores in at least 7 DF
25 < SDF ≤ 50	Weak activities in creating a mind-set of lean thinking	Focus on improving scores in at least 3 DF	Focus on improving scores in at least 5 DF
50 < SDF ≤ 75	Moderate activities in creating a mind-set of lean thinking	Focus on improving scores in at least 1 DF	Focus on improving scores in at least 3 DF
SDF > 75	Strong activities in creating a mind-set of lean thinking	N/A	Preserve or continuously improve the behavior
SRF			
SRF > 75	No or minimal activities in creating a mind-set of lean thinking	Focus on decreasing scores in at least 5 RF	Focus on decreasing scores in at least 7 RF
50 < SRF ≤ 75	Weak activities in creating a mind-set of lean thinking	Focus on decreasing scores in at least 3 RF	Focus on decreasing scores in at least 5 RF
25 < SRF ≤ 50	Moderate activities in creating a mind-set of lean thinking	Focus on decreasing scores in at least 1 RF	Focus on decreasing scores in at least 3 RF
SRF ≤ 25	Strong activities in creating a mind-set of lean thinking	N/A	Preserve or continuously improve the behavior

Table 6.7 Pillar VI: Action Plan to Increase Self-Driving Forces (SDFs)

Name: _____ Date: _____

No.	Driving Force	Current Score	Goal (Target Score) ⬇	Action Plan to Increase DF Score	Complete by (Date)	Required Resources
1	I have significant expertise in lean and I truly believe in lean thinking and in making things simple.					
2	I have implemented lean in manufacturing and business processes.					
3	I always focus on activities that add value to customers while trying to eliminate all activities that are NVA.					
4	My teams and I focus on identifying and eliminating or reducing all NNVA activities and all NVA activities.					
5	I regularly use lean tools like 5S, kaizen events, and value stream mapping.					
6	I take care not to gold plate or provide more to the customer than they are willing to pay for, as it is a form of a waste and scope creep.					
7	I proactively eliminate the eight wastes identified by TIM E. WOOD so that I can focus on using my intellect, creativity, and talent on more VA things.					

8	I believe that a major portion of the total time of the project is NVA time (waiting, motion) and should be reduced or eliminated.					
9	To eliminate the *muda* of "waiting" for an expert resource, I gladly use the help from a capable "expert's apprentice" to keep the project moving.					
10	I strongly believe that lean thinking is applicable to eliminating waste from projects.					
	Total SDF					

Table 6.8   Pillar VI: Action Plan to Decrease Self-Resisting Forces (SRFs)

Name: _____   Date: _____

No.	Resisting Forces	Current Score	Goal (Target Score) ⬇	Action Plan to Decrease RF Score	Complete by (Date)	Required Resources
1	I think that lean is used primarily to eliminate jobs or make people work faster.					
2	I have not formally used lean in any aspects of my work.					
3	I focus on results, and I do not try to analyze the activities as VA or NVA activity.					
4	My teams and I focus on all activities irrespective of their classification.					
5	I have not used any lean tools like 5S, kaizen events, and value stream mapping.					
6	We tend to provide more features, functionality, and services to the customers than they require but do not consider it an example of waste or scope creep.					
7	I do not focus on eliminating any wastes as I do not believe that it has any impact on me using my intellectual capability.					

8	I believe that there is not a significant amount of waste in most projects, and even if it is identified, there is not much that can be done about it.					
9	I prefer to wait for the expert resources even if it significantly delays my projects.					
10	I do not believe we need lean thinking for projects.					
	Total SRF					

Pillar VI   Exercises

PILLAR VI: ORGANIZATIONAL-LEVEL SKILL SET–ENHANCEMENT EXERCISES

GROUP EXERCISES

These exercises are best completed within a group of project managers, project leaders, executives, and stakeholders from within a department or an organization.

1. Using Table 6.9, identify at least five advantages to your organization in creating a culture of lean thinking and rate them from 1 (least important) to 5 (most important).
2. Using Table 6.10, identify at least five roadblocks within your organization in creating a culture of lean thinking for your projects and rate them from 1 (least difficult to overcome) to 5 (most difficult to overcome).
3. Identify a recent complex project completed by one of the experienced project managers in your organization. Get the team together and request them to use Table 6.11 to fill in at least three examples of each activity on their projects, which were (a) VA, (b) NNVA, and (c) *muda* based on the principles of Pillar VI. What would have been a benefit to them to identify these at the beginning of the project or each project phase?
4. Identify a recent complex project completed by one of the experienced project managers in your organization. Get the core team together and based on the principles of Pillar VI, using Table 6.12,

Table 6.9   Pillar VI: Five Advantages of Applying Principles of Pillar VI to Your Organization

No.	Advantages of Applying Principles of Pillar VI to Enhance Your Organization Culture	Rating (from 1 = Least Important to 5 = Most Important)	Explain the Rating
1			
2			
3			
4			
5			

Table 6.10 Pillar VI: Five Roadblocks to Creating a Culture of a Lean Thinking Using Pillar VI

No.	Roadblocks to Applying Principles of Lean Thinking Described in Pillar VI to Your Organization	Rating (from 1 = Least Difficult to Overcome to 5 = Most Difficult to Overcome)	Explain the Rating
1			
2			
3			
4			
5			

Table 6.11 Pillar VI: Classification of Activities Based on Pillar VI

	At Least Three Examples from Recently Completed Project	Benefits of Identifying Them at Start of Projects
VA activities		
NNVA activities		
Muda activities		

Table 6.12 Pillar VI: Identification of Muda Based on the Principles of Pillar VI

Eight Wastes	At Least Three Examples from a Recently Completed Project	Identify One Way to Reduce or Eliminate Each Waste
T—Transport		
I—Information (excess)		
M—Motion		
E—Energy		
W—Waiting		
O—Overprocessing		
O—Overdocumentation		
D—Defects		

request them to identify at least one example of each of the eight wastes (TIM E. WOOD) they encountered during the course of the project. Identify at least one way they would have reduced or eliminated each *muda*.

5. *Scenario analysis*: 4-1-MOMS2B is a global nonprofit organization that is self-sustaining and working to help poor single pregnant women around the world get healthy nutrition and medicines for prenatal and postnatal care. During the first 3 years after birth of the child, the single mothers are also provided with employment opportunities in the manufacturing plants run by 4-1-MOMS2B. Free housing and full health benefits are provided to the infants and new mothers. A generous donor started the nonprofit 4-1-MOMS2B with a self-sustaining business model as follows: There are 15 manufacturing plants owned by the nonprofit organization in underdeveloped countries, which make specialty handmade rugs that are of great quality and in-demand, and at least 200,000 rugs are sold annually for a hefty profit to developed countries. Because of the nonprofit status of this organization, they do not have to pay any taxes or import/export tariffs, and their profit margins on each of the rug are approximately 60%. They use this money to provide meals, nutrition, health care, and employment to poor and needy and to purchase the raw materials and run their business. It is estimated that without the support of this nonprofit organization, approximately 100,000 mothers and children around the world would be at a significant risk of diseases or even death annually.

Current situation: Because of the sustained global recession, 4-1-MOMS2B is facing significant shortage of funds with more mouths to feed and more bodies to keep warm. The board of trustees of the nonprofit organization is in a dilemma to reduce their operating costs significantly or has to deny care to at least 50,000 mothers and infants. The board feels that there is significant waste in the operations, and with significant cost cutting, they can save enough to make sure that they do not need to deny care to even one single mother. The following is the process.

The raw materials for the rugs are imported from China, and raw material costs account for at least 20% of the operating costs. A similar quality raw material is available locally in underdeveloped countries at a comparable cost, but the supplier in China provides a 5% discount on supplies of more than 6 months. However, to get good rates on the shipping costs, 4-1-MOMS2BE need to order at least one container full of raw material, which lasts them for approximately 9 months. They receive the raw material in a port in Indonesia, store it in a big warehouse (accounting for 15% of operating costs), and then transport the materials by smaller boats or trolleys or handcarts to all 15 manufacturing plants. The transport cost accounts for another 5% of total operating expenses.

Within the manufacturing plants, the raw material, and other supplies like needles and other fixtures required are placed in one corner of an environment-safe factory, and the mothers walk an average of approximately 20 minutes daily from their living quarters, pick up the raw materials and fixtures, and weave the rugs at home. At the end of the day, they walk 20 minutes to drop off the finished rugs and fixtures. There are no standards, and some mothers take 2 days per very intricate rug, whereas others weave simple designs and are able to complete two per day. To keep the accounting simple, all rugs are priced the same amount. At the end of every month, the finished rugs are taken back to the warehouse in Indonesia through various means of transportation. There is a quality control department that inspects the finished rugs for defects just before shipping. Approximately 20% of rugs are rejected on a monthly basis. The finished goods warehouse usually holds up to 4 months worth of finished rugs, and it has to stay at a certain temperature year-round for optimal condition of the rugs. The heating costs are 6% of the operating budget. Usually 5% of raw material is also defective and is thrown away when encountered in the raw materials while weaving. Total defects and scrap account for 8% of operating costs. The finished rugs are shipped via air to various distribution centers around the world every 2 months. This accounts for almost another 12% of total operating costs. The rest of the operating expenses are used to pay the salary, housing, and benefits of the mothers. The profits are used to pay for the medicine and other charitable activities of the nonprofit organization and to replenish the initial donations/investments and maintain them at a stable level.

The board of trustees creates a committee to look into the wastes and to provide a report. Imagine that you and some of the team members of the organization are on the committee selected by the board. Using the principles of lean, discussed in Pillar VI, provide a report regarding the following to the board of trustees of 4-1-MOMS2B:

a. Identify the VA, NNVA, and *muda* and note in Table 6.13.
b. Estimate the percentages of the above three categories and draw a pie chart in Table 6.14.
c. Categorize the *muda* as TIM E. WOOD as discussed in Pillar VI using Table 6.15.

PILLAR VI: PERSONAL-LEVEL SKILL SET–ENHANCEMENT EXERCISES

Individual Exercises

These exercises are to be completed individually after reviewing Pillar VI in detail.

Table 6.13   Pillar VI: Scenario Analysis Based on the Organizational Skill-enhancement Principles of Pillar VI

Category	Activities Identified by the Committee Appointed by the Board of Trustees of 4-1-MOMS2BE
VA activities	
NNVA activities	
Muda activities	

Table 6.14   Pillar VI: Scenario Analysis Percentages and Pie Chart of Activities

	Identification of Percentages of the Activities of VA, NNVA, and Muda Categories by the Committee Appointed by the Board of Trustees Of 4-1-MOMS2BE
Estimated percentages	1. VA activities _____ % 2. NNVA activities _____ % 3. *Muda* _____ %
Draw a pie chart of VA, NNVA, and *muda* activities of the operations of 4-1-MOMS2BE	

Table 6.15   Pillar VI: Identification of *Muda* for 4-1-MOMS2BE Operations

Eight Wastes	Identified Muda from 4-1-MOMS2B Operations
T—Transport	
I—Information (excess)	
M—Motion	
E—Energy	
W—Waiting	
O—Overprocessing	
O—Overdocumentation	
D—Defects	

Table 6.16 Pillar VI: Five Advantages of Applying Principles of Pillar VI to Your Career

No.	Advantages of Applying Principles of Lean Thinking from Pillar VI to All Future Projects	Rating (from 1 = Least Important to 5 = Most Important)	Explain the Rating
1			
2			
3			
4			
5			

1. Using Table 6.16, list at least five advantages of applying the principles of Pillar VI detailing lean thinking to your future projects. Rate the advantages from 1 (least important) to 5 (most important) and explain the rating.
2. Using Table 6.17, identify at least five roadblocks to applying the principles of lean thinking from Pillar VI on all your future major projects. Rate the identified roadblocks from 1 (least difficult to overcome) to 5 (most difficult to overcome) and explain the rating.
3. Using Table 6.18, select a project you worked on as a project manager/leader that did not meet the criteria and timeline created for project completion. Looking back on the project, answer following questions:
   a. For each phase of the project, estimate the percentage spent on one of the following: (i) VA activities, (ii) NNVA activities, and (iii) *muda*.
   b. Identify at least one example for each of the eight wastes defined by TIM E. WOOD during each phase.
4. Using Table 6.19, select a future project you have been assigned to. Answer the following questions:
   a. For each phase of the project, estimate the percentage of time you think you should spend on one of the following: (i) VA activities, (ii) NNVA activities, and (iii) *muda*.
   b. Identify at least one example for each of the eight wastes defined by TIM E. WOOD during each phase that you will eliminate or reduce to ensure you meet the estimated percentage of *muda* on the future project.
5. Scenario analysis: As seen in scenario analysis for operational assessment, 4-1-MOMS2B is a global nonprofit organization that is facing significant shortage of funds. The board of trustees created

Table 6.17   Pillar VI: Five Roadblocks to Applying Principles of Pillar VI

No.	Roadblocks to Applying Principles of Lean Thinking Detailed in Pillar VI to All Future Projects	Rating (from 1 = Least Difficult to Overcome to 5 = Most Difficult to Overcome)	Explain the Rating
1			
2			
3			
4			
5			

Table 6.18   Pillar VI: Reflecting on a Completed Project to Identify the Waste

Name of failed project		
Your role in the project		
Phase	Estimated Percentage of Time Spent	Identify At Least One Example For Each of the Eight Wastes Defined by TIM E. WOOD
1. Project start-up	1. VA activities: _____% 2. NNVA activities: _____% 3. *Muda*: _____%	T: I: M: E: W: O: O: D:
2. Project preparation	1. VA activities: _____% 2. NNVA activities: _____% 3. *Muda*: _____%	T: I: M: E: W: O: O: D

3. Project implementation	1. VA activities: _____% 2. NNVA activities: _____% 3. *Muda*: _____%	T: I: M: E: W: O: O: D
4. Project monitoring	1. VA activities: _____% 2. NNVA activities: _____% 3. *Muda*: _____%	T: I: M: E: W: O: O: D
5. Project closure	1. VA activities: _____% 2. NNVA activities: _____% 3. *Muda*: _____%	T: I: M: E: W: O: O: D

a committee to look into the wastes. The committee provided the following reports to the board of trustees:

a. Table 6.13: VA, NNVA, and *muda* activities
b. Table 6.14: Estimation of the percentages of the above three categories
c. Table 6.15: *Muda* categorized as TIM E. WOOD as discussed in Pillar VI

As you have some expertise regarding the lean principles based on understanding of Pillar VI, imagine that the board of trustees has assigned you as a voluntary project leader to get the 4-1-MOMS2BE profitable enough to be able to serve approximately 120,000 mothers and infants in the next year, which is also expected to be mired in recession woes. Using the principles of lean technology

Table 6.19 Pillar VI: Reflecting on a Future Project to Identify the Waste

Name of future project		
Your role in the project		
Phase	*Estimated Percentage of Time Spent*	*Identify At Least One Muda for the Eight Wastes (TIM E. WOOD) You Plan to Reduce or Eliminate*
1. Project start-up	1. VA activities: _____ % 2. NNVA activities: _____ % 3. *Muda:* _____ %	T: I: M: E: W: O: O: D:
2. Project preparation	1. VA activities: _____ % 2. NNVA activities: _____ % 3. *Muda:* _____ %	T: I: M: E: W: O: O: D:
3. Project implementation	1. VA activities: _____ % 2. NNVA activities: _____ % 3. *Muda:* _____ %	T: I: M: E: W: O: O: D:
4. Project monitoring	1. VA activities: _____ % 2. NNVA activities: _____ % 3. *Muda:* _____ %	T: I: M: E: W: O: O: D

5. Project closure	1. VA activities: _____% 2. NNVA activities: _____% 3. *Muda:* _____%	T: I: M: E: W: O: O: D

Table 6.20   Pillar VI: Scenario Analysis—Action Plan Based on the Self Skill-Enhancement Principles of Pillar VI

% Category per Table 6.14	*Activities Identified by the Committee Appointed by the Board of Trustees of 4-1-MOMS2BE per Table 6.13*	*Plan of Action to Increase VA and Reduce or Eliminate NNVA and Muda*
VA activities: _____%		
NNVA activities: _____%		
Muda: _____%		

discussed in Pillar VI, provide a report regarding the following to the board of trustees of 4-1-MOMS2B:

a. Using Table 6.20, create a plan of action to increase the VA and to decrease the NNVA and *muda* as per finding in Tables 6.13 and 6.14.

b. Using Table 6.21, create a plan of action to reduce or eliminate the eight wastes based on the acronym TIM E. WOOD as identified in Table 6.15.

c. Using Table 6.22, create a new detailed operations plan for 4-1-MOMS2BE based on the collective action plans of Tables 6.20 and 6.21.

Table 6.21   Pillar VI: Action Plan to Reduce or Eliminate Eight Types of Muda for 4-1-MOMS2BE Operations Based on the Principles of Pillar VI

Eight Wastes	Identified Muda from 4-1-MOMS2B Operations Based on Table 6.15	Plan of Action to Reduce or Eliminate the Eight Types of Muda
T—Transport		
I—Information (excess)		
M—Motion		
E—Energy		
W—Waiting		
O—Overprocessing		
O—Overdocumentation		
D—Defects		

Table 6.22   Pillar VI: Action Plan to Update the Operations for 4-1-MOMS2BE Based on the Principles of Pillar VI

Pillar VI References

1. Einstein, A. (2010). BrainyQuote.com, Xplore Inc., http://www.brainyquote.com/quotes/quotes/a/alberteins103652.html (accessed December 3, 2010).
2. da Vinci, L. (1452–1519). (2010). Quoteworld, http://www.quoteworld.org/quotes/3358 (accessed August 10, 2010).
3. Dalal, A. F. (May 2009). "Go lean, save green," *Six Sigma Forum Magazine*, 34.
4. Ohno, T., and Shingo, S. (2010). *Value Stream Mapping Method: Identifying and Decreasing Waste,* http://www.valuebasedmanagement.net/methods_value_stream_mapping.html (accessed November 11, 2010).
5. Krueger, K. (2004). *Value-Added vs. Non-Value-Added-Actvities,* http://www.wisc-online.com/Objects/ViewObject.aspx?ID=eng11104 (accessed November 11, 2010).
6. Yunus, M. (2007). *Creating a World Without Poverty: Social Business and the Future of Capitalism. PublicAffairs.* New York: Perseus Books Group.
7. Counts, A. (2008). *Small Loans, Big Dreams.* Hoboken, NJ: John Wiley & Sons, Inc.
8. Lee, Q. (2004). *Kaizen—What Does It Mean,* http://www.strategos-inc.com/ kaizen.htm (accessed November 11, 2010).
9. International Labor Organization. *Good Practice Guide, Factory Improvement Programme, What is 5S?* http://www.ilofip.org/GPGs/What%20is%205S.pdf (accessed November 11, 2010).

Chapter 7

Pillar VII: Minimize Meeticide™

Meeticide™, death of resource efficiency by meetings, is the leading cause of fatality for most global projects and countless aspiring project careers.

7.1 Introduction

7.1.1 Reasons for Waste

Waste is at epidemic proportions in the United States. In a 2005 report by Dan Malachowski, called *Wasted Time at Work Costing Companies Billions*,[1] he states that Salary.com calculated that employees waste at least 2.09 hours per 8-hour day and employers spend at least $759 billion per year on salaries for which real work was expected, but not actually performed, as shown in Figure 7.1.

The 10 top time wasting activities and percentages according to the survey are shown below:

1. Surfing the Internet for personal use (44.7%)
2. Socializing with coworkers (23.4%)
3. Conducting personal business (6.8%)
4. Spacing out (3.9%)
5. Running errands off-premises (3.1%)
6. Making personal phone calls (2.3%)
7. Applying for other jobs (1.3%)
8. Planning personal events (1.0%)
9. Arriving late/leaving early (1.0%)
10. Other (12.5%).

All these wastes are equally applicable to team members on projects. These wastes can be controlled by human resources, department heads, and project

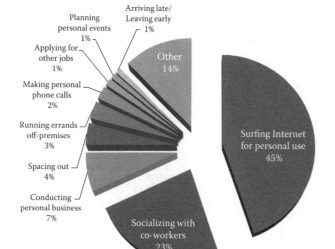

Top 10 time wasting activities in businesses

Figure 7.1   Top 10 time wastes in businesses. (Adapted from Salary.com and American online survey, July 11, 2005. http://www.salary.com/sitesearch/layoutscripts/sisl_display. asp?filename=&path=/destinationsearch/par485_body.html.)

managers and the guilty can be reprimanded as seen fit. However, there is a waste that is bigger. There are two reasons this crime goes unpunished; the first reason is that the leaders have not yet realized that a major portion of this is a waste, and second reason is that the managers and leaders are unknowingly the primary suspects of this crime. Have you guessed the waste yet? Yes, it is **"unnecessary meetings."**

7.1.2 Meetings—Sources for Waste

Thus, the death of resource efficiency by meetings (Meeticide™) is one of the cardinal offenses that go unpunished in most organizations. The dilemma for project leaders is how to make communication effective and yet keep meetings to a minimum? This is a million-dollar question. If only leaders could answer this question correctly, not only could they make a huge impact on their project but also on their careers.

> **The death of resource efficiency by meetings (Meeticide™) is one of the cardinal offenses that go unpunished in most organizations.**

According to research conducted in the United States, approximately 11 million meetings take place each and every day. A research study conducted on professionals who are regular meeting attendees (a.k.a. hostages) resulted in the following list of the biggest and most common time wasters during the meetings[2]:

1. Daydreaming
2. Missing parts of meetings
3. Bringing other work to meetings
4. Dozing off during meetings (as shown in Figure 7.2).

With so many meetings taking place on a daily basis, why is communication still the leading cause of project failures? Do we require more meetings? The answer is obviously—no, we cannot afford to have more meetings. Then, how do project leaders distribute the required information to all stakeholders? Well, the project leader needs to make meetings more productive using the lean approach. They need to find ways to communicate important project information in more productive ways without wasting the valuable time of project stakeholders.

7.2 Lean Approach to Meetings

Not all meetings are of equal importance. Some meetings are obviously critical and cannot be eliminated. However, there are many meetings that are not

Figure 7.2   Cost of dozing off during meetings.

productive and waste time. There are two categories of meetings—value-added meetings and non-value-added meetings. Let us conservatively assume that each day, there are at least 10 meetings of 1 hour each in various parts of an organization attended by at least 10 people. Thus, the organization expends 100 work hours per day on meetings. Considering an average wage of $30/hour per employee, the meetings are costing your organization $3000/day or $750,000 annually, considering 250 work days in a year.

In this example, the project leader has two options to reduce overall meeting costs:

1. Completely eliminate non-value-added meetings:
   In the above example with annual meeting costs being approximately $750,000, even if we can reduce the meetings by only 50% by eliminating some non-value-added meetings, the organization can save approximately $375,000 annually.
2. Minimize/eliminate non-value-added time each team member spends in meetings. Even if only 30 hours of daily meeting time is identified as non-value-added time in the meetings per day, just reducing this non-value-added time by half (15 hours/day) can save approximately $112,500 for the organization annually.

How many project managers think about project savings in this manner? In my experience, the answer is "some to none." Corporations and project managers rarely think of the cost of meetings and thus there is no attempt to analyze and subsequently reduce it. Thus, it is very essential for project leaders to focus on these two ways to reduce overall project costs by eliminating non-value-added elements related to meetings.

7.3 Components of a Project Meeting

The next section explains the details behind each solution described above to eliminate non-value-added meetings and non-value-added time during meetings. Before diving into the details, let us look at the fundamental makeup of a meeting process. To know the components that make up the meeting, we should look at the meeting from a different perspective.

> Consider each meeting as a process. Like a process, the three components that create a meeting are:
>
> 1. Input
> 2. Tools and techniques
> 3. Output or results.

Let us analyze these three components first and then try to understand the basic relationship between the value-added and non-value-added meeting time.

7.3.1 Input

A meeting is a structured process for producing results. However, the success of a meeting occurs when inputs to the meeting are selected carefully. As the saying goes, "garbage in, garbage out"—if we fail to begin the process using value-added inputs, how can we expect to get any value-added outputs? There are three elements that make up the input to a meeting

1. Meeting agenda
2. Required information
3. Meeting attendees.

The agenda of the meeting decides the needs of the meeting. Therefore, a project leader should carefully design the agenda and send it ahead of time to all people attending the meeting.

Information consists of documents, reports, statistics, and data on various project activities or project-related activities. The information needs of a project are decided by the basic purpose of the meeting. For example, the information needs of a requirement-gathering meeting are completely different from the information needs of phase gate meeting. Some of the information may be essential and mandatory for particular meetings. Therefore, project leaders should make sure the information brought to the meeting is valid, accurate, and nonambiguous.

Meeting attendees are the most critical element of the input to a meeting. Because attendees also bring information regarding the project to meetings, meeting attendees and information go together. Project leaders should identify mandatory, required, and optional people while sending the meeting request. Attendees include stakeholders, team members, sponsor, customer, technical leaders, and experts if required. Project leaders must not invite those attendees who are not affected by the project. While inviting the attendees for the meeting, the project leader should set a very specific objective for the meeting. This is especially true when virtual meetings are used for the attendees who are globally dispersed.

7.3.2 Tools and Techniques

Tools and techniques are used in the meeting to analyze and investigate the information and to explore possible options to generate the outputs or results. Various tools and techniques are available to present, monitor, and control information. Project management information system and other presentation tools are used to present the information in systematic way. Meeting rules and a time-keeper can be used to control people and time in the meeting. If the meeting is about brainstorming ideas, a facilitator or facilitating tools are generally required to stay focused on the agenda. Every person in the meeting is required to identify options or proposals as a team to represent shared vision. Some online tools have been used to keep everybody in the loop and keep the meeting on track. In virtual meetings, the tools and techniques play a significant role in running an effective meeting. Teleconferences, virtual meeting tools, are used to distribute and analyze the information. There are several "web meetings" tools available in the market today that make the task of scheduling, facilitating, and recording meetings quite easy.

7.3.3 Output (Results)

The results of a meeting are decisions, task assignments, or clarifications. Without these three, the meeting process is not productive. Because information is used to make such decisions or assignments, it is essential for a project manager to maintain the quality of the information and appropriate tools to make quick and meaningful decisions. Improper and invalid information and tools can lead to inappropriate decisions or ambiguity in work assignments. Inappropriate decisions and assignments can lead to more meetings, thus wasting project time. Figure 7.3 shows the fundamentals of the meeting process.

So far, we have discussed the inputs, tools, and techniques and outputs of the meeting. Now, let us look at the lean approach to meetings. The approach to eliminate waste in the meetings is a two-step process. Step 1 involves identifying

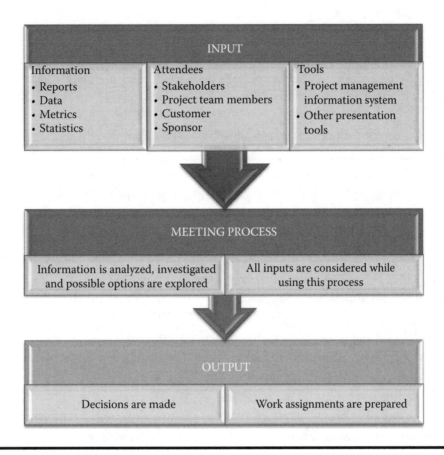

Figure 7.3   Fundamentals of a Meeting Process.

and eliminating all non-value-added meetings, and step 2 involves identifying and eliminating the non-value-added time in the other meetings.

7.4 Steps to Eliminate Waste in Meetings

7.4.1 Step 1: Identify and Eliminate Non-Value-Added Meetings

Successful project leaders are extremely mindful of the impact of meetings on the project metrics and on team morale. They will only hold meetings that can add value to the project to delight the customers/stakeholders and help the team grow. According to a survey conducted by Microsoft, people spend 5.6 hours in meetings each week and 69% feel the meetings are not productive.[3] This means that people think that the meeting itself is useless, nonproductive, and does not deliver results. Therefore, in some situations, the project leader should look for ways to eliminate the meeting itself. When is the best time to eliminate the meeting? The answer to this question will come from the fundamental components of the meeting. As seen from Figure 7.3, the meeting is essential when the meeting process delivers appropriate results. The criteria for eliminating meetings are explained below.

A meeting can be eliminated, if attendees cannot analyze and investigate the information and deliver any result using the available tools and techniques.

This does not mean that all meetings with no results can be eliminated. There are some instances when a meeting may not deliver results because of a lack of consensus between people. However, project leaders should certainly consider eliminating such meetings, if consensus is always very difficult to achieve in that particular meeting format. Project leaders diligently look at each meeting and analyze if the meeting is useful. Table 7.1 gives the list of non-value-added and value-added meetings in a project. The best example of a non-value-added meeting can be a status meeting. If a project leader wants to show only the progress of the project, with discussion, no analysis, or no investigation from the attendees, it is very much appropriate to not conduct such a meeting. The critical question is how to eliminate the non-value-added meetings without having a negative impact on the project? As stated in Table 7.1, most status reporting meetings are non-value-added. These meetings can be easily avoided if there are other means to gather and report the information in the form of a dashboard. The dashboard can be made available in a common location on the intranet of a corporation with appropriate read and write access privileges to the authorized team members. The project leader needs to create a schedule for updates so the information is timely and accurate. This requires significant discipline from those entrusted with updating the dashboard regularly, or else the dashboard reporting technique will fail and the team will have to go back to scheduling the costly, information-gathering meetings. If core stakeholders, sponsors, and decision makers are missing from the meeting when decisions are to be made, the meeting process becomes obsolete. In such situations, the meeting can be eliminated or rescheduled.

Recently, dashboard came into existence as a new meeting tool to present critical information of the project without the initiation of a meeting. The key first step to creating the dashboard is to identify the required data to be reported. For example, Figure 7.4 shows a sample of an executive dashboard.

Table 7.1 Value-added and Non-value-added Meeting Types

Value-added Meeting Types	Non-value-added Meeting Types
Project kick-off	Information (noncritical) gathering
Strategic planning and risk assessment	Information (noncritical) sharing
Problem solving	Regular status reporting
Brainstorming	Meetings with no output or results
Team building, consensus building	Stakeholder updates
Recognition and special occasions	Meetings with no agenda
Vendor meetings	Meetings with less or no team participation

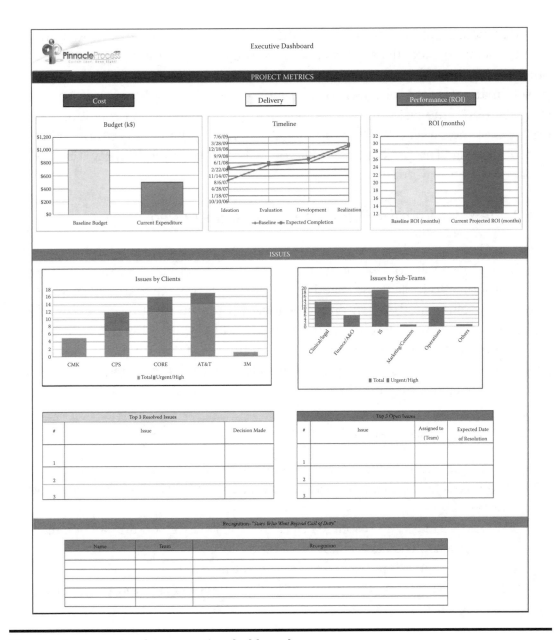

Figure 7.4   Example of an executive dashboard.

The elements of the executive dashboard are

1. Project metrics
   a. Cost
   b. Delivery
   c. Performance
2. Critical issues
   a. Issues by clients
   b. Issues by subteams
   c. Top three resolved issues
   d. Top three open issues
3. Recognition (stars who went beyond call of duty).

This dashboard can be customized to the project and by the levels communicated to include executives, project leaders, project teams, and clients. Many other tools are used to eliminate non-value-added meetings. A bulletin board, project management tools, and workspace collaboration tools are used to share the progress of the tasks, milestone information, deliverable information, and progress of the project. What is the ultimate result of eliminating a non-value-added meeting? The project costs will come down, and more time will be spent by the team on real project issues.

7.4.2 Step 2: Minimize/Eliminate Non-Value-Added Time

There are instances when project leaders cannot eliminate a meeting because of the absolute necessity of that particular meeting or meeting type. In such cases, it is appropriate to look at the meeting and see how non-value-added meeting time can be eliminated. When project leaders set up the meetings, they should diligently look for ways to eliminate non-value-added time. This can be done by carefully evaluating each input and analyzing the results of a meeting. Successful project leaders use the following techniques to ensure that meetings are efficient and productive, and meeting time is kept to a minimum.

7.4.2.1 Before the Meeting

1. Train the team on identifying and avoiding all time wasters
2. Have a detailed, clear, and "practical" agenda that is e-mailed out ahead of time
3. Always request key resources to be responsible for sending a back-up person when they are unable to attend any meetings
4. Keep undesirable people out of the meeting input
5. Prevent inaccurate, unwanted, and ambiguous information from going into the meeting process

7.4.2.2 During the Meeting

1. Bring awareness during meetings to all time wasters
2. Focus key meetings on critical path items
3. Do not exceed 60 minutes timeline for any single meeting
4. Include people on "need to know" basis
5. Ask questions during the meeting to check for understanding and awareness
6. Choose right technological tools to present the information
7. Have skilled facilitator to control the brainstorming meetings
8. Make effective decisions, assignments in the meeting process

7.4.2.3 After the Meeting

1. Send out minutes soon after the meeting
2. Create a common repository for project data with adequate security access for all team members
3. Request feedback from the recipients

By following the action items described above, non-value-added time can be drastically reduced in meetings.

7.5 Determination of Productive Meetings

In addition to the tasks listed above, the project leader should look for the ratio between value-added meeting time (VAMT) and non-value-added time (NVAMT). Meeting time can be divided into two segments value-added time and non-value-added time. But the ratio of non-value-added time to value-added time (VAMT/NVAMT) makes a significant difference. If this ratio is more than 0.6, the meetings are productive and add value to the project. If the ratio of VAMT/NVAMT is lower than 0.6, the non-value-added time is more, resulting in nonproductive meetings. **Hence, the task of project leader is to keep the VAMT/NVAMT ratio to the maximum in meetings as shown in Equation 7.1.**

$$0.6 < \frac{\text{VAMT}}{\text{NVAMT}} \qquad (7.1)$$

A good meeting process is possible when inputs are optimum, the agenda is clear, and attendees are prepared. Needless to say, the meeting time plays an important role in effective meetings.

7.6 Non-Value-Added Time in Complex Projects

The methods we discussed thus far have been very effective in small and medium-sized projects. However, in a complex organizational structure, the situation is completely different. Project organization structure plays an important role in meeting management. In a small organizational structure, fewer communication paths exist between the team members. The distribution of information is easier and simpler with a fewer number of meetings. In a complex organizational structure, as the number of communication paths increase, the number of meetings increases, resulting in more non-value-added meetings. In complex projects, the meetings are attended by both lower level staff and top-level executives whose time is valuable. Therefore, wasting their time is not advisable in such projects.

The percentage of project return on investment (ROI) will be much lower if high-level executives are involved in a non-value-added meeting (as explained in ROI calculations hereafter). Project leaders should try to split meetings into two different categories.

1. Air support meeting
2. Ground troops meeting

Meetings with "air support" include high-level executives in the meeting. Hence, project leaders should conduct air support meeting when executive's decisions are important and required. Efforts should be made by project leaders to keep the VAMT/NVAMT ratio to a maximum possible in such meetings. During air support meetings, the project leader should present the information in a clear and concise method. If possible, very effective presentation tools can be used to summarize the information. Decision points can be described in the agenda so that executives can make quick decisions. When discussing the project information, it is advisable to show cost performance index, schedule performance index, cost variance, and other related metrics. For executives, correct, valid, and relevant information is essential in air support meetings.

Ground support meetings are organized with lower level staff to make work assignments. These types of meetings follow the same principles discussed in the previous section. Figure 7.5 shows the value-added and non-value-added elements of a meeting.

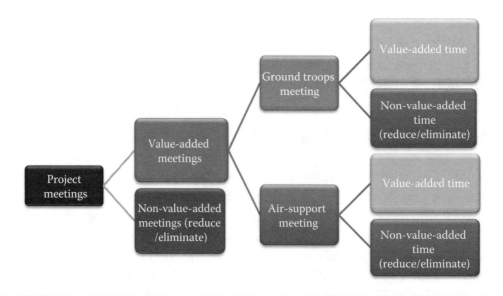

Figure 7.5 Value-added and non-value-added elements of a meeting.

7.7 The Right Approach to Calculate the Project ROI Using Meeting Costs

Advanced project leaders also consider meeting expenses in the Return on Investment (ROI) of their projects. They are aware that if they do not consider these expenses, the organization would miss a critical piece of information. The following examples illustrate this point and demonstrate how to calculate the project ROI by including the approximate cost of meetings.

Advanced project leaders also consider meeting expenses in the Return on Investment (ROI) of their projects.

7.7.1 ROI Calculations without Considering Meeting Costs

ROI calculations are done using Equation 7.2.

Project ROI can be calculated as follows:

$$\text{Project ROI\%} = \frac{(\text{Project gains} - \text{project costs})}{\text{Project costs}}$$

For example, if

Project gains = $21,000

Project costs = $10,000

$$\text{Project ROI} = \frac{(\$21{,}000 - \$10{,}000)}{\$10{,}000} = \frac{\$11{,}000}{\$10{,}000} = 1.1 = 110\%$$

(7.2)

Conclusion: The ROI of the Project is 110% which is excellent.

7.7.2 ROI Calculations Considering Meeting Costs

ROI calculations are done using Equation 7.3.

$$\text{Project ROI} = \frac{(\text{Project gains} - \text{project costs})}{\text{Project costs}}$$

Project costs = Meeting costs + Other project costs

For example, if

Project gains	= $21,000
Other project costs	= $10,000
Meeting expenses (food, travel etc.)	= $1,000
No. of meetings	= 30
No. of employee hours per meeting	= 10
Average hourly wage	= $15

$$\text{Meeting costs} = \text{Meeting expenses} + \left\{ (\text{No. of meetings}) \times \left(\frac{\text{No. of employee hours}}{\text{Meetings}} \right) \times (\text{Average hourly wage}) \right\}$$

Meeting costs $= \$1,000 + (30 \times 10 \times 15) = \$5,500$

Since project costs $=$ Meeting costs $+$ other project costs

Project costs $= \$10,000 + \$5,500 = \$15,500$

Project ROI $= \dfrac{\text{Project gains } - \text{ project costs}}{\text{project costs}}$

Project ROI $= \dfrac{\$21,000 - \$15,500}{\$15,500}$

Project ROI $= \dfrac{\$5,500}{\$15,500} = 0.35 = 35\%$ (7.3)

Conclusion: Wow! Our ROI dropped from 110% to 35% by considering the cost of meetings during a project. Can we improve this by reducing the number of meetings to absolute minimum required without affecting the results? Let's see …

7.7.3 ROI Calculations Considering Meeting Costs but Reducing the Number of Meetings by 50%

ROI calculations are done using Equation 7.4.

For example, considering 50%** reduction meetings:

Project gains $= \$21,000$

Other project costs $= \$10,000$

**Meeting expenses $(\text{food, travel etc.}) = \$500$

** No. of meetings $= 15$

No. of employees hours per meeting $= 10$

Average hourly wage $= \$15$

Meeting costs $= \$500 + (15 \times 10 \times 15) = \$2,750$ (7.4)

Total project costs $= \$10,000 + \$2,750 = \$12,570$

Project ROI $= \dfrac{\text{Project gains} - \text{project costs}}{\text{project costs}}$

Project ROI $= \dfrac{\$21,000 - \$12,750}{\$12,750}$

Project ROI $= \dfrac{\$8,250}{\$12,750} = 0.647 = 65\%$

Conclusion: Thus, when we cut the number of meetings by 50%, the cost of meetings was reduced from $5500 to $2750. This had a significant impact on the ROI of the project. **By cutting the meetings by 50%, our ROI increased from 35% to 65%.**

Thus, it is clear that considering meeting costs gives us a much more accurate ROI. Also, cutting down meetings and keeping them to the absolute minimum as necessary, without affecting the results, has a significant positive impact on the project ROI.

Thus, it is true that project ROI is *inversely proportional* to the number of non-value-added meetings held during a project, as shown in Equation 7.5.

$$\text{Project ROI} \propto \left\{ \frac{1}{(\text{No. of non-value-added meetings})} \right\} \qquad (7.5)$$

Pillar VII Summary

Death of resource efficiency by meetings (Meeticide™) is one of the cardinal offenses that go unpunished in most organizations. The dilemma for project leaders is how to make communication effective and yet keep meetings to a minimum. If leaders learn the art of running efficient meetings, not only could they make a huge impact on their project but also on their careers.

Project leaders should look for opportunities to eliminate non-value-added and nonproductive meetings. If the meeting cannot be eliminated, project leaders should look for the options to reduce non-value-added time in the meetings. Every successful project leader must avoid the loss of resource efficiency caused by excessive meetings and keep the meetings to an absolute minimum as required to get the results, so as to have an optimal project ROI. The details of Pillar VII are shown in Figure 7.6.

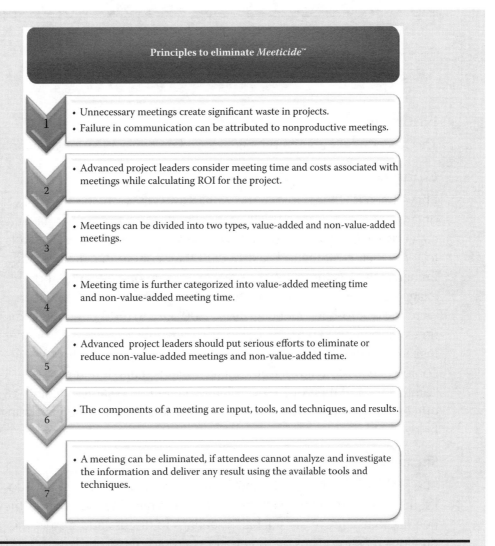

Figure 7.6 Principles to eliminate Meeticide.

Pillar VII   Case Study
Eliminate Non-Value-Added Meetings

INTRODUCTION

This case study is about non-value-added meetings in an organization.

CHALLENGE

I have been a witness to one the worst cases of Meeticide™ in an organization. I consulted briefly at the headquarters of a pharmaceutical corporation. The corporation was developing some new products to serve their customers. The aspect of their culture that amazed me immediately was the number of meetings everyone attended. I do not exaggerate when I tell you that the executives and project managers were in back-to-back meetings from 7:00 a.m. to 7:00 p.m. and sometimes even till 9:00 p.m. including attending lunch meetings. The meetings were either face-to-face or via phone conferencing. They would conference into meetings from home, airports, cars, lunch rooms, bathrooms, and their office even if they were in the same building, two offices down from the conference room where the meeting was being held.

SITUATION

The problem was that each meeting they attended generated a to-do list that they had to complete before the next meeting. Sometimes they needed to have several "sidebar" meetings to discuss and dissect the previous meeting. Thus, at the end of each day, most of them would be rushing from one meeting to the next and end up with a large laundry list of to-do items. When was the time to complete these? The only time available was at night or on weekends! The stress on these managers and executives was evident. The projects were falling way behind and as pressure from the top increased and some heads began to roll, every person on the team wanted to attend every possible meeting so that they could defend themselves in case someone tried to blame them for anything that went wrong. They did not want to risk their jobs so they even phoned in or attended meetings in person on their vacation days.

The saddest element for this organization was that they did not realize that although they were having excessive meetings, their Achilles heel was "lack of effective communication." The problem started right at the phase of defining customer specifications. They had absolutely no clue what the customer really wanted. They made several assumptions, and when they would go back to the customer for approvals, the customer would be upset at them for not understanding their specifications. They had lost more than one major account because of this problem. The lack of understanding of the customer's requirements led to incomplete product specifications, which led to several assumptions that, in turn, led to more chaos. All the meetings were just adding to the chaos and confusion—no one was truly communicating. No one stepped back and asked the tough questions—"What does the customer really want? Is that in line with our 3 to 5 year plan? When I asked them the latter, I was told "We do not have a 3 to 5 year plan, the executives want us to define it for them" Wow!

SOLUTION

It was quite clear to me that innocent project members were being punished, whereas the real culprit, their "culture was Meeticide" was creating havoc, not only was it going unpunished but it was also not even considered as a potential suspect. I gave them my recommendations but realized that I too was slowly becoming just another victim of their Meeticide™! Although the payments from them were quite good, I got myself fired and made a run for the door! I truly could not bear witness or be a party to this madness, unnecessary pain, and suffering of the employees and executives. My heart truly goes out to them and I wish them the best of luck.

If you are also in a similar situation, my advice is to openly discuss the problem of "Meeticide™" at all levels within your organization, before it is too late.

Pillar VII   Force Field Analysis

PILLAR VII: FORCE FIELD ANALYSIS OF ORGANIZATIONAL ASSESSMENT

Table 7.2 shows force field analysis of organizational assessment. The organizational assessment is conducted to assess if the culture of the organization is in alignment with the principles of Pillar VII. Tables 7.3 through 7.5 are used to develop and implement an action plan to increase the impact of the organizational driving forces and decrease the impact of the organizational resisting forces.

PILLAR VII: FORCE FIELD ANALYSIS OF SELF-ASSESSMENT

Table 7.6 shows force field analysis of self-assessment. The self-assessment is conducted to assess if your own strengths are in alignment with the principles of Pillar VII. Tables 7.7 through 7.9 are used to develop and implement an action plan to increase the impact of the self-driving forces and decrease the impact of the self-resisting forces.

PILLAR VII: RECOMMENDATIONS FOR OPTIMAL RESULTS FROM FORCE FIELD ANALYSIS

For optimal results and actual transformation of culture and strengths conducive to the creation of advanced master project leaders, the following three steps are necessary:

1. Both the organizational and self-evaluation assessments must be completed.
2. A well-designed action plan must be created and implemented to increase the driving forces and decrease the resisting forces.
3. The principles of each pillar must be constantly practiced and improved.

It is highly recommended that both the organizational assessments and self-assessments be conducted every year and the action plan be updated at least every 3 months.

Note: The sum of scores for Organizational Driving Force and Organizational Resisting Force for each point must be less than or equal to TEN.

The sum of scores for Self Driving Force and Self Resisting Force for each point must be less than or equal to TEN.

Table 7.2   Pillar VII: Force Field Organizational Analysis

Team Name: _____   Date: _____

	Does My Organization Drive or Resist a Culture of Eliminating Meeting Waste?			
	0 Never	5 Sometimes		7 Mostly
	3 Rarely	ODF + ORF ≤ 10		10 Always
No.	Driving Forces	*Score Organizational Driving Force (ODF)*	*Score Organizational Resisting Force (ORF)*	Resisting Forces
1	My organization recognizes the concept of Meeticide™ or death of resource efficiency by meetings as one of the primary wastes.			My organization does not understand the concept of Meeticide™ or death of resource efficiency by meetings nor recognize it as a form of waste.
2	Our organization encourages our leaders to keep meetings to the minimum necessary.			Our organization culture does not make any attempt to minimize meetings.
3	Our organizational culture encourages project leaders to use modern tools to present information and reduce meeting costs.			Our culture does not provide any modern tools to gather and present information needed to run efficient meetings.
4	Our leaders always strive to eliminate waste or non-value-added time in the meetings by having a clear agenda and correct information.			Our managers never make an attempt to either eliminate waste or non-value-added time in the meetings.
5	Our leaders encourage meeting attendees to come prepared for the meeting and to stay focused on the meeting agenda.			Our managers do not require participants to come prepared for meetings or stay focused on the meeting agenda.

6	Our leaders understand that meetings with high-level executives are necessary only for important decisions and critical updates.			Our managers often involve high-level executives in the meetings to keep them updated on details of the project or for making noncritical decisions.
7	Our project leaders identify mandatory, required, and optional attendees when sending the meeting request.			Our managers invite all team members to come to the meeting irrespective of the agenda.
8	Our leaders communicate and follow up with the participants by sending minutes and creating a repository for meeting minutes that can be easily accessed by participants.			Once the meeting is over, our managers do not send out timely meeting minutes or do not archive the minutes.
9	Our project leaders diligently look at each meeting and analyze if the meeting adds value to the project prior to scheduling it.			Our project managers do not evaluate the value of holding meetings and schedule meetings that do not add any value to the project.
10	Our project leaders and team members include meeting costs when calculating the project ROI.			Our managers have never heard of including meeting costs when calculating the project ROI.
	Total ODF Score			*Total ORF Score*

Result	Conclusion	Recommended Action Review and Update Every Quarter (3 months)
ODF >> ORF	My company culture strongly drives a culture of eliminating meeting waste.	Use Tables 7.3 through 7.5 to set goals and create an action plan to preserve or continuously improve the culture of eliminating meeting waste.
ODF > ORF	My company culture drives the culture of eliminating meeting waste.	Use Tables 7.3 through 7.5 to set goals and create an action plan to increase ODF to create a culture of eliminating meeting waste.
ORF >> ODF	My company culture strongly resists the culture of eliminating meeting waste.	Use Tables 7.3 through 7.5 to set goals and create an action plan to increase the ODF and reduce the ORF to create a culture of eliminating meeting waste.
ORF > ODF	My company culture resists the culture of eliminating meeting waste.	Use Tables 7.3 through 7.5 to set goals and create an action plan to reduce the ORF to create a culture of eliminating meeting waste.
ODF = ORF	My company culture does not drive or resist the culture of eliminating meeting waste.	Use Tables 7.3 through 7.5 to set goals and create an action plan to increase the ODF to create a culture of eliminating meeting waste.

Table 7.3 Pillar VII: Analysis of ODF and ORF Results

Result	Existing Organizational Culture	If the Goal is to Create a Moderately Strong Culture of Eliminating Meeting Waste	If the Goal is to Create a Very Strong Culture of Eliminating Meeting Waste
ODF			
ODF ≤ 25	No or minimal culture of eliminating meeting waste	Focus on improving scores in at least 5 DF	Focus on improving scores in at least 7 DF
25 < ODF ≤ 50	Weak culture of eliminating meeting waste	Focus on improving scores in at least 3 DF	Focus on improving scores in at least 5 DF
50 < ODF ≤ 75	Moderate culture of eliminating meeting waste	Focus on improving scores in at least 1 DF	Focus on improving scores in at least 3 DF
ODF > 75	Strong culture of eliminating meeting waste	N/A	Preserve or continuously improve the culture
ORF			
ORF > 75	No or minimal culture of eliminating meeting waste	Focus on decreasing scores in at least 5 RF	Focus on decreasing scores in at least 7 RF
50 < ORF ≤ 75	Weak culture of eliminating meeting waste	Focus on decreasing scores in at least 3 RF	Focus on decreasing scores in at least 5 RF
25 < ORF ≤ 50	Moderate culture eliminating meeting waste	Focus on decreasing scores in at least 1 RF	Focus on decreasing scores in at least 3 RF
ORF ≤ 25	Strong culture of eliminating meeting waste	N/A	Preserve or continuously improve the culture

Table 7.4   Pillar VII: Action Plan to Increase Organizational Driving Force (ODF)

Team Name: _____   Date: _____

No.	Driving Force	Current Score	Goal (Target Score) ⬆	Action Plan to increase DF Score	Complete by (Date)	Assigned to (Department Name or Initials of Person)
1	My organization recognizes the concept of Meeticide™ or death of resource efficiency by meetings as one of the primary wastes.					
2	Our organization encourages our leaders to keep meetings to minimum necessary.					
3	Our organizational culture encourages project leaders to use modern tools to present information and reduce meeting costs.					
4	Our leaders always strive to eliminate waste or non-value-added time in the meetings by having clear agenda and correct information.					
5	Our leaders encourage meeting attendees to come prepared for the meeting and to stay focused on the meeting agenda.					
6	Our leaders understand that meetings with high-level executives are necessary only for important decisions and critical updates.					

7	Our project leaders identify mandatory, required, and optional attendees when sending the meeting request.					
8	Our leaders communicate and follow up with the participants by sending minutes and creating a repository for meeting minutes that can be easily accessed by participants.					
9	Our project leaders diligently look at each meeting and analyze if the meeting adds value to the project prior to scheduling it.					
10	Our project leaders and team members include meeting costs when calculating the project ROI.					
	Total ODF					

Table 7.5 Pillar VII: Action Plan to Decrease Organizational Resisting Force (ORF)

No.	Resisting Force	Current Score	Goal (Target Score) ⬇	Action Plan to Decrease RF Score	Complete by (Date)	Assigned to (Department Name or Initials of Person)
1	My organization does not understand the concept of Meeticide™ or death of resource efficiency by meetings nor recognize it as a form of waste.					
2	Our organization culture does not make any attempt to minimize meetings.					
3	Our culture does not provide any modern tools to gather and present information needed to run efficient meetings.					
4	Our managers never make an attempt to either eliminate waste or non-value-added time in the meetings.					
5	Our managers do not require participants to come prepared for meetings or stay focused on the meeting agenda.					
6	Our managers often involve high-level executives in the meetings to keep them updated on details of the project or for making noncritical decisions.					
7	Our managers invite all team members to come to the meeting irrespective of the agenda.					

8	Once the meeting is over, our managers do not send out timely meeting minutes or do not archive the minutes.					
9	Our project managers do not evaluate the value of holding meetings and schedule meetings that do not add any value to the project.					
10	Our managers have never heard of including meeting costs when calculating the project ROI.					
	Total ORF					

Table 7.6 Pillar VII: Force Field Self-analysis

Name: _____   Date: _____

	Does My Behavior Drive or Resist the Principles of Eliminating Meeting Waste?				
	0 Never		5 Sometimes		7 Mostly
	3 Rarely		SDF + SRF ≤ 10		10 Always
No.	Driving Forces →	Score Self-Driving Force (SDF)	Score Self-Resisting Force (SRF)	← Resisting Forces	
1	I am very mindful of the tremendous waste in organizations because of unnecessary meetings.			I do not think that meetings result in organizational waste.	
2	I make an effort to eliminate all non-value-added meetings and organize productive meetings.			I do not differentiate between value-added and non-value-added meetings waste as I feel all meetings are important.	
3	I ensure that the non-value-added time in meetings is eliminated by encouraging team members to be active participants in the meetings.			I believe that all the time in meetings is always value-added time.	
4	I proactively prepare a detailed agenda for every meeting and invite only the required people.			I prefer to run meetings without a set agenda as it allows for an open exchange between all the team members who wish to attend these meetings.	
5	I understand the importance of presenting good quality project information during meetings and I present the required information in a clear and concise format to the meeting attendees.			I think it is the team member's job to decipher information and I present the information as available in the project documents.	
6	I personally use modern tools and techniques and also encourage my team members to use the same methods for presenting the information.			I use traditional methods and encourage team members to use those methods for presenting information in the meetings.	

7	I understand the importance of time and try to include high-level executives in the meeting only when key decisions are to be made.			I try to include high-level executives in every meeting to let them aware of the progress of the project.
8	To have the best results from meetings, the three critical inputs I focus on are a detailed agenda, accurate and unambiguous information, and appropriate meeting attendees.			I am not too worried about running efficient meetings or having meetings to follow up on meetings, as long as the project work is getting done.
9	I encourage feedback from the meeting attendees by sending minutes and request them to update the information, if necessary.			I send meeting minutes to the team when it is necessary to do so and rarely ask their feedback.
10	I consider time spent in meetings as a part of the ROI of a meeting and focus on improving the VAMT and reducing the NVAMT.			I never consider meetings while calculating the ROI for my projects.
	Total SDF score			*Total SRF score*

Result	Conclusion	Recommended Action Review and Update Every Quarter (3 months)
SDF >> SRF	My behavior strongly supports the principles of eliminating meeting waste.	Use Tables 7.7 through 7.9 to set goals and create an action plan to continuously enhance the behavior to create a culture of eliminating meeting waste.
SDF > SRF	My behavior supports the principles of eliminating meeting waste.	Use Tables 7.7 through 7.9 to set goals and create an action plan to increase SDF to allow a stronger behavior toward creating a culture of eliminating meeting waste.
SRF >> SDF	My behavior strongly resists the principles of eliminating meeting waste.	Use Tables 7.7 through 7.9 to set goals and create an action plan to increase SDF and reduce SRF to allow a stronger behavior toward creating a culture of eliminating meeting waste.
SRF > SDF	My behavior resists the principles of eliminating meeting waste.	Use Tables 7.7 through 7.9 to set goals and create an action plan to reduce SRF to allow a stronger behavior toward creating a culture of eliminating meeting waste.
SDF = SRF	My behavior does not drive or resist the principles of eliminating meeting waste.	Use Tables 7.7 through 7.9 to set goals and create an action plan to increase the SDF to allow a stronger behavior toward creating a culture of eliminating meeting waste.

Table 7.7   Pillar VII: Analysis of SDF and SRF Results

Result	Existing Behavior	If the Goal is to Create a Moderately Strong Behavior Toward Principles of Eliminating Meeting Waste	If the Goal is to Create a Very Strong Behavior Toward Principles of Eliminating Meeting Waste
SDF			
SDF ≤ 25	No or minimal activities in creating a culture of eliminating meeting waste	Focus on improving scores in at least 5 DF	Focus on improving scores in at least 7 DF
25 < SDF ≤ 50	Weak activities in creating a culture of eliminating meeting waste	Focus on improving scores in at least 3 DF	Focus on improving scores in at least 5 DF
50 < SDF ≤ 75	Moderate activities in creating a culture of eliminating meeting waste	Focus on improving scores in at least 1 DF	Focus on improving scores in at least 3 DF
SDF > 75	Strong activities in creating a culture of eliminating meeting waste	N/A	Preserve or continuously improve the behavior
SRF			
SRF > 75	No or minimal activities in creating a culture of eliminating meeting waste	Focus on decreasing scores in at least 5 RF	Focus on decreasing scores in at least 7 RF
50 < SRF ≤ 75	Weak activities in creating a culture of eliminating meeting waste	Focus on decreasing scores in at least 3 RF	Focus on decreasing scores in at least 5 RF
25 < SRF ≤ 50	Moderate activities in creating a culture of eliminating meeting waste	Focus on decreasing scores in at least 1 RF	Focus on decreasing scores in at least 3 RF
SRF ≤ 25	Strong activities in creating a culture of eliminating meeting waste	N/A	Preserve or continuously improve the behavior

Table 7.8 Pillar VII: Action Plan to Increase Self-Driving Forces (SDFs)

Name: _____   Date: _____

No.	Driving Force	Current Score	Goal (Target Score) ⬆	Action Plan to Increase DF Score	Complete by (Date)	Required Resources
1	I am very mindful of the tremendous waste in organizations because of unnecessary meetings.					
2	I make an effort to eliminate all non-value-added meetings and organize productive meetings.					
3	I ensure that the non-value-added time in meetings is eliminated by encouraging team members to be active participants in the meetings.					
4	I proactively prepare a detailed agenda for every meeting and invite only the required people.					
5	I understand the importance of presenting good quality project information during meetings and I present the required information in a clear and concise format to the meeting attendees.					
6	I personally use modern tools and techniques and also encourage my team members to use the same methods for presenting the information.					
7	I understand the importance of time and try to include high-level executives in the meeting only when key decisions are to be made.					

8	To have the best results from meetings, the three critical inputs I focus on are a detailed agenda, accurate and unambiguous information, and appropriate meeting attendees.					
9	I encourage feedback from the meeting attendees by sending minutes and request them to update the information, if necessary.					
10	I consider time spent in meetings as a part of the ROI of a meeting and focus on improving VAMT and reducing NVAMT.					
	Total SDF					

Table 7.9 Pillar VII: Action Plan to Decrease Self-Resisting Forces (SRFs)

Name: _____   Date: _____

No.	Resisting Force	Current Score	Goal (Target Score) ⬇	Action Plan to Decrease RF Score	Complete by (Date)	Required Resources
1	I do not think that meetings result in organizational waste.					
2	I do not differentiate between value-added and non-value-added meetings waste as I feel all meetings are important.					
3	I believe that all the time in meetings is always value-added time.					
4	I prefer to run meetings without a set agenda as it allows for an open exchange between all the team members who wish to attend these meetings.					
5	I think it is the team member's job to decipher information and I present the information as available in the project documents.					
6	I use traditional methods and encourage team members to use those methods for presenting information in the meetings.					
7	I try to include high-level executives in every meeting to let them aware of the progress of the project.					
8	I am not too worried about running efficient meetings or having meetings to follow up on meetings, as long as the project work is getting done.					

9	I send meeting minutes to the team when it is necessary to do so and rarely ask their feedback.					
10	I never consider meetings while calculating the ROI for my projects.					
	Total SRF					

Pillar VII Exercises

PILLAR VII: ORGANIZATIONAL-LEVEL SKILL SET–ENHANCEMENT EXERCISES

GROUP EXERCISES

These exercises are best completed within a group of project managers, project leaders, executives, and stakeholders from within a department or an organization.

1. Using Table 7.10, identify at least five advantages to your organization in creating a culture of eliminating meeting waste, rate them from 1 (least important) to 5 (most important) and explain the rating.
2. Using Table 7.11, identify at least five roadblocks within your organization in creating a culture of eliminating meeting waste for your projects, rate them from 1 (least difficult to overcome) to 5 (most difficult to overcome) and explain the rating.
3. As a group, identify a recently completed project within your organization that was successful. Using Table 7.12, identify the following during each phase of the project:
   a. Total number of hours spent in meetings
   b. Estimated number of hours in non-value-added meetings
   c. Average number of attendees per meeting
   d. Average hourly salary of attendees
   e. Calculate total amount of money wasted because of non-value-added meetings
4. As a group, identify a recently completed project within your organization. Using Table 7.13, document the following:
   a. Project Return on Investment (ROI)
   b. Total number of hours spent in meetings
   c. Average number of attendees per meeting
   d. Average hourly salary of attendees
   e. Calculate total amount of money spent on project meetings
   f. New ROI considering the amounts spent on meetings.
5. Scenario analysis: A world renowned organization called "ZALLUP," famous for conducting surveys and analyzing results, has just collected data regarding 10 projects over a billion dollars in various IT organizations in the United States. The data collected are shown in Table 7.14.
   a. Project gains
   b. Projects costs
   c. Total meeting costs (inclusive of meeting expenses)
   d. Total number of employee hours in meetings
   e. Average value-added time in the meetings.

Table 7.10   Pillar VII: Five Advantages of Applying Principles of Pillar VII to Your Organization

No.	Advantages of Applying the Principles of Pillar VII to Enhancing Your Organization Culture	Rating (from 1 = Least Important to 5 = Most Important)	Explain the Rating?
1			
2			
3			
4			
5			

Table 7.11   Pillar VII: Five Roadblocks to Creating a Culture of Eliminating Meeting Waste Using Pillar VII

No.	Roadblocks to Applying the Principles of Eliminating Meeting Waste as Described in Pillar VII to Your Organization	Rating (from 1 = Least Difficult to Overcome to 5 = Most Difficult to Overcome)	Explain the Rating
1			
2			
3			
4			
5			

Table 7.12   Pillar VII: Total Money Wasted in Meetings of a Successful Project

Project Phase	*No. of Hours Spent in Meetings*	*No. of Hours Spent in Non-Value-Added Meetings*	*Average No. of Attendees per Meeting*	*Average Hourly Salary of Attendees*	*Total Amount of Money Wasted on Project (No. of Hours in Non-Value-Added Meetings × Average No. of Attendees × Average Salary)*
1. Project initiation					
2. Project planning					
3. Project execution					
4. Project monitoring					
5. Project closing					

Project Name

Using Table 7.15, calculate the following:

a. Average non-value-added meeting percentage time (time lost in meetings because of daydreaming, missing parts of meetings, bringing other work to meetings, dozing off during meetings, inefficient meetings, and other reasons).

Note: Average non-value-added meeting percentage time = (100 − average value-added time).

b. Find the ratio between value-added time and non-value-added time.

Imagine that your team works for ZALLUP and is required to take the raw data and concert into meaningful statistics that can be published as final survey results.

Using Table 7.16, identify the following:

a. ROI on the 10 projects without considering the meeting costs. Use the formula shown in Equation 7.6.

Table 7.13   Pillar VII: Return on Investment Considering Meeting Time

Project Name				
Total Project Gain		*Total Project Costs*		
Project Return on Investment	*(Total Project Gain – Total Project Costs)/Total Project Costs*			
Project Phase	*No. of Hours Spent in Meetings*	*Average No. of Attendees Per Meeting*	*Average Hourly Salary of Attendees*	*Total Meeting Costs (No. of Hours in Non-Value-added Meetings * Average No. of Attendees *Average Salary)*
1. Project Initiation				
2. Project Planning				
3. Project Execution				
4. Project Monitoring				
5. Project Closing				
New Total Project Costs	(Total Project Costs + Total Meeting Costs)			
New Project ROI	(Project Gains – New Total Project Costs)/ New Total Project Costs			

Table 7.14   Pillar VII: Scenario Analysis: Costs from Project Survey

Project	Project Gains ($ millions)	Project Costs ($ millions)	Meeting Costs for Each Project ($ millions)	Total No. of Employee Hours in Meetings	Average Value-added Time per Meeting (%)
1.	250	200	1.0	20,000	40
2.	300	320	1.5	50,000	70
3.	150	125	0.75	16,000	40
4.	450	450	3.0	110,000	55
5.	700	500	1.5	50,000	30
6.	60	50	1.0	19,000	55
7.	25	30	1.0	32,000	25
8.	100	150	7.5	255,000	20
9.	350	200	0.3	10,000	55
10.	200	100	0.4	5,000	75

Table 7.15   Pillar VII: Scenario Analysis: Non-Value-Added Percentage Time from Survey

Project	Average Value-Added Time per Meeting (%)	Average Non-Value-Added Time per Meeting (%)	Ratio = Total Value-Added Time)/Total Non-value-added Time)	Identify the Meeting as Productive or Nonproductive (Ratio >0.6 is a Productive Meeting)
1	40	60	0.67	Productive
2	70			
3	40			
4	55			
5	30			
6	55			
7	25			
8	20			
9	55			
10	75			

Table 7.16   Pillar VII: Scenario Analysis: Project ROI Calculations

Project	Project Gains ($ millions)	Project Costs ($ millions)	Project ROI without Meeting Costs (%)	New Project ROI with Meeting Costs (%)	Comments
1.	250	200	0.25	0.24	
2.	300	320			
3.	150	125			
4.	450	450			
5.	700	500			
6.	60	50			
7.	25	30			
8.	100	150			
9.	350	200			
10.	200	100			

$$\text{Project ROI without meeting costs} = \frac{\left(\text{Project gains} - \text{project costs}\right)}{\text{Project costs}} \quad (7.6)$$

   b. ROI on the 10 projects considering the meeting costs. Use the formula shown in Equation 7.7 followed by the formula shown in Equation 7.8.

$$\text{New project costs} = \left(\text{Project costs} + \text{meeting costs}\right) \quad (7.7)$$

$$\begin{aligned} &\text{New project ROI with meeting costs} \\ &= \frac{\left(\text{Project gains} - \text{new project costs}\right)}{\text{New project costs}} \end{aligned} \quad (7.8)$$

   c. Comments regarding considering the meeting costs in project ROI. Using Table 7.17, identify the following:

   a. The amount of money lost because of non-value-added meeting time using the formula shown in Equation 7.9.

Total amount of money lost due to non-value-added time in the meetings

$$= \left\{ \begin{array}{l} \left[\left(\text{Total number of employee hours in meetings}\right)\right] \\ *\left(\text{Average employee salary}\right) \\ *\left(\text{Average non-value-added percentage}\right) \end{array} \right\} \quad (7.9)$$

Table 7.17 Pillar VII: Scenario Analysis: Non-Value-Added Percentage Time from Survey

Project	Total Number of Employee Hours in Meetings (1)	Average Employee Salary (2)	Average Non-Value-Added Time per Meeting (%) from Table 7.15	Total Amount Lost due to Non-Value-Added Time in the Meetings ($)
1	20,000	25	60	300,000
2	50,000	25		
3	16,000	25		
4	110,000	27		
5	50,000	25		
6	19,000	30		
7	32,000	25		
8	255,000	26		
9	10,000	20		
10	5,000	30		

PILLAR VII: PERSONAL-LEVEL SKILL SET–ENHANCEMENT EXERCISES

INDIVIDUAL EXERCISES

These exercises are to be completed individually after reviewing Pillar VII in detail.

1. Using Table 7.18, list at least five advantages of applying the principles of Pillar VII of value-added meetings to your future projects. Rate the advantages from 1 (least important) to 5 (most important) and explain the rating.
2. Using Table 7.19, identify at least five roadblocks to applying the principles of value-added meetings from Pillar VII on all your future major projects. Rate the identified roadblocks from 1 (least difficult to overcome) to 5 (most difficult to overcome) and explain the rating.
3. Using Table 7.20, select a project you worked on as a project manager/leader that was successful. Looking back on the project, answer the following questions for each phase of the project:
   a. The number of meetings in which the effective meeting techniques were used.
   b. If the technique was not used, explain why?
4. Using Table 7.21, select a failed project you worked on as a project manager/leader. Looking back on the project, answer the following questions for each phase of the project:
   a. Answer the number of meetings the effective meeting technique is used
   b. If the technique was not used, explain why?

Table 7.18 Pillar VII: Five Advantages of Applying the Principles of Pillar VII to Your Career

No.	Advantages of Applying Principles of Pillar VII of Eliminating Meeting Waste to All Future Projects	Rating (from 1 = Least Important to 5 = Most Important)	Explain the Rating
1			
2			
3			
4			
5			

Table 7.19 Pillar VII: Five Roadblocks to Applying the Principles of Pillar VII

No.	Roadblocks to Applying Principles of Eliminating Meeting Waste Detailed in Pillar VII to All Future Projects	Rating (from 1 = Least Difficult to Overcome to 5 = Most Difficult to Overcome)	Explain the Rating
1			
2			
3			
4			
5			

Table 7.20 Pillar VII: Identify the Effective Meeting Techniques Used in a Successful Project

	Technique	No. of Meetings in Which Technique Was Used	If the Technique Was Not Used, Explain Why?
1	Team members trained to identify time wasters		
2	Detailed, clear, and practical agenda e-mailed at least 1 day in advance		
3	Identified mandatory, required, and optional attendees for the meeting		
4	Team members instructed to bring accurate and clear information to the meeting		
5	Everyone focused on critical path items during the meeting		
6	Meeting duration of an hour or less		
7	Used right tools to present the information		
8	Skilled facilitator present during the brainstorming meetings		
9	Effective decisions and assignments during the meeting		
10	Feedback requested from the meeting attendees		

Table 7.21 Pillar VII: Identify the Effective Meeting Techniques Used in a Failed Project

No.	Technique	No. of Meetings in Which the Technique Is Used	Explain Why if Never Used
1	Trained team members to identify time wasters		
2	Detailed, clear, and practical agenda e-mailed 1 day before the meeting		
3	Identified mandatory, required, and optional attendees for the meeting		
4	Prepared team members to bring accurate and clear information to the meeting		
5	Focused on critical path items during the meeting		
6	Maintained the meeting for a duration of an hour or less		
7	Used right tools to present the information		
8	Have skilled facilitator to control the brainstorming meetings		
9	Made effective decisions and assignments in the meeting		
10	Requested feedback from the meeting attendees		

5. Scenario analysis: A world-renowned organization called ZALLUP, famous for conducting surveys and analyzing results, has just collected data regarding 10 projects over a billion dollars in various IT organizations in the United States. The data collected are shown in Tables 7.14 and 7.15, and the resulting calculations are shown in Tables 7.16 and 7.17.

The U.S. Department of Economic Advancement is worried about these data. They have selected your organization as a pilot to reduce or eliminate the revenue lost because of unnecessary meetings and because of non-value-added time during meetings. As a project leader with expertise in principles of Pillar VII of the book *12 Pillars of Project Excellence*, you have been selected by your organization to minimize or reduce the death of resource efficiency by meetings.

a. Using Table 7.22, identify and document the potential non-value-added meeting types and potential time wasters in meetings during each project phase.

b. Using Table 7.23, document the value-added agenda items for air support meetings and ground troops meetings.

c. Using Table 7.24, identify and document the techniques that you would like to use in your future meetings to maximize project ROI.

Table 7.22   Pillar VII: Scenario Analysis: Identify Potential Non-Value-Added Meeting Types and Potential Time Wasters in Meetings

Project Name		
Project Phase	*Potential Non-Value-Added Meeting Types*	*Potential Time Wasters in Meetings*
1. Project initiation		
2. Project planning		
3. Project execution		
4. Project monitoring		
5. Project closing		

Table 7.23   Pillar VII: Scenario Analysis: Determine the Value-Added Agenda Items in Each Meeting

No.		Value-Added Agenda Items
1	Air-support meetings	
2	Ground troops meetings	

Table 7.24   Pillar VII: Scenario Analysis: Identify the Effective Meeting Techniques That Will Be Used in Future Meetings to Maximize Project ROI

No.		Effective Meeting Techniques	Explain the Reason for Using the Technique
1	Before the meeting		
2	During the meeting		
3	After the meeting		

Pillar VII   References

1. *Survey from Salary.com and American online.* (2005). http://www.salary.com/sitesearch/layoutscripts/sisl_display.asp?filename=&path=/destinationsearch/par485_body.html (accessed November 11, 2010).
2. SMART Technologies. (2004). *The State of Meetings Today,* http://www.effectivemeetings.com/meetingbasics/meetstate.asp (accessed November 11, 2010).
3. Used with Permission from Microsoft. (2010). *Survey Finds Workers Average Only Three Productive Days per Week, News Press Release.* http://www.microsoft.com/presspass/press/2005/mar05/03-15threeproductivedayspr.mspx (accessed Nov. 11, 2010).

Chapter 8

Pillar VIII: Take Risks
But Do the Math Beforehand

Project Managers *react* to problems;
Project Leaders *prevent* them with "dynamic risk leadership."

8.1 Introduction

8.1.1 Risk Management

Risk management is a misleading term. It indicates trying to gain control over the risks, which we all know is impossible to achieve. The only way to address risk is not by managing it but by preparing in advance for the events, that is, proactively assessing, addressing, and eliminating major risks. The correct term to describe this process is **"dynamic risk leadership."** Albert Einstein understood this very well—he says *"Intellectuals solve problems, geniuses prevent them."*[1]

While teaching risk management to my students, I once asked them some questions relating risk management to real-life situations.

1. **What would you do if you were outside your armored vehicle in a war zone, taking light artillery fire, and saw a bullet coming in your general direction from a distance?** I received a range of answers from my students, some of which were

   a. *I would run away from there*

   b. *I would close my eyes and pray that it misses me*

   c. *I would dodge it by falling to the ground immediately*

   d. *I would protect myself by jumping behind any metal or heavy armor*

   e. *I don't know … maybe protect others from harm by getting hit in a non-fatal area*

I explained that all these options relate to the fundamentals of a traditional risk management strategy.

a. Run away	**RISK AVOIDANCE**
b. Close my eyes and pray that it misses me	**RISK ACCEPTANCE**
c. Dodge it by falling to the ground immediately	**RISK MITIGATION**
d. Protect myself by jumping behind any heavy armor	**RISK DEFLECTION**
e. Try to get hit in a nonfatal way	**RISK ABSORPTION**

Dynamic risk leadership in this scenario may include proactive assessment of the battle zone, if possible, by asking some basic questions, and based on the answers, creating a general procedure for exiting or staying in the vehicle in the war zone:

a. What type of ammunition does the enemy possess, i.e., caliber, range, impact?

b. Do we have the personal gear to protect against it?

c. Chances of survival from light artillery outside the armored vehicle?

Based on the answers to these questions, the best option may be to stay in the vehicle at all times or always protect your torso behind some part of the armored vehicle.

I also quizzed the students on risk planning. What if the risk comes to pass, how will they prioritize the action? The real-life scenario I used was an earthquake.

2. **What would you do if you and your family were in your house in California and encountered a major earthquake? What will you try to take with you?** Again the responses from the students ranged from

    a. My kids (leave the spouse behind, if possible, per one wise guy)
    b. Family and food
    c. Family, wallet, and other valuables
    d. Family, laptop, iPod
    e. Family, family pictures, and heirlooms

Thus, each of us may have totally different risk management plans based on the value we assign to animate and inanimate things. However, when the risk occurs, our judgment can be impaired by fear and we may end up inadequately responding to the risk, which may result in loss or even fatality. Dynamic risk leadership in this scenario may include having a plan of action, well rehearsed with the family on the strategy for exiting the house in case of a major earthquake. To clarify this point, I asked the students if they had played the computer game *Minesweeper*, in which the object is to identify/disarm the "land mines." Most of them raised their hands. I asked them about their approach to playing it and their record of winning the game. The responses varied from

    a. Started playing it and learning by trial and error and mostly lost the duel
    b. Read the instructions before playing, created a strategy and won most games

Bingo! I explained that they were correct, the fundamentals of the game are based on addressing risks and that there are two basic approaches to playing this game:

1. **The "try-and-die" approach**, where you keep clicking and if you are very lucky (ha, ha, ha …), you survive to play another game.
2. **The "learn-and-apply" approach**, where you learn to identify the land mines with awareness and skill, and eliminate them one-by-one to win every time.

Figure 8.1 shows the try-and-die approach and the learn-and-apply approach in playing *Minesweeper*.

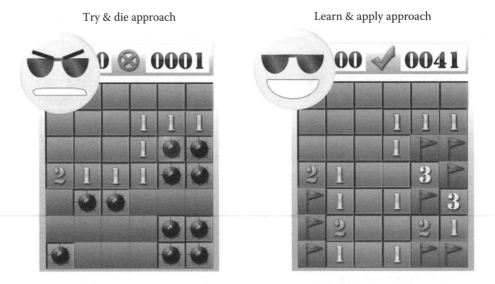

Figure 8.1 "Try-and-die" approach and "learn-and-apply" approach in playing *Minesweeper.*

8.1.2 Dynamic Risk Leadership

Traditional project risk management is very similar to the try-and-die approach.

Dynamic risk leadership is similar to the learn-and-apply approach.

Dynamic risk leadership is a critical trait to be learned and applied by all project leaders.

Dynamic risk leadership is the proactive assessment of risks and the development of methods to resolve those risks. Traditional project risk management is very similar to the try-and-die approach because project managers focus solely on addressing the risks during the particular project. I have seen some project managers use the risk management and mitigation tools and create "static" documents called "project risk analysis" only as an exercise—to allow them to check off a box on their project checklist. Dynamic risk leadership is similar to the learn-and-apply approach. Successful project leaders learn to have an ongoing approach to categorize, strategize, and neutralize various types of risks encountered in projects. They understand that a risk management document for a particular project is always a dynamic tool and has to be used and updated constantly throughout the course of the project and even beyond the project. They constantly document the risks encountered on various projects, their decisions, and the results of their decisions. They constantly build their self-confidence by the good decisions taken and learn valuable lessons from their poor decisions. They also evaluate the risk management plans of other project managers and learn from their wisdom or follies. Dynamic risk leadership is a critical trait to be learned and applied by all project leaders. As stated earlier, project leaders need to lead the team in gathering, analyzing, and documenting the risks, and need to be responsible for the quality of risk response plans throughout the life of the project. They need to follow a systematic approach and methodology to use the principles of dynamic risk leadership.

8.2 Methodology

Dynamic risk leadership involves the identification of risks, the prioritization of risks based on the probability and impact, the preparation of a risk assessment matrix, and a risk response plan. Because of the critical nature of risk assessment in the project, it is important to follow a systematic methodology to perform all these tasks. The methodology involves a three-step process.

1. **Creating a risk assessment team**
2. **Developing an assessment strategy**
3. **Preparing an action plan**.

Let us discuss each of these steps in more detail.

8.2.1 Create a Risk Assessment Team

Selecting and establishing a risk assessment team is the first step in the dynamic risk leadership. Even though high-level risks are established in the project charter, project managers do not pay much attention to the risks until the planning stage. They start digging into the project risks and take stakeholder feedback during the planning stage. However, it is already late by this time because the project is already surrounded by risks. Performing risk assessment in the early stages of the project's life cycle saves costs, avoids duplication of efforts, and prevents schedule overrun. To perform this assessment, a risk assessment team should be set up in the initial stage of the project. An immediate question that comes to mind is about the members of the team. Project leaders may not be experts in all areas of the project. If they do not know enough about a certain subject, they will not allow their ego to get in the way of approaching others for help. They also understand that the best people who can provide input into risks are those who are closest to the product or service. This may mean the end users, customers, key personnel, or service providers. They are not afraid to seek out those people and brainstorm the potential risk factors. The team should have persons who can clearly define the risks, who can perform important risk activities, and who can take decisions. The critical aspect is to select a balanced team represented by members from all levels of the project, that is, team members from the "air support" level and also from the "ground troops" level so that risks associated with and visible to various levels within an organization are considered for the dynamic risk leadership activity. Also, for complex projects, the knowledge about risks and risk factors may not be known by the organization and may need external experts.

> Thus, a risk assessment team may, in general, contain any of the following members:
>
> 1. Air support level: Customers, business owners, key stakeholders, project leader, and sponsors
> 2. Ground troops: Project subleaders, core team members, and technical leaders
> 3. Others (as required): Industry experts, suppliers, consultants, and organizational experts outside of the project team.

Project staff in the air support level can see the risk from a high level, which allows them to make decisions that affect the project as a whole. However, they cannot see lower level risks that can be seen by ground-level staff. Although lower level risks may have low impact on the project parameters, they can add up and create a big impact if not attended early. Hence, air support level and ground troops should work together to understand all project risks. Sometimes, they may need help from some subject matter experts to identify the risks. A dynamic leader not only creates a team but also leads the team through the decision-making process and gets executive support for important decisions made by the team. Figure 8.2 gives an example of various people involved in a dynamic risk assessment team.

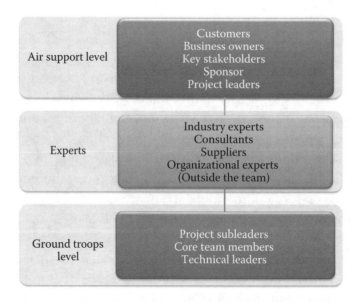

Figure 8.2   Dynamic risk assessment team.

8.2.2 Develop an Assessment Strategy

Developing an outstanding team does not guarantee a perfect plan for risk identification. What the team needs is a clear and well-defined assessment strategy. The strategy is required to determine the uncertainties in the project and map their effect on the overall objectives of the project.

The five tasks involved in this process are

1. Determine scope
2. Brainstorm risks at various levels (threats and opportunities)
3. Consolidate all ideas into risk themes
4. Prioritize risk themes based on the impact
5. Map the themes on a risk assessment matrix

8.2.2.1 Determine Scope

Creating a risk assessment team without a defined scope is like a calling a meeting without a defined agenda. Risk assessment scope clearly defines the areas of focus for the team. Some of the areas of focus include cost, resource, contracted product, schedule, and quality. Defining the scope is vital for assessing valid risks. Before determining the scope of the risk, the assessment team should ask questions such as

How much resilience does the project allow in cost and schedule changes?
What products are required from the vendor?
How dependent is this project on resource-level fluctuations?
What technologies are necessary to undertake this project?

Answers to these questions will determine negotiating terms for the project leader in establishing the scope of the risk and of the project. There is a close relationship between the scope of the risk and the scope of the project. In fact, having an accurate and clear scope of risk controls the scope of the project. For example, if a risk assessment team identifies storing credit card information as a serious risk to the project, the scope cannot have credit card payments as an option for payments. This identified risk can have a major impact on the scope of the project.

8.2.2.2 Brainstorm Risks at Various Levels (Threats and Opportunities)

Once the scope is identified, the risk assessment team should brainstorm ideas about threats and opportunities. This is a critical task in the risk assessment process. Threat is a negative risk that jeopardizes the objective of the project. An opportunity is a positive risk that adds value to the project. Project leaders should use the power of visualization, explained in Pillar I, to walk through the projects and visualize the risks and the possible actions to address them. The team can conduct several "mental drills" to create what-if scenarios of risks and can mentally walk through these to identify several options of addressing them proactively. This is a powerful tool no one is currently using for risk assessments but can pay rich dividends if used correctly.

Project leaders, leading the risk assessment team in the task of risk identification, should be smart enough to understand that they will never have adequate resources to address each and every risk identified. They, thus, learn to prioritize the risks by converting qualitative risks into quantitative risks. One of the simple strategies that are followed to generate threats and opportunities is by asking two simple questions.

1. What events/processes can adversely impact the project?
2. What events/processes can add value to the project?

By answering these two questions, it is easy to identify most threats and opportunities without complex analysis. The risk assessment team should generate ideas that negatively impact cost, schedule, scope, quality, product delivery, and resources. They should also generate ideas that benefit cost reduction, quality improvement, resource utilization, schedule compression, and product delivery. These ideas can be simple or complex, easy or difficult, but need to be all listed. Risk analysis using this technique is clearly explained in this chapter using a scenario. In addition to the technique that we discussed above, project leaders can also ask the team to use some simple to more sophisticated techniques to proactively generate threats and opportunities as follows:

1. Utilize knowledge of experts in the area
2. Failure mode and effects criticality analysis (FMECA)[2]
3. Fault Tree Analysis[3]
4. Reliability analysis.[4]

It is great to be able to get experts within the company, but that is not always possible. The experts need not always be internal to the company. A dynamic project leader should reach out to vendors, consultants, industry experts, and even professors at local universities when there is a need to have answers on the analysis techniques.

FMECA and Fault Tree Analysis are very common tools to look at potential failures from the bottom-up (component to final assembly) or top-down (final assembly to component level). For example, to design a medical instrument, creating an FMECA was a requirement. It helps the team understand potential modes of failures and the potential for these failures to result in catastrophic impact on the customer.

Reliability analysis can also be conducted over long periods by testing the equipment for performance under stress and by simulating actual working conditions. Risk identification tools are equally applicable to design and manufacturing and to software development and other business-systems-related projects.

8.2.2.3 Consolidate All Ideas into Risk Themes

Once all risk ideas are generated, the next step in the risk assessment process is to consolidate all those ideas into themes. What is a theme? A theme is a main idea or amalgamation of ideas. For example, if the risk assessment team generates 10 different risk ideas, and four of those 10 ideas target resources, then all those ideas can be combined into one theme. Similarly, if one team member generates various ideas to target cost reduction, all those ideas can be consolidated to form a single theme. The biggest advantage of consolidating themes is that the project leader or the assessment team can focus on the bigger picture of risks in the project. The team should be mindful of consolidating ideas into themes as some ideas can target more than one element of a project and need to be separated, if required.

8.2.2.4 Prioritize Risk Themes Based on the Impact

- After preparing the themes, they are prioritized based on the overall impact. The greater the impact of the risk theme, the greater is its priority. This phase is also known as *"doing the math."* Cost, schedule, or quality or all of these parameters are taken uniformly to prioritize the risk themes. Thus, the main task of a project leader and his/her team is to find ways to identify the impact of each theme. Some of the project management tools can be used to find the impact in a structured fashion. Traditionally, project managers identify risks and prepare potential impact documents and send it to the stakeholders. However, a project leader believing in dynamic risk leadership would use new methods to find the impact of risk themes. Preparing risk-based network diagram is an example of one such method. The impact of a risk theme on the schedule can be easily calculated by preparing a risk-based network diagram. Regular network diagram gives the start and end dates of each task, lag and lead times, and final task finish dates based on the critical path as shown in Figure 8.3. However, a risk-based network diagram gives projected finish dates and expected critical paths if all known risks are realized. Figure 8.4 gives a sample risk-based network diagram. By proactively preparing such a diagram, the changes in the schedule and the number of extra resources needed to complete the project can be calculated and the impact of the risk themes on the project can be measured.
- Preparing a risk-based work breakdown structure is another way to identify the impact of risk themes on the project. For example, if a risk theme is identified that adds three new tasks to the project plan, the time required for the resources to complete these additional tasks can be identified and its impact on the project parameters can be calculated by preparing a risk-based work breakdown structure.
- Changing regular status meetings to risk assessment meeting and creating an agenda item for the risks in regular status meetings are other methods to evaluate the impact of risk themes on the project.

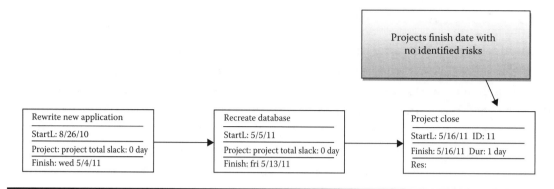

Figure 8.3   Network diagram with no identified risk.

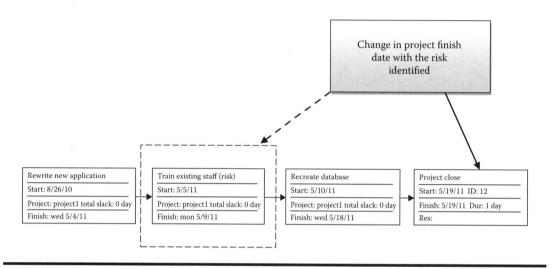

Figure 8.4   Sample risk-based network diagram.

Another key point in finding the impact in risk management is to understand that as your project matures, the potential gains for the project decrease, but the potential losses are significantly higher if the project fails because of negative risks. An easy way to understand this is using the analogy of retirement plan "vesting." Say, the policy of the company is to vest the corporate contribution portion of your retirement plan after 5 years. If you just started with a company, the risk of quitting within the first year is higher (project definition phase), but the amount at risk is low. However, during the fifth year of service (close-out phase), once you are used to the culture, have established credibility, and have formed relationships, the risk of quitting is low but the amount at stake is higher as the corporate has contributed to your retirement plan over 5 years. Another analogy would be: as the plant becomes a solid tree, the risk of losing the tree reduces; however, the potential loss of the time invested in growing the tree and the fruit increases significantly. Thus, risk management needs a proactive approach to find the negative impact (threat) of various risk themes on the project. Figure 8.5 gives the relation between project risks and potential losses in a project as it progresses through the life cycle.

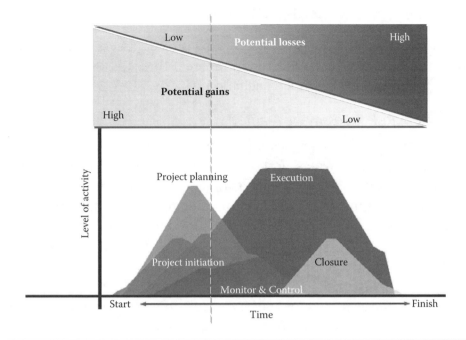

Figure 8.5 **Correlation of project maturity with potential gains and potential losses.**

8.2.2.5 Map the Themes on a Risk Assessment Matrix

This is the final step in risk assessment. The risk assessment team takes all prioritized risk themes (both threats and opportunities) and plots them on the matrix. While plotting the themes on the matrix, the assessment team should ask:

How difficult will it be to resolve the risk if it is realized on the project?

Based on the impact and difficulty of risk resolution, an assessment matrix can be prepared. Depending on the position of the risk theme on the matrix, the team can determine the risk response planning methods. Some of the risk response planning methods are risk absorption, risk acceptance, and risk mitigation.

We will now use a scenario and apply the principles of dynamic risk leadership explained above. The ultimate goal of this task is to prepare a risk assessment matrix and focus on significant risks in the project for risk assessment planning.

8.2.2.6 Scenario

A health department has seven different IT agencies working independently. Although each agency exchanges data between each other, the response time between each department is very slow, causing a lot of inconvenience to its customers. Executives of the department have decided to consolidate all agencies under one name called "Department of Health Information Technology," and agreed to maintain information systems at one location to reduce costs and improve response time. Initial cost estimate of the project is 5 million dollars.

Task

The task of the project leader is to analyze this project, assess threats associated with costs, resources, and schedule, and prepare a threat assessment matrix for this project based on the described scenario.

Step 1: Create a Risk Assessment Team

During Step 1, the project leader establishes a threat assessment team. This includes IT directors, key business owners, and subject matter experts from each agency, sponsor, and proposed core team members of the project. Because this project requires transfer of business knowledge from different agencies, the project includes individuals at all levels as described above to define and establish themes for threats.

Step 2: Establish the Scope of the Threats

Step 2 involves establishing the scope of the threats in the project. Because the team is analyzing only threats related to costs, resources, and schedule, the scope of the risk assessment includes hardware costs, software costs, resource costs, schedule changes, and resource allocations. Table 8.1 gives the scope of the threat assessment.

Step 3: Generate Threat Ideas

In Step 3, the primary focus is to generate ideas about the threats that can increase the cost of the project or increase the schedule time or create resource scarcity. Interviews can be conducted with subject matter experts to determine the

Table 8.1   Scope of the Risk Assessment

Risk Assessment Scope	Scope Description
Threats related to costs	• Scope covers threats related to costs involved in moving existing hardware and purchasing new hardware • Scope covers threats related to software licensing costs and maintenance costs • Scope covers threats related to costs incurred in training for the existing employees and costs associated in hiring experts
Threats related to schedule	• Scope covers threats related to preparing work breakdown structure, employee schedules, and delays in material delivery • Scope covers threats related to schedule due to quality problems, defects and rework
Threats related to resources	• Scope covers threats related to moving existing employees to a new location and recruiting new employees • Scope covers threats related to consultants and their availability • Scope covers conflicts between resources

vulnerabilities to the project. Questions can be asked to identify threats such as

- *What factors can increase the application development costs?*
- *Which of the tasks can take more time than the anticipated?*
- *What are the threats involved in procuring hardware?*

Table 8.2 lists all ideas generated on threats in the health department IT consolidation project.

Step 4: Consolidate Threat Ideas into Themes

In Step 4, all generated ideas for the threats from Table 8.2 can be consolidated into themes. Each idea is analyzed for its quantitative impact on the cost, schedule, resources, and scope. All these impacts are consolidated to form a theme, and each theme gives a forecast of impact in quantitative terms. Table 8.3 gives the themes (threats) developed for the health project.

Step 5: Prioritize Threats Based on the Impact

After preparing the themes, in Step 5, all threats are prioritized based on the impact on the project and the difficulty of resolution if the threat is realized, as shown in Table 8.4. Impact is calculated on a 1 to 10 scale, 1 being the lowest impact. Difficulty of threat resolution is also determined on a 1 to 10 scale, 10 being the high difficulty. Remember that impact is calculated based on the overall objectives of the project.

Table 8.2 Generated Lists of Ideas on Threats

No.	Threat Ideas—Things That Can Potentially Go Wrong
1	Software licensing costs may increase in 2 months
2	The current hardware may be obsolete due to new software
3	Few employees may go on vacation during the project
4	Consultants may not be available until the middle of the project
5	Hardware delivery may be delayed due to production problems
6	Subject matter experts may leave the company
7	New requirements may change the scope
8	New software may not handle huge health data
9	Cash flow in the initial stages may not be consistent
10	Resources may not have required knowledge to execute the project
11	Stakeholders may request new functionality during development
12	Hardware installation may be expensive in new location
13	Management's decisions will be delayed due to changeover
14	Company infrastructure may not handle project change management

Table 8.3   Threat Themes Developed from Ideas

Threat Ideas	Threat Themes	Code
Hardware and software costs (1, 2, 5, and 12)	Hardware and software costs can go up by 30%	T1
Schedule changes or delays (3 and 10)	Application development may be delayed by a month	T2
Expected scope changes (7, 11, and 14)	Scope changes may be increased by 20%	T3
Data transfer delays (8)	Data transfer from current system may be delayed by 2 weeks	T4
Planning or design delays (4 and 6)	Design sessions may be delayed by 2 weeks	T5
Installation delays (9)	Installation may be delayed by 3 weeks due to late payments	T6
Approval and decision delays (13)	Critical decisions will be delayed by 1 week	T7

Table 8.4   Impact and Difficulty of Threat Resolution

Threat	Impact (from 1 = Low to 10 = High)	Difficulty of Threat Resolution (from 1 = Low to 10 = High)
T1	8	7
T2	9	4
T3	3	3
T4	1	2
T5	3	7
T6	2	8
T7	7	2

Step 6: Plot Threat Themes on the Matrix

Each theme (threat) is then plotted on the threat assessment matrix, as shown in Figure 8.6, based on the impact and threat resolution.

8.2.3 Establish a Clear Risk Response Plan

After consolidating threat themes and plotting them on the matrix, a clear response plan is prepared to reduce the impact of negative risks or threats and gain from positive impacts of opportunities. In the scenario described above, different quadrants of threat assessment matrix are described in Table 8.5. The threat assessment team should realize that the threats in the red zone are critical. Because their impact is very high and the difficulty of resolution is also high, the

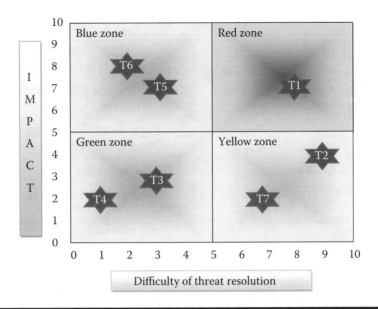

Figure 8.6   Threat assessment matrix for risk themes.

Table 8.5   Quadrants in Threat Assessment Matrix

Quadrant Zone	Threat	Action Required by Project Team
Red Zone	High impact and difficult to resolve	Deflect (avoid) the threat
Blue Zone	High impact and easy to resolve	Mitigate the threat
Yellow Zone	Low impact and difficult to resolve	Transfer the threat
Green Zone	Low impact and easy to resolve	Accept the threat

project team should make plans to avoid threats in the red zone. In this scenario, if an increase in software costs is very high, the project team should look for less expensive software for the development of a new health information system to completely avoid the threat. Threats in the green zone have low impact on the project, and the difficulty of resolution for those threats is also low. Therefore, accepting these threats will not jeopardize the objectives of the project. Accepting the threat means planning ahead to prevent the loss. In the given scenario, increase in scope changes has low impact on the project. Therefore, the project team should plan their budget early in the project to manage those changes. Because threats in the blue zone are easy to resolve, the project team should mitigate those threats and develop strategies to reduce the impact of the threat. Threats in the yellow zone have low impact on the project but the difficulty of resolution is high. As the project team cannot resolve these threats, these types of threats should be transferred. In this scenario, the chance of resolving delays in application development is very low. Hence, the project team should transfer the threat by outsourcing to a third party. Table 8.6 gives the risk response plan for different threats in each quadrant.

Table 8.6   Risk Response Plan for Each Quadrant

Quadrant Zone	Threat Ideas	Risk Response Plan
Red	Software licensing costs may increase in 2 months (T1)	• Negotiate with vendor on fixed price contract • Use another software with smaller licensing fees
Red	Hardware delivery may be delayed due to production problems (T1)	• Request early delivery of hardware • Upgrade existing hardware
Red	The current hardware may be obsolete due to new software (T1)	• Upgrade existing hardware
Red	Hardware installation may be expensive in new location (T1)	• Use existing location for installation
Blue	Consultants may not be available until the middle of the project (T5)	• Prepare project plan based on the availability • Train in-house technical team until consultants arrive at the location
Blue	Subject matter experts may leave the company (T5)	• Develop business continuity plan • Direct resources to learn from experts
Blue	Cash flow in the initial stages may not be consistent (T6)	• Establish reserves to cater the needs in the initial stages
Yellow	Resources may not have required knowledge to execute the project (T2)	• Outsource the project
Yellow	Management's decisions will be delayed due to changeover (T7)	• Create a core committee to make some important decisions during changeover
Yellow	Few employees may go on vacation during the project (T2)	• Employ consultants to perform some job duties
Green	Company infrastructure may not handle project change management (T3)	• Upgrade change management system • Train few team members on the software
Green	New requirements may change the scope (T3)	• Make sure the scope is well defined and all elements are captured in the initiation phase of the project
Green	New software may not handle huge health data (T4)	• Buy additional servers for data storage
Green	Stakeholders may request new functionality during development (T3)	• Establish a clear scope management plan. Assign resources, budget and schedule time to handle such requests

As a general rule, after preparing the risk (threat or opportunity) assessment matrix, the project risk assessment team should prepare a thorough risk response plan by assigning each risk to an individual or group with a clear response method. The team should realize opportunities as soon as possible to increase cost savings, and other risks should be managed efficiently to control the impact of risks on the project. In addition to these methods, dynamic risk leadership should prepare all team members ahead of time for the oncoming risk by conducting a risk response meeting at regular intervals.

8.3 Unknown Risks

Although risk planning is done very carefully, there is always a chance of unknown risks in a project. Project managers often prepare contingency plans or management reserves for unknown risks. However, dynamic project leaders motivate their team to prepare an unknown risk response plan. The unknown risk response plan contains risk response techniques that can be implemented when unknown risk happens. Project thresholds are used to prepare an unknown risk response plan. Because risk priorities are changed throughout the project, all risks and risk response plans should be evaluated frequently to keep the project team prepared on risks.

Thus, a dynamic project leader works with the project team to develop such methods to identify and plan for risks in each phase of the project to detect and prevent threats and realize opportunities as early as possible. The project leader should prepare a threat assessment matrix to reduce the impact of negative risks and an opportunity assessment matrix using the methods described above to gain the positive impact of opportunities. The difference between traditional risk management and dynamic risk leadership is shown in Figure 8.7.

The project leader should prepare a threat assessment matrix to reduce the impact of negative risks and an opportunity assessment matrix to gain the positive impact of opportunities.

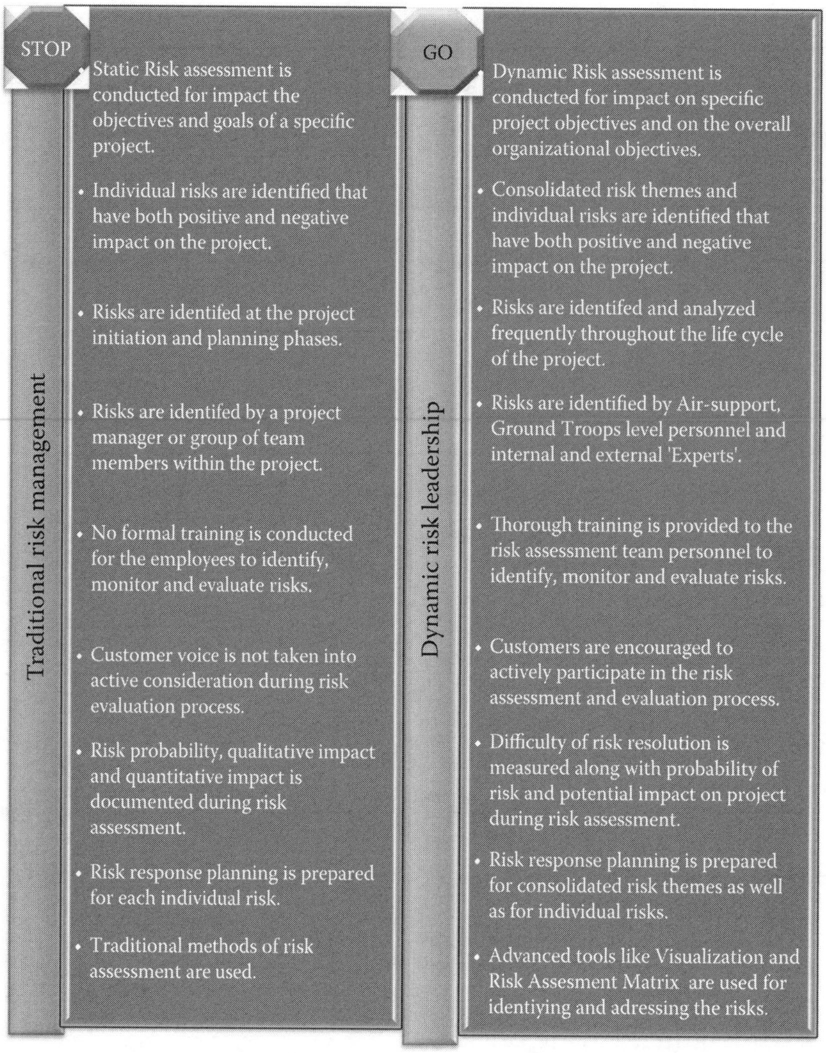

STOP — Traditional risk management

- Static Risk assessment is conducted for impact the objectives and goals of a specific project.

- Individual risks are identified that have both positive and negative impact on the project.

- Risks are identifed at the project initiation and planning phases.

- Risks are identifed by a project manager or group of team members within the project.

- No formal training is conducted for the employees to identify, monitor and evaluate risks.

- Customer voice is not taken into active consideration during risk evaluation process.

- Risk probability, qualitative impact and quantitative impact is documented during risk assessment.

- Risk response planning is prepared for each individual risk.

- Traditional methods of risk assessment are used.

GO — Dynamic risk leadership

- Dynamic Risk assessment is conducted for impact on specific project objectives and on the overall organizational objectives.

- Consolidated risk themes and individual risks are identified that have both positive and negative impact on the project.

- Risks are identifed and analyzed frequently throughout the life cycle of the project.

- Risks are identified by Air-support, Ground Troops level personnel and internal and external 'Experts'.

- Thorough training is provided to the risk assessment team personnel to identify, monitor and evaluate risks.

- Customers are encouraged to actively participate in the risk assessment and evaluation process.

- Difficulty of risk resolution is measured along with probability of risk and potential impact on project during risk assessment.

- Risk response planning is prepared for consolidated risk themes as well as for individual risks.

- Advanced tools like Visualization and Risk Assesment Matrix are used for identiying and adressing the risks.

Figure 8.7 **Difference between traditional risk management and dynamic risk leadership.**

Pillar VIII   Summary

Dynamic risk leadership is the proactive assessment of risks and the development of methods to resolve those risks. This approach focuses on learn-and-apply principles as opposed to the traditional risk assessment approach, which focuses on try-and-die principles. Dynamic risk leadership involves three basic steps: creating a risk assessment team, developing an assessment strategy, and preparing an action plan.

1. Create a risk assessment team
   - Creating a risk assessment team early in the project is essential for dynamic risk assessment. This team comprises of members from "air support" layer and "ground troops" layer, and experts external to the project.
2. Develop an assessment strategy
   - Risk assessment scope is defined based on cost, schedule, resources, contracted product, schedule, and quality.
   - Once the scope is identified, the risk assessment team should brainstorm ideas about threats and opportunities. This is a critical task in the risk assessment process.
   - The next step in the risk assessment process is to consolidate all those ideas into themes targeting resources, costs, or other elements of a project.
   - After preparing the themes, they are prioritized based on the overall impact. The greater the impact of the risk theme, the greater its priority. This phase is also known as "doing the math."
   - Risk assessment team takes all prioritized risk themes (both threats and opportunities) and plots them on the matrix. Based on the impact and difficulty of risk resolution, an assessment matrix can be prepared.
3. Create a risk response plan
   - Different quadrants of the threat assessment matrix are assessed and an action plan is prepared for threats and opportunities. This plan is updated frequently throughout the project.

Figure 8.8 gives the summary of dynamic risk leadership.

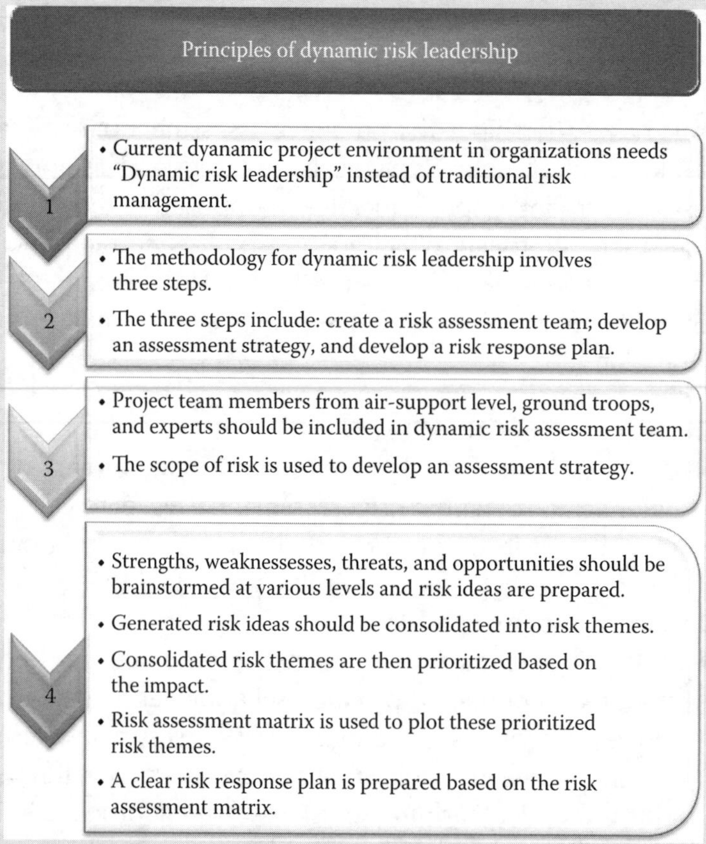

Figure 8.8 Principles of dynamic risk leadership.

Pillar VIII: Case Study 1

With Calculated Risks, Come Great Rewards

A RISK TAKEN BY TEAM DURING A KAIZEN PROJECT

INTRODUCTION

This case study is about risk taken by a team during a Kaizen project.

CHALLENGE

One of the most challenging Kaizen projects I have lead as a consultant was at a company manufacturing products for the housing industry. This was just the second event on their lean journey.

SITUATION

The diverse team consisted of 12 members—some from management, some from facilities, and other supervisors and operators. The leader of the team selected was a 6-ft. 6-in. gentle giant who was the manager of the facilities department. One of the projects identified by the team was to improve ergonomics, increasing the productivity and efficiency of the two machines. To accomplish that, we needed to have an automated packaging system between the two machines. However, this was not possible because the machines were currently facing away from each other, preventing the operator and automated packaging from being positioned between the machines. Thus, the charter of this project was to reposition three significantly large machines (~50 feet each) so we could implement automated packaging solutions during future projects. One of the machines was no longer required and had to be decommissioned. Another machine was to be moved in its place so that the two machines would now face each other and allow one operator to manage the two machines, increasing productivity and efficiency. This would also allow us to plan future ergonomic and automated solutions.

The major problem the team faced was that these were not ordinary machines but had several sections to them which fed about 12 wires—each on 0.5 ton rolls—through a series of spools, dies, and gears to weave, weld, and cut the final product. One of the companies' self-declared "experts" was at odds with the rest of the team. His diagnosis was that the machines should not be moved as it was an impossible undertaking without getting contractors. He estimated that the move and the set-up of the alignment would require special heavy-duty fork-lifts, take at least 1 month, and cost the company well over $300,000. He even got the president of the company involved in an attempt to stop our efforts. The president had just taken over the company. Although she was worried about potential short-term impact on their production, she knew that these moves would help increase productivity and help the division significantly in the long run. Based on the commitment of the team and with assurance from the Kaizen coordinator, she allowed us to go ahead.

SOLUTION

We called our team the "The Dirtiest Dozen" and divided the team into two subteams: team 1—the move team—was going to execute the move and included big, burly facilities personnel and operators, and team 2—the support team—would support them in getting all required equipment like forklifts, etc., clearing the areas, painting the machines, creating ergonomic material kanban, and most importantly, getting food and drinks. Our final charter: move three machines in 3 days. The two machines were needed to be operational and in perfect running condition by Friday for running some special-order products for key customers.

The team leader was risk averse, worried about the entire move, and started negotiating that they would only plan to move two machines. I knew that I had the Kaizen coordinator's support, and I stood my ground to stick to the original scope of moving three machines. I reasoned with him that the risk had to be taken and that I was absolutely positive that they could do it. The coordinator and I had already discussed our back-up plan. If by Wednesday, we had not moved and set up two machines, we would abort the move of the third and most difficult machine. I motivated the team and told them that if they pulled it off, I would make sure that they would be recognized as corporate heroes.

IMPLEMENTATION

On Tuesday morning, the team started moving the first machine and by late afternoon, the first machine was out of there—decommissioned. They started on the second machine move and it was quite complicated. The shop floor had a support beam that was blocking the move and they had to angle the machine section to move it. By Wednesday evening, the second machine was in place, and the start-up of the machine went quite well. It was producing good-quality product. Thus, the third and final move was on, with about 1 day to go. The team took another calculated risk—they knew that the alignment on, this machine had to be dead accurate for it to work correctly. They feared that if they were to separate the three sections, we may have a major task on our hands to align and set up the machines. The team took a calculated risk of moving the ~100-foot machine as one piece, without separating it into sections. We got three heavy-duty forklifts and about 12 wooden dollies with reinforced wheels to slip under the machine. The three forklifts had to be exactly synchronized to be able to lift the three sections simultaneously, and the synchronized forklifts were a great sight to see. When the dollies were placed under—we started hearing crackling sounds—bad news—the wheels were bending and some were even breaking. We now had only six good dollies supporting the machines.

Once we started the move and got the machine into the aisleway, there would be no turning back as it would block the forklift traffic. We had another decision to make—stop the show or press on. The team leader wanted to get my opinion. My question to him was "Does it have any impact on either the safety of the team members or the safety of the machine?" He assured me that it would be safe for the people and machine, but he was not sure of being able to complete the move in time. The Kaizen coordinator and I had seen the team in action and had full confidence in them. We also had some back-up equipment (two heavy-duty forklifts and six dollies) ready to be deployed from another close-by division of the corporation. We got another round of large pizzas for the team, plenty of soda, and made the decision to press on. We knew we had taken another risk but we had a mitigation strategy for the worst case scenario.

The move was very challenging, and we heard many voices from the team—like war cries of Chewbacca from *Star Wars*. After crossing our fingers, toes, and all other crossable parts of our bodies, and after shedding a few gallons of sweat, the machine was finally in place at around 10:45 p.m. on Thursday night. The electric drops and the water circulation were prepped and in place beforehand and everything was hooked up immediately. We had just 1 hour to set up and get the machine running for a customer order for the next day. The pressure was on. Once the machine was in place, the operators started conducting the set-up—stringing wires from 12 huge wire rolls through a series of rollers, dies, welders, and cutters. When the machine was finally ready to run, we all held our breath. As the clinking and clanking started, we saw the finished product coming out. The inspector inspected the product and gave us a thumbs-up sign. A roar of cheer went up—we had done it!!

RESULTS

We had moved three machines in 3 days and the time to set up after the move was a mere 18 minutes (instead of the predicted 1 month for move and set up). We did not use any contractors so the cost was minimal (compared to the $300,000 predicted). The machines had been painted and were looking great and performing great too! All our calculated risks paid off—the leader and the team could not believe they pulled it off—they were exhausted but very ecstatic! The potential productivity gain was approximately 50%.

I now had to stay true to my word of getting the team their very well-deserved recognition. During those 3 days, we had taken some video and pictures to document the move. That night, I took the files and made a small movie "The Dirtiest Dozen" on my laptop, complete with special effects, *Star Wars*–type music and credits, bloopers at the end, etc. We played the movie next day during the report for the executives of the division including the president. The look on the faces of the team members was truly priceless. To accomplish this task against all odds was great, but to have the president and others see them in a movie and cheer-on was something they never dreamed could be possible in their career. The movie was shown at all their divisions and was also aired at their headquarters in Canada for the corporate executives including their new CEO. The team had taken on a very challenging task against many odds and risked their reputation. The success and the kudos they got from this 1 week of effort were very well deserved— they truly were corporate heroes. How many operators and facilities personnel get to experience this during their careers? Not many.

LESSONS LEARNED

With great risks and responsibility, come greater rewards.

Pillar VIII: Case Study 2
A Risk to my Career as a Project Leader

INTRODUCTION

This case study is described here to understand the benefits of taking some personal risks. However, this does not mean taking up an unclear or vague personal risk. Sometimes, project leaders are thrown into such situations to take personal risks that can impact their career. Dynamic project leaders always take calculated personal risk and it is one of their best qualities.

CHALLENGE

I was asked to lead a project in another division of my corporation, to completely transform a medical business making nonintrusive surgical equipment to flow manufacturing.

SITUATION

Before I started this project, the president of the company and I happened to be in the same elevator and he candidly told me "Adil, I know that you have successfully used this technology in another division of our corporation, but my division is very different; our products and problems are much more sophisticated. I am quite sure you will be unsuccessful here." I was shaken by his "optimism in my impending failure." I knew for sure that by undertaking this project, I may be putting my career at risk. But my decision was made. I told him respectfully that I will put in extra effort to customize this technology to his division and ensure that the team is successful.

SOLUTION

With support from my sponsor and after a great deal of negotiations with the CFO, this project was budgeted at $650,000 including training, equipment, consulting, and inventory management software. Knowing the risks involved, I put in additional effort at every step to ensure that we were doing the right things.

IMPLEMENTATION

I even used a simulation modeling to optimize all the implementations on the computer itself so I could identify and eliminate all the bottlenecks virtually. We went through all the phases of the project with surgical precision.

RESULTS

The risk paid off handsomely—the project was not only completed on time but we completed the project at $250,000 ($400,000 below budget) by using many in-house experts to take care of training, and by creating our own inventory management software that dovetailed seamlessly into our AS400 system. The project also contributed significant productivity gains, best-in-class inventory management system, and an inventory reduction of approximately 4 million dollars within a year. The success of this project was even recognized in our corporate magazine and by our CEO and other corporate executives during their rare visit to our site.

LESSONS LEARNED

Thus, I have learned firsthand in my career that great rewards are not possible without taking some great risks.

Pillar VIII   Force Field Analysis

PILLAR VIII: FORCE FIELD ANALYSIS OF ORGANIZATIONAL ASSESSMENT

Table 8.7 shows force field analysis of organizational assessment. The organizational assessment is conducted to assess if the culture of the organization is in alignment with the principles of Pillar VIII. Tables 8.8 through 8.10 are used to develop and implement an action plan to increase the impact of the organizational driving forces and decrease the impact of the organizational resisting forces.

PILLAR VIII: FORCE FIELD ANALYSIS OF SELF-ASSESSMENT

Table 8.11 shows force field analysis of self-assessment. The self-assessment is conducted to assess if your own strengths are in alignment with the principles of Pillar VIII. Tables 8.12 through 8.14 are used to develop and implement an action plan to increase the impact of the self-driving forces and decrease the impact of the self-resisting forces.

PILLAR VIII: RECOMMENDATIONS FOR OPTIMAL RESULTS FROM FORCE FIELD ANALYSIS

For optimal results and actual transformation of culture and strengths conducive to the creation of advanced master project leaders, the following three steps are necessary:

1. Both the organizational and self-evaluation assessments must be completed.
2. A well-designed action plan must be created and implemented to increase the driving forces and decrease the resisting forces.
3. The principles of each pillar must be constantly practiced and improved.

It is highly recommended that both the organization assessments and self-assessments be conducted every year and the action plan be updated at least every 3 months.

Note: The sum of scores for Organizational Driving Force and Organizational Resisting Force for each point must be less than or equal to TEN.

The sum of scores for Self Driving Force and Self Resisting Force for each point must be less than or equal to TEN.

Table 8.7 Pillar VIII: Force Field Organizational Analysis

Team Name: _____   Date: _____

	Does My Organization Drive or Resist a Culture of Dynamic Risk Leadership?			
	0 Never	5 Sometimes		7 Mostly
	3 Rarely	ODF + DRF ≤ 10		10 Always
No.	Driving Forces	Score Organizational Driving Force (ODF)	Score Organizational Resisting Force (ORF)	Resisting Forces
1	My organization understands that risk cannot be managed, it has to be proactively assessed and a plan needs to be created to address and eliminate all major risks.			My organization uses the traditional methods of risk management by trying to gain control of the risks after they occur.
2	The organization culture rewards individuals and teams for preventing problems rather than wait and address them after they occur.			The organization culture rewards individuals and teams for "firefighting" or addressing the problems after they occur.
3	My organization integrates the principles of dynamic risk leadership in all aspects of the business.			My organization does not understand or follow the principles of dynamic risk leadership.
4	When managing risks, our leaders use the proactive learn-and-apply approach to dynamically addressing the risks versus using the try-and-die static approach of trial and error.			When managing risks, our leaders predominantly use the try-and-die approach of managing risks using trial and error.
5	In my organization, project leaders use an ongoing approach to learn from, categorize, strategize, and neutralize various types of risks encountered on projects.			In our organization, project leaders use a static project risk analysis checklist to check-off any risks encountered on a particular project but do not transfer these lessons learned to other projects.

6	My organization uses dynamic risk leadership to develop our future leaders by building their self-confidence from good decisions taken and learn valuable lessons from the poor decisions.			Our organization does not use risk assessment as a tool to develop our future leaders or to build their self-confidence.
7	Our leaders use the power of visualization not only to identify the events or processes that can adversely affect the project but also to identify the events of processes that can add value to the project.			Our leaders focus on traditional methods of risk assessment and do not use the power of visualization or attempt to identify the events of processes that can add value to the project.
8	My organization does not attempt to address each risk individually but focuses on simultaneously addressing several risks items that are combined into themes.			My organization does not create risk-related themes but addresses each risk individually.
9	My organization culture focuses on "doing the math" on the risk themes by prioritizing the risks based on the overall impact.			My organization culture focuses on identifying and attempting to address the impact of each risk.
10	My organization's leaders simplify the task of risk and opportunity assessment for projects by using risk and opportunity assessment matrices.			My organization's leaders use the traditional methods of risk assessment and do not use risk or opportunity assessment matrices.
	Total ODF Score			*Total ORF Score*

Result	Conclusion	Recommended Action Review and Update Every Quarter (3 months)
ODF ≫ ORF	My company culture strongly drives a culture of dynamic risk leadership.	Use Tables 8.8 through 8.10 to set goals and create an action plan to preserve or continuously improve the culture of dynamic risk leadership.
ODF > ORF	My company culture drives the culture of dynamic risk leadership.	Use Tables 8.8 through 8.10 to set goals and create an action plan to increase ODF to create a culture of dynamic risk leadership.
ORF ≫ ODF	My company culture strongly resists the culture of dynamic risk leadership.	Use Tables 8.8 through 8.10 to set goals and create an action plan to increase the ODF and reduce the ORF to create a culture of dynamic risk leadership.
ORF > ODF	My company culture resists the culture of dynamic risk leadership.	Use Tables 8.8 through 8.10 to set goals and create an action plan to reduce the ORF to create a culture of dynamic risk leadership.
ODF = ORF	My company culture does not drive or resist the culture of dynamic risk leadership.	Use Tables 8.8 through 8.10 to set goals and create an action plan to increase the ODF to create a culture of dynamic risk leadership.

Table 8.8 Pillar VIII: Analysis of ODF and ORF Results

Result	Existing Organizational Culture	If the Goal Is to Create a Moderately Strong Culture of Dynamic Risk Leadership	If the Goal Is to Create a Very Strong Culture of Dynamic Risk Leadership
ODF			
ODF ≤ 25	No or minimal culture of dynamic risk leadership	Focus on improving scores in at least 5 DF	Focus on improving scores in at least 7 DF
25 < ODF ≤ 50	Weak culture of dynamic risk leadership	Focus on improving scores in at least 3 DF	Focus on improving scores in at least 5 DF
50 < ODF ≤ 75	Moderate culture of dynamic risk leadership	Focus on improving scores in at least 1 DF	Focus on improving scores in at least 3 DF
ODF > 75	Strong culture of dynamic risk leadership	N/A	Preserve or improve the culture
ORF			
ORF > 75	No or minimal culture of dynamic risk leadership	Focus on decreasing scores in at least 5 RF	Focus on decreasing scores in at least 7 RF
50 < ORF ≤ 75	Weak culture of dynamic risk leadership	Focus on decreasing scores in at least 3 RF	Focus on decreasing scores in at least 5 RF
25 < ORF ≤ 50	Moderate culture of dynamic risk leadership	Focus on decreasing scores in at least 1 RF	Focus on decreasing scores in at least 3 RF
ORF ≤ 25	Strong culture of dynamic risk leadership	N/A	Preserve or improve the culture

Table 8.9 Pillar VIII: Action Plan to Increase Organizational Driving Force (ODF)

Team Name: _____ Date: _____

No.	Driving Force	Current Score	Goal (Target Score) ⬆	Action Plan to Increase DF Score	Complete by (Date)	Assigned to (Department Name or Initials of the Person)
1	My organization understands that risk cannot be managed, it has to be proactively assessed and a plan needs to be created to address and eliminate all major risks.					
2	The organization culture rewards individuals and teams for preventing problems rather than wait and address them after they occur.					
3	My organization integrates the principles of dynamic risk leadership in all aspects of the business.					
4	When managing risks, our leaders use the proactive learn-and-apply approach to dynamically addressing the risks versus using the try-and-die static approach of trial and error.					
5	In my organization, project leaders use an ongoing approach to learn from, categorize, strategize, and neutralize various types of risk encountered in projects.					
6	My organization uses dynamic risk leadership to develop our future leaders by building their self-confidence from good decisions taken and learning valuable lessons from the poor decisions made.					

7	Our leaders use the power of visualization not only to identify the events or processes that can adversely impact the project but also to identify the events of processes that can add value to the project.					
8	Due to limited resources, my organization does not attempt to address each risk individually but focuses on simultaneously addressing several risks items that are combined into themes.					
9	My organization culture focuses on "doing the math" on the risk themes by prioritizing the risks based on the overall impact.					
10	My organization leaders simplify the task of risk and opportunity assessment for projects by using risk and opportunity assessment matrices.					
	Total ODF					

Table 8.10 Pillar VIII: Action Plan to Decrease Organizational Resisting Force (ORF)

No.	Resisting Force	Current Score	Goal (Target Score) ⬇	Action Plan to Decrease RF Score	Complete by (Date)	Assigned to (Department Name or Initials of the Person)
1	My organization uses the traditional methods of risk management by trying to gain control of the risks after they occur.					
2	The organization culture rewards individuals and teams for firefighting or addressing the problems after they occur.					
3	My organization does not understand or follow the principles of dynamic risk leadership.					
4	When managing risks, our leaders predominantly use the try-and-die approach of managing risks using trial and error.					
5	In my organization, project leaders use a static project risk analysis checklist to check-off any risks encountered on a particular project but do not transfer these lessons learned to other projects.					
6	My organization does not use risk assessment as a tool to develop our future leaders or to build their self-confidence.					

7	Our leaders focus on traditional methods of risk assessment and do not use the power of visualization or attempt to identify the events of processes that can add value to the project.					
8	My organization does not create risk-related themes but addresses each risk individually.					
9	My organization culture focuses on identifying and attempting to address each risk individually.					
10	My organization's leaders use traditional methods of risk assessment and do not use risk and opportunity assessment matrices.					
	Total ORF					

Table 8.11 Pillar VIII: Force Field Self Analysis

Name: _____   Date: _____

No.	Driving Forces →	Score Self-Driving Force (SDF)	Score Self-Resisting Force (SRF)	← Resisting Forces
	Does My Behavior Drive or Resist the Principles of Dynamic Risk Leadership?			
	0 Never	5 Sometimes		7 Mostly
	3 Rarely	SDF + SRF ≤ 10		10 Always
1	I fully understand that it is impossible to manage risks and I thus use the approach of preparing in advance for them by proactively assessing, addressing, and eliminating major risks.			I use the principles of project management and attempt to gain control over the risks.
2	I consider myself a leader who uses the principles of dynamic risk leadership to proactively address risks on projects.			I consider myself a manager who needs to fulfill the obligations of risk management plan as required within the project charter and other project documents.
3	I encourage my teams to conduct mental risk drills to identify walk-through and address the risks.			For risk assessment planning, I only expect my teams to ensure that all items mentioned in the checklists are appropriately addressed.
4	I use the proactive learn-and-apply approach to keep learning from a dynamic database of potential risks and apply the lessons learned to address the risks on my current projects.			Because every project is different, I stay focused on the risks of the current projects only and prefer to use the trial-and-error method to managing the identified risks on the current projects.
5	I always spend more time training my teams to proactively identify and prevent the risks using the principles of dynamic risk leadership.			I spend very little time training my teams to plan ahead for risks as my team members are well trained to address any problems that may occur during projects.

6	I encourage a learning environment in my teams by allowing my team members to learn from both the good and bad decisions made on risk assessment on previous projects, thus raising their level of self-confidence.			I focus primarily on addressing risks on the current project and do not usually have time to encourage the team members to learn from their previous decisions.
7	I use the principles of power of visualization as a tool to walk through scenarios that can adversely affect or add value to the project.			I stick to traditional methods of risk assessment and do not attempt to identify the events or processes that can add value to the project.
8	I do not consider myself as an expert in identifying risks and create a risk assessment team to collectively take on the responsibility of identifying the risks and to create a dynamic risk leadership plan.			As a project manager, it is only my responsibility to identify the risks and generate a risk assessment plan to address the identified risks.
9	I encourage my teams to work smarter by arranging similar risks into themes that can be prioritized and addressed as a whole.			I tend to manage each identified risk individually without any prioritization.
10	I use the power of risk assessment matrix as a simple tool to quickly and efficiently categorize the risks based on the potential impact and difficulty of threat resolution.			I only use the traditional methods of risk assessment and do not use a risk assessment matrix.
	Total SDF Score			*Total SRF Score*

Result	Conclusion	Review and Update Every Quarter (3 months)
SDF ≫ SRF	My behavior strongly supports the culture of dynamic risk leadership.	Use Tables 8.12 through 8.14 to set goals and create an action plan to continuously enhance the behavior to create a mind-set of dynamic risk leadership.
SDF > SRF	My behavior supports the culture of dynamic risk leadership.	Use Tables 8.12 through 8.14 to set goals and create an action plan to increase SDF to allow a stronger behavior to create a mindset of dynamic risk leadership.
SRF ≫ SDF	My behavior strongly resists the culture of dynamic risk leadership.	Use Tables 8.12 through 8.14 to set goals and create an action plan to increase SDF and reduce SRF to allow a stronger behavior to create a mindset of dynamic risk leadership.
SRF > SDF	My behavior resists the culture of dynamic risk leadership.	Use Tables 8.12 through 8.14 to set goals and create an action plan to reduce SRF to allow a stronger behavior to create a mindset of dynamic risk leadership.
SDF = SRF	My behavior does not drive or resist the culture of dynamic risk leadership.	Use Tables 8.12 through 8.14 to set goals and create an action plan to increase the SDF to allow a stronger behavior to create a mindset of dynamic risk leadership.

Table 8.12   Pillar VIII: Analysis of SDF and SRF Results

Result	Existing Behavior	If the Goal Is to Create a Moderately Strong Behavior Toward Dynamic Risk Leadership	If the Goal Is to Create a Very Strong Behavior Toward Dynamic Risk Leadership
SDF			
SDF ≤ 25	No or minimal activities in creating a mindset of dynamic risk leadership	Focus on improving scores in at least 5 DF	Focus on improving scores in at least 7 DF
25 < SDF ≤ 50	Weak activities in creating a mindset of dynamic risk leadership	Focus on improving scores in at least 3 DF	Focus on improving scores in at least 5 DF
50 < SDF ≤ 75	Moderate activities in creating a mindset of dynamic risk leadership	Focus on improving scores in at least 1 DF	Focus on improving scores in at least 3 DF
SDF > 75	Strong activities in creating a mindset of dynamic risk leadership	N/A	Preserve or continuously improve the behavior
SRF			
SRF > 75	No or minimal activities in creating a mindset of dynamic risk leadership	Focus on decreasing scores in at least 5 RF	Focus on decreasing scores in at least 7 RF
50 < SRF ≤ 75	Weak activities in creating a mindset of dynamic risk leadership	Focus on decreasing scores in at least 3 RF	Focus on decreasing scores in at least 5 RF
25 < SRF ≤ 50	Moderate activities in creating a mindset of dynamic risk leadership	Focus on decreasing scores in at least 1 RF	Focus on decreasing scores in at least 3 RF
SRF ≤ 25	Strong activities in creating a mindset of dynamic risk leadership	N/A	Preserve or continuously improve the behavior

Table 8.13 Pillar VIII: Action Plan to Increase Self-Driving Force (SDF)

Name: _____   Date: _____

No.	Driving Force	Current Score	Goal (Target Score) ⬆	Action Plan to Increase DF Score	Complete by (Date)	Required Resources
1	I fully understand that it is impossible to manage risks and I thus use the approach of preparing in advance for them by proactively assessing, addressing, and eliminating major risks.					
2	I consider myself a leader who uses the principles of dynamic risk leadership to proactively address risks on projects.					
3	I encourage my teams to conduct mental risk drills to identify walk-through and address the risks.					
4	I use the proactive learn-and-apply approach to keep learning from a dynamic database of potential risks and apply the lessons learned to address the risks on my current projects.					
5	I always spend more time training my teams to proactively identify and prevent the risks using the principles of dynamic risk leadership.					
6	I encourage a learning environment in my teams by allowing my team members to learn from both the good and bad decisions made on risk assessment on previous projects, thus raising their level of self-confidence.					

7	I use the principles of power of visualization as a tool to walk through scenarios that can adversely impact the project or can add value to the project.					
8	I do not consider myself as an expert in identifying risks and create a risk assessment team to collectively take on the responsibility of identifying the risks and to create a dynamic risk assessment plan.					
9	I encourage my teams to work smarter by arranging similar risks into themes that can be prioritized and addressed as a whole.					
10	I use the power of risk assessment matrix as a simple tool to quickly and efficiently categorize the risks based on the potential impact and difficulty of threat resolution.					
	Total SDF					

Table 8.14 Pillar VIII: Action Plan to Decrease Self-Resisting Force (SRF)

Name: _____   Date: _____

No.	Resisting Force	Current Score	Goal (Target Score) ⬇	Action Plan to Decrease RF Score	Complete by (Date)	Required Resources
1	I use the principles of project management and attempt to gain control over the risks.					
2	I consider myself a manager who needs to fulfill the obligations of risk management plan as required within the project charter and other project documents.					
3	For risk assessment planning, I only expect my teams to ensure that all items mentioned in the checklists are appropriately addressed.					
4	Because every project is different, I stay focused on the risks of the current projects only and prefer to use the trial-and-error method to managing the identified risks on the current projects.					
5	I spend very little time training my teams to plan ahead for risks as my team members are well trained to address any problems that may occur during projects.					

6	I focus primarily on addressing risks on the current project and do not usually have time to encourage the team members to learn from their previous decisions.					
7	I stick to traditional methods of risk assessment and do not attempt to identify the events or processes that can add value to the project.					
8	As a project manager, it is only my responsibility to identify the risks and generate a risk assessment plan to address the identified risks.					
9	I tend to manage each identified risk individually without any prioritization.					
10	I only use the traditional methods of risk assessment and do not use a risk assessment matrix.					
	Total SRF					

Pillar VIII Exercises

PILLAR VIII: ORGANIZATIONAL-LEVEL SKILL SET–ENHANCEMENT EXERCISES

GROUP EXERCISES

These exercises are best completed within a group of project managers, project leaders, executives, and stakeholders from within a department or an organization.

1. Using Table 8.15, identify at least five advantages to your organization of using the principles of dynamic risk leadership and creating a culture of proactively addressing risks and rate them from 1 (least important) to 5 (most important) and explain the rating.
2. Using Table 8.16, identify at least five roadblocks within your organization using the principles of dynamic risk leadership and creating a culture of proactively addressing risks and rate them from 1 (least difficult to overcome) to 5 (most difficult to overcome) and explain the rating.
3. Identify a recent complex project completed by one of the experienced project managers in your organization. Get the core team together and ask them to fill out Table 8.17 to address the following:
a. Document five major risks identified during the risk assessment phase, which came to pass on the project
b. Explain in detail how the risks were addressed (avoidance, acceptance, mitigation, deflection, or absorption)
c. Discuss if a better strategy can be developed to proactively address these using the learn-and-apply approach?

Table 8.15   Pillar VIII: Five Advantages of Applying the Principles of Pillar VIII to Your Organization

No.	Advantages of Applying Principles of Pillar VIII to Enhancing Your Organization Culture	Rating (from 1 = Least Important to 5 = Most Important)	Explain the Rating
1			
2			
3			
4			
5			

Table 8.16   Pillar VIII: Five Roadblocks to Applying the Principles of Pillar VIII to Your Organization

No.	Roadblocks to Applying Principles of Lean Thinking Described in Pillar VIII to Your Organization	Rating (from 1 = Least Difficult to Overcome to 5 = Most Difficult to Overcome)	Explain the Rating
1			
2			
3			
4			
5			

Table 8.17   Pillar VIII: Identification and Mitigation of Risks Based on the Principles of Pillar VIII

No.	Five Major Risks Identified during Risk Assessment Phase, which Came to Pass On the Project	Explain in Detail How the Risks Were Addressed (Avoidance, Acceptance, Mitigation, Deflection, or Absorption)	How Would You Develop A Strategy to Proactively Address These Using the Learn-and-Apply Approach?
1			
2			
3			
4			
5			

4. Identify an upcoming future complex project within your organization where a traditional risk assessment approach is to be used. Have a team external to the project use the principles of dynamic project leadership detailed in Pillar VIII. Using Table 8.18, create a detailed dynamic risk assessment plan to identify risks, prioritize the risks based on the probability and impact, prepare the risk assessment matrix, and a risk response plan using the following three steps:
   1. Creating a risk assessment team
   2. Developing an assessment strategy
   3. Preparing an action plan.

   Compare the results of this plan to that created by the project team. What are the advantages of the dynamic assessment plan versus the traditional risk assessment plan?

5. Scenario analysis: NORTHERN AIRWAYS (NA) is a major airline that is growing tremendously in the western domestic market, especially in travel within adjoining states. They are considering the option to acquire WESTERN JETWAYS (WJ), a small regional airlines with a fleet of about 150 small jets, namely, DC-9–21/41/51 series planes with a seating capacity ranging from 70 to 122 passengers. It is estimated to cost NA close to $1.5 billion to acquire WJ and another $0.5 billion to integrate both the operations.

   DUE DILIGENCE SOLUTIONS (DDS), is a consulting company hired by NA to conduct due diligence and recommend the risks and threats in going ahead with the acquisition project:

Table 8.18 Pillar VIII: Prepare the Risk Assessment Matrix and Risk Assessment Plan

Create a Risk Assessment Plan	

The general threats to cost, scope, and resources identified by DDS is shown in Table 8.19A. Create a group of experts within your organization and imagine that you work for DDS. You are assigned the following responsibilities:

a. Using Table 8.19B, create a list of potential risks to NA for acquiring WJ.
b. Using Table 8.20, group the potential risks together to create a theme and assign a threat code (T1, 2, 3 ...) to each theme.
c. Using Table 8.21, for each theme/threat code, assign a rating to the impact of each theme from 1 (low) to 10 (high) and for difficulty of threat resolution from 1 (low) to 10 (high).
d. Using the guidelines provided in Table 8.22, create a response plan for each identified threat code and detail in Table 8.23.

What recommendations will you make to the board of directors of NA regarding the acquisition of WJ?

Table 8.19A   Pillar VIII: Scenario Analysis—General Threats Identified by DDS

Risk Assessment Scope	Scope Description
Threats related to costs	• WJ has not been profitable during the last three quarters • WJ has a debt of about $50 million • The existing employees of WJ have a union that is requesting a payout of benefits, etc., to each union member, which will cost NA close to $5 million
Threats related to schedule	• NA wants to complete the deal within the next 3 months to ensure that they are ready to account for passenger rush during the peak holiday season • WJ has recently had two regional jets make emergency landings due to engine problems causing an investigation by the Federal Aviation Administration. The acquisition cannot be finalized until WJ is cleared of any blame in the two incidents. It usually takes about 1 to 6 months for similar investigations to be complete
Threats related to resources	• The pilots of WJ are very inexperienced and will require considerable training to be on par with NA's pilot policies • The relationship between WJ executives and staff is very acrimonious and can delay the acquisition process • At least 40% of WJ's fleet of 150 jets are about 2 years from being retired

Table 8.19B   Pillar VIII: Scenario Analysis—Risk Identification

No.	Potential Risks to NA to Acquiring WJ
1	
2	
3	
4	
5	
6	
7	
8	
9	
10	
11	
12	

Table 8.20   Pillar VIII: Scenario Analysis—Themes Based on Identified Risks

Potential Risks	Theme	Code

PILLAR VI: PERSONAL-LEVEL SKILL SET– ENHANCEMENT EXERCISES

INDIVIDUAL EXERCISES

These exercises are to be completed individually after reviewing Pillar VIII in detail.

1. Using Table 8.24, list at least five advantages of applying the principles of dynamic project leadership of Pillar VIII, detailing the principles of dynamic risk leadership to your future projects. Rate the advantages from 1 (least important) to 5 (most important) and explain the rating.

Table 8.21   Pillar VIII: Impact and Difficulty of Resolution of Threats

Threat Code	Impact (from 1 = Low to 10 = High)	Difficulty of Threat Resolution (from 1 = Low to 10 = High)

Table 8.22   Pillar VIII: Quadrants in Threat Assessment Matrix

Quadrant Zone	Threat	Action Required by Project Team
Red zone	High impact and difficult to resolve	Deflect (avoid) the threat
Blue zone	High impact and easy to resolve	Mitigate the threat
Yellow zone	Low impact and difficult to resolve	Transfer the threat
Green zone	Low impact and easy to resolve	Accept the threat

2. Using Table 8.25, identify at least five roadblocks to applying the principles of dynamic project leadership of Pillar VIII on all your future major projects. Rate the identified roadblocks from 1 (least difficult to overcome) to 5 (most difficult to overcome) and explain the rating.

3. Using Table 8.26, select a project you worked on as a project manager/leader that failed or was affected because of risk that was not identified or because of an inadequate plan to address it. Looking back on the project, answer the following questions:
   a. For each phase of the project, list at least one risk that was not identified or an adequate plan was not developed to address it.
   b. Which principles or techniques from Pillar VIII would have helped identify the risks better or create a better plan for addressing the risks.

4. Using Table 8.27, select a future project you have been assigned to. Answer the following questions:
   a. Identify three principles or techniques that you will use from Pillar VIII to better identify the risks.

Table 8.23   Pillar VIII: Risk Response Plan for Each Quadrant

Quadrant/Zone	Potential Threats	Risk Response Plan
Red		
Red		
Red		
Red		
Blue		
Blue		
Blue		
Yellow		
Yellow		
Yellow		
Green		
Green		
Green		
Green		

Table 8.24   Pillar VIII: Five Advantages of Applying Principles of Pillar VIII to Your Career

No.	Advantages of Applying Principles of Dynamic Risk Leadership from Pillar VIII to All Future Projects	Rating (from 1 = Least Important to 5 = Most Important)	Explain the Rating
1			
2			
3			
4			
5			

Table 8.25   Pillar VIII: Five Roadblocks to Applying Principles of Pillar VIII

No.	Roadblocks to Applying Principles of Dynamic Risk Leadership from Pillar VIII to All Future Projects	Rating (from 1 = Least Difficult to Overcome to 5 = Most Difficult to Overcome)	Explain the Rating
1			
2			
3			
4			
5			

Table 8.26   Pillar VIII: Reflecting a Failed Project and Identifying Principles of Pillar VIII

Name of Failed Project		
Your Role in the Project		
Phase	List at Least One Risk That Was Not Identified or an Adequate Plan That Was Not Developed to Address It	Identify Principles or Techniques from Pillar VIII That Would Have Helped Identify the Risks Better or Create a Better Plan for Addressing the Risks
1. Project start-up		
2. Project preparation		
3. Project implementation		
4. Project monitoring		
5. Project closure		

Table 8.27   Pillar VIII: Reflecting on a Future Project and Identifying Principles of Pillar VIII

Name of Future Project		
Your Role in the Project		
No.	Identify Three Principles or Techniques Utilized from Pillar VIII to Better Identify the Risks	Describe Three Principles or Techniques Utilized from Pillar VIII to Better Plan for the Identified Risks
1.		
2.		
3.		

Table 8.28   Pillar VIII: Scenario Analysis—General Threats Identified by WJ's Project Leader

Risk Assessment Scope	Scope Description
Threats related to costs	• NA have been known to play hardball and short change smaller player (WJ) in acquisitions • NA usually will not take over the debt on the acquired company or deduct the debt from the total acquisition costs • WJ has a staff of three full-time senior employees dedicated to support the representatives from DDS and NA who are conducting due diligence at the WJ site. This is costing a considerable amount of time and money for WJ
Threats related to schedule	• The union contract is up for renegotiations and if the acquisition is not finalized in the next 2 months, it can cost WJ over 2 million dollars in additional salary and benefit increases as per default terms in the contract • NA is spending excessive time in due diligence at the WJ site and it is impacting daily operations
Threats related to resources	• The presence of NA and DDS representatives at the WJ site is causing considerable anxiety regarding job security and layoffs among WJ employees • Per WJ policies, the union has to sign off on all of WJ's union buyout terms before NA finalizes the acquisition. NA has a nonunion environment and has no experience negotiating with or dealing with union employees • NA's culture is very different from that of WJ. NA tends to have a limited staff and work them much harder. There is a major fear of layoffs at WJ if the acquisition is finalized

    b. Describe three principles or techniques that you will use from Pillar VIII to better plan for the identified risks.

5. Scenario analysis: WESTERN JETWAYS (WJ), a small regional airlines with a fleet of about 150 small jets, that is, DC-9–21/41/51 series planes with a seating capacity ranging from 70 to 122 passengers. NORTHERN AIRWAYS (NA) is a major airline that is growing tremendously in the western domestic market, especially in travel within adjoining states. There is another major carrier that, during some brief conversations with the WJ executives, has also indicated a verbal interest in acquiring WJ. WJ executives are expecting to get at least $2.5 billion for the merger with either major airline carrier. Because NA has shown significant interest in moving ahead with the acquisition, WJ has appointed an internal project leader who has some experience with acquisition projects. Imagine you are the project leader appointed by the executives of WJ to conduct due diligence and recommend the risks and threats in going ahead with the acquisition project:

The general threats to cost, scope, and resources identified by the executives of WJ are shown in Table 8.28. You are assigned the following responsibilities:

    a. Using Table 8.29, create a list of potential risks to WJ for being acquired by NA.

    b. Using Table 8.30, group the potential risks together to create a theme and assign a threat code (T1, 2, 3 …) to each theme.

    c. Using Table 8.31, for each theme/threat code, assign a rating to the impact of each theme from 1 (low) to 10 (high) and for difficulty of threat resolution from 1 (low) to 10 (high).

Table 8.29　Pillar VIII: Scenario Analysis—Risk Identification

No.	Potential Risks to NA in Acquiring WJ
1	
2	
3	
4	
5	
6	
7	
8	
9	
10	
11	
12	

Table 8.30   Pillar VIII: Scenario Analysis—Themes Based on Identified Risks

Potential Risks	Theme	Code

Table 8.31   Pillar VIII: Impact and Difficulty of Resolution of Threats

Threat Code	Impact (from 1 = Low to 10 = High)	Difficulty of Threat Resolution (from 1 = Low to 10 = High)

Table 8.32   Pillar VIII: Threat Assessment Matrix

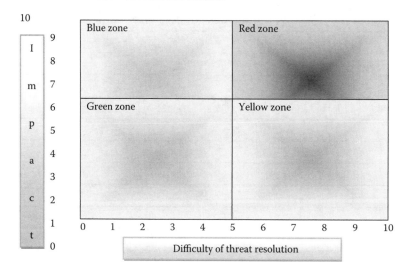

Table 8.33 Pillar VIII: Quadrants in Threat Assessment Matrix

Quadrant Zone	Threat	Action Required by Project Team
Red	High impact and difficult to resolve	Deflect (avoid) the threat
Blue	High impact and easy to resolve	Mitigate the threat
Yellow	Low impact and difficult to resolve	Transfer the threat
Green	Low impact and easy to resolve	Accept the threat

Table 8.34 Pillar VIII: Risk Response Plan for Each Quadrant

Quadrant/Zone	Potential Threats	Risk Response Plan
Red		
Red		
Red		
Red		
Blue		
Blue		
Blue		
Yellow		
Yellow		
Yellow		
Green		
Green		
Green		
Green		

d. Using Table 8.32, identify the quadrant for each of the identified threats within the threat assessment matrix based on the impact and difficulty of threat resolution.

e. Using the guidelines provided in Table 8.33, create a response plan for each identified threat code and detail in Table 8.34.

What recommendations will you make to the executives of WJ regarding being acquired by NA?

Pillar VIII   References

1. Einstein, Albert, 1879–1955. *Quotationsbook.com*, http://quotationsbook.com/quote/21311/ (accessed on November 10, 2010).
2. FMEA-FMECA.com. (2010). *FMEA and FMECA Information*, http://www.fmea-fmeca.com/index.html (accessed November 11, 2010).
3. Isograph Ltd. (2010). http://www.faulttree.org/ (accessed November 10, 2010).
4. Federal Aviation Administration. (2006). http://www.faa.gov/about/office_org/headquarters_offices/ast/media/ast_guide_to_software_safety_final_070706.pdf (accessed November 10, 2010).

Chapter 9

Pillar IX: Decode and Shield Your Data

> "Know where to find information, and how to use it. That is the secret of success."[1]
>
> "Information is not knowledge."[2]
>
> **Albert Einstein**

9.1 Introduction

Although this Pillar does not directly deal with project leadership, not following the guidelines presented in this Pillar can end the career of a project leader.

9.1.1 What Is Information?

In general, information is raw data that (1) has been verified to be accurate and timely, (2) is specific and organized for a purpose, (3) is presented within a context that gives it meaning and relevance, and (4) leads to an increase in understanding and a decrease in uncertainty.[3] Thus, information is any acquired or supplied knowledge that can be used to make a difference.

9.1.2 What Is Data?

Data is any information in its entirety, part, or as a part of the whole that may assist us in making decisions on taking the next steps.

Data is any information in raw or unorganized form (such as alphabets, numbers, or symbols) that refers to, or represents, conditions, ideas, or objects. Data is limitless and present everywhere in the universe.[4]

In other words, data is any information in its entirety, part, or as a part of the whole that may assist us in making decisions on taking the next steps. The decision may be to continue on the same path, to take an alternate path, to stop and proceed with caution, to end the journey, or any other alternatives. Thus, to make correct decisions, it is critical to have accurate information and data. General Colin Powell says, "Experts often possess more data than judgment."[4]

Data can be used as information only when it is applicable to the topic of interest.

9.1.3 Why Is Timely Availability of Data Critical?

Imagine that you are travelling to New York City with your family for the very first time. You are planning a week-long vacation of sightseeing, meeting friends, and making stops at various tourist attractions. You have confidently left home with your newly purchased GPS car navigation unit and you are completely relying on the GPS to help you plan and execute your trip. As you reach New York, you notice that the GPS is showing you incorrect directions. Shortly, you notice that the GPS does not show any data at all as it cannot find the satellites. The result is that your family vacation is spoiled and your family is very upset. You could have taken some hard copies for directions to continue your trip. However, your planning would not have been as easy as with GPS as you could not make quick decisions in case the plan suddenly changes. Thus, the mapping data was critical to the success of your family vacation. This simple example shows you how important data is in daily life. Project data is no different from GPS data. In projects, the importance of having the correct and timely data is imperative to its success. Presenting incorrect data or loss of critical data will not only delay the project but also terminate the project without a result. The failure of a project can have a major negative impact on the career of a project leader. Hence, data security, storage, access, and distribution are very important for the success of a project and for the sustainment of successful project leaders. Thus, this pillar supports project leaders by keeping the project on track on the path to ultimate success.

9.2 Data Availability through the Ages

Since the Stone Ages and through the agriculture age, very limited data was available to human beings. Also, there were no robust data storage or distribution systems during those ages. Data was transferred from generation to generation by memory or sometimes by the use of signs or symbols. But the storage and distribution of data began when human beings started writing and recording information. Mass data distribution began in the Industrial Age with the advent of TV and motion pictures, and data was in abundance in the Information Age because of the advent of the computer, the Internet, and the World Wide Web. Today, we are in the Information Overload Age or the Too Much Information Age. Figure 9.1 shows various aspects of data distribution technology, means of communication, speed, distribution group size, purpose, employee requirements, and data storage type over the various ages.[5]

9.2.1 Age of Information Overload or Age of Too Much Information

What is considered too much information or information overload? After a rigorous study, Bohn and Short concluded that Americans consumed 3.6 zettabytes in 2008. A zettabyte is equivalent to 1,000,000,000,000,000,000,000 bytes (21 zeroes), equating to approximately 10,845 trillion words. This translates into each American consuming approximately 34 gigabytes (approximately one-fifth of the storage in a standard laptop) per day. Also, according to Kathleen Parker, of the *Washington Post*, the total amount of data produced in 2006 was 3 million times more than the information contained in all the books ever written.[6]

Time Period	~Before 9000 B.C. Stone Age	~After 9000 B.C. Agricultural Age	~After 1800 A.D. Industrial Age	~After 1950 Information Age	~After 1990 Information Overload Age (TMI)
Available Technology	Sharp Rocks Sharp Objects Bones	Sharp Objects Writing stylus, made of metal, bone or ivory, to place	Typewriters Telegraph Telephone Paper made from vegetable fiber Lithography Personal Cameras Phonographic Disks Radio Signal	Computers Color TV, Color motion pictures Cell phones/ pagers Fax machines Microchips Camcorders, Point & shoot cameras CD ROMs Internet - Dial-up, Cable World Wide Web Holograms Fiber optics Microwaves	Smart Phones, Blackberry Laptops, Tablets 3D Movies, Cable TV 3G, 4G Technology Blue-ray, DVD Blue-Tooth Social Media E-Readers Ipod's, Ipad's Virtual Reality/Games Reality TV
Means of Communications	Oral Histories Storytelling Picto grams Petroglyphs (Images incised in Stones) Pictograph (Paining/Drawing on rocks) Cave Paintings Geoglyphs (drawings on ground)	Oral histories Fables Agricultural Record Tokens Scribes Seals Tablets	Television Motion Pictures Circulating Libraries Postal Services Phonographs Transc ontinental Telephone calls Wireless radio	Libraries Courier Mail E-mail Cell Phones Color Motion, TV CD's, Video Cassettes Holographic images	IM, Chat, Blog, Text, Twitter E-mail, Voice Mail E-books 3D Movies LinkedIn, FaceBook, My Space Video games, Virtual Games Reality TV
Speed of Communication	Very Slow	Very Slow	Slow-Fast	Fast	Instant
Approximate Distribution Size	2–30 people	2–50 people	Mass Distribution (Thousands)	Mass Distribution (Millions)	Global Distribution (Billions)
Purpose of Communication	Hunting, food related	Crop related records, Weather	Weather, Commerce, Politics, Sports, Entertainment	Weather, Commerce, Politics, Sports, Entertainment, World affairs	Everything under the sun including personal/private information
Empoyee Requirements	N/A	N/A	Low Discretion, Judgement requirements Little or no decision-making Simple tasks	High Discretion, Judgement requirements Considerable decision-making Compl ex tasks	Technology Savy, Superior discretion, Judgement Super-fast Decision making abilities Very Complex Tasks and Projects
Data Storage Type	Picto grams	Clay Tablets	Printed Paper	Optical Disks - Floppy, CD ROM, Databases, Servers	Microchips, HD's, CD's, DVD's, Blue-Ray, Thumb Drives, Databases, Servers

Figure 9.1 Technology and communication changes over ages. (Adapted from Jim Kinnie, *What is information,* **University of Rhode Island, 1994. http://www.uri.edu/library/staff_pages/kinnie/lib120/info.html#overload.)**

9.3 Dynamic Data Management Plan

The pendulum has had an extremely wide swing within the last 200 years, and we have gone from minimal data during the Industrial Age to an overkill of data in the "Age of information overload". So, what can we do when we have an overabundance of something and getting the right data is more like looking for a needle in the haystack?

Within the last 200 years, and we have gone from minimal data during the Industrial Age to an overkill of data in the "Age of information overload".

To utilize the best and most useful data in our projects, we need to understand the mechanics of data requirement and data usage, the data sources, the methods of data collection, the process of eliminating unnecessary data, and the science of data storage, security, retrieval, and change management. We also need to address the challenges of emerging technologies like "cloud computing" and also understand that the modes of communication and data collection have had extreme shifts in the last few decades. Today, we communicate via chat, text messages, Twitter, LinkedIn, Facebook, and several other channels of uncontrolled communications. How can we capture the information? How do we secure the information and ensure data sanctity? Thus, a normal data management plan does not work. We need to create a dynamic management plan that addresses the challenges posed by emerging technologies and an overabundance of means of communications.

9.4 Steps to Designing a Dynamic Data Management Plan

The following steps are critical to creating a dynamic data management plan:

  a. Analysis of project data requirements
  b. Selection of appropriate data types and data sources
  c. Appropriate data storage, security, retrieval, and distribution
  d. Data monitoring and change management.

As discussed previously, we are currently in an information overload age. There is a plethora of data everywhere. If we do not have a means to manage these data, separate the critical pieces from spam or just reference data, backup critical data regularly, and provide adequate access to authorized personnel, we are setting ourselves up for failure.

Thus, it is important to ask the following three questions:

  1. *How much data will my project require?*
  2. *What are the types of data available?*
  3. *Which type of data is most critical to make my project successful?*

These are important questions to ask ourselves in every project. However, the answers to these questions are not as straightforward as you would like them to be and thus *dynamic data selection* is a critical consideration in any project.

Let us use the power of visualization to understand how the dynamic data selection process can help the project leaders determine the appropriate types of data critical to achieving project goals.

Find a comfortable place where you can relax without being disturbed for the next 30 minutes. Close your eyes, or keep them open, as you wish. Now, visualize the following two scenarios:

Scenario 1: Visualize that you are a heavyweight bodybuilder weighing approximately 210 lbs. Visualize your rippling muscles and your massive biceps, arms, and legs. Visualize yourself as one of the athletes at a bodybuilding competition 1 day away from the event and sitting around a gigantic table of almost every kind of food available—meat, fish, dairy products, fruit, vegetables, bread, cereals, potatoes, nuts, pulses, and so forth. Every food type you can imagine as edible is available to you. Now, visualize your coach telling you that *"your nutrition is the key to your mental and physical success"* and that the basic formula is that you must have a balanced diet of proteins (15%), carbohydrates (55%), and fat (30%). The carbohydrates will provide energy, proteins will help repair the tissues, and the fats are a source of energy and protect vital organs. The coach has also cautioned you against eating foods made up of saturated fats (some oils like coconut and palm oil) and trans fats (vegetable shortening and margarine) as they are most unhealthy.

You are serious about winning the top prize, so you need to make sure that you should choose the right ingredients at the right quantities and decide how frequently you should eat. You have 5 minutes to visualize yourself and plan your menu so that you have the right nutrition to win the competition.

Now, visualize another scenario.

Scenario 2: Visualize that you are a 120-lb. jockey getting ready for the Kentucky Derby. Visualize your lean, small, and aerodynamic body. Visualize yourself as one of the jockeys at the Derby, 1 day away from the big race, sitting around a gigantic table of almost every kind of food available—meat, fish, dairy products, fruit, vegetables, bread, cereals, potatoes, nuts, pulses, and so forth. Every food type you can imagine as edible is available to you. Now, visualize your coach telling you that *"your nutrition is the key to your mental and physical success"* and that the basic formula is that you must have a balanced diet of proteins (15%), carbohydrates (55%), and fat (30%). The carbohydrates will provide energy, proteins will help repair the tissues, and the fats are source of energy and protect vital organs. The coach has also cautioned you against eating saturated fats (some oils like coconut and palm oil) and trans fats (vegetable shortening and margarine) as they are most unhealthy.

You are serious about winning the top prize, so you need to make sure that you plan what you are going to eat, in what quantity, and how frequently. You have 5 minutes to visualize yourself and plan your menu so that you have the right nutrition to win the competition.

Now, let us discuss your visualization experience in both scenarios. In both scenarios, what food did you visualize yourself eating? Was it the same food? Was it in the same quantity? Did you balance out the proportions of proteins, carbohydrates, and fat?

In scenario 1, for the 210-lb. bodybuilder, 456 g of carbohydrates, 252 g of protein, and 35 g of fat are required.[7] This diet provides enough energy to build muscles and perform daily activities for bodybuilders. Figure 9.2 gives balanced daily intake of meat, fish, milk, eggs, beans, lentils (proteins), or potatoes, rice, pasta, some fruits and vegetables, cakes (carbohydrates), and butter and oils (fats) for a bodybuilder. By calculating the percentage for each ingredient, it comes to 61% for carbohydrates, 34% for protein, and 5% for fat.

In scenario 2, for the 120-lb. jockey, 261 g of carbohydrates, 144 g of protein, and 20 g of fat are required. This diet provides enough nutrition to give him energy and stay lean and fit to compete in races. Figure 9.3 gives a balanced daily intake of meat, fish, milk, eggs, beans, lentils (proteins), or potatoes, rice, pasta, some fruits and vegetables, cakes (carbohydrates), and butter and oils (fats) for a jockey. By calculating the percentage for each ingredient, it comes to 61% for carbohydrates, 34% for protein, and 5% for fat.

Thus, it is apparent from this visualization exercise that to have a balanced diet and be successful as a bodybuilder or as a jockey, you require all the above foods, but depending on what you are trying to achieve, the quantity may differ, as shown in Figure 9.4. The visualization also shows that the source and type of data can also vary significantly from project to project. This visualization has allowed us to understand the first two critical points in creating a dynamic data

Bodybuider's (210 lbs.) nutrition plan

Body weight	210 Ibs
Protein	252
Carbohydrates	456
Fat	35

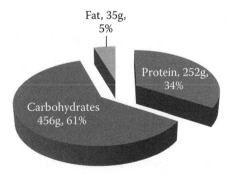

Figure 9.2   Nutrition plan for a body builder. (Adapted from Robert Thoburn, *The Body Builders Eating Plan,* 2010. http://www.nutritionexpress.com.)

Jockey's (120 lbs.) nutrition plan

Body weight	120 lbs
Protein	144
Carbohydrates	261
Fat	20

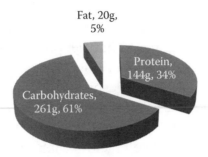

Figure 9.3   Nutrition plan for a jockey.

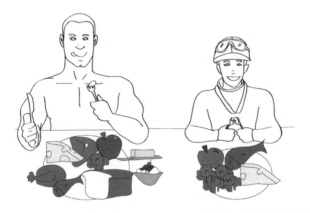

Figure 9.4   A balanced diet for different body types of a bodybuilder and a jockey.

management plan, namely, identifying the data requirements, type, and source of the required data.

9.4.1 Analysis of Project Data Requirements

Project data is no different from a nutrition plan; you need a timely, balanced data of the appropriate type to make your project successful while avoiding the wrong kind of data.

Project data is no different from a nutrition plan; you need a timely, balanced data of the appropriate type to make your project successful while avoiding the wrong kind of data. Also, it is to be understood that even if the bodybuilder eats some "junk" food, the impact on his performance may be minimal or none, whereas to the jockey, any "junk" food may result in a significant effect on the performance and may even result in his/her losing the race.

The estimation of how much data is the right amount is very challenging, and there is no science or formula to determine it. Advanced project leaders use their vast experience on projects to estimate these based on the following:

1. Duration of project—long, medium, or short
2. Type of project—complex or simple
3. Criticality to business—extremely critical, critical, not critical.

Thus, the first step in the process of analyzing the data requirements is to understand the data. Is the project long term or short term, simple or complex, or critical or noncritical? If the project is short term, simple, and noncritical, the data required may not be excessive. However, if the project is long term, complex, and very critical, it requires more data and it will be important to focus on the critical aspects of the value-added data and minimize the non-value-added or "junk" data.

9.4.2 Selection of Appropriate Data Type and Sources

It is clear from the visualization exercise that nutrition from various sources is critical for the success of both the bodybuilder and the jockey. Similarly, success in a project of any duration, complexity, and level of criticality depends on the appropriate quantity and type of data from reliable sources.

It is very critical for project leaders to identify and bucket the data in the appropriate categories. Thus, similar to nutritional diversity and required balance, project data types can be seen in Figure 9.5 and are categorized as follows.

9.4.2.1 Value-Added Data

Value-added data is the information that is required for the project and has an ability to affect a behavior, decision, or outcome within the project.

> Value-added data can include
>
> a. Critical project data
> b. Historical data
> c. Artifacts (electronic records/templates)
> d. Metadata (unique identifier for any artifact).

9.4.2.1.1 Importance of Value-Added Data to Projects

Critical data is very essential, just like "proteins" that are needed for a bodybuilder to build muscle tissue. This data is needed to maintain the project and to make important decisions during the project. Historical data is similar to

DATA ANALYSIS — TYPE, ELEMENTS, NUTRITION ANALOGY, RECOMMENDATION AND SOURCES

#	DATA TYPE	DATA ELEMENTS	ANALOGOUS TO FOOD TYPE	RECOMMENDATION ON DATA QUANTITY	DATA SOURCES
1	Value Added	a. Critical project data b. Historical data c. Artifacts (electronic records/templates) d. Metadata (unique identifier for any artifact)	PROTEINS FAT CARBOHYDRATES CARBOHYDRATES	As much as Needed In Moderation As Required As Required	Organization documents, historical databases, templates, metadata files, customers, consultants, suppliers, project documents—charter etc., experts, tribal knowledge, credible websites, books, articles.
2	Necessary Non-Value Added	a. Corporate policies and procedures b. Regulatory or industry related data c. Factual or Referenced data, and d. Analytical or Inferred Data (Subjective or Objective)	CARBOHYDRATES CARBOHYDRATES CARBOHYDRATES CARBOHYDRATES	As Required As Required As Required As Required	Corporate documents, mission statements, policies, procedures, task instructions, industry standards, regulatory agency documents, websites, books, articles, experts, customers, consultants, suppliers, project documents, risk analysis, quality plans.
3	Non-Value Added	a. False, Incorrect or Misleading information b. Irrelevant information	SAT OR TRANS FAT SAT OR TRANS FAT	Avoid Avoid	Sources which are not credible like personal blogs, open sources like Wikipedia, books, articles by unknown authors, inexperienced personnel.

Figure 9.5 Categories of project data.

"fat" in the nutrition plan. Although this data is required for carrying out the project, too much of it spoils the project. Artifacts and metadata, like "carbohydrates," can be helpful in providing energy to make the project more efficient.

9.4.2.1.2 Sources of Value-Added Data

Organization documents, historical databases, templates, metadata files, customers, consultants, suppliers, project documents (charter, etc.), experts, tribal knowledge, credible Web sites, books, and articles.

9.4.2.2 Necessary Non-Value-Added Data

Some non-value-added activities in a project are necessary and cannot be avoided. Necessary non-value-added data is information required to affect a behavior, decision, or outcome within the project related to that necessary non-value-added activity.

Non-value-added data can include

    a. Corporate policies and procedures
    b. Regulatory or industry-related data
    c. Factual or referenced data
    d. Analytical or inferred data (subjective or objective).

9.4.2.2.1 Importance of Eliminating Non-Value-Added Data from Projects

Corporate policies, regulatory data, industry data, referenced data, and inferred data are like "carbohydrates" in the nutrition plan. Just like carbohydrates give instant energy, this data is essential for proper functioning and completion of the project but may not add value to the project.

9.4.2.2.2 Sources of Necessary Non-Value-Added Data

Corporate documents, mission statements, policies, procedures, task instructions, industry standards, regulatory agency documents, Web sites, books, articles, experts, customers, consultants, suppliers, project documents, risk analysis, and quality plans.

9.4.2.3 Non-Value-Added Data

Non-value-added data is any extraneous information that is not required for the project and that has no ability to positively affect a behavior, decision, or desired outcome within the project. Non-value-added data can sometimes adversely affect a behavior, decision, or desired outcome within the project.

    a. False, incorrect, or misleading information
    b. Irrelevant information.

9.4.2.3.1 Importance of Eliminating Non-Value-Added Data from Projects

Non-value-added data is similar to "junk" food. Adding more junk in the diet not only creates unhealthier, saturated, and trans fats but also creates unwanted problems. Similarly, adding junk or invalid data into the project prevents the project team from making accurate decisions.

9.4.2.3.2 Sources of Non-Value-Added Data

Sources that are not credible like personal blogs, open sources like Wikipedia, books, articles by unknown authors, unnecessary project data, and inexperienced personnel are considered non-value-added data.

    Although all three types of data exist in any project, the ratio of the three types of data may vary significantly based on the type and duration of the project. It is important to keep the non-value-added data to a minimum, or it will

Ideal project data

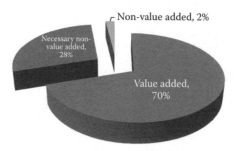

Figure 9.6   Ideal project data.

cause the project to fail because of misleading information. Also, it is critical to understand that a higher percentage of non-value-added data may not have a significant impact on a long-term project, but the same percentage of non-value-added data may result in failure on some short-term projects. Ideal project data should have very little non-value-added data, as shown in Figure 9.6.

9.4.3 Appropriate Data Storage, Security, Retrieval, and Distribution

Once the distinction between value-added data, necessary non-value-added data, and non-value-added data is clearly understood and the process of collecting the required project data from appropriate sources has begun, it is important to focus on some other critical elements regarding data, such as storage, security, and distribution because project data is very crucial for making important decisions during the project. For complex and critical projects, the data needs to be secured and access should be restricted based on permissions. There are several case studies of situations of data losses and unauthorized access to data leading to disasters.

The following are some critical elements to consider when the organization is dealing with excessive project or process data:

1. **Data storage and retrieval**—safe storage, backup, and easy retrieval of data
2. **Data security**—securing data against access by unauthorized personnel, software viruses, and so forth.
3. **Data access**—fast access of data to personnel with access rights and permissions
4. **Data monitoring**—monitoring file size, data type, and appropriate filing protocols
5. **Data distribution**—ensuring data goes to authorized distribution lists that are kept current
6. **Data change management**—reliable and user-friendly change management system.

Figure 9.7 Elements in the project data management plan.

Project managers sometimes do not give adequate importance to these elements. However, project leaders consider these elements critical to success and prepare a data management plan as part of the overall project plan. Various elements in the project data management plan are explained in Figure 9.7. The data management plan gives guidance to the project team regarding data administration and usage throughout the life cycle of the project. If project leaders do not possess expertise in data management, they should make sure that experts are available within the project team to help them prepare the data management plan document. Because the majority of documentation effort takes place in the project planning stage, project leaders should prepare a data management plan well in advance in the planning stage to store planning documents. Now, let us discuss, in detail, the elements to be included in a good data management plan.

9.4.3.1 Data Storage and Retrieval

Storing data in a safe place is essential in projects. Projects contain many documents such as the charter, project plans, project management documents, quality

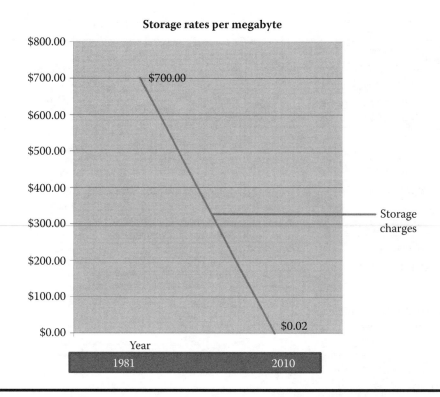

Figure 9.8 Fall of costs over the years per megabyte of digital storage. (Adapted from David M. Smith, *Data Loss and Hard Drive Failure: Understanding the Causes and Costs,* **Ace Data recovery Engineering Inc., 2010. http://www.deepspar.com/wp-data-loss.html.)**

documents, and budget documents. As the projects progress, several new data elements, files, and documents are added to the project. These documents are important not only to that project but also to future projects as historical knowledge. The dramatic growth of the amount of data stored within corporate servers, workstations, and user's machines is primarily due to the decreasing costs per megabyte of data storage. On an average, the cost of 1 MB of data storage has gone from $700 to 0.002 cents (see Figure 9.8).[8]

However, there are several cases of data loss in major corporations and agencies. On an average, an incident of lost data can cost an organization several thousand dollars in lost productivity and may also result in other costs like litigation and data recovery costs to the tune of millions of dollars. For example, recently, a reputable medical insurance company lost 7 years' worth of encrypted data containing personal, financial, and medical information of 1.5 million customers in four different states. This loss lead to a government investigation followed by lawsuits and millions of dollars for monitoring the credit reports for those individuals whose data were lost.[9]

The importance of storage requirements is often ignored by project managers while initiating a project. An advanced project leader should make sure that the data is stored in one centralized location and similar data is consolidated within one virtual or physical location. Moreover, a project leader should also consider managing data growth efficiently, including archiving of unused data and elimination of redundant data files. To determine efficient data storage methods, project leaders should ask the following questions.

- *What type of project data needs to be stored for the project?*
- *Is there a detailed plan to back up the project data?*
- *Is there a well-defined strategy to restore the data, in case of a disaster?*

The answers to these questions will guide the project leader and his/her team in making important decisions regarding data storage. For example, individual project data can be stored on the hard disk of a computer or other media; for critical project data, external storage and backup devices are used. If the amount of data is really enormous, it can be stored in databases, on servers, and so forth. The advantage of storing data in a database is that metadata (data about data) can also be stored in a database, which helps in easy retrieval of data in future. In addition to these tools, there are many data storage tools and file formats available to collect data records, and use of these tools is determined during the initiation of the project. Project leaders should make storage decisions based on four important elements of a project as shown in Figure 9.9.

1. **Project documents**
2. **Project duration**
3. **Project resources**
4. **Project tasks.**

Project documents are considered while making storage decisions. As the number of documents in the project increase, the space required to store those documents increases significantly. Project duration also plays an important role in storage decisions. The longer the duration of the project, the higher the required storage space. A higher number of resources always creates more documents compared with fewer resources. Hence, the number of resources

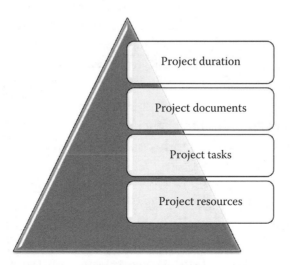

Figure 9.9   Four important elements for data storage considerations.

is also important in making storage decisions. Project tasks also determine the storage requirements. A project with thousands of tasks requires higher storage compared with a project with fewer tasks.

From our visualization exercise, it is clear that the important requirement for a bodybuilder is not to just consume higher quantities of food but it is critical to eat the right amount of nutrients. In the same way, storage requirements should be decided not on the amount of data but based on the amount of value-added data. The ratio of value-added data to non-value-added data decides the storage requirements. Project leaders should always create methods to eliminate redundant or invalid data from the databases to reduce the expenses involved in data storage.

I was at a multibillion dollar global company that manages data and other IT requirements for large client organizations. During investigations of some issues in the project management department, the executives of this company and I were horrified, to put it mildly, to find out that the project teams did not have their project management data stored in a central repository. All their project-related team communications within the United States, India, China, and other European locations were via e-mails and voice mails. No wonder some managers stopped responding to e-mails. Their mail box had more than 200 e-mails per day, and the critical project information got buried under the FYI's. The executives immediately mandated a central data storage system.

Every complex project must have data that is centrally accessible to all the required and authorized personnel. There is an initial investment, but the team leader and teams will reap significant benefits on every project. The project timeline, number of meetings, and the project costs will decrease and quality of the output will be significantly improved.

9.4.3.2 Data Security

Data security is the practice of keeping data protected from corruption. The protection of data can be done to prevent unauthorized access and accidental distribution. The main emphasis for data security is to ensure privacy and protect critical information.[10] In a recent high-profile incident, U.S. Government Transportation and Security Administration (TSA) accidentally posted secret information detailing its airline screening practices on their Web site. This information contained settings for x-ray machines and explosive detectors, as well as procedures with diplomats and other high officials.[11] In this case, the implications if this document falling into the wrong hands could be devastating to national security.

According to the Ponemon Institute, *"The average information leak costs organizations approximately $182 per record, averaging roughly $4,800,000 per breach in total."* On the basis of a 2005 survey, 49% of companies have experienced an internal security breach. Out of those companies, approximately 31% experienced a breach because of virus or worm attack, 28% had insider fraud, and 18% experienced security breach because of data leakage, as shown in Figure 9.10.[12]

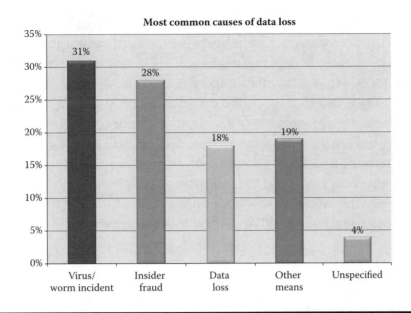

Figure 9.10 Most common causes of data loss. (Adapted from Ironport Systems, *Data Loss Prevention Best Practices: Managing Sensitive Data in the Enterprise*. Cisco Systems, 2007, accessed on November 29, 2010. pp. 7 and 15. Inc. http://www.ironport.com/pdf/ironport_dlp_booklet.pdf.)

A majority of the project decisions are based on data. Critical decisions cannot be taken if the data is corrupted or missing. Project managers routinely keep their data in Excel spreadsheets and Word documents and store their data in shared drives. Because shared drives can be used by anybody in the department, there is every chance of data getting corrupted accidentally by employees. In many organizations, project managers do not put much focus on the data security and assume that because data security and backup is the duty of the network administrator or data administrator, they are solely responsible for the safety and maintenance of the project data. The case study at the end of this chapter shows that this assumption is often untrue. Never make the mistake of trusting non–project resources for the security of project data as the ultimate accountability and responsibility of data security related to the project data rests solely on the shoulders of the project leader.

What Is the Project Leader's Role in Securing the Project Data?

Project leaders need to be proactive and should plan in advance to protect the data from unauthorized access. As more complex projects are carried out, organization readiness for handling critical data is more critical than ever. Project leaders should think about data security upfront and plan for it. There are two important elements that a project leader should focus on. The first is collecting data using secured tools, and the second element is to secure the data using encryption to prevent data loss. Collecting data securely can be done using existing in-house tools or utilizing new tools available in the market. Project leaders should look for in-house tools in organizational process assets and enterprise environmental factors. The latest software tools such as project management information systems and scheduling software tools are also available to collect data securely and store it in the database. Once the data is collected and stored securely, regardless of the type of tools used, project leaders should take steps to ensure that the data is shared only when absolutely necessary. If other applications need critical information, protocols should be followed for this information to be destroyed by the other party after its purpose is achieved. Project data security is breached when critical or confidential data is shared with other applications. A project leader should keep the following points in mind to secure project data.

- Data encryption
- Virus and hacker protection
- Strong user authentication
- Data loss prevention
- Backup solution.

9.4.3.2.1 Data Encryption

Data encryption converts data into unreadable text using certain mathematical algorithms that make it unreadable by other computer programs.[10] The encrypted data will be converted into readable text by a decrypting mechanism. The critical data in the project should be stored with the encryption mechanism to shield the data from changes.

9.4.3.2.2 Virus and Hacker Protection

Most serious threats to data in recent years have come from hackers and viruses. The problems associated with viruses or hacker attacks are twofold. The first problem is access to critical data, and the second problem is the loss of critical data. Software manufacturers are giving utmost importance to preventing intruders from corrupting the data by updating the software frequently. Project leaders should make sure that their project software is up to date and all virus protection patches are applied on a timely basis.

9.4.3.2.3 Strong User Authentication

User authentication is a key element to prevent unauthorized access.[10] There are varieties of authentication techniques such as using passwords, passcodes, CAPTCHA (Completely Automated Public Turing test to tell Computers and Humans Apart), fingerprints, and sometimes, by asking access questions. Project leaders can set different authentication mechanisms for different users to access project information, project plans, project documents, and deliverables.

9.4.3.2.4 Data Loss Prevention

Data loss can happen by virus attack or by accidental deletes or updates by team members. This really ties back to the points discussed earlier. Project leaders should diligently work on access mechanism to make sure that critical data is not updated or deleted unintentionally.

9.4.3.2.5 Backup Solution

Data security would not be complete without a solution to back up your critical information.[10] Although it may seem secure while confined away in a machine, there is always a chance that your data can be compromised.[10] Therefore, project files, tasks, plans, changes, resource information, deliverables, and contract information must be backed up. The frequency of data backup can be determined on the basis of the criticality of the data and the frequency of updates.

9.4.3.3 Data Access

Securely storing value-added information does not help the project team if the right information cannot be accessed quickly by the right individuals or departments at the appropriate time when needed.

Thus, data access should be

  a. "Quick"
  b. To the "right people"
  c. At the "right level"
  d. At the "right time."

Missing any of these key elements can delay or adversely impact the project and also the organization.

9.4.3.3.1 Quick

Speed of access is critical because if it is too slow or too cumbersome to access, project performance will be affected as people may get frustrated and avoid looking at the required information.

9.4.3.3.2 To the "Right People"

Data access can be divided into three elements. Noncritical project data access, critical project data access, and corporate data access. Noncritical project data can be accessed by anyone in the project team. It is freely available for interpretation. Critical project data related to customer discussions and other sensitive information is important and cannot be disclosed to all project team members. Therefore, the project leader should take precautions to not give access to this information to all team members. Corporate data access uses the same rules with care taken to providing limited or no access to consultants, vendors, and other external resources that are part of the core project team. Corporate data has same critical and noncritical elements in it. Because project data is stored in project repositories, whereas corporate data is stored outside of project repositories, if a project requires critical corporate information, it should be accessed from the corporate database. A project leader must ensure that right permissions are given to the people to quickly access both corporate and project data.

9.4.3.3.3 At the "Right Level"

Project data access varies depending on the type of project and the type of data. In general, data access usually takes place to accomplish one or all of the following tasks:

i. **Decoding the available information.** Data is frequently accessed either by the project leader or by the project team members to decode or interpret the information. This type of access is usually done before "ground support" meetings, phase-end meetings, and at critical points during the project to present the information and to update the status of the project on the basis of the interpretation of the information. This type of access does not require any updates to the available information. The individuals and teams who are only required to access this information as an "FYI" should be given "read only" access to the project data.

ii. **Making decisions using the available information.** Sometimes, data is accessed by the project leader to make decisions on the basis of the interpretation of the available data. This type of access can often be seen before executive or "air support" meetings, phase-end meetings, and other critical decision points during the project. The individuals and teams who are only required to access this information for decision making and are not required to update any information should also be given "read only" access to the project data.

iii. **Updating the available information.** Many times during the project, data access is done to update the information. This type of access is done when task information, resource information, or project information is updated. This type of access is done more frequently by the lower level or "ground-level" project team on a daily basis to update the project data. The individuals and teams who are required to update the information should be given "read and write" access to the project data.

iv. **Archiving the available information.** Some individuals or departments are tasked with archiving the old project data so that the database stays fresh and less storage is required in the primary servers. These individuals should be given the appropriate rights to archive the data. AutoArchive is not recommended on long-term projects as human judgment may be critical to determining the information to be archived. Some software like Microsoft Outlook have a built-in feature which allows the users to auto-archive the old correspondence.

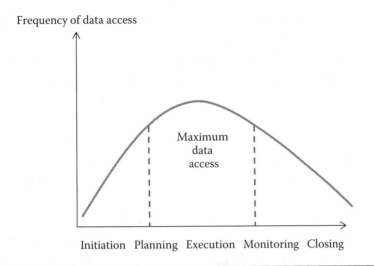

Figure 9.11   Frequency of data access in various project phases.

9.4.3.3.4 At the "Right Time"

The frequency of data access changes with the phases of the project. Data access is less frequent during the initial phases of the project and increases in the planning phase, reaches its maximum during execution and monitoring phases of the project, and decreases at the end of the project, as shown in Figure 9.11. Also, the people involved may change as the project progresses from phase to phase. Therefore, a project leader should make sure that data is current and readily available to the team during those phases while ensuring that the access is withdrawn for people who are no longer working on that project.

Thus, data access is a critical aspect, and a proactive plan needs to be created to ensure that appropriate access is granted only to the appropriate individuals at the appropriate phases during the project so that they can quickly accomplish their tasks without adversely affecting the sanctity of the available information.

9.4.3.4 Data Monitoring

One of the key factors project managers fail to plan for about data during a project is that it is dynamic and constantly growing. If the project is simple and of short duration, then there is not much to fear about data growth, but if the project is complex and of a longer duration, it is crucial that the team members monitor data and plan for the growth. Modern project management tools are beneficial and worthwhile to use when the project scope is vast. Project data grows exponentially from initiation phase into planning phase. Therefore, assessing data growth gives an idea on the storage requirements, data access requirements, and security requirements. A few things that can help project leaders and team members stay on top of the data monitoring challenge in complex projects are as follows.

a. **Standardize file nomenclature.** A standard for folder and file nomenclature is a powerful tool in the arsenal of project leaders working on complex projects. Also, linking similar records can be helpful to save time in trying to locate the appropriate files. The nomenclature can include the initials of the person who last updated the file and a revision level.

b. **Periodically update security protocols and data access rights.** It is critical for project leaders to periodically update the security protocols on the basis of actual or potential threats to the project data and also review the data access permissions closely to ensure that the right people are provided access at the right permission levels.

c. **Create rules for periodic data purging.** A recommended approach while monitoring the data is to delete redundant information, removing unnecessary information at frequent intervals.

d. **Create rules for periodic data archiving.** Once data is purged, the rest of the "good and current" reference and other data can be archived once it is not needed. All project-related documents like the charter, risk management plan, and communication plan should never be archived away as they are critical documents for project success and should be used dynamically throughout the project's life cycle.

9.4.3.5 Data Distribution

The large barrel theory (and black hole corollary) states that "It is a lot easier to archive data than to disseminate it!"[13] Data distribution is a critical element in a project. It is the responsibility of the project leader to provide accurate data to customers, stakeholders, sponsor, and the entire project team in a timely fashion. The project data is so important that it drives almost all major activities in a project.

Project data contains:

- Historical data from past projects
- Risk-related project data
- Earned value data
- Issue and defect data
- Cost, schedule, and quality data
- Project-related progress data.

9.4.3.5.1 Importance of Selective Data Distribution

The data can be distributed into two instances. One instance is a request and the other is a response. A request can occur from a stakeholder, customer, or a team member to send project data. A request can also come from a project leader. A response can occur from a project leader or from other members of the team based on the request. A response can also be voluntary. In either case, information is distributed to the parties involved. It is quite common for some project managers to send project data to everybody in the project team just to update them on the project. This method of distribution has serious problems. The first problem is disclosing confidential or critical data to all team members, and the second problem is in creating confusion among team members because of the overwhelming data that is unnecessary to them. In simple projects, sending project data to everybody all the time is not a problem. As the project grows bigger in size, data distribution grows exponentially. The potential number of communication channels is $n(n-1)/2$, where n is the total number of stakeholders in a team. Thus, a project with 10 stakeholders or team members will have 45 communication channels,[14] whereas for a team with 30 members, the number of communication channels grows to 435 and maintaining data distribution in all 435 channels or paths is really cumbersome. A dynamic project leader follows certain methods to distribute the data to the right people at the right time. The communication methods that were discussed in the previous chapter are very useful in data distribution. Project leaders must ensure that data distribution lists are maintained in the project and kept current throughout the project. As soon as the project team is finalized, the project leader should prepare a data distribution plan as part of the data management plan.

9.4.3.6 Project Data Change Management

Change is inevitable in projects. Changes not only have an impact on the project but also have an impact on the project data. Change management has been the Achilles heel for many project managers, and there are several case studies on how poor change management led to project disasters. Entire volumes can be easily written on this topic alone, and several software tools are available on the market, which allows project managers to put change management on autopilot. However, sometimes this is not so easy.

Changes cost money. In one company, the estimated cost to initiate, execute, and complete a change in the project ranged from $500 for a simple change request to more than $2000 for a complicated change requiring several internal and external authorizations, print changes, and supplier communications. Yes, changes do take up time and resources, and project leaders need to manage them very carefully. The need to control project data changes is very essential when projects are complex or resources are globally distributed. The project leader should develop a data change management plan in the planning stage of the project and indicate how a data change is to be carried out in subsequent phases of the project. If project leaders adhere to the following simple rules, they can significantly improve their change management ability.

The five rules of change management are as follows:

1. **All changes are not equal or urgent.** Changes can be initiated by the customer, sponsor, stakeholder, project team, or the project leaders themselves. Customer- and sponsor-requested changes should always take priority for consideration. Next, any changes to the critical path or quality-related

items need to be prioritized, and then any other changes affecting functionality should be considered. Changes need to be evaluated, and changes that may have little or no value to add to the project can be eliminated.

2. **Changes will mostly impact more than one area of multiple personnel.** Changes to one element of the project data can have a ripple effect on other data elements and resources involved within the project. The project leaders need to identify the impact upfront by having a template that asks leading questions to the person requesting the change to identify the individuals or groups affected by that change. The document control is then required to request an authorization signature from the groups that are affected to ensure that they are on board with the change. This is very critical and can prevent any misgivings and finger-pointing in case the changes result in some unforeseen issues in the business area that did not initiate the change.

3. **Changes must be authorized in a timely manner.** This is very critical. Expectations need to be set on expected completion time of changes for Priority 1, 2, and 3 changes. On critical, complex projects, a change control board consisting of department heads and their backups can be assigned. The change control board can meet on a weekly, biweekly, or monthly basis to review or set priorities and approve the changes in a timely manner. Sometimes, this can also be accomplished virtually and electronically through workflow solutions.

Just like every change request is processed through a change control board, project data changes should also go through a data change management board. Unlike the change control board, the project data change management board can be a single person or group of persons who should authorize data changes. Sometimes, a change management tool can also work as a data change management board. Change management tools maintain different versions of the project data and record the credentials of the person doing the updates. This makes it very easy to see who made the updates and when those updates were made.

4. **Changes require accurate documentation, timely communication, and training.** Making the change is not enough. It is critical to document the change accurately and communicate the change in a timely manner to all affected by the change. If the change entails significant updates, training should be scheduled for all those affected, as part of completing the implementation of that change.

5. **Change management should be an assigned responsibility.** A person or a group needs to be given the authority and responsibility for change control. It is a very specialized function requiring significant attention to detail and has to be conducted by trained personnel.

9.5 Why Is Dynamic Data Management Critical for the Future Success of Project Leaders?

Project leaders will need to keep updating their skills in data management as communication and data distribution channels are constantly being updated. Today, almost everyone has a data-capable cell phone or a smart phone. Communication is wide open, and data is accessed via blogs, social media like LinkedIn, Facebook, instant messaging, and several other ways. How does one manage data from so many sources? About three decades ago, we did not

Today, there is an over-abundance of data, the only way we can address the issue is by using the concepts of dynamic data management and using the process of elimination at the source level for non-value-added data.

have this problem, in fact, the problem was the opposite—"Where can we get the information?" was the primary question, and so it was acceptable to collect the limited data available and use as required for the project. Today, there is an overabundance of data, the only way we can address the issue is by using the concepts of dynamic data management and using the process of elimination at the source level for non-value-added data. If we do not allow "bad" data to infiltrate and enter into our projects, we will definitely have fewer issues and it will take us less time to evaluate the available data and cost us less to store it. The other challenge will be to keep up with the ever-changing technology. The concept of "cloud computing," is an emerging technology that aims to enhance the capacity and capabilities of the current PC or laptop by not requiring us to store data or use applications on the hard drive. Instead, it delivers an application through the browser to thousands of customers using a multitenant architecture. A great example of this is Google's Google Docs. In Google Docs, a user creates an account for free and can log on and an interface much like Microsoft Word pops up in their Web browser. The user can now create and save text documents. Microsoft is actually considering taking a similar approach and making the next Microsoft Office to be released accessible only online.

Thus, it is the use of Internet-based ("cloud") computer technology for doing what we do today on the PC. All data and applications will be stored on a server. According to Oracle CEO, Larry Ellison, cloud computing is … "on-demand access to virtualized IT resources that are housed outside of your own data center, shared by others, simple to use, paid for via subscription, and accessed over the Web."[15] There are obviously advantages to the project leaders as they do not have to worry about storage space and other issues. One of the major advantages of cloud computing is that it is very cost-effective for the user, as there are lower upfront costs, and it is a "pay-as-you-go" service and the project budget will not require funds for a new server, server installation, or server maintenance. Other benefits of using cloud computing are faster time to market, reduced financial risk, lower capital expenses, lower operating expenses, decreased downtime and costly delays, and additional services that are included such as software, security, and bandwidth. However, if the project data is of a sensitive nature, how can they make sure that their information is supersecure and cannot be broken into by hackers or be compromised in some other way. Speed of Internet access, overwriting of data, and other issues and aspects of the new technologies need to be thought out clearly and addressed upfront. A dynamic data management plan is shown in Figure 9.12.

Thus, project leaders will need to approach data management very differently in the future and will need to use the concept of dynamic data management if they want to be successful.

Every successful project leader must have a reliable system to secure, monitor, distribute, control, access, and store project data.

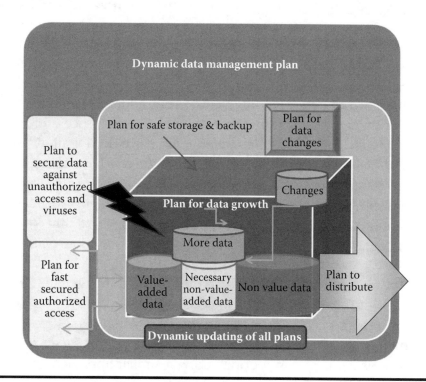

Figure 9.12   Dynamic data management plan.

Pillar IX   Summary

Presenting incorrect data or loss of critical data will not only delay the project but also terminate the project without a result. Data has played an important role in the development of human beings since the beginning of time. However, the data distribution, technology, the means of communication, speed, distribution group size, and purpose and data storage type have changed tremendously over the ages. It is very important for the project leader to select an appropriate data source and type to bucket the data into different categories. Data is categorized into value-added data, such as critical project data, historical data, and artifacts, and non-value-added data, such as false or incorrect information or irrelevant information. In addition to these two data elements, corporate data, regulatory data, and reference data constitute necessary non-value-added data. The following data elements are critical to consider when dealing with project data.

- **Data storage and retrieval**
- **Data security**
- **Data access**
- **Data monitoring**
- **Data distribution**
- **Data change management**

Every successful project leader must have a reliable system to secure, monitor, distribute, control, access, and store project data. Figure 9.13 outlines the concepts in dynamic data management plan.

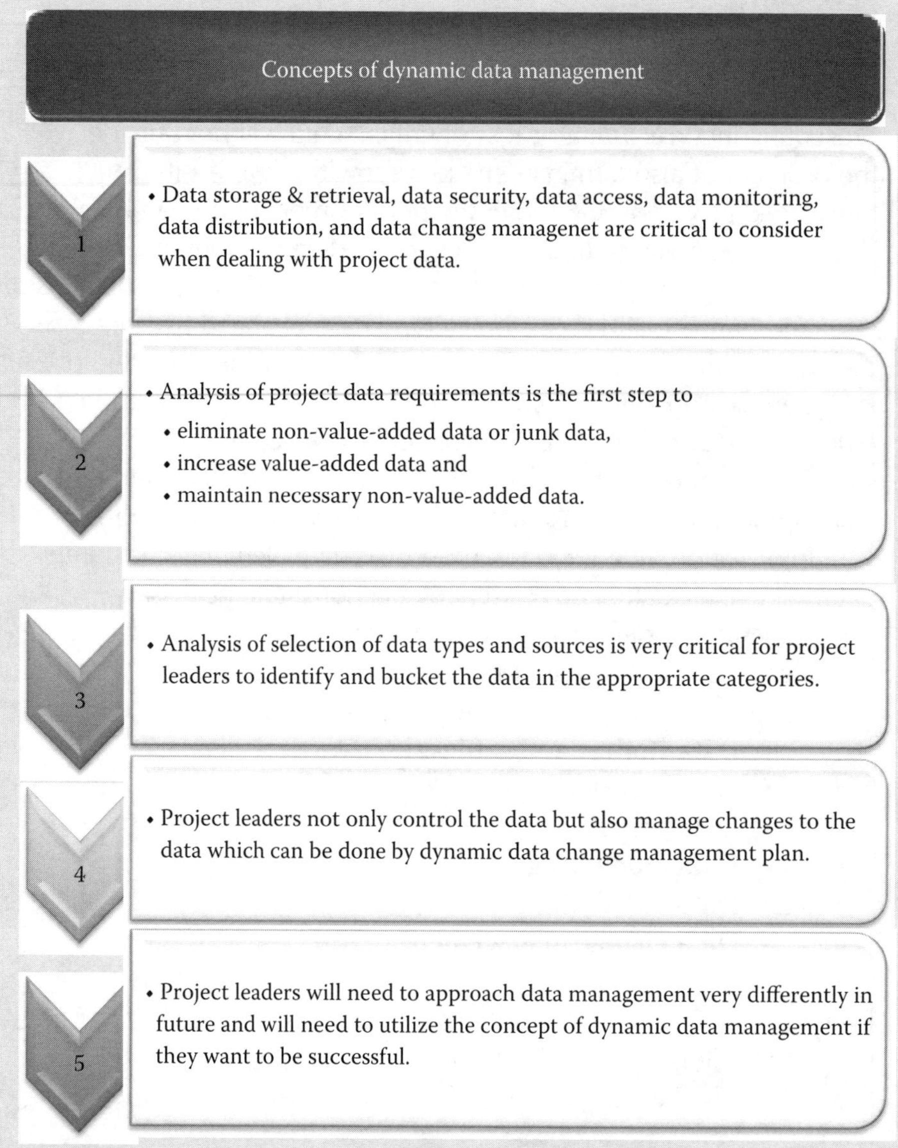

Figure 9.13   Concepts of dynamic data management.

Pillar IX   Case Study 1
Solving the "Data Noise" Problem

INTRODUCTION

This case study is about using the principles described in Pillar IX to solve the problem of "low, low signal, high noise" data due to the information overload at a call center site.

CHALLENGE

A classic example of a "low signal, high noise" data ratio at a call "command" center of a global IT company for identifying and separating critical severity (priority 1 and 2) customer service issues from other lower severity issues and nonissues.

SITUATION

At a command center of a multibillion dollar IT corporation, there were some major issues regarding missing a major portion of critical customer issues (priority 1 and 2) by an experienced team of operators and supervisors. Missing these critical priority 1 and 2 issues had to lead to downtime on systems at customer sites—a very serious problem for the client and the IT company. Upon further investigation, it was identified that at any time, for each priority 1 or 2 issue (signal), the command center was inundated with 155 nonissues (noise). The nonissues were mostly just "chatter" and should not even have been submitted to them in the first place. As shown in Figure 9.14, the signal-to-noise ratio was $1/150 = 0.65\%$, which is very low and it was not a surprise that the customer service team was unable to catch these as each item stays on the screen for a few seconds and if there is no action taken and a priority is not assigned, it scrolls off the screen and is automatically classified as a nonissue. While the operators were looking at the "noise" (nonissues), the "signal" (priority 1 and 2) had already slipped and was classified as a nonissue in the system, thus creating performance issues and creating "red alert" situations for operations or completely shutting down operations. It was getting to a point where the executives of this multibillion dollar company were receiving calls from the executives of their client companies furious at how the situation was being handled. The directors of the call center did not understand what the issue was as the situation was never this bad. In fact, they had just opened up five new data input centers in Brazil, five new centers in India in addition to the five each in the United States and in Canada, two in Brazil, and two in Bangalore, India—all with the purpose of increasing customer satisfaction in the growing international market.

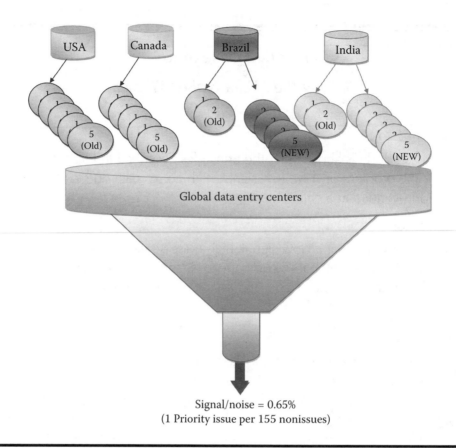

Figure 9.14   Very low signal-to-noise ratio.

PROBLEM

Upon data analysis, it was identified that almost 90% of the "noise" (135 items) was originating from the newly opened data entry centers. These items were internal issues, not customer related, and should not have been entered into the system as potential issues at all. After conducting root cause analysis, it was found that considerable experience was required to know the difference between internal and customer-related issues, and the new hires obviously lacked that experience and then entered everything into the system to "play it safe."

SOLUTION

Although training the new hires would help reduce the noise level, many items really needed significant experience to make the right call. Also, there was no way these employees could be taken off their jobs for classroom-type training. On the basis of the analysis, the company realized that spreading the data entry responsibilities over several locations was not a great idea to begin with and that their experiment had failed. A decision was made to consolidate the new hires into the original locations of the respective countries and focus on on-the-job training by allocating them to more experienced supervisors who were able to act as mentors and also help make the call if there were questions or concerns regarding the data entry. If the supervisors could not make the call, the managers were also in the area to jump in and help out in making the decision immediately. Although many newly hired employees could not make the physical move, several new hires agreed to the consolidation. Within 1 month, the company consolidated the operations to the original number of five each in the United States and in Canada, two in Brazil, and two in Bangalore, India, with a bigger staff.

RESULTS

The results were almost immediate. The month after the newly consolidated operations began, the command center had missed only a single priority 1 item, which was on par with historical monthly averages. On re-evaluating the noise-to-signal ratio, it was found that for every one priority 1 or 2 item, five nonissues or "noise" items were being entered, making the signal-to-noise ratio 20%, which translated to a 3000% improvement, as shown in Figure 9.15. The IT company was very pleased as the customer complaints had dropped off completely, as they had hoped it would.

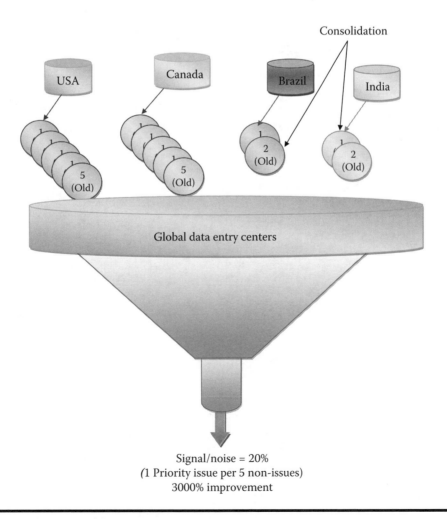

Figure 9.15   Significantly improved signal-to-noise ratio.

LESSONS LEARNED

A critical lesson learned is that if the signal-to-noise ratio is not evaluated and monitored when excessive data is being collected on a project, it can result in significant issues. It is important to maintain the signal (value-added data) to noise (non-value-added data) ratio as high as possible on all projects, and it is imperative that project leaders pay close attention to this ratio on critical projects.

Pillar IX: Case Study 2

The following is a two-part critical case study relating to data loss and change control problems I faced in my career—both due to two different reasons but surprisingly during the same project. Luckily, I have never had to live through these issues ever again because these lessons are very difficult and it would be extremely irresponsible to have these repeat during the course of one's career.

1. Loss of critical data

   I remember the only time in my career I had to walk into my vice president's office completely heartbroken, shaken, and shattered to let him know that my team had forgotten to back up the system during a software upgrade resulting in loss of approximately 1 month of data. I told him "We have no choice, we will have to push back the 'line live' (when the new Flow line goes live) date." He heroically came back with, "Cheer up Adil. We still have 2 weeks—let me know what you need from me to make the date." My team worked hard through the next few nights and managed to pull through on this project—we did not have to move the deadline after all. We learned our lesson, and we put our database on automatic backup every midnight.

2. Lack of change control

   Another bigger debacle was actually during the same project 2 days before "line live," when the project manager in charge of materials accidently printed more than a thousand labels from a test database. The materials team worked over the entire weekend to find out that we had pulled material for our kanban from the incorrect business unit. Thus, to add to the pressure we were already under, we had to return the 1000 parts to their respective locations, remove old labels from the bins, print and apply new labels, and pull new parts before the 6 a.m. start on Monday morning. The irony was that to take care of this "nightmare," 15 of us had to be fully "awake the entire night" before D-day. We never ever had to go through that again as we had multiple steps of validation and quality control procedures put immediately in place for future label printing. We learned our lesson here too, and we made sure that, in the future, all our databases had approvals and revision levels to ensure that the latest database was used in similar situations.

Pillar IX   Force Field Analysis

PILLAR IX: FORCE FIELD ANALYSIS OF ORGANIZATIONAL ASSESSMENT

Table 9.1 shows force field analysis of organizational assessment. The organizational assessment is conducted to assess if the culture of the organization is in alignment with the principles of Pillar IX. Tables 9.2 through 9.4 are used to develop and implement an action plan to increase the impact of the organizational driving forces and decrease the impact of the organizational resisting forces.

PILLAR IX: FORCE FIELD ANALYSIS OF SELF-ASSESSMENT

Table 9.5 shows force field analysis of self-assessment. The self-assessment is conducted to assess if your own strengths are in alignment with the principles of Pillar IX. Tables 9.6 through 9.8 are used to develop and implement an action plan to increase the impact of the self-driving forces and decrease the impact of the self-resisting forces.

PILLAR IX: RECOMMENDATIONS FOR OPTIMAL RESULTS FROM FORCE FIELD ANALYSIS

For optimal results and actual transformation of culture and strengths conducive to the creation of advanced master project leaders, the following three steps are necessary:

1. Both the organizational and self-evaluation assessments must be completed.
2. A well-designed action plan must be created and implemented to increase the driving forces and decrease the resisting forces.
3. The principles of each pillar must be constantly practiced and improved.

It is highly recommended that both the organization assessments and self-assessments be conducted every year and the action plan be updated at least every 3 months.

Note: The sum of scores for Organizational Driving Force and Organizational Resisting Force for each point must be less than or equal to TEN.

The sum of scores for Self Driving Force and Self Resisting Force for each point must be less than or equal to TEN.

Table 9.1 Pillar IX: Force Field Organizational Analysis

Team Name: _____ Date: _____

Does My Organization Drive or Resist the Principles of Dynamic Data Management?				
0 Never		5 Sometimes		7 Mostly
3 Rarely		ODF + ORF ≤ 10		10 Always
No.	Driving Forces	Score Organizational Driving Force (ODF)	Score Organizational Resisting Force (ORF)	Resisting Forces
1	My organization understands the importance of dynamic data management while leading projects for effectively dealing with the present-day challenges posed by emerging technologies and an overabundance of means of communications.			My organization does not consider data management as an important aspect of project management.
2	My organization deals with the information overload on projects by proactively providing means to manage the data, separate the critical pieces from spam, regularly back up critical data, and provide adequate access to authorized personnel.			My organization does not plan for any information overload on projects.
3	Leaders within my organization understand that data, just like balanced nutrition, has to be provided to projects based on the duration, complexity, and criticality of the project and it has to be from reliable sources.			Project managers do not consider the project duration, complexity, criticality, and sources while providing data for various projects.
4	Our leaders categorize project data as value added, necessary non-value added, and non-value added (or waste).			Our managers do not see the need to bucket project data in appropriate categories.

5	As project data is very crucial for making important decisions during a project, for complex and critical projects, the leaders secure the data and restrict the access based on permissions.			Project data is usually openly and equally accessible to all team members.
6	If project leaders do not possess expertise in data management, they make sure that experts are available within the project team to help them prepare the data management plan document.			The project manager prepares and manages the data management plan document.
7	At the onset of the project, project leaders ensure that the data is stored in one centralized location and data growth, archiving of unused data, and elimination of redundant data files are managed effectively.			Project managers do not consider it important to plan for data storage requirements during the project initiation phase.
8	Project leaders create and dynamically manage detailed custom plans for data security, protection from data corruption, prevention of unauthorized access, accidental distribution, and ensuring privacy of critical information.			Project managers use a basic data management plan that is standardized.
9	Project leaders actively assess the exponential growth of data from the initiation to planning phases of projects to plan for storage, data access requirements, and security requirements.			Project managers plan for a standard data storage capacity and security that stays static during the entire project.

10	Project leaders keep updating their skills in data management as the communication and data distribution channels are constantly being updated.			Project managers usually depend on standard forms of communications and do not see the need to update their skills in data management.
	Total ODF score			*Total ORF score*

Results	Conclusions	Recommended Action Review and Update Every Quarter (3 months)
ODF >> ORF	My company culture strongly drives a culture of dynamic data management.	Use Tables 9.2 through 9.4 to set goals and create an action plan to preserve or continuously improve the culture of dynamic data management.
ODF > ORF	My company culture drives the culture of dynamic data management.	Use Tables 9.2 through 9.4 to set goals and create an action plan to increase ODF to create a stronger culture of dynamic data management.
ORF >> ODF	My company culture strongly resists the culture of dynamic data management.	Use Tables 9.2 through 9.4 to set goals and create an action plan to increase the ODF and reduce the ORF to create a stronger culture of dynamic data management.
ORF > ODF	My company culture resists the culture of dynamic data management.	Use Tables 9.2 through 9.4 to set goals and create an action plan to reduce the ORF to create a stronger culture of dynamic data management.
ODF = ORF	My company culture does not drive or resist the culture of dynamic data management.	Use Tables 9.2 through 9.4 to set goals and create an action plan to increase the ODF to create a stronger culture of dynamic data management.

Table 9.2   Pillar IX: Analysis of ODF and ORF Results

Result	Existing Organizational Culture	If the Goal is to Create a Moderately Strong Culture of Dynamic Data Management	If the Goal is to Create a Very Strong Culture of Dynamic Data Management
ODF			
ODF ≤ 25	No or minimal culture of creating dynamic data management	Focus on improving scores in at least 5 DF	Focus on improving scores in at least 7 DF
25 < ODF ≤ 50	Weak culture of dynamic data management	Focus on improving scores in at least 3 DF	Focus on improving scores in at least 5 DF
50 < ODF ≤ 75	Moderate culture of dynamic data management	Focus on improving scores in at least 1 DF	Focus on improving scores in at least 3 DF
ODF > 75	Strong culture of dynamic data management	N/A	Preserve or continuously improve the culture
ORF			
ORF > 75	No or minimal culture of dynamic data management	Focus on decreasing scores in at least 5 RF	Focus on decreasing scores in at least 7 RF
50 < ORF ≤ 75	Weak culture of dynamic data management	Focus on decreasing scores in at least 3 RF	Focus on decreasing scores in at least 5 RF
25 < ORF ≤ 50	Moderate culture of dynamic data management	Focus on decreasing scores in at least 1 RF	Focus on decreasing scores in at least 3 RF
ORF ≤ 25	Strong culture of dynamic data management	N/A	Preserve or continuously improve the culture

Table 9.3   Pillar IX: Action Plan to Increase Organizational Driving Forces (ODFs)

Team Name: _____   Date: _____

No.	Driving Force	Current Score	Goal (Target Score) ⬆	Action Plan, to increase DF Score	Complete by (Date)	Assigned to (Department Name or Initials of Person)
1	My organization understands the importance of dynamic data management while leading projects for effectively dealing with the present-day challenges posed by the emerging technologies and an overabundance of means of communications.					
2	My organization deals with the information overload on projects by proactively providing means to manage the data, separate the critical pieces from spam, regularly back up critical data, and provide adequate access to authorized personnel.					
3	Leaders within my organization understand that data, just like balanced nutrition, has to be provided to projects based on the duration, complexity, and criticality of the project and it has to be from reliable sources.					
4	Our leaders categorize project data as value added, necessary non-value added and non-value added (or waste).					
5	As project data is very crucial for making important decisions during the project, for complex and critical projects, the leaders secure the data and restrict the access based on the permissions.					

6	If project leaders do not possess expertise in data management, they make sure that experts are available within the project team to help them prepare the data management plan document.					
7	At the onset of the project, project leaders ensure that the data is stored in one centralized location and data growth, archiving of unused data, and elimination of redundant data files are managed effectively.					
8	Project leaders create and dynamically manage detailed custom plans for data security, protection from data corruption, prevention of unauthorized access, accidental distribution, and ensuring privacy of critical information.					
9	Project leaders actively assess the exponential growth of data from the initiation to planning phases of projects to plan for storage, data access requirements, and security requirements.					
10	Project leaders keep updating their skills in data management as the communication and data distribution channels are constantly being updated.					
	Total ODF					

Table 9.4 Pillar IX: Action Plan to Decrease Organizational Resisting Forces (ORFs)

No.	Resisting Force	Current Score	Goal (Target Score) ⬇	Action Plan to Decrease RF Score	Complete by (Date)	Assigned to (Department Name or Initials of Person)
1	My organization does not consider data management as an important aspect of project management.					
2	My organization does not plan for any information overload on projects.					
3	Project managers do not consider the project duration, complexity, criticality, and sources while providing data for various projects.					
4	Our managers do not see the need to bucket project data in appropriate categories.					
5	Project data is usually openly and equally accessible to all team members.					
6	The project manager prepares and manages the data management plan document.					
7	Project managers do not consider it important to plan for data storage requirements during the project initiation phase.					
8	Project managers use a basic data management plan that is standardized.					
9	Project managers plan for standard data storage capacity and security, which stays static during the entire project.					
10	Project managers usually depend on standard forms of communications and do not see the need to update their skills in data management.					
	Total ORF					

Table 9.5 Pillar IX: Force Field Self Analysis

Name: _____   **Date:** _____

	*Does My Behavior Drive or Resist the Principles of Dynamic Data Management?*				
0 Never		5 Sometimes		7 Mostly	
3 Rarely		SDF + SRF ≤ 10		10 Always	
No.	Driving Forces →	*Score Self-Driving Force (SDF)*	*Score Self-Resisting Force (SRF)*	← Resisting Forces	
1	I am not overwhelmed by the present-day challenges of data management as I understand and adhere to the principles of dynamic data management while leading projects.			Data management is one of the aspects of project management that frustrates me.	
2	I understand the pros and cons of the emerging modes of communication and have used chat, blogs, text messages, Twitter, LinkedIn, Facebook, and several other channels of communications.			I prefer to stick to simple modes of communications like phone, e-mail, and other standard forms.	
3	I follow the principles of dynamic data selection on projects and only use reliable and balanced data based on the duration, complexity, and criticality of the project.			I use as much data as is available and from any source irrespective of the duration, complexity, and criticality of the project.	
4	While leading projects, I categorize project data as VA, NNVA, and NVA and try to reduce or eliminate the NNVA and NVA data types.			I do not categorize or attempt to reduce the project data while managing projects.	
5	On every project, I create a dynamic data management plan that provides guidance to the project team regarding data security, administration, and usage throughout the life cycle of the project.			On my projects, I do not create a data management plan or just use a standard checklist to fulfill the requirements of data planning.	
6	I usually delegate the task of creating a comprehensive data management plan document to the data management experts on my team.			Although I am not an expert on data management, I prepare and manage the data management plan document.	

7	I use the ratio of value-added data to non-value-added data to decide the storage requirements and create methods to eliminate redundant or invalid data from the databases to reduce the expenses involved in data storage.			I do not consider data storage requirements while creating a project plan.
8	I encourage my team members to store critical project-related data in a secure, centralized location with appropriate access permissions.			I do not mandate the location of storage of project data and the team members are allowed to store all data on their hard drives or on their personal network drives.
9	I proactively plan for securing the project data using data encryption, virus and hacker protection, data loss prevention, user authentication, and backup solutions.			I depend on the IT department to provide security for my project data.
10	I understand the cost and resources involved in project data changes and proactively create a data change management plan for the life cycle of the project.			I depend on the document control department for the project data changes and do not create a data change management plan on my projects.
	Total SDF Score			*Total SRF Score*

Results	Conclusions	Recommended Action *Review and Update Every Quarter (3 months)*
SDF >> SRF	My behavior strongly supports the culture of dynamic data management.	Use Tables 9.6 through 9.8 to set goals and create an action plan to continuously enhance the behavior toward dynamic data management.
SDF > SRF	My behavior supports the culture of dynamic data management.	Use Tables 9.6 through 9.8 to set goals and create an action plan to increase SDF to allow a stronger behavior toward dynamic data management.
SRF >> SDF	My behavior strongly resists the culture of dynamic data management.	Use Tables 9.6 through 9.8 to set goals and create an action plan to increase SDF and reduce SRF to allow a stronger behavior toward dynamic data management.
SRF > SDF	My behavior resists the culture of dynamic data management.	Use Tables 9.6 through 9.8 to set goals and create an action plan to reduce SRF to allow a stronger behavior toward dynamic data management.
SDF = SRF	My behavior does not drive or resist the culture of dynamic data management.	Use Tables 9.6 through 9.8 to set goals and create an action plan to increase the SDF to allow a stronger behavior toward dynamic data management.

Table 9.6   Pillar IX: Analysis of SDF and SRF Results

Results	Existing Behavior	*If the Goal is to Create a Moderately Strong Behavior Towards Principles of Dynamic Data Management*	*If the Goal is to Create a Very Strong Behavior Towards Principles of Dynamic Data Management*
SDF			
SDF ≤ 25	No or minimal activities supporting dynamic data management	Focus on improving scores in at least 5 DF	Focus on improving scores in at least 7 DF
25 < SDF ≤ 50	Weak activities supporting dynamic data management	Focus on improving scores in at least 3 DF	Focus on improving scores in at least 5 DF
50 < SDF ≤ 75	Moderate activities supporting dynamic data management	Focus on improving scores in at least 1 DF	Focus on improving scores in at least 3 DF
SDF > 75	Strong activities supporting dynamic data management	N/A	Preserve or continuously improve the behavior
SRF			
SRF > 75	No or minimal activities supporting dynamic data management	Focus on decreasing scores in at least 5 RF	Focus on decreasing scores in at least 7 RF
50 < SRF ≤ 75	Weak activities supporting dynamic data management	Focus on decreasing scores in at least 3 RF	Focus on decreasing scores in at least 5 RF
25 < SRF ≤ 50	Moderate activities supporting dynamic data management	Focus on decreasing scores in at least 1 RF	Focus on decreasing scores in at least 3 RF
SRF ≤ 25	Strong activities supporting dynamic data management	N/A	Preserve or continuously improve the behavior

Table 9.7   Pillar IX: Action Plan to Increase Self-Driving Force (SDF)

Name: _____   Date: _____

No.	Driving Force	Current Score	Goal (Target Score) ⬆	Action Plan, to increase DF Score	Complete by (Date)	Required Resources
1	I am not overwhelmed by the present-day challenges of data management as I understand and adhere to the principles of dynamic data management while leading projects.					
2	I understand the pros and cons of the emerging modes of communication and have used chat, blogs, text messages, Twitter, LinkedIn, Facebook, and several other channels of communication.					
3	I follow the principles of dynamic data selection on projects and only use reliable and balanced data based on the duration, complexity, and criticality of the project.					
4	While leading projects, I categorize project data as VA, NNVA, and NVA and try to reduce or eliminate the NNVA and NVA data types.					
5	On every project, I create a dynamic data management plan that provides guidance to the project team regarding data security, administration, and usage throughout the life cycle of the project.					
6	I usually delegate the task of creating a comprehensive data management plan document to the data management experts on my team.					

7	I use the ratio of VA data to NVA data to decide the storage requirements and create methods to eliminate redundant or invalid data from the databases to reduce the expenses involved in data storage.					
8	I encourage my team members to store critical project-related data in a secure, centralized location with appropriate access permissions.					
9	I proactively plan for securing the project data using data encryption, virus and hacker protection, data loss prevention, user authentication, and backup solutions.					
10	I understand the costs and resources involved in project data changes and proactively create a data change management plan for the life cycle of the project.					
	Total SDF					

Table 9.8 Pillar IX: Action Plan to Decrease Self-Resisting Forces (SRFs)

Name: _____   Date: _____

No.	Resisting Force	Current Score	Goal (Target Score) ⬇	Action Plan to Decrease RF Score	Complete by (Date)	Required Resources
1	Data management is one of the aspects of project management that frustrates me.					
2	I prefer to stick to simple modes of communications like phone, e-mail, and other standard forms.					
3	I use as much data as is available and from any source irrespective of the duration, complexity, and criticality of the project.					
4	I do not categorize or attempt to reduce the project data while managing projects.					
5	On my projects, I do not create a data management plan or just use a standard checklist to fulfill the requirements of data planning.					
6	Although I am not an expert at data management, I prepare and manage the data management plan document.					
7	I do not consider data storage requirements while creating a project plan.					
8	I do not mandate the location of storage of project data, and the team members are allowed to store all data on their hard drives or on their personal network drives.					
9	I depend on the IT department to provide security for my project data.					
10	I depend on the document control department for the project data changes and do not create a data change management plan on my projects.					
	Total SRF					

Pillar IX   Exercises

PILLAR IX: ORGANIZATIONAL-LEVEL SKILL SET–ENHANCEMENT EXERCISES

Group Exercises

These exercises are best completed within a group of project managers, project leaders, executives, and stakeholders from within a department or an organization.

1. Using Table 9.9, identify at least five advantages to your organization in creating a culture of dynamic project data management, rate them from 1 (least important) to 5 (most important), and explain the rating.

2. Using Table 9.10, identify at least five roadblocks within your organization in creating a culture of dynamic project data management, rate them from 1 (least difficult to overcome) to 5 (most difficult to overcome), and explain the rating.

3. Identify a complex project that is in the planning stages. Get the core team together and ask them to use Table 9.11 to fill in the method used to accomplish the following on the project.
   a. Analysis of project data requirements
   b. Selection of appropriate data types and data sources
   c. Appropriate data storage, security, retrieval, and distribution
   d. Data monitoring and change management.

Next, have them make improvements to the plan in each of these categories on the basis of the principles of dynamic data management of Pillar IX.

4. Identify a recently completed complex project. Get the core team together and ask them to use Table 9.12 to fill in at least three examples where their project was adversely affected or failed because of lack of any aspects of data management. Next, for each of the three items, have them reflect on the principles of dynamic data management and mention which principles from Pillar IX could have helped prevent the adverse impact or failure of the project.

5. Scenario analysis: DOCUTV is a major Documentary TV channel with a central global hub in San Francisco, CA, with satellite offices in Paris, Berlin, Prague, Beijing, Delhi, and Dubai. Every clip of news is digitally recorded and transferred to the newsroom in San Francisco for editing, approval, and archiving before being released on the air. DOCUTV does not do any live broadcast transmissions. The San Francisco location also serializes labels and catalogs each clip. Some clips are sensitive in nature as release permissions have not been granted by the third parties, and the clip is quarantined until all required permissions are obtained.

Table 9.9   Pillar IX: Five Advantages of Applying Principles of Pillar IX to Your Organization

No.	Advantages of Applying Principles of Pillar IX to Enhancing Your Organization Culture	Rating, 1 (Least Important) to 5 (Most Important)	Explain the Rating
1			
2			
3			
4			
5			

Table 9.10   Pillar IX: Five Roadblocks to Creating a Culture of Dynamic Data Management

No.	Roadblocks to Applying Principles of Dynamic Data Management as Described in Pillar IX to Your Organization	Rating, 1 (Least Difficult to Overcome) to 5 (Most Difficult to Overcome)	Explain the Rating
1			
2			
3			
4			
5			

Table 9.11   Pillar IX: Comparison of Current Method with Principles of Pillar IX

Aspects of Data Management	Methods Used to Accomplish These Aspects	Improvements Made Based on Principles of Pillar IX
1. Analysis of Project Data Requirements		
2. Selection of Appropriate Data Types and Data Sources		
3. Appropriate Data Storage, Security, Retrieval, and Distribution		
4. Data Monitoring and Change Management		

Table 9.12   Pillar IX: Application of Principles of Pillar IX to a Failed Project

Name of Failed Project	
Examples Where Project Was Adversely Affected or Failed due to Lack of Any Aspects of Data Management	Principles of Dynamic Data Management from Pillar IX Which Could Have Helped Prevent the Adverse Effect or Failure of the Project
1.	
2.	
3.	

DOCUTV is considering creating a central repository of all footage that can be remotely accessed from anywhere in the world by the management in the San Francisco location. They are also considering "cloud computing" by hosting the expensive editing software on the network that can be accessed globally for immediate editing by each satellite office before having it checked-in for automated cataloging. The cloud computing costs are $10/TB of data exchanged, and the archiving costs are $1/TB of data. Monthly digital video footage for DOCUTV is approximately 100,000 TB. DOCUTV has contracted a company, XPRTDATA, to plan and execute the project to create a bulletproof dynamic data management system on the basis of the principles of Pillar IX. Assuming your team is part of XPRTDATA, make the necessary assumptions using Tables 9.13 through 9.15, and provide a detailed plan for dynamic data management with focus on the following:

    i. Appropriate data storage
   ii. Appropriate data security
  iii. Appropriate data retrieval, distribution, and monitoring.

Table 9.13   Pillar IX: Scenario Analysis Based on Principles of Pillar IX

Focus Area	XPRTDATA's Plan for Dynamic Data Management Based on Principles of Pillar IX
Data Storage	1. 2. 3. 4. 5. 6. 7. 8. 9. 10.

Table 9.14   Pillar IX: Scenario Analysis Based on Principles of Pillar IX

Focus Area	XPRTDATA's Plan for Dynamic Data Management Based on Principles of Pillar IX
Data Security	1. 2. 3. 4. 5. 6. 7. 8. 9. 10.

Table 9.15 Pillar IX: Scenario Analysis Based on Principles of Pillar IX

Focus Area	XPRTDATA's Plan for Dynamic Data Management Based on Principles of Pillar IX
Data Retrieval Distribution and Monitoring	1. 2. 3. 4. 5. 6. 7. 8. 9. 10.

PILLAR IX: PERSONAL-LEVEL SKILL SET–ENHANCEMENT EXERCISES

INDIVIDUAL EXERCISES

These exercises are to be completed individually after reviewing Pillar IX in detail.

1. Using Table 9.16, list at least five advantages of applying the principles of Pillar IX detailing dynamic data management to your future projects. Rate the advantages from 1 (least important) to 5 (most important) and explain the rating.

2. Using Table 9.17, identify at least five roadblocks to applying the principles of dynamic data management from Pillar IX on all your future major projects. Rate the identified roadblocks from 1 (least difficult to overcome) to 5 (most difficult to overcome) and explain the rating.

3. Using Table 9.18, select a project you worked on as a project manager/leader that had issues related to data. Looking back on the project, answer the following questions for each phase of the project.

    a. Provide an example of the following: (a) value-added data, (b) necessary non-value-added data, and (c) data categorized as *muda*.

    b. Provide an estimation of percentage of the following: (a) value-added data, (b) necessary non-value-added data, and (c) data categorized as *muda*.

4. Using Table 9.19, select a future project requiring significant amounts of data that you have been assigned to. How will you

Table 9.16   Pillar IX: Five Advantages of Applying Principles of Pillar IX to Your Career

No.	Advantages of Applying Principles of Lean Thinking from Pillar IX to All Future Projects	Rating, 1 (Least Important) to 5 (Most Important)	Explain the Rating
1			
2			
3			
4			
5			

Table 9.17   Pillar IX: Five Roadblocks to Applying Principles of Pillar IX

No.	Roadblocks to Applying Principles of Lean Thinking Detailed In Pillar IX to All Future Projects	Rating, 1 (Least Difficult to Overcome) to 5 (Most Difficult to Overcome)	Explain the Rating
1			
2			
3			

4			
5			

Table 9.18 Pillar IX: Reflecting on a Failed Project and Identifying Principles of Pillar IX

Name of Failed Project		
Your Role in the Project		
Phase	*Identify at Least One Example for Each of the Data Categories—VA, NNVA, and Muda*	*Estimate Percentage of Each Category of Data*
1. Project start-up	VA: _____ NNVA: _____ *Muda:* _____	1. VA data: _____% 2. NNVA data: _____% 3. *Muda* data: _____%
2. Project preparation	VA: _____ NNVA: _____ *Muda:* _____	1. VA data: _____% 2. NNVA data: _____% 3. *Muda* data: _____%
3. Project implementation	VA: NNVA: *Muda:* _____	1. VA data: _____% 2. NNVA data: _____% 3. *Muda* data: _____%
4. Project monitoring	VA: _____ NNVA: _____ *Muda:* _____	1. VA data: _____% 2. NNVA data: _____% 3. *Muda* data: _____%
5. Project closure	VA: _____ NNVA: _____ *Muda:* _____	1. VA data: _____% 2. NNVA data: _____% 3. *Muda* data: _____%

Note: VA: value added; NNVA: necessary non-value added, *Muda*: Waste

ensure that you will use the principles Pillar IX for achieving the following on the project:

a. Safe storage, backup, and easy retrieval of data
b. Securing data against access by unauthorized personnel, software viruses, and so forth.
c. Fast access of data to personnel with access rights and permissions
d. Monitoring file size, data type, and appropriate filing protocols

Table 9.19   Pillar IX: Principles of Pillar IX Applied to Future Project with Excessive Data

Critical Elements of Data Management	Principles of Pillar IX Applied to Future Project
1. Data Storage and Retrieval	
2. Data Security	
3. Data Access	
4. Data Monitoring	
5. Data Distribution	
6. Data Change Management	

e. Ensuring data goes to authorized distribution lists that are kept current

f. Reliable and user-friendly change management system.

5. Scenario analysis: DOCUTV is a major Documentary TV channel with a central global hub in San Francisco, CA, with satellite offices in Paris, Berlin, Prague, Beijing, Delhi, and Dubai. Every clip of news is digitally recorded and transferred to the newsroom in San Francisco for editing, approval, and archival before being released on the air. DOCUTV does not do any live broadcast transmissions. The San Francisco location also serializes, labels, and catalogs each clip. Some clips are sensitive in nature as release permissions have not been granted by the third parties, and the clip is quarantined until all required permissions are obtained.

DOCUTV is considering creating a central repository of all footage that can be remotely accessed from anywhere in the world by the

Table 9.20   Pillar IX: Scenario Analysis Based on Principles of Pillar IX

a. Data encryption	
b. Virus and hacker protection	
c. Strong user authentication	
d. Data loss prevention	
e. Backup solution	

management in the San Francisco location. They are also considering "cloud computing" by hosting the expensive editing software on the network that can be accessed globally for immediate editing by each satellite office before having it checked-in for automated cataloging. The cloud computing costs are $10/TB of data exchanged, and the archiving costs are $1/TB of data. Monthly digital video footage for DOCUTV is approximately 100,000 TB. DOCUTV has contracted a company, XPRTDATA, to plan and execute the project to create a bulletproof dynamic data management system on the basis of the principles of Pillar IX. Assuming you are the project leader at XPRTDATA, make the necessary assumptions, and using Table 9.20, provide the detailed plan for the following critical elements using the principles of dynamic data management:

    i. Data encryption
   ii. Virus and hacker protection
  iii. Strong user authentication
  iv. Data loss prevention
   v. Backup solutions.

Pillar IX   References

1. Albert Einstein. (1879–1955). http://www.great-quotes.com/quote/980332 (accessed November 29, 2010).
2. Albert Einstein. (2010). BrainyQuote.com, Xplore, Inc., http://www.brainyquote.com/quotes/quotes/a/alberteins163057.html (accessed November 29, 2010).
3. Luthra, V. (2010). *Information*. http://www.businessdictionary.com/definition/information.html (accessed November 29, 2010).
4. Luthra, V. (2010). *Data*. http://www.businessdictionary.com/definition/data.html (accessed November 29, 2010).
5. Kinnie, J. (2004). *What is Information? Is There Anything That Isn't Information?* http://www.uri.edu/library/staff_pages/kinnie/lib120/info.html#overload (accessed November 29, 2010).
6. Slome, W. (2010). *TMI: The Age of Information Overload*, http://investingcaffeine.com/2010/01/07/tmi-the-age-of-information-overload (accessed November 29, 2010).
7. Thoburn, R. (2010). *The Body Builders Eating Plan*, http://www.nutritionexpress.com/supplements/whey+protein/showarticle.aspx?articleid=266 (accessed November 29, 2010).
8. Smith, D. M. (2010). *Data Loss and Hard Drive Failure: Understanding the Causes and Costs*, http://www.deepspar.com/wp-data-loss.html (accessed November 29, 2010).
9. Info security. (2009). *Health Net Comes Under Scrutiny for Data Loss*, http://www.infosecurity-us.com/view/5422/health-net-comes-under-scrutiny-for-data-loss (accessed November 29, 2010).
10. Spam Laws. (2009). *What is Data Security?* http://www.spamlaws.com/data-security.html (accessed November 29, 2010).
11. McCaney, K. (2009). *In Wake of TSA Breach, A Refresher on Redacting PDFs*, http://gcn.com/articles/2009/12/09/tsa-breach-pdf-redaction-refresher.aspx (accessed November 29, 2010).
12. Ironport Systems. (2007). *Data Loss Prevention Best Practices: Managing Sensitive Data in the Enterprise*. Cisco Systems. Inc., http://www.ironport.com/pdf/ironport_dlp_booklet.pdf, pp. 7 and 15 (accessed November 29, 2010).
13. Data Management Working Group. (2010). *Project Data Management Criteria*, http://www.eol.ucar.edu/projects/ghp/dm/documents/criteria.html (accessed November 29, 2010).
14. Project Management Institute. (2008). *A Guide to the Project Management Body of Knowledge (PMBOK Guide)*, 4th Ed., p. 253. 14 Campus Boulevard, Newtown Square, PA 19073–3299 USA.
15. Foley, J. (2008). *A Definition of Cloud Computing*, http://www.informationweek.com/cloud-computing/blog/archives/2008/09/a_definition_of.html (accessed November 29, 2010).

Chapter 10

Pillar X: Learn from Failures

Past lessons learned can affect future successes earned.

True leaders treat successes as strangers and failures as
faithful friends.

10.1 Introduction

How many times did Thomas Alva Edison (1847–1931) fail in his search for the perfect filament for the incandescent lamp? The answer is approximately 1799 times. Edison tried anything he could think of including bamboo, animal hair, and even whiskers from a friend's beard. In all, he tried approximately 1800 things. After approximately 1000 attempts, someone asked him if he was frustrated at his lack of success.[1] He said, *"Results! Why, man, I have gotten a lot of results. I know several thousand things that won't work".*[2]

Wow! Would you agree with me that Edison was cool for his time! He had a totally fresh and different perspective of failure. But because of his fresh perspective and the knowledge gained from his failures, Edison's eventual success was in inventing not only the perfect incandescent light bulb but also an electric lighting system that contained all the elements necessary to make the incandescent light practical, safe, and economical. After 1.5 years of failures, he was finally successful when he used a filament of carbonized sewing thread for the incandescent lamp, which glowed for a total of 13.5 hours[3] (Figure 10.1).

What motivated Edison to persevere through his "failures?" To understand this, we need to first understand the definition of the word "failure" and contrast it with Edison's interpretation of the meaning of the word "failure."

The question I ask myself is, if Thomas Edison was part of a project team or a project manager in the corporate environment today, would he have been as successful as before? Would he have been able to persevere in his quest of find-

Figure 10.1   Thomas Edison with his invention, the incandescent bulb.

ing the perfect filament? Would Thomas Edison have had an opportunity to truly change the world forever if he worked for any corporation today?

Sadly, my conclusion is that today's corporate environment may not have been able to tolerate the number of "failures" that Thomas Edison had in inventing the incandescent light bulb. The instant gratification demands of Wall Street and the intense pressures for "speed to market" spurred by global competition encourage a culture of instant wins and short-term successes versus long-term breakthroughs and life-changing innovations. Edison persevered through his 1799 "failures" because he or others did not label any of his findings as "failures" but looked at them as another step toward achieving the ultimate success. Thus, just as beauty is in the eye of the beholder, success is in the heart of the seeker.

> **Just as beauty is in the eye of the beholder, success is in the heart of the seeker.**

10.2 What Is a Failure?

In simple terms, a failure is not reaching or accomplishing the intended objective one set out to achieve at the start. Generally, failure is considered as a converse of success.

10.2.1 The Difference between a Task Failure and a Project Failure

A task is an element of the project that is assigned to a particular resource or team member. Generally, if the task is not successful, it is called task failure.

In any project, a project manager is tasked with balancing the following competing objectives, such as scope, time, cost, quality, resources, and risks. At the onset of the project, a baseline is created for all of the above and goals are set to accomplish the outcomes of the project within the constraints set. If any of the objectives set above are not met, the project is considered a failure.

A task failure can be a minor failure that may delay the project, increase the budget, affect resource availability, or interrupt communications; sometimes, it can be significant enough to result in a project failure. Let us look at an example to understand a task failure in a project. A team member implemented a change request that was not approved by the change control board. The task failure resulted in affecting the timeline of the task by 1 week because of the time lost in correcting the change request. The longest time taken to complete the project, which is also known as the critical path of a project, is the collective timeline of various tasks that can affect the end date of the project. If the failed task is not on the critical path of the project, this task failure may just delay the task timeline but may not affect the overall project timeline. However, if the failed task is on the critical path, the task failure may result in project failure by increasing the overall timeline of the project.

10.2.2 What Do "Success" and "Failure" Mean to a Project Manager

For project managers, "failure" and "success" are the two opposite sides of a coin; to them "failure" is the opposite of "success."

For project managers, "failure" and "success" are the two opposite sides of a coin; to them "failure" is the opposite of "success." They consider a failure as a task failure if any of the team members are unable to achieve success in any of the assigned tasks, and consider a failure as a project failure if a project does not achieve all the objectives one sets out to achieve. Project managers also consider the lack of ability of the team to successfully plan or execute the project as a project failure. Thus, project managers attribute any type of failure to the team or individual ability. Depending on the culture of the organization and on the criticality of the project to the business results, some failures are considered acceptable, whereas others might be severe enough to be considered fatal to the project and to the career of the individual or project manager.

10.2.3 What Do "Success" and "Failure" Mean to a Project Leader

Just like Thomas Edison, true leaders, innovators, and philosophers have a very progressive view of failures. Let's look at some quotes from some well-known and highly respected personalities:

> *Failure is simply the opportunity to begin again, this time more intelligently*[4]

Henry Ford

> *Failure is the foundation of success . . . success is the lurking place of failure*[5]

Ancient Chinese philosopher, Lao-Tzu

All successful leaders have also definitely tasted failures. The only difference is that they consider every failure as a friend trying to provide candid opinion on the gaps in their skill-set or style or other aspects of their performance. Every failure for them is a "new lesson learned" to build on so that the current and future projects never encounter this failure ever again.

True leaders, innovators, and philosophers also have a more practical and humbling view of success and thus they do not dwell too long on their successes either. Their reaction to successes is similar to their reaction to strangers in the street—they acknowledge and move on. Here are some quotes from some other well-known and highly respected personalities:

> *Success is 99 percent failure.*[5]

Soichiro Honda, Founder, Honda Motor Co., Ltd.

Failure is inevitable. Success is elusive.[6]

Steven Spielberg, Director/Producer

All glory is fleeting.[7]

General George Patton

Thus, to true leaders, successes are strangers and even minor failures are true friends as they are continuously providing feedback that helps them become better leaders. They consider every failure as an essential stepping-stone on their road to the pinnacle of ultimate success.

> To true leaders, successes are strangers and even minor failures are true friends as they are continuously providing feedback that helps them become better leaders. They consider every failure as an essential stepping-stone on their road to the pinnacle of ultimate success.

Project leaders also have a progressive view of project success and project failure, and the role they play in both these. For example, even if their project is a tremendous success and project leaders always know that they are far from perfect and there are definitely some areas they can improve on. Also, even if their project or some portions of their project have failed, successful project leaders learn from mistakes throughout the project and conduct lessons learned meetings at the end of each critical project phase. They also use the "closing phase" of the project to effectively gather this information. The fundamental point that a project leader focuses on is identifying failures, analyzing the root causes of the failures, and learning from each and every failure. They believe that, *"Past lessons learned, impact the future successes earned."*

10.3 The Three Modes of Project Failure

Once we have an understanding of the definition of project success and project failure, let us look at the three modes of project failure. In an organization, failures can occur because of a variety of reasons. Thus, if we need to learn from failures, all failures must be categorized on the basis of the root cause of the failures. Let us ask a question, "What are the most common modes of projects failure?"

There are three basic modes of failure:

1. System-level failure
2. Process-level failure
3. Human-level failure

10.3.1 System-Level Failure

A "system-level failure" mode of a project can be defined as the failure of a project caused by the gaps in overall constitution, strategy, organizational culture, expertise, corporate readiness, or a gap in organizational or project leadership.

A "system-level failure" mode of a project can be defined as the failure of a project caused by the gaps in overall constitution, strategy, organizational culture, expertise, corporate readiness, or a gap in organizational or project leadership. This mode of failure is the most serious as it can affect all the projects and initiatives within an organization. Also, the root cause(s) of this mode of failure are not readily visible and have to be investigated carefully. To find the root cause of system-level mode of failure, the question to ask is:

"Why Did It Fail?"

Consider a situation in an aggressive sales-driven software organization where the project leaders are consistently failing to deliver the advanced functionality and conflicting features promised to the customers within the contractual timeline. The project leaders are not involved until the contract is signed with the customers. One of the system-level root causes of this failure could be that the sales team very frequently sells "vapor-ware" to the client promising functionalities that do not exist among the core competencies within the organization. On investigating further, it was found out that the sales team is measured and rewarded solely on the number of sales made and as a result they are exceedingly aggressive in "overpromising" functionality, quality, and timeline to the customers. This can only be corrected at the executive level of the organization by adjusting the metrics of performance for the sales team, authorizing project leaders to evaluate the contract before signing, or allowing project leaders to acquire resources and expertise needed to complete the software development project.

10.3.2 Process-Level Failure

A "process-level failure" mode of a project can be defined as the failure of the project caused by gaps in, inadequate resources for, lack of documentation of, lack of capability within, or lack of foolproof methods to implement any process.

A "process-level failure" mode of a project can be defined as the failure of the project caused by gaps in, inadequate resources for, lack of documentation of, lack of capability within, or lack of foolproof methods to implement any process. This mode of failure can be serious, depending on the impact on the project. The root cause(s) of this mode of failure need to be investigated to identify them correctly. To find the root cause of process-level modes of failure, the question to ask is:

"What Caused It to Fail?"

Consider an instance in which there are several customer complaints regarding defects for almost all new products sold by the organization. An increase in product defects indicates a failure of the quality control process. One of the process-level root causes for this could be that quality management processes used to control the quality of new products are not adequate to design and manufacture quality products. This can be corrected at the process level by updating the design specifications, better managing supplier quality, updating manufacturing process and tolerance specifications, and updating the inspection criteria for final inspections. Similarly, not resolving stakeholder issues in a timely manner shows a failure of the stakeholder management process.

10.3.3 Human-Level Failure

A "human a level" failure mode can be defined as the failure of the project caused directly or indirectly by human error, supervision, negligence, inability, or by any kind of unnecessary human intervention. This mode of failure can be serious, depending on the effect on the personnel and on the project. Although this mode of failure is commonly observed, care must be taken to correctly identify the human level failure as an effect, cause, or the root cause of project failure because it is quite easy to mistake the system level and process level root causes as human level if a true root cause, deeper level analysis is not conducted. To find the root cause of human level mode of failure, the question to ask is:

> **A "human-level" failure mode can be defined as the failure of the project caused directly or indirectly by human error, supervision, negligence, inability, or any kind of unnecessary human intervention.**

"Who Caused It to fail?"

Some of the examples of human failures in a project are failure to complete a task by a team member, failure to make the right decisions, and failure of managing conflicts by the team leaders. Human failure can also lead to accidents or safety issues. Human failures can occur because of a variety of reasons. Human failures can also be caused by overlooking facts, sheer negligence, and carelessness. Human failures can also be possible because of errors during interactions with processes or existing systems, such as entering incorrect data in a database. Figure 10.2 explains the classification of each type of failure.

10.4 Approach to Investigate and Address Project Failures

Thus far, we have discussed the definition of a failure and various modes of failure. However, root cause analysis of a failure is required to identify the true

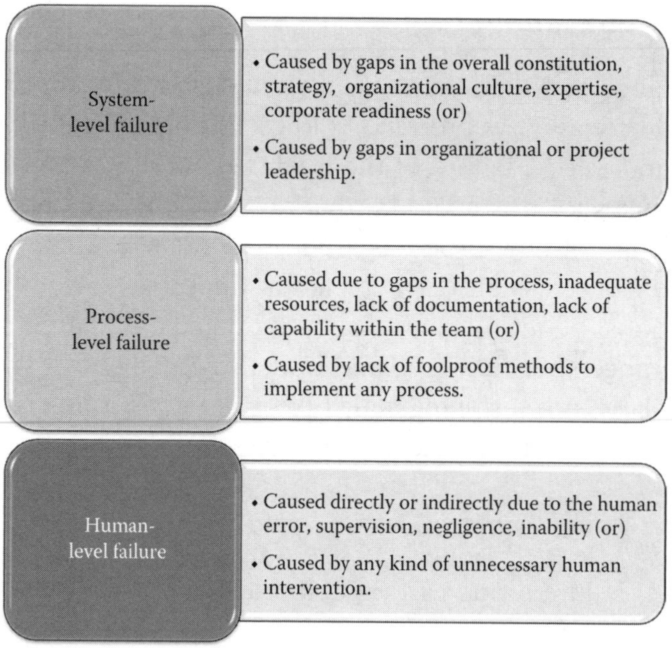

Figure 10.2   Classification of failures in projects.

cause of the failures so that we can learn from it and prevent it from ever happening again. Merely investigating failures is not enough; it is critical to learn lessons from the mistakes so we never have to repeat them. Thus, it is essential for the project team to thoroughly examine the failures and to conduct failure analysis in order to arrive at a full understanding of the root cause(s) of the failures. To determine this, the lessons learned process should examine each failure from the systems, processes, and human level of failure modes. There are two different approaches followed in failure analysis.

These two approaches focus on different type of failures.

1. A reactive analysis using the "who" approach with a primary focus on the human-level mode of failure.
2. A proactive analysis using the "why" approach with a focus on system- and process-level modes of failure.

10.4.1 Reactive Analysis Using the "Who" Approach with a Focus on Human-Level Failure

As discussed earlier, project managers who have not yet developed the five powers of project leadership, especially the power of lean thinking, are constantly in the reactive mode. Project managers try to analyze and investigate reasons

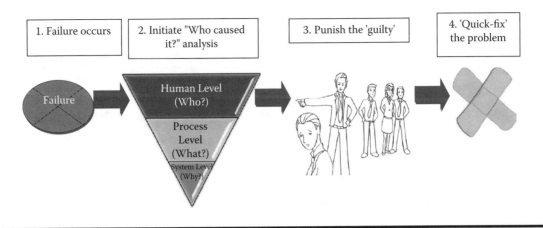

Figure 10.3 A project manager's approach to failure resolution.

for failures only after each failure has already happened. Also, during project execution, because of the intense pressures of time, the level of interest among project managers in conducting lessons learned analysis for failures is very low. Thus, project managers take the quickest and easiest approach to addressing the failures by trying to find "Who caused it to fail?" and fix it fast using a Band-Aid solution.

As shown in Figure 10.3, the following are the steps project managers generally take to find the quick fix for the identified failures.

1. Failure occurs
2. Initiate "who caused it?" analysis
3. Punish the guilty
4. Quick-fix the problem

The project manager's approach toward project failures is described below.

10.4.1.1 Failure Occurs

Failures usually occur on projects because of the lack of upfront planning, incorrect or insufficient assessment of risks, insufficient time to train resources, or a number of other reasons. In a poorly planned project, these failures are usually reported to the project manager only after they occur, and only after some damage has been done to the project. Once the failure occurs, because of the intense stress on project managers, they react with a "who" approach with a focus on human-level mode of failure. Project managers who lack adequate experience also use the same approach to fix the problem.

10.4.1.2 Initiate "Who Caused It?" Analysis

After the failure occurs, project managers make an attempt to conduct a quick analysis of the project failure.

As shown in Figure 10.4, project managers focus on failure analysis in the following order of priority:

1. Human-level mode of failure
2. Process-level mode of failure
3. System-level mode of failure

Thus, after every failure, the project managers focus on asking "Who caused it to fail?" till there is an individual or a team identified as the one responsible for the failure. If the failure is critical, the project manager will request the individual or team to conduct an analysis and find out "What caused it to fail?", that is, focus on the process-level mode of failure. Unless it is absolutely necessary and is mandated from above, the project manager and the team rarely have time to investigate the root cause(s) of the failure by asking "Why did it fail?", as shown in Figure 10.5.

10.4.1.3 Punish the Guilty

Because of pressures on time and resources, it becomes important for project managers to demonstrate to the rest of the team that the "failures" are not acceptable on the project and that "heads may roll" if a team member is identified as someone who caused a major negative effect on the project timeline, budget, scope, or quality. Thus, the next step after discovering the failure and conducting "Who caused it" analysis is to identify the culprit responsible for the failure. The team members whose tasks were not completed on time and whose previous decisions resulted in delays in the work will come under intense scrutiny. Also,

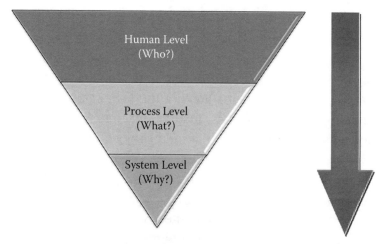

Figure 10.4   Project manager's failure analysis using the "who" approach with a focus on human-level mode of failure.

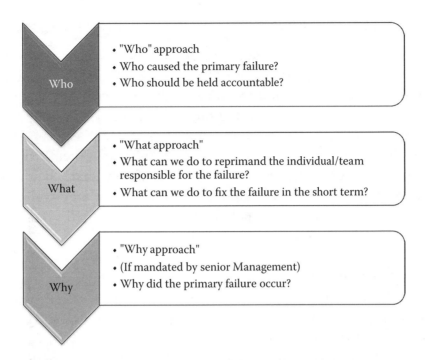

Figure 10.5   Project manager's reactive approach to investigate and resolve failures.

the team members at the lowest level of the task can usually be wrongly identified as the culprit who does not have a voice in the project. The punishment can range from a simple reprimand to a censure in the project performance appraisal affecting pay and bonus, to demotion of rank, removal from project team, and sometimes even from the organization.

10.4.1.4 Quick-Fix the Problem

The final step in closing out the failure is to identify the resources that can be put in a Band-Aid solution so that it cannot cause any more harm to the project. Sometimes, the "quick fix" fails before closing out the project and another Band-Aid solution is found and implemented. Project managers knowingly or unknowingly follow this approach believing that this is how the lessons learned process is carried out.

10.4.1.5 Effect of the Reactive Approach

Project and organization culture can be severely affected by the project manager's approach to failure analysis by focusing on human-level modes of failure.

The fundamental flaw of the reactive approach focused on the human-level mode of failure is that it results in

    a. Culture of fear
    b. Culture of distrust
    c. Culture of risk aversion, lacking creativity and innovation

10.4.1.4.1 Culture of Fear

Using the human-level failure mode approach, the project managers, without even realizing, create an environment of fear resulting in individuals and teams hiding any issues encountered in the course of the project. There is general fear of "the messenger being killed," and the project manager is blindsided until a failure occurs. In projects, the fear arises from two different aspects. The first aspect is that team members or project managers think that their abilities will be questioned and their expertise will be doubted if they share their failure with others. The second aspect is that team members think that they will be made responsible for the loss because of failure and will be removed from the project. This makes the team members fearful of failures.

10.4.1.4.2 Culture of Distrust

Another problem with this approach is that team members blame each other and point fingers for their own mistakes and make few people responsible for their failure. This type of behavior may also be expected from the project manager. As a result of this, team cohesiveness is reduced and significant performance problems will be encountered. Because project team members do not trust each other, the project team disintegrates into small groups of individuals, leading to project failure. Very few project managers realize the adverse effect of this approach on the project team.

There may also be a culture of a negative attitude or a culture of "being looked down upon" by the rest of the project team members, sponsors, or stakeholders if a certain individual or team is allegedly identified to have issues or have been allegedly identified as the root cause of failures. Thus, there is a possibility of project critical communication in the lateral and vertical directions being completely closed-off, having a major negative effect on the project performance. This may lead to the project manager, knowingly or unknowingly, also closing off failure-related communications with the sponsor and other stakeholders, leading to an inability to satisfy the end customer as a result of project failures.

Thus, this creates a negative atmosphere, finger-pointing disharmony, closed project communications, and intense fear among the project team.

10.4.1.4.3 Culture of Risk Aversion, Lacking Creativity and Innovation

This approach also results in the loss of creativity and changes in the ability of risk-taking among the team members. Because project managers focus on human failures in this approach, team members become averse to taking the slightest risk in their projects. They fear that each decision they make on their project may lead to failure and result in more responsibilities, reprimand, or dismissal. Subsequently, they tend to hide everything from the project team and like to neither discuss nor learn from their failures. The result of this approach is loss of risk-taking capability by the project team. Because the team does not learn from its mistakes, the same mistakes and failures could happen again and again, resulting in more project failures.

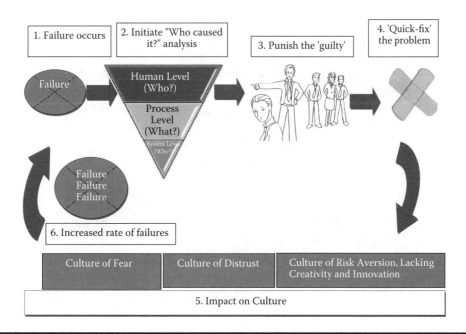

Figure 10.6   Impact on culture with project manager's reactive approach to failure resolution.

Figure 10.6 describes the culture effect of a project manager's focus on human failure. This can become a never-ending cycle, repeated project after project, keeping the project manager in a reactive mode. This can sometimes become a detriment to their career advancement within an organization and may even lead to a career-ending, high-profile failure, on any project.

Let us look at a real example to understand the severity of the effect of the reactive mode of failure analysis at National Aeronautics and Space Administration (NASA). The U.S. General Accounting Office conducted a survey on NASA's lessons learned process. This represented 192 managers overseeing approximately 240 programs and projects. The survey indicates a key point in lessons learned process, which is "Managers are reluctant to share failures with others." The survey also states that "There is an unwillingness to share information or air dirty laundry. If you made a mistake you might not be deemed to be a good project manager."[9] The survey clearly indicates lack of enthusiasm among project managers to discuss failures. Thus, the consequences of this approach can have a significant negative effect on the culture of the project team and also on the performance of the organization. Figure 10.7 shows the potential consequences of the human-level mode of failure analysis.

Thus far, we have discussed the reactive approach from project managers. Let us discuss the proactive approach from project leaders.

10.4.2 A Proactive Analysis Using the "Why" Approach with a Focus on System- and Process-Level Modes of Failure—A Lean Approach

As discussed earlier, project leaders who possess the five powers of project leadership, especially the power of lean thinking, use a proactive approach to failure

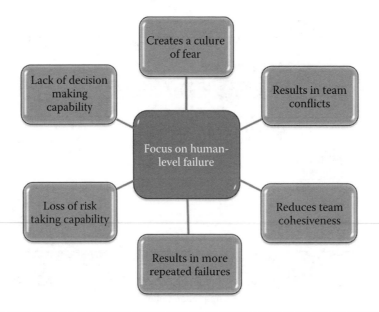

Figure 10.7   Potential consequences of focus on human failures.

analysis. Project leaders focus on proactively trying to assess potential modes of failure by conducting a thorough risk analysis. This does not mean that project leaders do not encounter any failures during projects; they most certainly do, but the approach project leaders take in resolving them is very different and progressive. They use failures as opportunities to address the root causes at the system or the organizational level. They show immense interest in conducting lessons learned analysis for failures as they are curious to understand the primary cause for failure so that they and the entire organization can learn to avoid similar outcomes in the future. Advanced project leaders strongly believe that, "Failure to eliminate the root cause of the identified failure is a more critical failure than the initial failure itself."

Thus, project leaders take the lean approach to address the failures by using a technique called "5 Why's," which requires the team to go to a deeper level of failure analysis each time by asking "Why?" until they find the root cause(s), which they can fix using a systematic approach so that it can never occur again on their projects or other projects undertaken by their organization.

As shown in Figure 10.8, the following are the steps project leaders generally take to find and address the root cause(s) for the failures.

1. Identify potential or actual failure
2. Conduct "5 Why" analysis
3. Find the root cause(s)
4. Eliminate the root cause(s)
5. Update lessons learned databases.

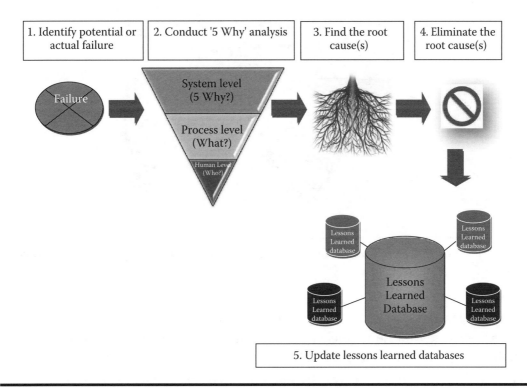

Figure 10.8   Project leader's approach to failure resolution.

10.4.2.1 Identify Potential or Actual Failure

The project leader and the project team members are constantly evaluating the project risks and are always on a lookout for potential failures. They are fully aware that no project is immune from minor failures and their motto is "be prepared" so that none of the minor failures should affect the overall objectives of the project. They use several tools like failure modes and effects analysis, fault tree analysis, and dynamic risk assessment tools to proactively identify failures. They also review the lessons learned databases from previous projects to ensure that they have considered some of the lessons learned by other project leaders so that they do not have to suffer the same failures.

10.4.2.2 Conduct "5 Why" Analysis

After the failure is identified, the project leader and team members take a very systematic approach to conduct a root cause analysis of the project failure.

As shown in Figure 10.9, project managers focus on failure analysis in the following order of priority:

1. System-level mode of failure
2. Process-level mode of failure
3. Human-level mode of failure

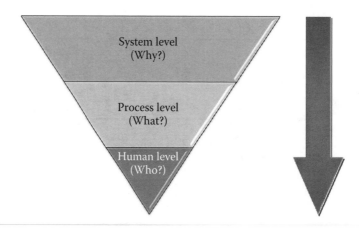

Figure 10.9   Project leader's root cause analysis using the "5 why" approach with a focus on system-level mode of failure.

The project leaders understand that even when it seems that the failure has occurred because of a human-level mode, that may not be the true root cause of the failure and that the root cause may be at the system level. Human errors may actually stem from various issues such as lack of training, lack of procedures, poor supervision, and other issues that may be at a system or organizational level. They understand that just like weeds that are visible above the ground, cutting off the leaves just provides a temporary fix; if we need to prevent the weed from growing back ever again, we need to dig the ground deep enough to get to the roots and then remove the weed along with the root. Thus, they understand that when failure occurs, it is important to start at the systems level and dig as deep as required to reach the root cause(s).

Thus, project leaders focus on taking a team through an analysis called the "5 Why" analysis, which involves asking "why" did the failure occur until they are able to identify the actual cause of the failure at the system level.

"5 Why" Analysis

In "5 Why" analysis, the question "Why did this happen" is repeatedly asked for each valid reason of the failure. The root cause of the problem is determined and efforts are taken to eliminate the root cause.

Benefits of "5 Why Analysis"

- Helps identify the root cause of a failure
- Determines the relationship between different root causes of a failure
- One of the simplest tools; easy to complete without statistical analysis.

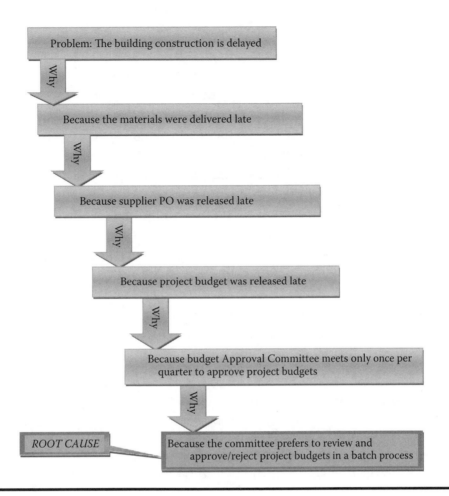

Figure 10.10   An example of "5 why" analysis.

How to Complete the "5 Whys"

1. Write down the specific failure. Writing the issue helps you formalize the failure and describe it completely. It also helps a team focus on the same failure.
2. Ask "Why the failure happens" and write down the answer below the problem.
3. If the answer you just provided does not identify the root cause of the problem that you wrote down in step 1, ask "Why" again and write that answer down.
4. Loop back to step 3 until the team is in agreement that the problem's root cause has been identified. Again, this may take fewer or more times than five "whys."[10] The entire process of "5 why analysis" is shown in Figure 10.10 using an example. The root cause analysis shows "the committee's preference to approve budgets in a batch process" as the real reason for the delayed building construction.

10.4.2.3 Find the Root Cause(s)

Thus, unlike project managers, dynamic project leaders take a lean approach by first focusing on system failures to uncover the problems associated with existing systems. As discussed previously, focusing on existing systems means focusing on the direction, strategy, and vision provided by the leadership in managing the project. Because these elements are disseminated from the air support level to the ground troops level, the ground troops do not have any control in changing those systems even if they have any flaws. Project leaders look at the entire system flow to discover weaknesses in the system that caused the project to fail. Once the system failures or root causes are identified, project leaders focus on process failure to see if any of the existing project management processes caused failures and give least importance to human failures. Although the root cause of failures are identified with "5 Why" analysis, the project leaders can also use other tools like the Fishbone diagram or Ishikawa diagram (this diagram uses "why-why" and "how-how" approach) and other tools as long as the tool meets the following three key criteria of root cause analysis:

1. The tool is easy to use and is designed to get to the root cause of the failure
2. Allows input from team members, stakeholders, and experts
3. Data can be easily entered into a database for lessons learned.

10.4.2.4 Eliminate the Root Cause(s)

Once the root cause is identified, a plan is put into place to address the failure in the short term and eliminate the root cause(s) identified by updating the systems, processes, and procedures so that the failure never occurs again.

10.4.2.5 Update Lessons Learned Databases

The team members responsible for updating the systems, processes, and procedures are identified, databases are updated and the team members are trained on the new systems and procedures. The lessons learned are also shared with the entire organization and are used as inputs for future projects. This is shown in Figure 10.11.

Effect of the Proactive Approach Focused on System-Level Mode of Failure Analysis

By focusing on root cause analysis at the systems level rather than at the human level, project leaders use failures as a learning and growing opportunity for the team members, and for the organization as a whole. They engage the team members in the entire process of problem solving using scientific methods and allow them to grow in competence and confidence in solving problems proactively. This, in turn, creates a truly "open-learning" culture that allows for creativity and innovation during the entire project life cycle. Thus, the project leaders turn the stigma of failure into an opportunity to keep improving as per lean thinking.

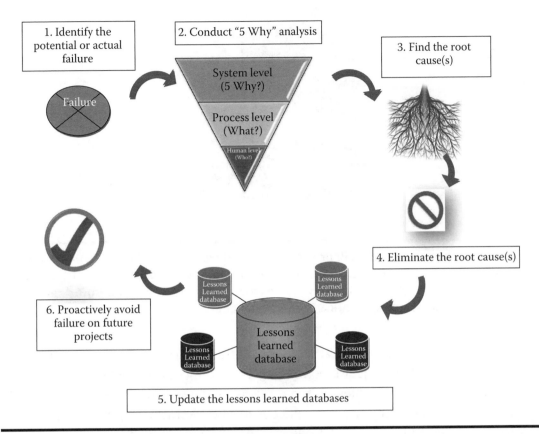

Figure 10.11   Project leader's proactive approach to failure resolution.

This approach results in

  a. Culture of team member engagement
  b. Culture of scientific problem solving—focus on issues not on people
  c. Proactive human error prevention: poka-yoke
  d. Culture of "open learning," creativity, and innovation

10.4.2.5.1 Culture of Team Member Engagement

Towers Perrins' 2007 to 2008 global workforce study regarding employee engagement in organizations reveals that only 21% of their employees are highly engaged in their work, 41% of are partially engaged, 30% are partially disengaged (this means that ~71% of them are in the massive middle), and 8% are fully disengaged, as shown in Figure 10.12.[11] This means that the majority of the employees are not highly engaged in their work.

Project leaders should strive hard to involve partially engaged people and fully disengaged people in the problem-solving and the subsequent learning process. During the brainstorming stages, the project leaders truly believe that "no idea is a bad idea" and "every opinion counts," thus encouraging maximum engagement. Project leaders use the end of the project meeting not only to celebrate successes

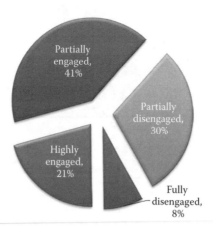

Figure 10.12   Team engagement in projects. (Adapted from Towers Watson, *An Interview with Julie Gebauer on Towers Perrin's Just Released Global Workforce Study*, Part 2. 2008, accessed November 11, 2010. http://www.towersperrin.com/tp/showhtml.jsp?url=global/ publications/gws/key-findings_2.htm&country=global.)

but also conduct an "autopsy" of their project, that is, conduct a "lessons learned" meeting. Out of all the project meetings, this is the most critical to project leaders. Just like a mirror never lies, this process is used to highlight all the outstanding qualities, but most importantly, exposes all the blemishes, spots, cracks, and fissures that need to be addressed before future projects begin.

During the closing phase meeting, the leaders must invite all team members, stakeholders, and senior executives who supported the project in the minutest way to celebrate the successful project and to conduct a lessons learned process. They recognize the key personnel with some customized tokens of appreciation and/ or certificates that remind the members that they were a part of this project. They create a feedback form for the team to be candid about their experience on this project. Many "Ah, Ahs!!" come from this and it helps the leaders in three ways:

1. Helps them improve their own leadership skills and areas needing refinement.
2. Helps them get a deeper understanding of team members and so they can manage their expectations better on future projects.
3. Builds respect and loyalty from team members—they will be excited to work on any future projects with this project leader.

These meetings also help team members in three different ways:

1. Helps them understand the effect of their mistakes or failures on the elements of a project
2. Helps them understand that they are part of the project team and their opinions are valued
3. Learn from their past mistakes and help improve their skills.

The case study at the end of this chapter discusses a "failure" I had early on in my career as a manufacturing engineer as a result of not engaging the people in the problem solving and process improvement step.

10.4.2.5.2 Culture of Scientific Problem Solving— Focus on Issues Not on People

As we discussed before, project managers always resolve failures on the basis of human mistakes and project leaders resolve failures on the basis of system faults. Unlike project managers who focus on human failures first, dynamic project leaders focus on human failures last. Although project leaders also focus on human failures, they focus on the root causes related to human failures instead of trying to blame resources. The critical issues related to failures during the course of the project may be associated with costs, resources, or schedule. Project managers document the problems and update the lessons learned database and take action on some underperformed resources at the end of the project. Thus, there is no way for the team members to learn during the execution of the project. However, project leaders try to document the failure in each phase and prevent such failures from happening in subsequent phases and in future projects. At the end of each phase, and also at the end of the project, project leaders ask questions, such as "What went wrong in the project?" and "What problems could have been preventable?" to fix the problems associated with each failure.

Project leaders use the following methods to fix the root cause of the problem:

1. Project leaders use project data and project baselines to identify and fix the source of the failure. A project baseline is set in the beginning of the project execution. If the actual project plan changes during execution, then the deviation of the plan from the baseline is calculated. Project variations are also calculated on the basis of the baseline data. These deviations can be used to fix the problems associated with project failures.
2. Project leaders also use an issue register to find out the real reasons behind resource failure. Project leaders dig into different documents to discover the reasons for resource failures and task failures across each project phase, and develop methods to fix those.
3. Project leaders use lean method, such as dynamic risk assessment, to analyze the risk as early as possible in the project and fix the problem at the system level to eliminate the failure. They encourage team members to take calculated risks on the basis of the risk assessment from previous phases.
4. Project leaders use a Pareto chart to determine the causes that generated most of the failures. A Pareto chart is based on an 80/20 principle, which says that 80% of the failures are due to 20% of the causes. Therefore, establishing the reasons for such failures will prevent it from happening in the next phase.

5. For failures that have already occurred, the root cause analysis gives the root cause of the problem by asking questions like why this did happen and how did this happen. Corroborating the root causes of the problem gives the project leader the ability to fix those errors for the next phases of the project.

10.4.2.5.3 Proactive Human Error Prevention: Poka-Yoke

Poka-yoke is a lean tool that helps any operator avoid (yoke) mistakes (poka). Poka-yoke is a technique for avoiding simple human error in the workplace. Also known as mistake-proofing, goof-proofing, and fail-safe work methods, poka-yoke is simply a system designed to prevent inadvertent errors made by workers performing a process. The idea is to take overrepetitive tasks that rely on memory or vigilance and guard against any lapses in focus.[12] Poka-yoke can be used not only manufacturing but also in construction, process industries, business processes, and software development.

Sometimes, simple, errors result in big failures. Therefore, preventing them early in the process really saves time, money, and effort. We encounter poka-yoke systems in daily life, for example, the modern automobile has several poka-yoke systems like the beeping alarm when we do not wear our seat belts, the oil change light, the engine check light, the door open signal, and several others. A simple example of poka-yoke in computers is the "save" button. When files are opened, if people forget to save the file and close the program, it would result in loss of important data if the poka-yoke is not in place. To prevent such human mistakes, when files are closed, the system asks the person to click on the "save" or "don't save" button to inform them of the file's closing. This is a very simple example of poka-yoke used to prevent human errors. To use this technique, project leaders make an attempt to identify potential human errors in the projects in repeatable processes. After the identification of such mistakes, they narrow their focus on each mistake to find out the different components causing the mistakes. Then they apply poka-yoke fixes to the system to eliminate such mistakes.

10.4.2.5.4 Culture of "Open Learning," Creativity, and Innovation

Project leaders could create a powerful open-learning environment by leading the charge in creating a positive environment for the lessons learned process.

The biggest advantage of the proactive approach focused on system level mode of failure is the elimination of fear and improvement in team learning. With this approach, project leaders can develop a positive relationship with the team members, allowing the team members to openly discuss failures with the project leader and others on the team. Project leaders could create a powerful open-learning environment by leading the charge in creating a positive environment for the lessons learned process. In a learning organization, leaders are designers, stewards, coaches, and teachers. They focus on using the lessons learned not only for the good of their own future projects but are open to sharing their findings with other project leaders and stakeholders within the entire organization. Thus, they are responsible for building organizations in which people continually expand their capabilities to understand complexity,

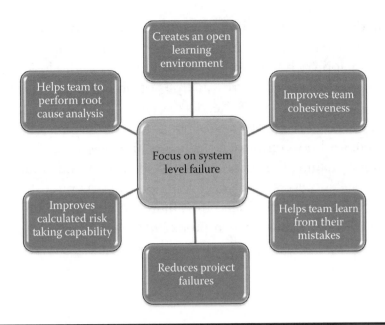

Figure 10.13 Benefits of project leader's focus on system failure.

clarify vision, and improve shared mental models, that is, they are responsible for open learning.

Learning organizations will just remain a "good idea" until more project leaders focus on taking a strong stand for building and establishing this concept in

Table 10.1 Different approached used by the Project Manager and Project Leader to Manage Failures

Project Manager	Project Leader
Focuses on human failures ("who")	Focuses on system failures ("why")
Spends more time to analyze the failure	Spends more time to prevent the failure
Believes that 80% of the failures are caused by 20% of the people	Believes that 80% of the failures are avoidable by 20% of planning
Performs criminal investigation to analyze failures	Performs root cause analysis to prevent failures
Implements risk analysis techniques to confront the failure	Implements dynamic risk assessment to identify and plan for failures
Use Act-Check-Do-Plan cycle to assess failures	Use Plan-Do-Check-Act cycle to prevent failures
Creates mundane and trustless environment for lessons learning	Establish a creative and open environment for lessons learning
Team members working under project manager fail to take decision due to fear of failure	Team members working under project leaders take wise decisions with an opportunity to success

their organizations. Taking this stand is the key action requird to "breathe life into" the vision of creating a sustainable open-learning organization.[13]

Thus, the lean approach followed by project leaders in the lessons learned process helps the project team in true analysis of project failures. Figure 10.13 describes the benefits of the project leader's focus on system failure.

No matter how good the projects are managed, failures are unavoidable. The significant difference between project managers and project leaders lies in the approach of not managing the successes but dealing with the failures. Project managers celebrate successes and ignore failures, whereas project leaders not only enjoy the successes but also lead the failures to acquire future successes. Table 10.1 lists the difference between project managers and project leaders in failure analysis.

Pillar X   Summary

For project managers, "failure" and "success" are the two oppo-site sides of a coin; to them, "failure" is the opposite of "success." All successful leaders consider every failure as a friend trying to provide candid opinion on the gaps in their skill-set, style, or other aspects of their performance. Every failure for them is a "new les-son learned" to build on so that current and future projects never encounter this failure ever again. Every successful project leader learns from failures during the project, at the end of every phase, and at the end of each project so that they can continually fine-tune their leadership skills.

There are three basic modes of failure: system-level failure, process-level failure, and human-level failure. Project managers focus on human-level failures first and other failures later, whereas project leaders focus on system-level failures first and on other failures later. Because project managers use a reactive approach by focusing on human failures, they create a team environment with fear. The proactive approach of the project leader creates an open-learning environment. The real difference between a project manager and project leader can be seen in failure analysis. Project managers look at the surface and perform Band-Aid solutions for failures. However, a project leader focuses on the root causes of the problem and fixes it at the system level. Figure 10.14 highlights important points in project failure analysis.

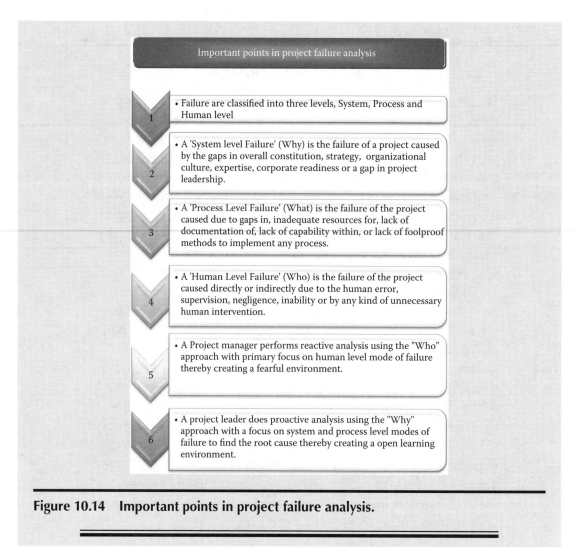

Figure 10.14 Important points in project failure analysis.

Pillar X   Case Study 1
Learn From Failures

INTRODUCTION

This case study discusses two failures in the history of NASA, one that was a tragic failure and the other that was an embarrassing mistake for the organization.

1. The Space Shuttle *Challenger* tragedy on the fateful morning of January 28, 1986
2. The Mars Climate Orbiter crash-landing on the Red Planet on September 23, 1999

THE CHALLENGER TRAGEDY (MISSION 51-L)

On January 28, 1986, the Space Shuttle *Challenger* (Mission 51-L) experienced a catastrophic explosion 73 seconds into the flight and disintegrated over the Atlantic Ocean off the coast of Florida, causing the deaths of seven crew members. The initial cause of the explosion was determined to be an O-ring failure and cold weather was determined to be the contributing factor for that failure. The U.S. Government created the Rogers Commission to investigate the reasons behind this space shuttle failure. The commission identified the initial root cause of the failure as the "failure of communication" and "decisions based on conflicting or incomplete information" that led to the O-ring failure. The U.S. House Committee also conducted hearings on the disaster. Although the committee agreed with the Rogers Commission on the technical causes of the accident, it disagreed with the root cause of the problem. The committee identified the root cause of the failure as a weakness in the decision-making processes in NASA and in contract organizations that have been working with them over the period. Therefore, it is imperative that the root cause of the challenger tragedy conclusively lead to systems or organizational failure instead of human or mechanical failures. The details of "The Challenger Tragedy" are shown in Table 10.2. The root cause diagram is shown in Figure 10.15.

THE MARS CLIMATE ORBITER CRASH-LANDING ON THE RED PLANET (125 MILLION DOLLAR FAILURE)

The Mars Climate Orbiter, with an estimated cost of $125 million, and whose objective was to orbit Mars as the first interplanetary weather satellite and provide a communications relay for the Mars Polar Lander, was launched on December 11, 1998, and was lost some time following the spacecraft's entry into Mars occultation during the Mars Orbit Insertion maneuver on September 23, 1999.

Table 10.2   Case Study and Root Cause Analysis on the Challenger Tragedy

The Challenger Tragedy (Mission 51-L)		Reference
The failure	On January 28, 1986, the Space Shuttle *Challenger* on Mission 51-L experienced a catastrophic explosion, 73 seconds into the flight, and disintegrated over the Atlantic Ocean off the coast of Florida, causing the deaths of seven crew members including the first member of the Teacher in Space Program, Christa McAuliffe	*Source*: Rogers Commission report (1986). Report of the Presidential Commission on the Space Shuttle *Challenger* accident, Chapters 2 and 3. http://history.nasa.gov/ rogersrep/genindex.htm (accessed November 11, 2010)
Initial findings	The loss of the Space Shuttle *Challenger* on Mission 51-L was caused by a failure in the seal in the joint between the two lower segments of the right solid rocket motor. The seal was designed to prevent hot gases from leaking through the joint during the propellant burn of the rocket motor and it failed, resulting in hot gases escaping past the seal and contacting an external tank causing the explosion. It was also found that no other element of the space shuttle system contributed to this tragedy	*Source*: Rogers Commission report (1986). Report of the Presidential Commission on the Space Shuttle *Challenger* accident, Chapter 4. http:// history.nasa.gov/rogersrep/ v1ch4.htm (accessed November 11, 2010)
Initial analysis of cause of failure		
Why did the joint fail?	The O-ring, which is designed to seal the joint, failed	*Source*: Rogers Commission report (1986). Report of the Presidential Commission on the Space Shuttle *Challenger* accident, volume 2, Appendix F. http://history.nasa.gov/ rogersrep/v2appf.htm
Why did the O-ring compress and ultimately fail?	The diameters of the two solid rocket motor segments had grown due to prior use and the O-ring in the joint was compressed to the extent that it pressed against all three walls of the O-ring retaining channel. The O-ring seal failure was caused by the unusually cold temperatures close to or below freezing, which was close to or below the minimum temperature permitted for launch	*Source*: Rogers Commission report (1986). Report of the Presidential Commission on the Space Shuttle *Challenger* accident, Chapter 4. http:// history.nasa.gov/rogersrep/ v1ch4.htm (accessed November 11, 2010).
Initial assessment	Thus, the apparent conclusion was that the shuttle tragedy was a direct result of a mechanical failure caused by a flaw in the O-ring design	

The root cause analysis		
Why was the shuttle launched in questionable temperature conditions?	As per a member of the Rogers Commission, theoretical physicist, Richard Feynman, the safety factors used in the systems design suggest that the management of NASA exaggerates the reliability of its product, to the point of fantasy	*Source*: Rogers Commission report (1986). Report of the Presidential Commission on the Space Shuttle *Challenger* accident, Volume 2, Appendix F. http://history.nasa.gov/rogersrep/v2appf.htm
Root cause found by the Rogers Commission	The root cause is the failures in communication that resulted in a decision to launch 51-L based on incomplete and sometimes misleading information, a conflict between engineering data and management judgments, and a NASA management structure that permitted internal flight safety problems to bypass key shuttle managers	*Source*: Rogers Commission report (1986). Report of the Presidential Commission on the Space Shuttle *Challenger* accident, Volume 1, chapter 5. http://history.nasa.gov/rogersrep/v1ch5.htm
Root cause found by the U.S. House Committee on Science and Technology (disagreeing on some key points with the Rogers Commission's findings)	Committee concludes that the underlying problem that led to the *Challenger* accident was not poor communication or underlying procedures, as discovered by the Rogers Commission conclusion. Rather, the fundamental problem was poor technical decision making over a period of several years by top NASA and contractor personnel, who failed to act decisively to solve the increasingly serious anomalies in the solid rocket booster joints	*Source*: U.S. House Committee on Science and Technology (October 29, 1986). Investigation of the *Challenger* accident; Report of the Committee on Science and Technology, House of Representatives, pp. 4–5. http://www.gpoaccess.gov/challenger/64_420.pdf
Conclusions	The root cause of the problem is not human failure or mechanical failure but system-level or organizational failure within NASA and the contractors working with them. The decision-making process is flawed in different ways	

Jet Propulsion Laboratory engineers failed to convert rocket thruster data from English units of a pound of force to Newtons, the metric system of measurement used by NASA. These data were provided by contractor who work with NASA. The difference in force calculation resulted in inaccurate landing calculations that led to the crash of the Mars Climate Orbiter. The error was not sensed by ground computers. Therefore, the initial conclusion was that the Mars orbiter crash was a direct result of human failure in converting the scientific data. But

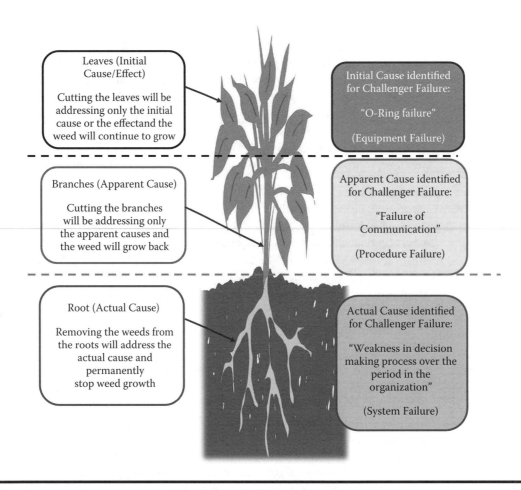

Figure 10.15   Root cause analysis of the challenger disaster.

it was later determined, with root cause analysis, that even the processes in place in the Mars project were not able to catch the error for 9 months. The chairman of the investigation board on mission failures concluded that all these failures happened because of not following the procedures, improper communication methods, peer review protocols, and other measures. Although there were meetings between the teams on unit conversion problems, the problem was never resolved. Thus, the actual root cause was not a human-level failure but a system-or organization-level failure with a culture of poor communications, inadequate training, and significant stress caused by multitasking, which truly led to the failure of the Mars Climate Orbiter mission—a $125 million failure. The details of "The Mars Climate Orbiter Crash Landing" are shown in Table 10.3. The root cause diagram is shown in Figure 10.16.

Therefore, as seen in both these case studies, it is critical to identify and correct the root causes of the problems to correct the errors. In both these cases, although it seemed that failures were caused at the human level, a thorough "5 Why" analysis was required to determine that the true root causes that were ultimately responsible for the Space

Table 10.3 Case Study and Root Cause Analysis on the Crash of NASA's Mass Climate Orbiter (MCO)

	Crash of NASA's MCO—A $125 Million Failure	Reference
The failure	On September 23, 1999, the MCO, with an estimated cost of $125 million, went off course by approximately 60 miles and crashed into the atmosphere of the Red Planet and was lost in space. The primary mission of the MCO was to monitor the Martian atmosphere, surface, and polar caps for 1 Martian year, or 687 Earth days	*Source:* Dan Sorid, September 30, 1999. Human Error Doomed Mars Climate orbiter (MCO). http://www.space.com/news/orbiter_error_990930.html (accessed November 11, 2010)
Initial findings	The review board says that project teams in Colorado and California were using different measurement systems—one in feet and pounds, and the other in metric units—to measure "critical" information for the spacecraft's maneuvers	*Source:* Dan Sorid, September 30, 1999. Human Error Doomed Mars Climate orbiter (MCO). http://www.space.com/news/orbiter_error_990930.html (accessed November 11, 2010)
Initial analysis of cause of failure		
Why did the Mars Orbiter crash?	JPL engineers failed to convert rocket thruster data from English units of a pound of force to Newtons, a metric system of measurement used by NASA. Because one pound of force is equal to approximately 4.48 Newtons, the small difference in conversion caused the orbiter to approach Mars at a lower altitude than planned, causing the $125 million orbiter to crash into the Mars atmosphere	*Source:* Mars Climate Orbiter Mishap Investigation Board, Phase I Report. November 10, 1999. ftp://ftp.hq.nasa.gov/pub/pao/reports/1999/MCO_report.pdf (accessed November 11, 2010)
Why did NASA's engineers fail to convert the English units to metric units?	The error was not detected in NASA's ground-based computers, and the JPL, the mission's navigation team, did not understand how the Orbiter was pointed in space while descending into the Martian atmosphere	
Initial assessment	Thus, the apparent conclusion was that the Mars Orbiter crash was a direct result of a human-level failure due to error in conversion of critical data from English to metric units	*Source:* Mishap Investigation Board, Phase I Report. November 10, 1999. ftp://ftp.hq.nasa.gov/pub/pao/reports/1999/MCO_report.pdf (accessed November 11, 2010)

The root cause analysis

Why was NASA unable to synchronize the metrics between Lockheed Martin and JPL or catch the unit conversion error?	The output data from the SM_FORCES software was a file called Angular Momentum Desaturation and was required to be in metric units per existing software interface documentation. JPL navigation teams of trajectory modelers falsely assumed the data was provided in metric units per the requirements. The MCO was launched on December 11, 1998, and for 9 months, this error was not caught by the processes in place in the MCO project, resulting in the crash.	*Source:* Mishap Investigation Board, Phase I Report. November 10, 1999. ftp://ftp.hq.nasa.gov/pub/pao/reports/1999/MCO_report.pdf (accessed November 11, 2010)
Root cause and contributing causes found by the MCO MIB Commission	Root cause: Failure to use metric units in the coding of a ground software file, "small forces," used in trajectory models. The contributing causes: 1. Undetected mismodeling of spacecraft velocity changes, unfamiliarity with spacecraft, and lack of adequate system engineering process. 2. Inadequate communication between project elements and inadequate verification and validation process and other process failures.	*Source:* Mishap Investigation Board, Phase I Report. November 10, 1999. ftp://ftp.hq.nasa.gov/pub/pao/reports/1999/MCO_report.pdf (accessed November 11, 2010)
Comments by Arthur Stephenson, Chairman of the Mission Failure Investigation Board and Director of NASA's Marshall Space Flight Center	1. The JPL navigators had already realized that contractors were providing data in different units and although there was even a meeting between the teams, the situation was never resolved. 2. Procedures and peer review protocols were not followed. 3. Training and communication between the teams was inadequate.	*Source:* Greg Clark, November 10, 1999. Navigation Team was Unfamiliar with Mars Climate Orbiter. http://www.space.com/news/mco_report-b_991110.html
Conclusions	Thus, the actual root cause was not a human-level failure but a system-or organization-level failure with a culture of poor communications, inadequate training, and significant stress caused by multitasking, which truly led to the failure of the MCO mission—a $125 million failure.	

Note: MCO: Mars Climate Orbiter; MIB: Mishap Investigation Board; JPL: Jet Propulsion Laboratory.

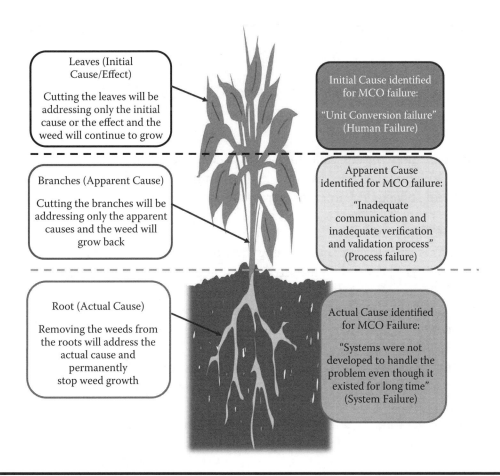

Figure 10.16 **Root cause analysis of the mars climate orbiter disaster.**

Shuttle *Challenger* tragedy and the failure of the Mars Climate Orbiter mission were at the system or organizational levels. To prevent similar failures in the future, the project leaders of NASA and their contractors needed to fix these at the system or culture level and also be proactive in identifying other causes of failures.

Pillar X: Case Study 2
Engage Your Team in the Problem Solving

INTRODUCTION

This case study discusses a "failure" I had early on in my career as a manufacturing engineer, as a result of not engaging the people in the problem-solving and process improvement step.

CHALLENGE

This is my favorite case study! During my early years of "trying to manage projects," I created a situation that may seem like an episode from the television series *I Love Lucy*, but almost ended my dreams to be a project leader. I had just moved from the research and development department to the manufacturing department. I was the "green" manufacturing engineer in the clean room. Susan had just taken over the role as the unit manager. She was an excellent manager and was well known for her quick and tough decisions. One evening, as a rite of passage for new engineers trying to make a positive impression, I was hanging around after hours to get some face time and brownie points from the new manager. Susan came up to my desk and mentioned that she was unhappy with the layout of the assembly area for a new product line in the clean room.

SITUATION

She said she had tried to explain to the ladies in the clean room about her concerns but they did not want to make the changes. Some of them had worked in the clean room more years than I had lived on this planet at that time. I knew some of them were set in their ways and were hardheaded.

SOLUTION

As I began agreeing with her viewpoint, I tried to impress her by starting to draw some potential layouts on a piece of paper. Before I knew it, we had left my desk, suited up outside the clean room and were inside at the site of our discussion. She held my layout, took some measurements, and asked me to go ahead with the move—right now! What? She assigned me two operators who were on overtime in the clean room. They were not very happy at the prospect of being roped in but Susan was very determined—she was going to pull the trigger (while the gun was in my hand).

IMPLEMENTATION

At that time, I felt quite powerful that my manager was showing trust in me and without thinking again, we started moving the assembly tables and some equipment around. Within 20 minutes, the area was looking great and I was sure would help increase productivity as it reduced the move times between stations. I went home satisfied and proud at my accomplishments.

RESULTS

The next morning, I went to work thinking that the ladies may have come in at 6:00 a.m., complaining a little, but by the time I got to work at 7:30 a.m., they would have settled in their new area and will thank me for the improvements made last night. As soon as I walked past the clean room, I saw that no one was working in the assembly area. I went to my desk to leave my laptop bag, and I heard some loud voices coming out of Susan's closed-door office. Upon peering through the glass window, I saw that there were approximately 10 ladies in Susan's small office. One of them saw me looking in. That was the last normal moment I enjoyed for the rest of the day. As soon they saw me they left Susan alone and shifted their attention, me. They opened the door, and one of them literally dragged me in and I heard the door close behind me. I felt like a small mouse trapped in by 10 fully grown cats. I felt like I was in a scene from a horror movie. They were talking loudly, pointing fingers at me, giving me the evil look and I was expecting the fatal blow at any time. I meekly sat through their tirade that lasted for approximately 15 minutes. They had even used up their break—I guess I was the breakfast as they were eating me alive. When I noticed that they were beginning to lose steam, I said the most brilliant words I could have under the circumstances—"I am sorry!" Then I followed it up with "I should not have changed the layout without involving you all. What can I do right now for you that will make all of you happy?" All of them calmed down, took a deep breath, and the team leader spoke "Remember, the clean room is our home. If you want to rearrange our furniture ever again, ask our permission first and take our opinions into consideration. Regarding the new layout—it is not bad so we are willing to try it. If it does not work, we will go back to the way we had it!" All I could say is, "OK, no problem" and was very glad to leave Susan's office alive and in one piece. After that, once we got to know each other, we got along very well and learned how to respect each other's opinions. I ended up spending two more years there making some major updates to the clean room including helping design and get manufactured two automated labeling machines that reduced the manual labeling operations (one of the main complaints used to be stress on the wrists and hands of the ladies due to repetitive motion of labeling more than 10,000 packages/day). The project helped increase productivity by more than 1000% for the labeling operation. Later, I also implemented lean/flow in the area. I did all this, of course, with "their permission and involvement."

Lessons Learned

Although it was a traumatic experience at that time, I am very glad this happened to me at an early stage in my career. I have never repeated that mistake ever again. I learned this lesson very well. Since then, I have been involved in more than 50 relayout projects. Whenever I have to re–layout an area or a facility, I go the extra mile to make sure that I involve all key personnel as I always remember "It is their home and I need their involvement in rearranging their furniture."

Pillar X   Force Field Analysis

PILLAR X: FORCE FIELD ANALYSIS OF ORGANIZATIONAL ASSESSMENT

Table 10.4 shows force field analysis of organizational assessment. An organizational assessment is conducted to assess if the culture of the organization is in alignment with the principles of Pillar X. Tables 10.5 through 10.7 are used to develop and implement an action plan to increase the effect of the organizational driving forces and decrease the effect of the organizational resisting forces.

PILLAR X: FORCE FIELD ANALYSIS OF SELF-ASSESSMENT

Table 10.8 shows force field analysis of self-assessment. The self-assessment is conducted to assess if your own strengths and are in alignment with the principles of Pillar X. Tables 10.9 through 10.11 are used to develop and implement an action plan to increase the effect of the self-driving forces and decrease the effect of the self-resisting forces.

PILLAR X: RECOMMENDATIONS FOR OPTIMAL RESULTS FROM FORCE FIELD ANALYSIS

For optimal results and actual transformation of culture and strengths conducive to the creation of advanced master project leaders, the following three steps are necessary:

1. Both the organizational and self-evaluation assessments must be completed.
2. A well-designed action plan must be created and implemented to increase the driving forces and decrease the resisting forces
3. The principles of each pillar must be constantly practiced and improved.

It is highly recommended that both the organizational assessments and self-assessments be conducted every year and the action plan be updated at least every 3 months.

Note: The sum of scores for Organizational Driving Force and Organizational Resisting Force for each point must be less than or equal to TEN.

 The sum of scores for Self Driving Force and Self Resisting Force for each point must be less than or equal to TEN.

Table 10.4   Pillar X: Force Field Organizational Analysis

Team Name: _____   Date: _____

	Does My Organization Drive or Resist a Culture of Learning from Failures?			
	0 Never	5 Sometimes		7 Mostly
	3 Rarely	ODF + ORF ≤ 10		10 Always
No.	Driving Forces	*Score Organizational Driving Force (ODF)*	*Score Organizational Resisting Force (ORF)*	Resisting Forces
1	My organization understands that creating an environment where failures are considered as stepping-stones to success is critical to long-term innovation and growth.			My organization does not tolerate failures and the focus is on short-term wins.
2	Our leaders consider every failure as a "new lesson learned" to build on so that the current and future projects never encounter the same failure ever again.			Our managers consider every failure as a failure of a team member to plan or execute the project correctly.
3	Our leaders consider every success as a "fleeting achievement" to be acknowledged briefly with humility.			Our mangers rely on the past successes and hold on to them as long as they can.
4	Our leaders consider even minor failures are true friends as they are continuously providing feedback that helps them to be better leaders.			Our managers try to distance themselves from any failures, as much as possible.
5	Our project leaders learn from mistakes throughout the entire project and use the "closing phase" to focus on identifying failures, analyzing the root causes, and learning from each and every failure.			Our project managers conduct a brief "lessons learned" meeting at the end of projects as a part of the requirement for closing out projects.

6	Our leaders categorize failures based on the root cause analysis as "system level," "process-level," and "human-level" failures.			Our managers categorize failures based on end effect on the project as high, medium, and low severity failures.
7	Our leaders use a proactive method of failure analysis using the "why" approach with a focus on system-and process-level modes of failure.			Our managers use a reactive method of failure analysis using the "who" approach with a focus on human-level modes of failure.
8	Our leaders believe that "failure to eliminate the root cause of the identified failure is a more critical failure than the initial failure itself."			Our managers are reluctant to share failure information or air dirty laundry for the fear that they might not be deemed to be a good project manager.
9	Our project leaders and team members are fully aware that no project is immune from minor failures and are thus proactively on the lock out for potential failures that can affect the overall objectives of the project.			Project managers hope that they do not encounter failures and prefer to have the team members react to failures when they occur.
10	Our leaders use "system-level" thinking and focus on issues, not on people, by asking "why" the failure occurred to determine and eliminate the root cause of failures.			Our managers use "human-level" thinking and focus their primary effort on finding the people "who" caused the failure.
	Total ODF score			*Total ORF score*

Results	Conclusions	Recommended Action Review and Update Every Quarter (3 months)
ODF ≫ ORF	My company culture strongly drives a culture of learning from failures.	Use Tables 10.5 through 10.7 to set goals and create an action plan to preserve or continuously improve the culture of learning from failures.
ODF > ORF	My company culture drives the culture of learning from failures.	Use Tables 10.5 through 10.7 to set goals and create an action plan to increase ODF to create a culture of learning from failures.
ORF ≫ ODF	My company culture strongly resists the culture of learning from failures.	Use Tables 10.5 through 10.7 to set goals and create an action plan to increase the ODF and reduce the ORF to create a culture of learning from failures.
ORF > ODF	My company culture resists the culture of learning from failures.	Use Tables 10.5 through 10.7 to set goals and create an action plan to reduce the ORF to create a culture of learning from failures.
ODF = ORF	My company culture does not drive or resist the culture of learning from failures.	Use Tables 10.5 through 10.7 to set goals and create an action plan to increase the ODF to create a culture of learning from failures.

Table 10.5 Pillar X: Analysis of ODF and ORF Results

Result	Existing Organizational Culture	If the Goal is to Create a Moderately Strong Culture of Learning from Failures	If the Goal is to Create a Very Strong Culture of Learning from Failures
ODF			
ODF ≤ 25	No or minimal culture of learning from failures	Focus on improving scores in at least 5 DF	Focus on improving scores in at least 7 DF
25 < ODF ≤ 50	Weak culture of learning from failures	Focus on improving scores in at least 3 DF	Focus on improving scores in at least 5 DF
50 < ODF ≤ 75	Moderate culture of learning from failures	Focus on improving scores in at least 1 DF	Focus on improving scores in at least 3 DF
ODF > 75	Strong culture of learning from failures	N/A	Preserve or continuously improve the culture
ORF			
ORF > 75	No or minimal culture of learning from failures	Focus on decreasing scores in at least 5 RF	Focus on decreasing scores in at least 7 RF
50 < ORF ≤ 75	Weak culture of learning from failures	Focus on decreasing scores in at least 3 RF	Focus on decreasing scores in at least 5 RF
25 < ORF ≤ 50	Moderate culture of learning from failures	Focus on decreasing scores in at least 1 RF	Focus on decreasing scores in at least 3 RF
ORF ≤ 25	Strong culture of learning from failures	N/A	Preserve or continuously improve the culture

Table 10.6 Pillar X: Action Plan to Increase Organizational Driving Forces (ODFs)

Team Name: _____   Date: _____

No.	*Driving Force*	Current Score	Goal (Target Score) ⬆	Action Plan to Increase DF Score	Complete by (Date)	Assigned to (Department Name or Initials of Person)
1	My organization understands that creating an environment where failures are considered as stepping-stones to success is critical to long-term innovation and growth.					
2	Our leaders consider every failure as a "new lesson learned" to build on so that the current and future projects never encounter this failure ever again.					
3	Our leaders consider every success as a "fleeting achievement" to be acknowledged briefly with humility.					
4	Our leaders consider even minor failures as true friends as they are continuously providing feedback that helps them be better leaders.					
5	Our project leaders learn from mistakes throughout the entire project and use the "closing phase" to focus on identifying failures, analyzing the root causes and learning from each and every failure.					

6	Our leaders categorize failures based on the root cause analysis as system-level, process level and human level failures.					
7	Our leaders use a proactive method of failure analysis using the "why" approach with a focus on system and process-level modes of failure.					
8	Our leaders believe that "failure to eliminate the root cause of the identified failure is a more critical failure than the initial failure itself."					
9	Our project leaders and team members are fully aware that no project is immune from minor failures and are thus proactively on a lookout for potential failures that can affect the overall objectives of the project.					
10	Our leaders use "system level" thinking and focus on issues, not on people, by asking "why" the failure occurred to determine and eliminate the root cause of failures.					
	Total ODF					

Table 10.7   Pillar X: Action Plan to Decrease Organization Resisting Forces (ORF)

No.	Resisting Force	Current Score	Goal (Target Score) ⬇	Action Plan to Decrease RF Score	Complete by (Date)	Assigned to (Department Name or Initials of Person)
1	My organization does not tolerate failure and the focus is on short-term wins.					
2	Our managers consider every failure as a failure of a team member to plan or execute the project correctly.					
3	Our managers rely on past successes and hold on to them as long as they can.					
4	Our managers try to distance themselves from any failures, as much as possible.					
5	Our project managers conduct a brief "lessons learned" meeting at the end of projects as a part of the requirement for closing out projects.					
6	Our managers categorize failures based on end effect on the project as high-, medium-, and low-severity failures.					
7	Our managers use a reactive method of failure analysis using the "who" approach with a focus on human-level modes of failure.					
8	Our managers are reluctant to share failure information or air "dirty laundry" for the fear that they might not be deemed to be good project managers.					

9	Project managers hope that they do not encounter failures and prefer to have the team members react to failures when they occur.					
10	Our managers use "human-level" thinking and focus their primary effort on finding the people "who" caused the failure					
	Total ORF					

Table 10.8   Pillar X: Force Field Self-Analysis

Name: _____   Date: _____

	Does My Behavior Drive or Resist the Principles of Learning from Failures?			
	0 Never	5 Sometimes	7 Mostly	
	3 Rarely	SDF + SRF ≤ 10	10 Always	
No.	Driving Forces	Score Self–Driving Force (SDF)	Score Self–Resisting Force (SRF)	Resisting Forces
1	I do not fear failures as I consider them as stepping-stones to my long-term success.			I consider failure as "bad word" and hope I never encounter it in any of my projects during my career.
2	I consider every failure as an opportunity to learn a new lesson so that we can fix the root cause and never have to encounter a similar failure again.			I consider every failure as a reflection of inability or incompetence to plan or execute correctly.
3	I do not "rest on my successes" and celebrate my successes briefly with humility.			I rely on my past successes and celebrate them as long as I can.
4	I consider even minor failures as true friends as they are continuously providing me with invaluable feedback to be a better leader.			I consider failures as detriments and distance myself from any failures, as much as possible.
5	I encourage my team to learn from mistakes throughout the entire project and use the "closing phase" to focus on identifying failures, analyzing the root causes, and learning from each and every failure.			I conduct a brief "lessons learned" meeting at the end of projects as a part of the requirement for closing them out.
6	At the end of projects, I encourage candid feedback on my performance from my team members, as it is invaluable to my growth as a leader and allows me to be aware of my "blind spots."			I evaluate my team members at the end of project but do not find it valuable to solicit feedback on my own performance as a project manager.
7	I use a proactive method of failure analysis using the "5 Why" analysis with a focus on system level and process level modes of failure.			I use a reactive method of failure analysis using the "Who" analysis with a focus on human-level modes of failure.

8	I believe in openly discussing failures in order to find and eliminate the true root causes of the failures so that similar failures are never encountered again.			I am reluctant to share failure information with others as it may reflect badly on my project management abilities.
9	I believe in finding and eliminating the system-level failures first, as they can be serious and can have an adverse affect on more than one project within the organization.			I believe in primarily finding who caused the failure as it is easy to fix with a simple reprimand or suspension so that the team can continue on with the project.
10	By using "system-level" analysis on my projects, I create a culture of "open learning," creativity, and innovation.			I observe a culture of fear, mistrust, and risk aversion on my projects.
	Total SDF Score			*Total SRF Score*

Results	Conclusions	Recommended Action *Review and update every quarter (3 months)*
SDF ≫ SRF	My behavior strongly supports the principles of learning from failures.	Use Tables 10.9 through 10.11 to set goals and create an action plan to continuously enhance the behavior to create a culture of learning from failures.
SDF > SRF	My behavior supports the principles of learning from failures.	Use Tables 10.9 through 10.11 to set goals and create an action plan to increase SDF to allow a stronger behavior toward creating a culture of learning from failures.
SRF ≫ SDF	My behavior strongly resists the principles of learning from failures.	Use Tables 10.9 through 10.11 to set goals and create an action plan to increase SDF and reduce SRF to allow a stronger behavior toward creating a culture of learning from failures.
SRF > SDF	My behavior resists the principles of learning from failures.	Use Tables 10.9 through 10.11 to set goals and create an action plan to reduce SRF to allow a stronger behavior toward creating a culture of learning from failures.
SDF = SRF	My behavior does not drive or resist the principles of learning from failures.	Use Tables 10.9 through 10.11 to set goals and create an action plan to increase the SDF to allow a stronger behavior toward creating a culture of learning from failures.

TABLE 10.9   Pillar X: Analysis of SDF and SRF Results

Result	Existing Behavior	If the Goal is to Create a Moderately Strong Behavior toward Principles of Learning from Failures	If the Goal is to Create a Very Strong Behavior toward Principles of Learning from Failures
SDF			
SDF ≤ 25	No or minimal activities in creating a culture of learning from failures	Focus on improving scores in at least 5 DF	Focus on improving scores in at least 7 DF
25 < SDF ≤ 50	Weak activities in creating a culture of learning from failures	Focus on improving scores in at least 3 DF	Focus on improving scores in at least 5 DF
50 < SDF ≤ 75	Moderate activities in creating a culture of learning from failures	Focus on improving scores in at least 1 DF	Focus on improving scores in at least 3 DF
SDF > 75	Strong activities in creating a culture of learning from failures	N/A	Preserve or continuously improve the behavior
SRF			
SRF > 75	No or minimal activities in creating a culture of learning from failures	Focus on decreasing scores in at least 5 RF	Focus on decreasing scores in at least 7 RF
50 < SRF ≤ 75	Weak activities in creating a culture of learning from failures	Focus on decreasing scores in at least 3 RF	Focus on decreasing scores in at least 5 RF
25 < SRF ≤ 50	Moderate activities in creating a culture of learning from failures	Focus on decreasing scores in at least 1 RF	Focus on decreasing scores in at least 3 RF
SRF ≤ 25	Strong activities in creating a culture of learning from failures	N/A	Preserve or continuously improve the behavior

Table 10.10   Pillar X: Action Plan to Increase Self–Driving Forces (SDFs)

Name: _____   Date: _____

No.	Driving Force	Current Score	Goal (Target Score) ⬆	Action Plan to Increase DF Score	Complete by (Date)	Required Resources
1	I do not fear failures as I consider them as stepping-stones to my long-term success.					
2	I consider every failure as an opportunity to learn a new lesson so that we can fix the root cause and never have to encounter a similar failure again.					
3	I do not "rest on my successes" and celebrate my successes briefly with humility.					
4	I consider even minor failures as true friends as they are continuously providing me with invaluable feedback to be a better leader.					
5	I encourage my team to learn from mistakes throughout the entire project and use the "closing phase" to focus on identifying failures, analyzing the root causes, and learning from each and every failure.					
6	At the end of projects, I encourage candid feedback on my performance from my team members, as it is invaluable to my growth as a leader and allows me to be aware of my "blind spots."					
7	I use a proactive method of failure analysis using the "5 Why" analysis with a focus on system-level and process level modes of failure.					

8	I believe in openly discussing failures in order to find and eliminate the true root causes of the failures so that similar failures are never encountered again.					
9	I believe in finding and eliminating the system-level failures first as they can be serious and can have an adverse affect on more than one project within the organization.					
10	By using "system-level" analysis on my projects, I create a culture of "open learning," creativity, and innovation.					
	Total SDF					

Table 10.11   Pillar X: Action Plan to Decrease Self–Resisting Forces (SRFs)

Name: _____   Date: _____

No.	Resisting Force	Current Score	Goal (Target Score) ⬇	Action Plan to Decrease RF Score	Complete by (Date)	Required Resources
1	I consider failure as "bad word" and hope I never encounter it in any of my projects during my career.					
2	I consider every failure as a reflection of inability or incompetence to plan or execute correctly.					
3	I rely on my past successes and celebrate them as long as I can.					
4	I consider failures as detriments and distance myself from any failures, as much as possible.					
5	I conduct a brief "lessons learned" meeting at the end of projects as a part of the requirement for closing them out.					
6	I evaluate my team members at the end of project but do not find it valuable to solicit feedback on my own performance as a project manager.					

7	I use a reactive method of failure analysis using the "who" analysis with a focus on human-level modes of failure.					
8	I am reluctant to share failure information with others as it may reflect badly on my project management abilities.					
9	I believe in primarily finding who caused the failure as it is easy to fix with a simple reprimand or suspension so that the team can continue on with the project.					
10	I observe a culture of fear, mistrust, and risk aversion on my projects.					
	Total SRF					

Pillar X   Exercises

PILLAR X: ORGANIZATIONAL-LEVEL
SKILL SET–ENHANCEMENT EXERCISES

GROUP EXERCISES

These exercises are best completed within a group of project managers, project leaders, executives, and stakeholders from within a department or an organization.

1. Using Table 10.12, identify at least five advantages to your organization in creating a culture of learning from failures, rate them from 1 (least important) to 5 (most important), and explain the rating.
2. Using Table 10.13, identify at least five roadblocks within your organization in creating a culture of learning from failures for your complex projects, rate them from 1 (least difficult to overcome) to 5 (most difficult to overcome), and explain the rating.
3. Identify a complex project within your organization that failed. Get the core team together and ask them to use Table 10.14 to identify the following on the project.

Table 10.12   Pillar X: Five Advantages of Applying Principles of Pillar X to Your Organization

No.	Advantages of Applying Principles of Pillar X to Enhancing Your Organization Culture	Rating (from 1 = Least Important to 5 = Most Important)	Explain the Rating
1			
2			
3			
4			
5			

a. Describe three major things that failed the project.
b. Was root cause analysis conducted on the failed aspects of the project?
c. Using best judgment, identify the root causes as system-level, process-level, or human-level failures.

Table 10.13   Pillar X: Five Roadblocks to Creating a Culture of Learning from Failures Using Pillar X

No.	Roadblocks to Applying Principles of Learning from Failures As Described In Pillar X to Your Organization	Rating (from 1 = Least Difficult to Overcome to 5 = Most Difficult to Overcome)	Explain the Rating
1			
2			
3			
4			
5			

Table 10.14   Pillar X: Failed Project Analysis Using Principles of Pillar X

Three Major Failures on the Project	Was a Root Cause Analysis Conducted on the Failed Aspects of the Project? (Yes/No)	Root Cause due to System Level, Process Level, or Human Level Failures?
1.		
2.		
3.		

4. Identify a complex project in the planning phase. Get the core team together and ask them to use Table 10.15 to fill in at least risk themes that were identified using the risk assessment matrix or any other methods. Next, for each of the three items, conduct a proactive root cause analysis to determine the potential root causes if the failure occurred during the project. Create a plan of action to proactively address the potential root causes using the key principles from Pillar X.

5. Scenario Analysis: The largest oil spill in the history of the United States happened on Tuesday, April 20, 2010, as a result of an explosion that occurred at 11:00 p.m. eastern standard time on British Petroleum's (BP) Deepwater Horizon oil rig in the Gulf of Mexico, 52 miles southeast of the Louisiana port of Venice. Fifteen human lives were lost aboard the rig as result of the blast, and millions of barrels of oil spill have killed countless number of species of ocean life in the Gulf of Mexico.

Your company has been hired to conduct a thorough root cause analysis of this disaster based on your research of all the reports in the media. Complete the following:

a. Using Table 10.16, note the key findings based on research regarding the BP oil spill following the explosion on Deep Water Horizon on April 20, 2010.

b. Using Table 10.17, conduct a "5 Why" analysis on the BP oil spill tragedy.

c. Using Table 10.18, fill in the details regarding the following, including appropriate references when necessary:
   i. Initial findings
   ii. Initial analysis of the cause of failure

Table 10.15   Pillar X: Proactive Application of Principles of Pillar X to a Failed Project

Name of Project		
Potential Risks Identified Using Risk Assessment Matrix or by Any Other Methods	*Potential Root Causes Based on the Proactive Root Cause Analysis if the Failure Was to Come to Pass*	*Plan of Action to Proactively Address the Potential Root Causes Using the Key Principles from Pillar X*
1		
2		
3		

        iii. Root cause analysis
        iv. Conclusions
    d. Using Table 10.19, show the root cause analysis as a visual
       representation.

Table 10.16   Pillar X: BP Oil Spill Tragedy Scenario Analysis Based on Principles of Pillar X

Key findings based on research regarding the BP oil spill following the explosion on Deep Water Horizon on April 20, 2010

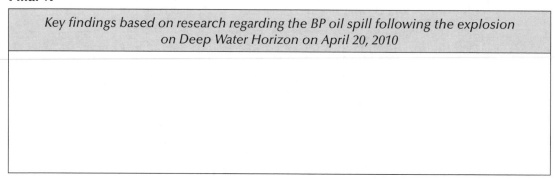

Table 10.17   Pillar X: "5 Why" Analysis for BP Oil Spill Tragedy

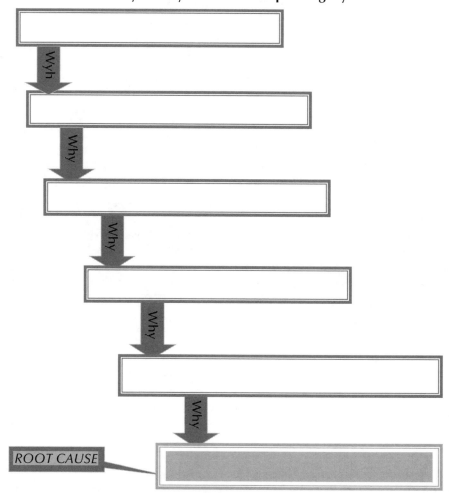

Table 10.18   Pillar X: BP Oil Spill Tragedy Scenario Analysis

The BP Oil Spill Tragedy		Reference
The failure		
Initial findings		
Initial analysis of cause of failure		
Initial assessment		
The root cause analysis		
Root causes		
Conclusions		

Table 10.19   Pillar X: Visual Representation of BP Oil Spill Tragedy Scenario Analysis

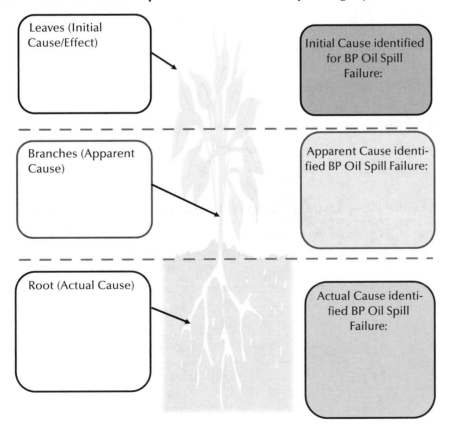

Leaves (Initial Cause/Effect)

Initial Cause identified for BP Oil Spill Failure:

Branches (Apparent Cause)

Apparent Cause identified BP Oil Spill Failure:

Root (Actual Cause)

Actual Cause identified BP Oil Spill Failure:

PILLAR X: PERSONAL-LEVEL SKILL SET–ENHANCEMENT EXERCISES

INDIVIDUAL EXERCISES

These exercises are to be completed individually after reviewing Pillar X in detail.

1. Using Table 10.20, list at least five advantages of applying the principles of Pillar X in learning from failures to your future projects. Rate the advantages from 1 (least important) to 5 (most important) and explain the rating.
2. Using Table 10.21, identify at least five roadblocks to applying the principles of learning from failures from Pillar X on all your future major projects. Rate the identified roadblocks from 1 (least difficult to overcome) to 5 (most difficult to overcome) and explain the rating.
3. Using Table 10.22, select a project you worked on as a project manager/leader or as team member that had issues related to multiple failures. Looking back on the project, answer the following questions for each phase of the project:
   a. Estimate the total number of small, medium, or large failures experienced during each project phase.
   b. Provide a best judgment on the percentage of each category of the root cause of the failure: (a) system level, (b) process level, or (c) human level.
4. Using Table 10.23, select a project you worked on as a project manager/leader or as team member that had issues related to multiple failures. Looking back on the project, answer the following questions for each phase of the project:
   a. Provide at least one example of the failure experienced during each project phase.
   b. Provide a best judgment on the category of the root cause of the failure as either: (a) system level, (b) process level, or (c) human level.

Table 10.20 Pillar X: Five Advantages of Applying Principles of Pillar X to Your Career

No.	Advantages of Applying Principles of Pillar X of Learning from Failures to All Future Projects	Rating (from 1 = Least Important to 5 Most Important)	Explain the Rating
1			
2			
3			
4			
5			

Table 10.21 Pillar X: Five Roadblocks to Applying Principles of Pillar X

No.	Roadblocks to Applying Principles of Learning from Failures Detailed in Pillar X to All Future Projects	Rating (from 1 = Least Difficult to Overcome to 5 = Most Difficult to Overcome)	Explain the Rating
1			
2			
3			
4			
5			

Table 10.22 Pillar X: Reflecting on a Failed Project—Estimate the Failures

Name of Failed Project	
Your Role in the Project	

Phase	Estimate Total Number of Small, Medium, and Large Failures	Best Judgment on Percentage of Root Causes as System Level, Process Level, or Human Level?
1. Project start-up		1. System _____ % 2. Process _____ % 3. Human _____ %
2. Project preparation		1. System _____ % 2. Process _____ % 3. Human _____ %
3. Project implementation		1. System _____ % 2. Process _____ % 3. Human _____ %

4. Project monitoring		1. System _____ % 2. Process _____ % 3. Human _____ %
5. Project closure		1. System _____ % 2. Process _____ % 3. Human _____ %

Table 10.23   Pillar X: Reflecting on a Failed Project—Estimate the Failures

Name of Failed Project		
Your Role in the Project		
Phase	*Identify at Least One Example of Failure*	*Best Judgment on Root Cause—System Level, Process Level, or Human Level?*
1. Project start-up		1. System _____ 2. Process _____ 3. Human _____
2. Project preparation		1. System _____ 2. Process _____ 3. Human _____
3. Project implementation		1. System _____ 2. Process _____ 3. Human _____
4. Project monitoring		1. System _____ 2. Process _____ 3. Human _____
5. Project closure		1. System _____ 2. Process _____ 3. Human _____

5. Scenario Analysis: The largest oil spill in the history of the United States happened on Tuesday, April 20, 2010, as a result of an explosion that occurred at 11 p.m., eastern standard time on BP's Deepwater Horizon oil rig in the Gulf of Mexico, 52 miles southeast of the Louisiana port of Venice. Fifteen human lives were lost aboard the rig as result of the blast, and millions of barrels of oil spill have killed countless number of species of ocean life in the Gulf of Mexico.

A root cause analysis has been conducted by an independent company to identify the root reasons for one of the biggest tragedies in the Gulf of Mexico and is noted in Tables 10.16 through 10.19.

You have been selected as an independent project leader by the U.S. Government to provide recommendations to BP, Transocean Ltd., the operator of the ill-fated Deepwater Horizon oil rig, and oil services company Halliburton, which cemented the deep-sea well that ruptured on April 20, 2010. Your recommendations need to include the following:

a. Using Table 10.24, identify all the "system-level" failures based on the findings and recommend a plan of action to prevent them from ever happening again.
b. Using Table 10.25, identify all the "process-level" failures based on the findings and recommend a plan of action to prevent them from ever happening again.
c. Using Table 10.26, identify all the "human-level" failures based on the findings and recommend a plan of action to prevent them from ever happening again.
d. Using Table 10.27, make overall recommendations and suggest a plan of action to prevent any of the failures from ever happening again because of similar reasons.

Table 10.24   Pillar X: "System-Level" Analysis of BP Oil Spill Tragedy

"System-Level" Failures of BP Oil Spill Tragedy	*Recommended Plan of Action to Prevent the "System-Level" Failures from Happening Ever Again*

Table 10.25 Pillar X: "Process-Level" Analysis of BP Oil Spill Tragedy

"Process-Level" Failures of BP Oil Spill Tragedy	Recommended Plan of Action to Prevent the "Process-Level" Failures from Happening Ever Again

Table 10.26 Pillar X: "Human-Level" Analysis of BP Oil Spill Tragedy

"Human-Level" Failures of BP Oil Spill Tragedy	Recommended Plan of Action to Prevent the "Human-Level" Failures from Happening Ever Again

Table 10.27 Pillar X: "Overall Recommendations" to Prevent Another BP Oil Spill Tragedy

Overall Recommended Plan of Action to Prevent Another BP Oil Spill Tragedy

Pillar X   References

1. Fisher, R. (2002). *Creative Minds: Building Communities of Learning for the Creative Age*, paper presented at Teaching Qualities Initiative Conference, Hong Kong Baptist University, 2002, http://www.teachingthinking.net/thinking/web resources/robert_fisher_creativeminds.htm (accessed November 11, 2010).

2. Thomas A. Edison. (1847–1931). http://www.quotationspage.com/quote/1914.html (accessed November 11, 2010).

3. Bellis, M. (2010). *The Inventions of Thomas Edison*, http://inventors.about.com/library/Inventors/bledison.htm (accessed November 11, 2010).

4. Henry Ford. (1863–1947). http://quotationsbook.com/quote/13723 (accessed November 11, 2010).

5. Lao-Tzu. (1905). http://www.sacred-texts.com/tao/salt/salt10.htm (accessed November 11, 2010).

6. Steven Spielberg. (2010). http://refspace.com/quotes/success (accessed November 11, 2010).

7. General George S. Patton Jr. (1885–1945). http://www.military-quotes.com/Patton.htm (accessed November 11, 2010).

8. Confucius. (551–497). http://quotationsbook.com/quote/13704/ (accessed November 11, 2010).

9. U.S. General Accounting Office. (September 5, 2001). *GAO-01-101R Survey of NASA's Lessons Learned Process,* http://www.gao.gov/new.items/d011015r.pdf. pp. 1, 12 (accessed November 11, 2010).

10. iSixSigma. (2010). *Determine the Root Cause: 5 Whys*, http://www.isixsigma.com/index.php?option=com_k2&view=item&id=1308:&Itemid=49 (accessed November 11, 2010).

11. Towers Watson. (2008). *An Interview with Julie Gebauer on Towers Perrin's Just Released Global Workforce Study*, Part 2, http://www.towersperrin.com/tp/showhtml.jsp?url=global/publications/gws/key-findings_2.htm&country=global (accessed November 11, 2010).

12. Inman, R. A. (2010). Poka-Yoke, http://www.referenceforbusiness.com/management/Or-Pr/Poka-Yoke.html (accessed November 11, 2010).

13. Smith, M. K. (2001) *Peter Senge and the Learning Organization, the Encyclopedia of Informal Education*, http://www.infed.org/thinkers/senge.htm (accessed: September 3, 2009).

Chapter 11

Pillar XI: Make Projects Less Stressful

(Hard work + Fun – Stress) is a guaranteed formula for
long-term success. Pinnacle Performance Zone™ is where
perfection goes on cruise control!

11.1 Introduction

Stress is a term in psychology and biology, borrowed from physics and engineering and first used in the biological context in the 1930s, which has in more recent decades become commonly used in popular parlance. It refers to the consequence of the failure of an organism—human or other animal—to respond adequately to mental, emotional, or physical demands, whether actual or imagined.[1]

The key point to understand is that everyone responds to *stressors* (the condition causing stress) differently in type of the response and in intensity of the response. Upon encountering a stressor, the instinctive response to stress is usually "flight or flight" which is caused by the following sequence of physiological events:

a. Adrenaline in blood releases blood sugar in liver
b. Less blood flows to skin and intestines and more blood flows to muscles causing acid to build up in stomach
c. Breathing gets faster and shallower
d. Pupils dilate creating tunnel vision
e. Person becomes hyperalert and hyperactive resulting in an abnormal response to the stress

Stress can cause physiological disorders and can also lead to diseases in people. Prolonged acute stress can also lead to permanent damage for some individuals. In the present day, most new product development and some other projects are mostly global, multicultural, and critical to the growth and survival of corporations due to intense competition. This adds to the several factors already in play that can create significant stress in team members and project leaders.

According to the National Opinion Research Center at the University of Chicago, more than 30% of workers say they are "always" or "often" under stress at work. About half of Americans (48%) feel that their stress has increased over the past 5 years (according to an American Psychological Association study, 2007). According to American Institute of Stress, NY, work place (job-related) stress costs more than $300 billion each year in health care, missed work in stress reduction.[2]

Approximately 30% of workers say they are living with extreme stress.

11.2 The Impact of Stress—A Personal Experience

Let me narrate an extreme case of the impact of stress on the life of a friend. Many years ago, my friend found himself in a very stressful situation in a start-up company dealing with import/export in Texas. The company had a few employees and was on a significant growth curve. As a manager, my friend had numerous responsibilities, and because of his conscientious attitude toward work, he took on extreme amount of workload and the resulting stress on behalf of his organization. During an extremely busy cycle of the fiscal year, my friend suddenly collapsed and had to be rushed to the hospital. They found that his body had literally crumpled up and he had lost all functions of the body—he could no longer walk or even lift anything with his fingers. The doctor's diagnosis was that the extreme stress had a devastating impact on his physical self and that he would be in a wheelchair for the rest of his life. It has taken my friend several decades of various kinds of therapy to recover slightly. Today, although he can walk on his own, his body still displays the impact of the stress he experienced at work more than 30 years ago. This is an extreme example but clearly shows that the project leader cannot underestimate the impact of stress on the lives of their team members.

11.3 What Causes Stress?

Stress is caused by many factors within and outside of the human body. However, in this chapter, we are going to discuss about how projects create stress and what should project leaders do to avoid or reduce stress. To get started, let us discuss the reasons for the development of stress in the projects. Stress in the projects cannot be eliminated unless the root causes have been properly understood and acknowledged and appropriate remedial actions are taken. For many stress-related problems, the root cause of the problem is not always apparent. However,

> Project stress is always built on solid foundation of three critical factors:
>
> 1. Ambiguous requirements
> 2. Poor or inadequate project planning
> 3. Lack of emphasis on understanding individuals on the project team

11.3.1 Ambiguous Requirements

Unambiguous requirements and clear directions are a must for stress-free project planning, execution, and closeout. Ambiguous requirements or unclear charter on a project is a major cause for anxiety, fear, and stress for project managers and team members.

Just imagine Yogi Berra, the iconic Yankee baseball player most famous for his Yogi-isms or quotes, as your project sponsor who is responsible for creating the project charter. His directions will be something like *"If you come to a fork in the road, take it,"* and he may caution you with *"You've got to be very careful if you don't know where you're going, because you might not get there."* When you are helpless and confused with his directions and about to be fired for the chaos on the project, Yogi may defend himself with, *"I didn't really say everything I said."* When you are finally fired for the failed project, he may apologize to you with *"I made a wrong mistake,"* or give you confidence with, *"It ain't over 'til it's over"* or try to console you with *"The future ain't what it used to be."*[3]

Thus, if Yogi were to try to explain this concept to you, he might have said something like, *"It is important to add here that if your project directions are minus clarity, stress will continuously multiply you into several divisions."* The same in plain English—ambiguity regarding project requirements results in significant stress.

11.3.2 Poor Project Planning

Poor planning, in addition to causing project failure, leads to stress within the project team.

Poor planning is another top reason for project failure. Poor planning, in addition to causing project failure, leads to stress within the project team. Planning is the most significant phase of a project. Majority of project work occurs during the project planning process, and approximately 75% of documents are prepared during the planning phase. Planning phase lays out the road map for all the nine processes within a project including integration, scope, cost, time, risk, quality, HR, communication, and procurement management. Therefore, effective planning is critical to getting best results during the project execution phase. However, as discussed in Pillar IV, the approach many project managers take is "fire, ready, aim" and completely overlook the importance of planning and create significantly more problems in the subsequent phases of the project.

One of the consequences of poor planning often ignored by the project managers is the development of stress in individuals on the team.

One of the consequences of poor planning often ignored by the project managers is the development of stress in individuals on the team. The seeds of stress are planted at the onset of the planning phase. As the seeds germinate and the project environment provides the right amount of fertilizer in the form of poor planning techniques and project manager's lack of understanding of the team, the weeds of stress grow unabated throughout the project. The consequences of poor planning are unrealistic schedule estimates, inaccurate requirements, scope creep, and inadequate budget. Unrealistic schedule estimates create unreachable goals for the team and will build intense pressure on the team. Scope creep creates additional work load on the project team members resulting in severe stress on the team.

The weeds then take over the trunk and the branches of the entire project tree, causing a buildup of intense stress in all aspects of the project and impact all team members to some extent.

11.3.3 Lack of Emphasis on Understanding the Individuals on the Project Team

Another major factor that leads to increased project stress is the lack of emphasis by the project managers in understanding the individuals on the team and in allocating the right resources to the appropriate roles and responsibilities. Let us look at the impact of stress on individuals using an insightful anecdote.

11.4 Impact of Stress—An Anecdote

When stress fills the project because of inadequate planning and lack of understanding, the impact can be readily seen on all the team members. However, what should a dynamic project leader do to reduce the team stress and to create an open, stress-free environment under those circumstances? Before looking into the details, let me explain the impact of stress in detail with an anecdote.

11.4.1 Introduction

On a critical software development project, a recently promoted project manager's career was in complete shambles because of immense stress created by project deliverables. Some of his key team members were burnt out. One of his best team leader was even hospitalized; her diagnosis was stress-induced ulcers. Some of the team members became quite agitated and were rude and insulting to other team members. Only a handful of the team members were being able to meet their objectives and a few were even ahead of the objectives. Overall, the team was not making much progress. With the team completely falling apart and his career at risk, his mentor, an executive in the organization, came to his rescue. He advised the project manager to get some help from an experienced executive coach. The executive even recommended a coach but warned the project manager that this coach had a reputation of using unconventional methods of coaching.

11.4.2 Experiment

The project manager lost no time in setting up an appointment with the coach and explained to him the plight of the team and his career. The coach smiled and asked if they could get permission to use the executive kitchen at the organization. The coach and the project manager went to the corporate kitchen and saw that there were three stoves. The coach asked for three identical vessels. He filled one with a gallon of water, another with a gallon of oil, and the third with a gallon of milk. The coach then put each of the vessels on a stove and turned them on to low heat. The project manager was by now wondering if the coach was hungry or just plain crazy. However, he let him continue with this madness. The coach then set the timer for an hour and asked the project manager to observe the three vessels carefully, shut off the stoves after an hour, and report back to him. The coach then left the kitchen. After approximately 2 hours, the project manager met up with the coach. *"What took you so long?"* asked the coach looking at the project manager who was disheveled and dirty. *"I was just cleaning up after your silly experiment"* retorted the project manager sarcastically. It was evident that the coach was enjoying this.

11.4.3 Observation

Without holding back the grin, he asked the project manager, *"So what did you observe?"*

The project manager told him that after approximately 30 minutes, the water surface began to be unstable and some bubbles started escaping. The oil was stable and calm. The milk was also starting to bubble. After a while, the water started boiling violently and some of it was escaping as steam, the oil was beginning to show some instability, and the milk was also boiling and foam was beginning to appear as shown in Figure 11.1. After approximately 60 minutes, the water had disappeared and the vessel was actually turning black, the oil was boiling violently and was splashing some drops of hot oil around the stove, and the milk had a thick layer formed at the top—it was cream. After shutting off the stove for the next 1 hour, he had to clean up the vessels and the mess.

11.4.4 Results

The coach then said, *"All that is well, but did you learn anything?"* "Yes," said the project manager, *"It is nearly impossible to get a burnt vessel shining again and jumping around the kitchen trying to avoid the hot splashing oil is no picnic either."* The coach became quite serious and initially seemed disappointed with the answer, but then with a Zen-like peace on his face began to explain to the project manager as follows:

Figure 11.1   Water, oil, and milk being heated on stoves.

"You missed the point of this little experiment. All three, water, oil, and milk were in the same environment—in the kitchen, on the stove, and in the vessel; they were all subjected to the same stress and adversity—fire; but all there reacted completely differently. The water was at an optimal point but could not take the heat for too long and disappeared; the oil reached an optimal level but after that was violently agitated; the milk reached an optimal point and then it boiled over—but after a while transformed itself into cream."

11.4.5 Lessons Learned

The kitchen represents this organization; the stove and the vessel represent your project environment; the water, the oil, and the milk represent the different people on your team; and lastly the fire represents the stress they were under. Water, oil, and milk reached an optimal point after which they reacted differently to the fire.

Similarly, there are basically three kinds of people who react differently to stress as follows and as shown in Figure 11.2.

1. People who reach a stress point much faster and after a certain point, with prolonged stress, get burnt out completely—these are represented by water.
2. People who reach a stress point much later but upon reaching that break point can be agitated and violent and can hurt others around them—these were represented by oil.
3. People who also react to stress but upon reaching a certain stress point instead of burning out or hurting others, they learn to transform themselves into something more worthy and valuable—these were represented by milk transforming itself to cream. However, beyond a certain point, even cream would be charred.

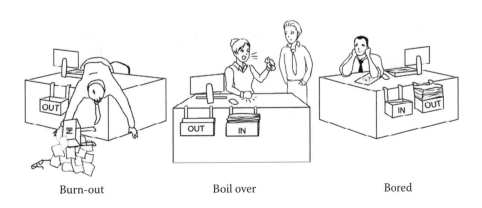

Burn-out   Boil over   Bored

Figure 11.2   Three types of individuals reacting differently to stress.

Your job as a project manager is to identify and separate the individuals who react like water, like oil, and like milk. You then need to put them only in roles and under the stress they are designed to handle.

He continued, "You too have the 3 kinds of people on this team. They each have a different tolerance level and different reaction to the same stress. Your job as a project manager is to identify and separate the individuals who react like water, like oil, and like milk. You then need to put them only in roles and under the stress they are designed to handle" (as shown in Figure 11.3):

- The individuals who have a tendency to burnout should be put in environments and be given tasks that do allow them to stay well below their burnout point.
- The individuals who have a tendency to be agitated and rude under stress should be put in environments where they never encounter the agitation point.
- The individuals who want to take on challenges and transform themselves under stress making them more valuable to the project and to the organization must be put in roles where they can always thrive and continually improve and transform.

The project manager eyes became brighter than two 100 watt lightbulbs. His face was as if he had heard the most profound truth. He had realized his mistake. In all the rush after his "coronation" as a project manager, he had forgotten to understand that his team was made of individuals who were unique and he had not taken the time to understand them enough. He had randomly assigned them to roles and given them responsibilities without knowing them completely.

Figure 11.3   Three different types of individuals excelling in their appropriate roles.

He thanked the coach profusely and rushed back to the project office to "get to know his team—member by member." Within a month of this revelation, the right individuals were assigned to appropriate duties on the basis of their individual abilities to handle the responsibility and stress, and project was back on track. Not only was his career saved, but he had learned a very important lesson in life about diversity.

From this anecdote, it is quite clear that stress can develop on projects because of the project manager's lack of emphasis on understanding the team members as individuals and allocating work according to the work potential and stress thresholds of different team members. Project managers incorrectly assume that all resources working in a project team are motivated equally and will be able to perform optimally at the same stress level. Therefore, they assign tasks to the project team without considering the ability of the individual's stress thresholds. However, each individual's reaction to stress may be quite different. Some team members are least impacted by the stress, whereas some are heavily impacted. Knowing the limitations of individual stress, bearing potential is very much needed in a project environment. The project manager's lack of such understanding will result in work overload and will generate conflicts among team members. Figure 11.4 shows the elements responsible for project stress.

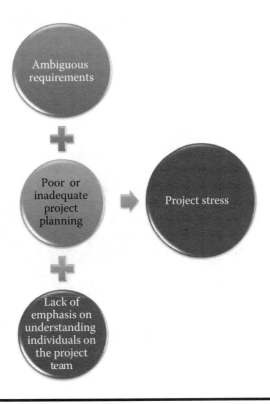

Figure 11.4   Elements responsible for project stress.

11.5 Stress and Human Function Curve

Do you recognize the individuals who react like water, oil, and milk within your own teams?

Do you recognize the individuals who react like water, oil, and milk within your own teams? If not, it is very critical that you understand these differences. A tool that helps us understand the "science of stress" is the human function curve based on Nixon's model of "eustress," with five basic zones between good stress (eustress) and bad stress (distress) as shown in Figure 11.5.[4]

These five zones represents the areas of stress levels that every person goes through while working:

1. Zone of boredom
2. Zone of safe work
3. Zone of fatigue
4. Zone of exhaustion
5. Zone of injury or breakdown

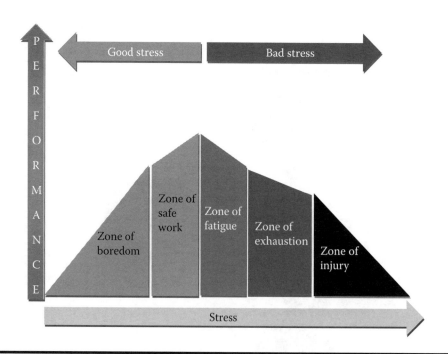

Figure 11.5   Nixon's human performance curve. (Adapted from Posen, D.B. Stress Management for Patient and Physician, *Can. J. Cont. Med. Educ.*, April 1995.)

What differentiates project leaders from project managers is the way they deal with stress on various team members. The project managers use the "one-size-fits-all" approach to stress reduction, whereas the project leaders take a more enlightened approach when alleviating stress on various individuals on the project team.

The project managers use the "one-size-fits-all" approach to stress reduction, whereas the project leaders take a more enlightened approach when alleviating stress on various individuals on the project team.

11.6 Project Managers—A "One-Size-Fits-All" Approach

Because project managers assume the same stress level to every team member, they push all team members to show the same level of performance or output in the work. In the initial stages of the project, all team members start in the zone of boredom or zone of safe work. As the project progresses and goes into execution phase, project managers unknowingly follow the "one-size-fits-all" approach and build more pressure on the team members by creating tight schedules, overallocating work, and choosing tight deadlines. Furthermore, they create a closed environment in which team members are not given a chance to express their opinions on the stress levels they were experiencing. As a result, some team members will be initially pushed into the zone of fatigue and subsequently into zone of exhaustion, as shown in Figure 11.6. Because too much pressure reduces the performance and productivity of team members, they are ultimately pushed further into zone of injury or breakdown. Often times, the project managers who are unable to delegate effectively take too much upon themselves and are also equally liable to succumb to the stress and experience burnout and injury.

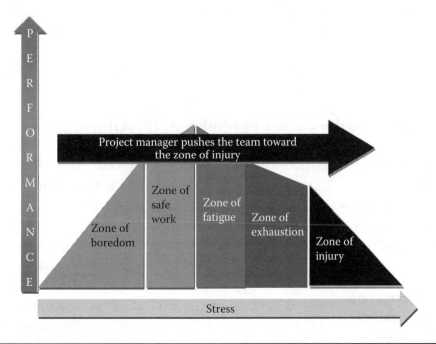

Figure 11.6   Project manager's "one-size-fits-all" approach.

Table 11.1 Stressful Aspects and Impact on Projects

Stressful Aspects of a Project	*Impact on a Team*
• Tight schedule	• Team member burnout
• Close deadlines	• Lack of performance
• Overallocation	• Poor quality
• Scope creep	• Increased defects
• Strict procedures	• Increased failure rate
• Closed project environment	• Physical and emotional problems
• Lack of direction	• Team conflicts
• Disproportionate responsibilities	• Lack of cohesion

Although it is difficult to quantitatively express the impact of stress, the implication of excessive stress on the team members is tremendous. In a study, it is estimated around one-third of employees reported feeling frustrated or demotivated by the amount of stress on the job. That means around one-third of the workforce is not completely participating in corporate initiatives and projects. When subjected to severe stress levels, team members burn out completely and break down mentally, physically, and emotionally. Slowly, they start to disengage themselves from the project work to avoid stress. The symptoms of team burnout and their disengagement can be seen in projects in many ways. Lack of attention in the meetings, lack of involvement in the work, and conflicts with other team members are some of the negative effects caused by disengagement and severe stress. As we discussed in earlier chapters, because project managers focus on blaming human errors instead of eliminating processes and systems problems, the stress still stays at the same level throughout the project. Projects will reach the brink of failure because of complete disengagement of the team and lack of motivation.

Various activities that create team stress in a project are listed in Table 11.1.

11.7 Project Leaders—An "Enlightened" Approach

Leaders take the time to understand individuals and put them in situations where they can truly "soar with their strengths."

Successful project leaders know that there is one more zone to this called the "Zone of Pinnacle Performance™."

Successful project leaders are aware that all resources cannot be motivated with an identical stimulus. Thus, leaders take the time to understand individuals and put them in situations where they can truly "soar with their strengths." There are some resources that tend to get bored easily and need to be challenged constantly; others do not do well under stress and some have a meltdown at the slightest level of stress. Successful project leaders also know that just getting an average performance from their team members is not enough. They need the members to be operating at the pinnacle of their performance, that is, reach an optimal point. Thus, successful project leaders know that there is one more zone to this called the "Zone of Pinnacle Performance™," that is, overlap between the "safe work zone" and the "fatigue zone," as shown Figure 11.7. They challenge their team just enough so that they stretch and go beyond their envelope of comfort. Great athletes train exactly the same way—making measurable improvements in small steps until they reach their pinnacle performance. Project leaders motivate their team and create an open environment to improve their performance in the project. They ensure that the project team members are within the zone of pinnacle performance during all the phases of the project life cycle. Project leaders follow the "enlightened approach" to creating an environment that automatically gravitates the team toward the zone of pinnacle performance, which results in optimal performance. For example, the team members who thrive on stress and who do not burnout easily are provided more challenging opportunities and responsibilities within the project, which allows them to move into the zone of pinnacle performance. When team members move into the zone of fatigue or exhaustion on few occasions, the project leaders reverse the trajectory and bring them back into the zone of pinnacle performance by fine-tuning the amount of workload and the level of responsibility, by motivating them, and by creating a fun environment. Project leaders think that celebration and fun is one more ingredient that is critical to the success of the team. Creating a fun environment, free of blame and worries, can make a huge difference in teams willing to take more risks and expanding their zone of comfort.

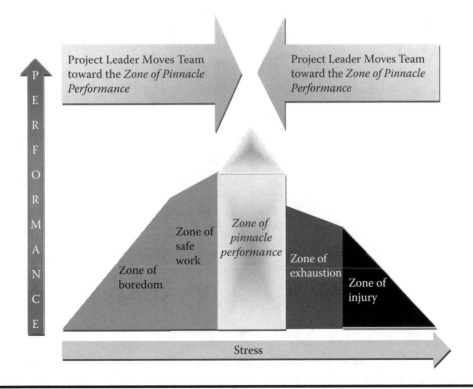

Figure 11.7   Project leader's "enlightened approach" to optimal team performance.

Celebrating small and big successes and thanking team members who "go the extra mile" pay huge dividends.

> The Pinnacle Performance Zone™ is where the new ideas flow, breakthroughs happen, and successes are celebrated with fun and joy for the project and for personal growth of team members.

11.8 Formula for Success

During any project, long-term or week-long kaizen project, one of the key advices I always give my team is—have fun! I was consulting at a company in Canada. The company had some fairly strong-minded individuals who did not mind taking verbal shots at each other, mostly in jest. During kaizen events, we implemented a unique way to have fun and keep it interesting while allowing them to perform at their best. We had a "kaizen violation jar," as seen in Figure 11.8, and the following amounts were accrued and deposited in the jar on the basis of the type of violation, as shown in Table 11.2.

The money collected sometimes reached more than $100 during a single week and was donated to a local charity. This kept the event fun, did not inhibit the natural tendencies of the team members, but also kept them in check as they had to pay for every violation. I thoroughly enjoyed playing

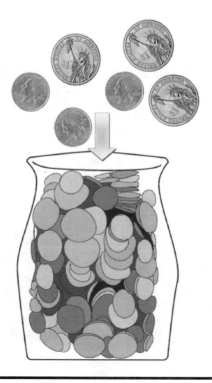

Figure 11.8 Kaizen violation jar.

Table 11.2 Kaizen Violation Game

Taking verbal shots at other team member	$0.25
Being late for meetings	$0.50
Saying "can't" to any solution without trying	$1.00
Not having any violations by end of the week— "being a big bore"	$2.00

along and would sometimes pay upfront so I could know how many shots I had to take at my "favorite" team members before the end of the week. I can tell you for sure that *fun* was a very critical ingredient in the success of this and other teams I have led.

Successful project leaders know that the formula for success is, "Project success is directly proportional to the challenging environment and quality of celebrations":

Project success $\propto$ (Challenging Environment + Celebrations).

Pillar XI   Summary

Stress can cause physiological disorders and can also lead to diseases in people. Prolonged acute stress can also lead to permanent damage for some individuals. Stress in the projects has become part of the project team's work life. However, stress in the project can be avoided or reduced by eliminating ambiguous requirements, by careful and proper planning, and by the project manager's emphasis on individual ability in the team.

Every successful project leader must understand the unique nature of individuals on their team and give them appropriate roles and responsibilities and create a fun environment that allows them to stretch and grow without any adverse effects so that they completely transform themselves. Project managers transform themselves into project leaders by changing their thinking from one-size-fits-all approach to "the enlightened" approach and try hard to keep the team in zone of pinnacle performance. Figure 11.9 provides valuable insights into project stress management.

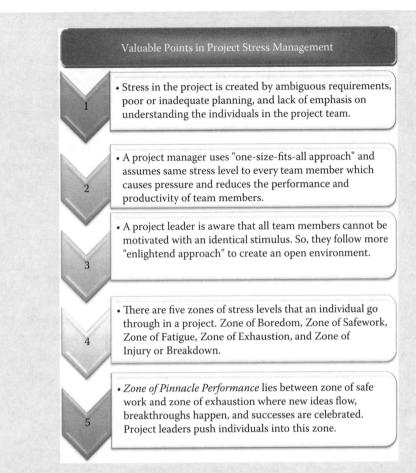

Valuable Points in Project Stress Management

1. • Stress in the project is created by ambiguous requirements, poor or inadequate planning, and lack of emphasis on understanding the individuals in the project team.

2. • A project manager uses "one-size-fits-all approach" and assumes same stress level to every team member which causes pressure and reduces the performance and productivity of team members.

3. • A project leader is aware that all team members cannot be motivated with an identical stimulus. So, they follow more "enlightend approach" to create an open environment.

4. • There are five zones of stress levels that an individual go through in a project. Zone of Boredom, Zone of Safework, Zone of Fatigue, Zone of Exhaustion, and Zone of Injury or Breakdown.

5. • *Zone of Pinnacle Performance* lies between zone of safe work and zone of exhaustion where new ideas flow, breakthroughs happen, and successes are celebrated. Project leaders push individuals into this zone.

Figure 11.9 Valuable points in project stress management.

Pillar XI   Case Study
My Favorite Role Model

INTRODUCTION

This is one of my favorite case studies about my hero and role model, Lonny. This case study discusses how great project leaders can motivate the team and create an open and stress-free environment to flourish team member ideas.

LONNY—THE KING OF MOTIVATORS

During my employment at a Fortune 500 company, I had the greatest luck to work with the vice president of operations—Lonny. Lonny's leadership is a model worth studying by anyone who wishes to be successful. Lonny is the king of motivators. He is well liked by people at all levels in the organization. He has a charm and a style I have seen few people possess. When you work for him, you can be assured of 110% support from him. He is humble and encourages others to make their own decisions, but when the situation requires it; he can be very demanding and does not hesitate to hold people accountable. He makes each person he interacts with feel genuinely special, and that person always leaves feeling that their specific role and talent is important to the overall mission of the project and to the organization. He discusses issues, coaches anyone who seeks his guidance, or have a chat with new hires and with the shop floor operators. People see Lonny as a boss, a coach, a friend, a master motivator, and sometimes even as their continuous challenge as he stretches them out of their comfort zone.

His "work ethics" and "loyalty" to the organization would be a great topic for a Harvard research paper because the significance of those two words has slowly faded from our corporations. He is at work before 6:00 am every day, no matter what, and can be found working in his office way past office hours. But he is not a workaholic at all; in fact, he is one of the greatest family man I know of and admire. I can still remember the beautiful pictures in his office of him rolling in the grass with his family. He truly believes in "giving his very best" to whatever he is doing at that time. I was once sitting next to him on a flight, and as a junior project engineer, eager to learn from an executive, I asked him what was it that motivated him. I still remember his profound answer, he told me "Adil, I just live each day as if it is my very last." I knew he walks his talk; he always lives in the present moment.

GO BABY GO!

The greatest quality Lonny possesses is to make every project fun and get the best out of everyone, every time—no matter what the situation, no matter how much pressure, Lonny is always able to see the humor of the situation and in the process diffuse some very tense situations. He thoroughly enjoys playing practical jokes on his peers and is also a target of some. These qualities, which demonstrate the "human touch," are critical to have in the arsenal of successful leaders.

He leads from the front and with his heart. He has taught me to catch people doing the right thing and recognize them for it. He encourages everyone to celebrate small victories and not wait for the big ones. His favorite motivational line is "Go baby go!" The appreciation reinforces the behavior, and the people exhibit that behavior more often. He customizes nicknames for everyone. If they were funny or ego busters, he uses them to keep people in line during meetings, and if they were positive, he uses the nicknames to motivate them.

When you start working for him, you have to answer some personal questions like your birthday, your spouse's birthday, what motivates you, your hot buttons, your pet peeves, and so forth. He uses these data to customize his rewards for individuals. If your passion is to vacation with your family, when he catches you going the extra mile, he gives you a day off to spend with your family or sometimes tickets to a theme park or movies. If you like good food, you could get gift certificates to the best restaurant in town for you and your spouse.

When he promoted me from an engineer to a manager, he had his secretary call my wife at home without my knowledge and asked her to be at a certain restaurant for lunch with me. He then pretended to have an off-site meeting and took me to the same place. After I got over the surprise of finding my wife at the same restaurant, as we were about to eat lunch, he toasted me and announced my promotion in her presence. He knew that I liked to involve my family at special occasions and in major decisions. His actions truly touched me and my wife, and we still remember this after a decade has passed.

COMFORTABLE IN HIS OWN SKIN

One quality about Lonny that I always felt made him a "leader of leaders" and allows him to enjoy whatever he does and shares the joy with all, is that—he is always completely comfortable in his own skin. During my career, I have met many managers and leaders who do not share credit or do not provide enough opportunities for others to grow and shine for the fear it may somehow diminish their own worth. Lonny is the complete opposite—he is so comfortable and confident of his abilities that he does not feel threatened by others successes but encourages them to take on more challenges and looks forward to celebrating their successes as his own. He creates an environment of trust and encouragement that allows us to soar without fear knowing that he will be there in case we stumble. There were occasions when he was challenged by his peers, but he was always cool, calm, and confident and never rattled. He knew where he stood, and I have never seen him threatened by power plays or any other negative situations.

In my case, he saw something in me, which made him trust me with some critical projects, including acquisitions and complete reorganization of manufacturing areas, which at that time I felt were way beyond my capabilities. His confidence in my abilities made me dig to the deepest levels of my courage and abilities. He celebrated my small successes by his encouraging e-mails and notes titled "Go baby go!" and gave me the confidence to stretch for the next victory. Once he saw my confidence soar, he just stretched me further until I and others truly believed I was a champion among project leaders in my organization. I consider myself very lucky to have found the jeweler of Lonny's ability to take me in his hands and polish off my great many rough spots and share his light with me until I could see my own light shine through—I owe a lot to him.

Learn from the Best But Be Original

I admire him to this day and learned a lot of my early motivational skills by observing him and studying his style, However, I do not think I ever tried to imitate him. On the basis of some fundamentals I learned from him, I developed my own style of leading and motivating teams for success. For example, I liked his idea of personalized rewards, so I excelled in the organization at personalizing gifts for end-of-project celebrations. Each project team member got something very unique, original, and customized. When we completed a clean room packaging project, I gave each member a blade with their name engraved on it, packaged, sealed, and custom labeled with the project name, logo, and mission statement.

When I completed the acquisition project of a specialized cauterizing needle, I had the company gold plate it and engrave the name of each of my teammates on it. I then had it encased in clear crystal-like plastic and had it signed by the project sponsors and also signed it myself. This was presented to each team member at the successful completion of the project. I am sure my team members still have these on their desks. Thus, I had people who followed me from one project to another although they had full-time functional department roles. They knew that they were on board for a wild ride as I expected them to always stretch beyond their comfort zone and achieve top-quality results. However, I always made sure that we also had fun while achieving the breakthrough results, a lesson from my hero, Lonny, I will always remember and apply.

Lonny is now a president in a Fortune 500 company. I cannot think of anyone else more deserving than him for this critical role. Go baby go!

Pillar XI Force Field Analysis

PILLAR XI: FORCE FIELD ANALYSIS OF ORGANIZATIONAL ASSESSMENT

Table 11.3 shows force field analysis of organizational assessment. The organizational assessment is conducted to assess if the culture of the organization is in alignment with the principles of Pillar XI. Tables 11.4 through 11.6 are used to develop and implement an action plan to increase the impact of the organizational driving forces and decrease the impact of the organizational resisting forces.

PILLAR XI: FORCE FIELD ANALYSIS OF SELF-ASSESSMENT

Table 11.7 shows the force field analysis of self-assessment. The self-assessment is conducted to assess if your own strengths are in alignment with the principles of Pillar XI. Tables 11.8 through 11.10 are used to develop and implement an action plan to increase the impact of the self-driving forces and decrease the impact of the self-resisting forces.

PILLAR XI: RECOMMENDATIONS FOR OPTIMAL RESULTS FROM FORCE FIELD ANALYSIS

For optimal results and actual transformation of culture and strengths conducive to the creation of advanced master project leaders, the following three steps are necessary:

1. Both the organizational and self-evaluation assessments must be completed.
2. A well-designed action plan must be created and implemented to increase the driving forces and decrease the resisting forces.
3. The principles of each pillar must be constantly practiced and improved.

It is highly recommended that both the organization assessments and the self-assessments be conducted every year and the action plan be updated at least every 3 months.

Note: The sum of scores for Organizational Driving Force and Organizational Resisting Force for each point must be less than or equal to TEN.

The sum of scores for Self Driving Force and Self Resisting Force for each point must be less than or equal to TEN.

Table 11.3   Pillar XI: Force Field Organizational Analysis

Team Name: _____   Date: _____

	Does My Organization Drive or Resist a Culture of Stress-Free Projects Leadership?			
	0 Never	5 Sometimes		7 Mostly
	3 Rarely	ODF + ORF ≤ 10		10 Always
No.	Driving Forces	Score Organizational Driving Force (ODF)	Score Organizational Resisting Force (ORF)	Resisting Forces
1	My organization fully understands that stress on their employees can result in psychophysiological disorders or several diseases.			My organization focuses on results and believes that stress is an essential component of a demanding corporate environment.
2	Our organization is constantly trying to reduce the increasing stress levels among employees caused by intense global competition and downturn in the economy.			Our organization considers employees' stress level as a personal problem of the employees, which they need to learn to manage so that they can be competitive in this tough economy.
3	Our sponsors provide clear and unambiguous project requirements so that there is no unnecessary stress on the project leaders and the project teams.			Our project requirements are not well defined, but the project managers and the projects teams are used to the anxiety it creates.
4	Our project leaders pay immense attention to project planning and spend considerable amount of time to make sure that inadequate planning, which causes undue stress, is avoided at all costs.			Our culture is of "Fire, Ready, Aim," and we spend very little time planning although the poor planning may cause some stress later on in the project.
5	Our organization avoids scope creep on projects as they understand that it results in severe stress on the team members.			Our organization is not opposed to scope creep and often adds work even during later stages of the project as they know that the team will somehow manage to complete it.

6	Our leaders fully understand the importance of assigning work based on individual abilities of team members and their varied levels of tolerance to stress.			Our managers treat everyone on the team equally and distribute work without considering their tolerance to stress.
7	Our organization has a "work hard, play hard" culture and encourages a fun, stress-free environment on projects.			Our organization has a culture of "burnout" and tends to overload the team members with excessive work.
8	Our leaders take the time to understand individuals on their team and put them in situations where they can truly "soar with their strengths."			Our project managers push all team members to the same level of performance or output in the work.
9	Project leaders understand the concept of Zone of Pinnacle Performance,™ and they challenge themselves and their team members just enough so that they stretch, that is, go beyond their envelope of comfort.			Project managers tend to overwork themselves and the team members and go beyond the "zones of fatigue" into the zone of injury, burnout, and breakdown.
10	Our leaders create a fun-filled environment where new ideas flow freely, breakthroughs happen, and successes are celebrated for the project and for personal success of team members.			Our managers focus on creating a serious work-oriented environment and sometimes celebrate if there are big successes on projects.
	Total ODF score			*Total ORF score*

Result	Conclusion	Recommended Action Review and Update Every Quarter (3 months)
ODF >> ORF	My company culture strongly drives a culture of stress-free project leadership.	Use Tables 11.4 through 11.6 to set goals and create an action plan to preserve or to continuously improve the culture of stress-free project leadership.
ODF > ORF	My company culture drives the culture of stress-free project leadership.	Use Tables 11.4 through 11.6 to set goals and to create an action plan to increase ODF to create a culture of stress-free project leadership.
ORF >> ODF	My company culture strongly resists the culture of stress-free project leadership.	Use Tables 11.4 through 11.6 to set goals and to create an action plan to increase the ODF and to reduce the ORF to create a culture of stress-free project leadership.
ORF > ODF	My company culture resists the culture of stress-free project leadership.	Use Tables 11.4 through 11.6 to set goals and to create an action plan to reduce the ORF to create a culture of stress-free project leadership.
ODF = ORF	My company culture does not drive or resist the culture of stress-free project leadership.	Use Tables 11.4 through 11.6 to set goals and to create an action plan to increase the ODF to create a culture of stress-free project leadership.

Table 11.4 Pillar XI: Analysis of ODF and ORF Results

Result	Existing Organizational Culture	If The Goal Is to Create a Moderately Strong Culture of Stress-Free Projects	If The Goal Is To create a Very Strong Culture of Stress-Free Projects
ODF			
ODF ≤ 25	No or minimal culture of stress-free projects	Focus on improving scores in at least 5 DF	Focus on improving scores in at least 7 DF
25 < ODF ≤ 50	Weak culture of stress-free project leadership	Focus on improving scores in at least 3 DF	Focus on improving scores in at least 5 DF
50 < ODF ≤ 75	Moderate culture of stress-free project leadership	Focus on improving scores in at least 1 DF	Focus on improving scores in at least 3 DF
ODF > 75	Strong culture of stress-free project leadership	N/A	Preserve or continuously improve the culture
ORF			
ORF > 75	No or minimal culture of stress-free project leadership	Focus on decreasing scores in at least 5 RF	Focus on decreasing scores in at least 7 RF
50 < ORF ≤ 75	Weak culture of stress-free project leadership	Focus on decreasing scores in at least 3 RF	Focus on decreasing scores in at least 5 RF
25 < ORF ≤ 50	Moderate culture stress-free project leadership	Focus on decreasing scores in at least 1 RF	Focus on decreasing scores in at least 3 RF
ORF ≤ 25	Strong culture of stress-free project leadership	N/A	Preserve or continuously improve the culture

Table 11.5 Pillar XI: Action Plan to Increase Organizational Driving Forces (ODFs)

Team Name: _____   Date: _____

No.	Driving Force	Current Score	Goal (Target Score) ⬆	Action Plan to Increase DF Score	Complete by (Date)	Assigned to (Department Name or Initials of the Person)
1	My organization fully understands that stress on their employees can result in psychophysiological disorders or several diseases.					
2	Our organization is constantly trying to reduce the increasing stress levels among employees caused by intense global competition and downturn in the economy.					
3	Our sponsors provide clear and unambiguous project requirements so that there is no unnecessary stress on the project leaders and on the project teams.					
4	Our project leaders pay immense attention to project planning and spend considerable amount of time to make sure that inadequate planning, which causes undue stress, is avoided at all costs.					
5	Our organization avoids scope creep on projects as they understand that it results in severe stress on the team members.					

6	Our leaders fully understand the importance of assigning work based on individual abilities of team members and their varied levels of tolerance to stress.					
7	Our organization has "work hard, play hard" culture and encourages a fun, stress-free environment on projects.					
8	Our leaders take the time to understand individuals on their team and put them in situations where they can truly "soar with their strengths."					
9	Project leaders understand that concept of Zone of Pinnacle Performance™ and they challenge themselves and their team members just enough so that they stretch, that is, go beyond their envelope of comfort.					
10	Our leaders create a fun-filled environment where new ideas flow freely, breakthroughs happen, and successes are celebrated for the project and for personal success of team members.					
	Total ODF					

Table 11.6 Pillar XI: Action Plan to Decrease Organizational Resisting Forces (ORFs)

No.	Resisting Force	Current Score	Goal (Target Score) ⬇	Action Plan to Decrease RF Score	Complete by (Date)	Assigned to (Department Name or Initials of the Person)
1	My organization focuses on results and believes that stress is an essential component of a demanding corporate environment.					
2	Our organization considers the employees' stress level as a personal problem of the employees, which they need to learn to manage so that they can be competitive in this tough economy.					
3	Our project requirements are not well defined, but the project managers and the project teams are used to the anxiety it creates.					
4	Our culture is of "Fire, Ready, Aim," and we spend very little time planning although the poor planning may cause some stress later on in the project.					
5	Our organization is not opposed to scope creep and often adds work even during later stages of the project as they know that the team will somehow manage to complete it.					

6	Our managers treat everyone on the team equally and distribute work without considering their tolerance to stress.					
7	Our organization has a culture of "burnout" and tends to overload the team members with excessive work.					
8	Our project managers push all team members to the same level of performance or output in the work.					
9	Project managers tend to overwork themselves and the team members and go beyond the "zones of fatigue" into the zone of injury, burnout and breakdown.					
10	Our managers focus on creating a serious work-oriented environment and sometimes celebrate if there are big successes on projects.					
	Total ORF					

Table 11.7   Pillar XI: Force Field Self Analysis

Name: _____   Date: _____

	Does My Behavior Drive or Resist the Principles of Stress-Free Project Leadership?				
	0 Never		5 Sometimes		7 Mostly
	3 Rarely		SDF + SRF ≤ 10		10 Always
No.	Driving Forces ➡	Score Self-Driving Force (SDF)	Score Self-Resisting Force (SRF)	⬅ Resisting Forces	
1	I am very careful not to allow excessive stress to buildup for myself and others as I am aware that it can lead to several disorders and diseases.			I believe that stress in a demanding corporate environment is imminent and is to be expected.	
2	As a leader, it is my duty to ensure that the team members are mentally and physically in best shape so that they can effectively counter the intense global competition and downturn in the economy.			As a manager, it is my duty to get best project results and not to worry about what stress levels, competition, or economy issues our team members are facing.	
3	I use the project charter, project vision statements, and active communications to ensure that all project requirements are clear and unambiguous to avoid any unnecessary stress on the project.			I spend little time in communicating all project requirements as the team usually figures it out, plus the resulting project anxiety helps keep the team members on their toes at all times.	
4	I spend considerable amount of time in detailed project planning efforts early on in the project.			I spend little time planning as it is critical to get the project started without wasting too much time upfront on detailed requirements.	
5	If I see anyone on my team being chronically stressed, I immediately try to understand the cause and try my best to alleviate the stress, if it is related to work or to work–life balance.			If I see anyone on my team being chronically stressed, I ask their team leader to replace them before they adversely impact the project.	

6	I spend adequate time with my core team members so that I fully understand their tolerance levels to stress and allocate work that allows them to perform at their optimal levels.			I do not have time to try to decipher the stress tolerance levels of my core team members, and I distribute work as required to them.
7	I attempt to make coming to work enjoyable for my team and encourage a culture of healthy competition, fun, less stress, and creativity on projects.			My team members have a tendency to "burnout" and constantly complain about being overloaded with excessive work.
8	I spend adequate informal time with team members and try to understand their strengths so that I can allocate them to assignments that allow them to "soar with their strengths."			I expect team members to deliver best results on assigned tasks, irrespective of their strengths and weaknesses.
9	I encourage my team members to always perform within the Zone of Pinnacle Performance™, which stretches them enough beyond their envelope of comfort that they constantly excel in their performance and continuously grow in self-confidence.			My teams usually operate within the "zone of fatigue" and some members even operate in the "zone of injury and breakdown" as there are always very limited resources on my projects.
10	I always celebrate the successes of my team and team members and personalize rewards for my team members who go the extra mile.			I only celebrate team successes when there are some major breakthroughs or big savings on my project.
	Total SDF score			*Total SRF score*

Result	Conclusion	Recommended Action Review and Update Every Quarter (3 months)
SDF ≫ SRF	My behavior strongly supports the principles of stress-free project leadership.	Use Tables 11.8 through 11.10 to set goals and create an action plan to continuously enhance the behavior to create a culture of stress-free project leadership.
SDF > SRF	My behavior supports the principles of stress-free project leadership.	Use Tables 11.8 through 11.10 to set goals and create an action plan to increase SDF to allow a stronger behavior toward creating a culture of stress-free project leadership.
SRF ≫ SDF	My behavior strongly resists the principles of stress-free project leadership.	Use Tables 11.8 through 11.10 to set goals and create an action plan to increase SDF and reduce SRF to allow a stronger behavior toward creating a culture of stress-free project leadership.
SRF > SDF	My behavior resists the principles of stress-free project leadership.	Use Tables 11.8 through 11.10 to set goals and create an action plan to reduce SRF to allow a stronger behavior toward creating a culture of stress-free project leadership.
SDF = SRF	My behavior does not drive or resist the principles of stress-free project leadership.	Use Tables 11.8 through 11.10 to set goals and create an action plan to increase the SDF to allow a stronger behavior toward creating a culture of stress-free project leadership.

Table 11.8 Pillar XI: Analysis of SDF and SRF Results

Result	Existing Behavior	*If the Goal Is to Create a Moderately Strong Behavior Toward Principles of Stress-Free Project Leadership*	*If the Goal Is to Create a Very Strong Behavior Toward Principles of Stress-Free Project Leadership*
SDF			
SDF ≤ 25	No or minimal activities in creating a culture of stress-free project leadership	Focus on improving scores in at least 5 DF	Focus on improving scores in at least 7 DF
25 < SDF ≤ 50	Weak activities in creating a culture of stress-free project leadership	Focus on improving scores in at least 3 DF	Focus on improving scores in at least 5 DF
50 < SDF ≤ 75	Moderate activities in creating a culture of stress-free project leadership	Focus on improving scores in at least 1 DF	Focus on improving scores in at least 3 DF
SDF > 75	Strong activities in creating a culture of stress-free project leadership	N/A	Preserve or continuously improve the behavior
SRF			
SRF > 75	No or minimal activities in creating a culture of stress-free project leadership	Focus on decreasing scores in at least 5 RF	Focus on decreasing scores in at least 7 RF
50 < SRF ≤ 75	Weak activities in creating a culture of stress-free project leadership	Focus on decreasing scores in at least 3 RF	Focus on decreasing scores in at least 5 RF
25 < SRF ≤ 50	Moderate activities in creating a culture of stress-free project leadership	Focus on decreasing scores in at least 1 RF	Focus on decreasing scores in at least 3 RF
SRF ≤ 25	Strong activities in creating a culture of stress-free project leadership	N/A	Preserve or continuously improve the behavior

Table 11.9   Pillar XI: Action Plan to Increase Self-Driving Forces (SDFs)

Name: _____   Date: _____

No.	Driving Force	Current Score	Goal (Target Score) ⬆	Action Plan to Increase DF Score	Complete by (Date)	Required Resources
1	I am very careful not to allow excessive stress to buildup for myself and others as I am aware that it can lead to several disorders and diseases.					
2	As a leader, it is my duty to ensure that the team members are mentally and physically in best shape so that they can effectively counter the intense global competition and downturn in the economy.					
3	I use the project charter, project vision statements, and active communications to ensure that all project requirements are clear and unambiguous to avoid any unnecessary stress on the project.					
4	I spend considerable amount of time in detailed project planning efforts early on in the project.					
5	If I see anyone on my team being chronically stressed, I immediately try to understand the cause and try my best to alleviate the stress, if it is related to work or to work–life balance.					

6	I spend adequate time with my core team members so that I fully understand their tolerance levels to stress and allocate work, which allows them to perform at their optimal levels.					
7	I attempt to make coming to work enjoyable for my team and encourage a culture of healthy competition, fun, less stress, and creativity on projects.					
8	I spend adequate informal time with team members and try to understand their strengths so that I can allocate them assignments that allow them to "soar with their strengths."					
9	I encourage my team members to always perform within the Zone of Pinnacle Performance™, which stretches them enough beyond their envelope of comfort that they constantly excel in their performance and continuously grow in self-confidence.					
10	I always celebrate the successes of my team and team members and personalize rewards for my team members who "go the extra mile."					
	Total SDF					

Table 11.10   Pillar XI: Action Plan to Decrease Self-Resisting Forces (SRFs)

Name: _____   Date: _____

No.	Resisting Force	Current Score	Goal (Target Score)	Action Plan to Decrease RF Score	Complete by (Date)	Required Resources
1	I believe that stress in a demanding corporate environment is imminent and is to be expected.					
2	As a manager, it is my duty to get best project results and not worry about what stress levels, competition, or economy issues our team members are facing.					
3	I spend little time in communicating all project requirements as the team usually figures it out, plus the resulting project anxiety helps keep the team members on their toes at all times.					
4	I spend little time planning as it is critical to get the project started without wasting too much time upfront on detailed requirements.					
5	If I see anyone on my team being chronically stressed, I ask their team leader to replace them before they adversely impact the project.					

6	I do not have time to try to decipher the stress tolerance levels of my core team members, and I distribute work as required to them.					
7	My team members have a tendency to "burnout" and constantly complain about being overloaded with excessive work.					
8	I expect team members to deliver best results on assigned tasks, irrespective of their strengths and weaknesses.					
9	My teams usually operate within the "zone of fatigue" and some members even operate in the "zone of injury and breakdown" as there are always very limited resources on my projects.					
10	I only celebrate team successes when there are some major breakthroughs or big savings on my project.					
	Total SRF					

Pillar XI   Exercises

PILLAR XI: ORGANIZATIONAL-LEVEL SKILL SET–ENHANCEMENT EXERCISES

GROUP EXERCISES

These exercises are best completed within a group of project managers, project leaders, executives, and stakeholders from within a department or an organization.

1. Using Table 11.11, identify at least five advantages to your organization in creating a culture of stress-free project leadership, rate them from 1 (least important) to 5 (most important), and explain the rating.
2. Using Table 11.12, identify at least five roadblocks within your organization in creating a culture of stress-free project leadership

Table 11.11   Pillar XI: Five Advantages of Applying Principles of Pillar XI to Your Organization

No.	Advantages of Applying Principles of Pillar XI to Enhancing Your Organization Culture	Rating (from 1 = Least Important to 5 = Most Important)	Explain the Rating
1			
2			
3			
4			
5			

Table 11.12 Pillar XI: Five Roadblocks to Creating a Culture of Stress-Free Project Leadership Using Pillar XI

No.	Roadblocks to Applying Principles of Stress-Free Project Leadership as Described in Pillar XI to Your Organization	Rating (from 1 = Least Difficult to Overcome to 5 = Most Difficult to Overcome)	Explain the Rating
1			
2			
3			
4			
5			

for your complex projects, rate them from 1 (least difficult to overcome) to 5 (most difficult to overcome) and explain the rating.

3. Identify a complex project within your organization that was recently completed. Get the core team together and request them to use Table 11.13 to identify the following on the project.
   a. Approximate average stress levels during various project phases (0 = no stress, 5 = neutral stress, 10 = extreme stress)
   b. Factors that contributed to stress during each phase
4. Identify two projects of approximately equal complexity and duration within your organization that were led by different project leaders: Project A, which failed to meet all the project requirements, and Project B, which was successful in meeting all project

Table 11.13   Pillar XI: Reflecting on a Project and Identifying principles of Pillar XI

Name of Completed Project		
Phase	*Approximate Average Stress Levels during Various Project Phases (0 = No Stress, 5 = Neutral Stress, 10 = Extreme Stress)*	*Factors That Contributed to the Stress*
1. Project start-up		
2. Project preparation		
3. Project implementation		
4. Project monitoring		
5. Project closure		

requirements. Get the core teams of both Project A and Project B together and request them to use Table 11.14 to fill in the factors that increased stress and factors that relieved stress during the projects. Ask them to also reflect on the impact of both factors on the project results.

5. Scenario analysis: Divine Heart Hospital (DHH), a major hospital in the Detroit area, is launching a major project to modernize its emergency room (ER) with the latest technology equipment. Because the ER operations cannot be impacted at all, they have created a makeshift ER in a location approximately 1 mile from where the ER currently is located. The project is estimated to take at least 10 months to complete. They have hired the leading experts in the area of ER technology, "ERial," which will manage the entire

Table 11.14   Pillar XI: Factors That Increase or Relieve Stress during Project and Their Impact on Project Results

Projects	Factors That Increased Stress during the Project	Factors That Relieved Stress during the Project	Impact of Both Factors on the Project Results
Project A (failed project)			
Project B (successful project)			

project for DHH. Three nurses from DHH have also been assigned to the project. They are as follows:

- Karen, who as the newly hired chief registered nurse (RN), is the ring leader and is called "Kween Karen" because of her "know-it-all" attitude and also for being the young girlfriend of good old Doctor Don, who is the director of the ER at DHH.
- Ben, who is the male RN in the ER. He is also known as "Busy Bee Ben" because he seems to be always zipping around the ER and always seems to be on a mission.
- Wendy, another experienced RN who is also known as "Worry Wart Wendy" because of her obsession for details and perfection.

All three of these DHH employees are going to act as the voice of the customer and communication liaison between DHH and ERial. They will be responsible to ensure that the project is on track because after 10 months, the lease at the new location will be up and they will have to vacate it, even if the new ER is not ready. Because of a hiring freeze, Karen, Wendy, and Ben will also be required to help in the ER when they are short staffed. Dr. Don has asked Karen, Ben, and Wendy to jointly make all the required decisions and involve him only if they face serious issues.

All three RNs will report to Dr. Don and to Mario, the project manager from ERial.

The project kickoff goes off well, but within 3 months, the following issues are encountered:

- All suggestions by the more experienced RNs Wendy and Ben have been tossed out by Karen, the 35-year-old chief RN, and she has decided the new layout and the vendors for all the equipment, which are 180° opposed to the suggestions made by Wendy and Ben, who collectively have 45 years of experience in the ER. Also, they are many questions posed by DHH about the facilities, which have either been unanswered or Karen has provided directions on the basis of her "guesstimates." Karen does not like to take the back seat and is even overruling Mario in some of the decisions that he has made.
- Mario, although a good project manager, does not have good planning skills and has made several assumptions in his project plans and risk assessments. He seems already concerned about the 10-month deadline as his ERial team seems to be moving very slowly. Also, he commutes weekly for this project from Juarez, Mexico, and he and his wife are expecting their first child around the same time as that of the project deadline.
- Ben has been asked to deal with the equipment vendors to ensure that they provide the equipment on time and with the right specifications. Ben has no experience in this and is putting in 18-hour days to ensure he does not miss anything that he can be blamed for.
- Worry Wart Wendy has already had two meltdowns and was once herself rushed to the ER for severe hypertension.

Although Karen reported a rosy picture of the project, during the quarterly project status review meeting, Dr. Don sensed that something was amiss as he had not seen much activity at the ER site. Dr. Don has assigned your team as the secret "investigative committee" so that you can provide him with an unbiased opinion of the situation on the basis of the following:

a. Using Table 11.15, identify the strengths and weaknesses of all the key individuals on the project.
b. Using Table 11.16, identify the major themes and the major factors causing stress on this project. Rate them from 1 (very low impact) to 5 (very high impact).
c. Using Table 11.17, identify the major roadblocks to achieving success on this project and rate them from 1 (least difficult to overcome) to 5 (most difficult to overcome).

Table 11.15　Pillar XI: Scenario Analysis—Strengths and Weaknesses of Project Individuals

Name	Strengths	Weaknesses
Morio (PM, ERial)		
Karen (Chief RN, DHH)		
Wendy (RN, DHH)		
Ben (RN, DHH)		

Table 11.16　Pillar XI: Scenario Analysis—Factors Causing Project Stress

Major Stress Themes	Major Factors Causing Project Stress	Rating (from 1 = Very Low Impact to 5 = Very High Impact)

Table 11.17　Pillar XI: Scenario Analysis—Roadblocks to DHH project Success

Major Roadblocks to DHH Project Success (Themes)	Major Roadblocks to DHH Project Success (Factors)	Rating (from 1 = Least Difficult to Overcome to 5 = Most Difficult to Overcome)

PILLAR XI: PERSONAL-LEVEL SKILL SET–ENHANCEMENT EXERCISES

INDIVIDUAL EXERCISES

These exercises are to be completed individually after reviewing Pillar XI in detail.

1. Using Table 11.18, list at least five advantages of applying the principles of Pillar XI of stress-free project leadership to your future projects. Rate the advantages from 1 (least important) to 5 (most important) and explain the rating.

2. Using Table 11.19, identify at least five roadblocks to applying the principles of stress-free project leadership from Pillar XI on all your future major projects. Rate the identified roadblocks from 1 (least difficult to overcome) to 5 (most difficult to overcome) and explain the rating.

Table 11.18   Pillar XI: Five Advantages of Applying Principles of Pillar XI to Your Career

No.	Advantages of Applying Principles of Pillar XI of Stress-Free Project Leadership to All Your Future Projects	Rating (from 1 = Least Important to 5 = Most Important)	Explain the Rating
1			
2			
3			
4			
5			

Table 11.19   Pillar XI: Five Roadblocks to Applying Principles of Pillar XI

No.	Roadblocks to Applying Principles of Stress-Free Project Leadership Detailed in Pillar XI to All Your Future Projects	Rating (from 1 = Least Difficult to Overcome to 5 = Most Difficult to Overcome)	Explain the Rating
1			
2			
3			
4			
5			

3. Using Table 11.20, select a project you worked on as a project manager/leader or as team member that had issues related to significant stress. Looking back on the project, answer the following questions for each phase of the project:
   a. Major factors that contributed to the project stress and were within your control
   b. Major factors that contributed to the project stress but were beyond your control
4. Using Table 11.21, select a complex project you are working on currently as a project manager/leader or as team member and answer the following questions for each phase of the project:
   a. What are the expected stress factors for you and for the team members on the project during each phase?

Table 11.20 Pillar XI: Reflecting on a Failed Project with Excessive Stress and Identifying Principles of Pillar XI

Name of Failed Project		
Your Role in the Project		
Phase	*Major Factors That Contributed to the Project Stress That Were Within My Control*	*Major Factors That Contributed to the Project Stress That Were Beyond My Control*
1. Project start-up		
2. Project preparation		
3. Project implementation		
4. Project monitoring		
5. Project closure		

   b. Which principles of Pillar XI can be applied to reduce or eliminate the factors resulting in project stress?

   c. What are the expected improvements in the project results?

5. Scenario analysis: DHH, a major hospital in the Detroit area, is launching a major project to modernize its ER with the latest technology equipment. Because the ER operations cannot be impacted at all, they have created a makeshift ER in a location approximately 1 mile from where the ER currently is located. The project is estimated to take at least 10 months to complete. They have hired the leading experts in the area of ER technology, ERial, whose project manager Mario will manage the entire project for DHH. Three nurses, Karen, Wendy, and Ben, from DHH have also been assigned to the project. As seen, Dr. Don, the director of the ER at

Table 11.21   Pillar XI: Proactive Stress Reduction on an Upcoming Project using Principles of Pillar XI

Name of Failed Project			
Your Role in the Project			
Phase	*Expected Stress Factors for Yourself and for the Team Members on the Project*	*Principles of Pillar XI That Can be Applied to Reduce or Eliminate the Factors Resulting in Project Stress*	*Expected Improvements in the Project Results*
1. Project start-up			
2. Project preparation			
3. Project implementation			
4. Project monitoring			
5. Project closure			

DHH, is concerned about the project on the basis of the reports received from his secret investigative team, as seen in Tables 11.5 through 11.7.

Upon Dr. Don's insistence, ERial has hired you to be the senior project leader on this project. Mario will now be reporting to you. You have been asked to provide the following to Dr. Don:

  a. A human performance curve with symbols indicating current state zone for Mario, Karen, Wendy, and Ben in Table 11.22.

b. A human performance curve with ideal state zones for Mario, Karen, Wendy, and Ben in Table 11.23.

c. Using Table 11.24, create a plan of action to allow Mario, Karen, Wendy, and Ben to be in the zone as identified in Table 11.23.

d. Using Table 11.25, provide other recommendations to get the project back on the path to success.

Table 11.22   Pillar XI: Scenario Analysis—Identifying Zone of Performance—Current State

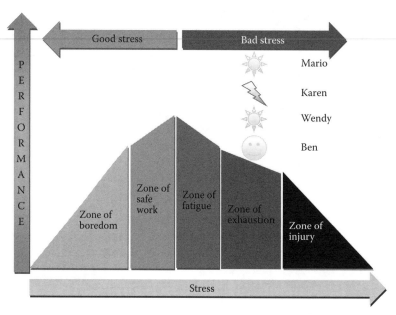

Table 11.23   Pillar XI: Scenario Analysis—Identifying Zone of Performance—Future State

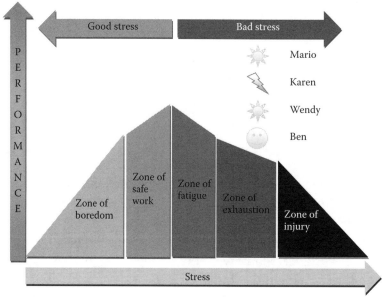

Table 11.24 Pillar XI: Scenario Analysis—Plan of Action for DHH Project Success

Name	Plan of Action for DHH Project Success
Morio (PM, ERial)	
Karen (Chief RN, DHH)	
Wendy (RN, DHH)	
Ben (RN, DHH)	

Table 11.25 Pillar XI: Scenario Analysis—Other Recommendations for DHH Project Success

Other Recommendations for DHH Project Success

Pillar XI   References

1. Selye, H. (1956). *The Stress of Life*, New York: McGraw-Hill.
2. Proactive Change. *Stress & Burnout Statistics: Physical & Psychological Symptoms of Anxiety Stress,* http://www.proac-tivechange.com/stress/statistics.htm (accessed Nov 11, 2010).
3. Stoddard, S. (2010). *Yogi Berra Quotes*, http://www.rinkworks.com/ said/yogiberra.shtml (accessed November 11, 2010).
4. Posen, D. B. (April 1995), "Stress management for patient and physician," *Canadian Journal of Continuing Medical Education*, http:// www.mentalhealth.com/mag1/p51-str.html (accessed Nov 11, 2010).

Chapter 12

Pillar XII: Invest in Your Appreciating Assets

Things Do Not Appreciate, Only People Do

12.1 Introduction

Project leaders who gain expertise and apply the 11 pillars discussed in the previous chapters stand a significantly better chance of achieving success in enterprise-level projects than those project managers who do not. However, without the use of last and final pillar, no project or no other initiative can be successful. Pillar XII is primarily focused on what truly makes a project successful—"The people."

> This pillar is focused on answering three critical questions:
>
> 1. What is a true appreciating asset and how can an organization invest in this asset?
> 2. Should the organization continue to invest in these assets in tough economic times?
> 3. What should be the final objective for a project leader?

Let us explore these critical questions together. Let us take a leap into the future by using our power of visualization. I want you to envision yourself in a job interview with "Pinnacle Process," one of the biggest, most progressive, and most reputable organizations in this world. You are in the final stage of selection for the role of a Project Sensei (*Sensei* is a Japanese title used to refer to or address teachers, professors, and professionals such as doctors and other figures of authority).[1]

The interviewer, Susan, is a very elegant, charming, wise lady. Her white hair and beautiful pale skin have the sheen of wisdom, and she radiates an aura of complete tranquility. Visualize yourself looking into her deep-blue eyes and all your uneasiness and anxiety has completely disappeared. You are immersed in a "Zen-like state" and all you desire is to work for this organization—even if they were to offer you a position of a junior janitor. Susan asks you if you are comfortable. Visualize yourself smiling and answering in the affirmative.

Susan then says, "Mr. _____ (your name) I am very pleased that you are among our finalists for the position of Project Sensei. Today, I will ask you three questions only. After each reply, I will discuss the culture of our organization. At the end, I will allow you to rate your answers from 1 (least fit for our culture) to 5 (best fit for our culture). I will do the same. If we come up with similar scores, I will tell you immediately if you will be joining us or not."

Question 1

Assume that you are starting with Pinnacle Process on Monday as a Project Sensei. Assume that the organization had significant success and has about a million dollars to invest in the growth of the company. As the Project Sensei, on the first day of taking over the responsibilities, what will you invest those million dollars into so that you can show a significant appreciation of that investment?

Question 2

Assume that Pinnacle Process, just like the rest of the corporations, is facing some economic challenges. You are coming on board as our "turnaround expert" to show us the way out of these tough economic times. On the first day of taking over the responsibilities of a Project Sensei, you will be assigned a project team of seasoned project experts who have had to take pay cuts and whose motivation level is at an all time low. We currently have two major projects you can deploy these resources on. The two options are a simple departmental project, which will allow us to work more efficiently, or a very challenging strategic project, which has many unknowns and if successful, can have a significant effect on the growth of our corporation. You also have an option to let some of them go to save money. Will you let them go or will you get them engaged on one of the projects? If your choice is to engage them, which project will you choose to lead using these expert resources?

Question 3

Imagine yourself, 20 years from now, on the day of retirement from this organization. Imagine that you are on the stage and the people who have been trained by you or have worked with you on several occasions are coming up one by one and saying a few words about their experiences working with you. What would you want them to say about you?

Now, visualize yourself being jolted by these three questions. You have been through several interviews but no one has ever asked you these questions. This truly is a different organization and you are determined to be a part of it. Visualize Susan sitting in front of you and yourself answering the first question—what will you invest a million dollars into so that you can show a significant appreciation of that investment? Take your time to provide her with an insightful and honest answer.

After answering your first question, Susan patiently engages you in a conversation about the corporate culture at Pinnacle Process. The ideas she reveals in her conversation are unique and you are amazed that an advanced culture like this even exists in the corporate world.

12.2 Valuing Our True Appreciating Assets

Within our organization, our appreciating assets are not the millions-worth of top-of-the line servers and computers we have just purchased for our projects, nor the 2-million-dollar equipment we purchased for manufacturing, or even the 10-million-dollar building. Our team members or employees are truly the only appreciating assets we will ever have. The motto of our company is "Things do not appreciate; only people do."[2] This axiom is true not only from a tax perspective of depreciation but also from pure logic—it is our way of life. We realize that our buildings and equipment can only provide us a structure; but only our employees can help us define our culture.

People should be considered as the prime appreciating assets in any organization. Some companies use this notion as a slogan, but only a few organizations truly believe it.

Listen to what Teruyuki Minoura, managing director of global purchasing at Toyota, has to say about this—"Developing people is the starting point for *monozukuri* (making things) at Toyota. There can be no successful *monozukuri* without *hitozukuri* (making people)."[3]

In a vast majority of cases, the success or failure of any initiative will depend on the people who execute it rather than on any equipment, consultant, software, or other tools and techniques.

In a vast majority of cases, the success or failure of any initiative will depend on the people who execute it rather than on any equipment, consultant, software, or other tools and techniques. We invest adequate time, effort, and money in hiring and developing the right people and get unmatched results.

12.3 People: The Real Appreciating Assets

People generally perform their work at a level equivalent to the how much we value them at.

People generally perform their work at a level equivalent to the how much we value them at. Here, we value our people enough to consider them as our only appreciating asset and they deliver optimal performance, sometimes even beyond our expectations. We feel that every manager, leader, or executive who is not optimizing the human potential within our organization is literally throwing away talent and millions of dollars with it. One hundred percent of our projects and initiatives are extremely successful, and the successes have helped shape and transform the DNA of our organizational culture. This is the major factor differentiating us from the rest of our competitors who are struggling to survive in our industry.

We are a profit-driven organization and are not naïve, and do not proclaim by any means that we are in a utopian state of operations. Although we take great care in hiring the right people, we do have human resources–related issues. The difference is how we deal with them. Our policy is to use the "human touch" in all difficult situations. For a company of our size, it is very easy to use the heavy hand on our employees who do not fit in. We, however, believe in finding the best fit for the individual with the organization and if it still does not work out, we counsel them and provide resources for them to find an employment that is better suited to them and their family needs. The care we show has paid off for us because we still have employees who have been with us for more than 35 years and have not forgotten the "L" word, which has been lost from the corporate vocabulary. Yes, we still believe in "loyalty" toward our people and they, in turn, are very "loyal" to this organization—it is a simple act of truly caring that promotes loyalty—and we start at the shop-floor levels with our supervisors and it continues on all the way to the top levels of the board of directors. At Pinnacle Process, we are all humans first, employees a distant second. In short, our management and employees share a symbiotic relationship—the employees have complete trust that management will take care of their well being, and management has complete trust that the employees will take care of the customers and the organization, and they both work hard to keep enhancing the trusting relationship.

Thus, the Project Senseis in our organization do not focus on investing, beyond what is absolutely necessary, in assets like software, hardware, building, and machinery as they are all depreciating assets and their value only comes down with time. We focus on investing in improving the skills of our project team members and develop them into the future leaders as we value our team members and their skills as the true appreciating assets. Figure 12.1 clearly describes the philosophy of appreciating and depreciating assets in our organization.

Visualize Susan's face beaming with radiance as she shared her insights into the workings of the organization. Visualize yourself thinking—what a powerful culture—if I could afford it, I would pay them to allow me to work for them. Susan's deep-blue eyes are indicating that the interview must continue and her looks suggests that it is time for me to respond to her second question—Visualize yourself answering this question—Will you let the expert resources go or will you get them engaged on one of the projects? If your choice is to engage them, which project will you choose to lead using these expert resources? Take your time to provide her with an insightful and honest answer of what you would truly do to prove your worth as a "turnaround expert" in these tough economic times for Pinnacle Process.

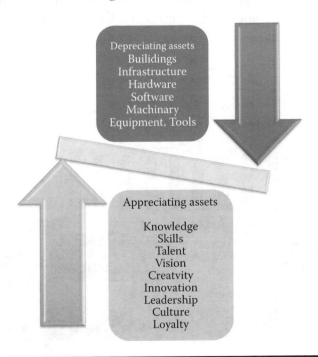

Figure 12.1   Appreciating and depreciating assets in an organization.

After you provide a game plan of what you would do, Susan smiles and provides a deeper insight into the philosophy of their corporation regarding managing resources during tough economic times.

12.4 Pinnacle House of Project Excellence

Susan continues providing some more insight into what she refers to as **"The Pinnacle House of Project Excellence."** She mentions that Pinnacle Process considers the organization as **made of three key elements:**

1. **The Foundation**
   Pinnacle Process thinks that people, their knowledge, and their skills and talents are the real foundation of an organization.
2. **The 12 Pillars**
   The 12 pillars consist of the principles of project leadership, which the organization lives by.
3. **The Roof of Excellence**
   The roof of excellence is delighted customers, excellent results, and employee loyalty.

In normal times, the foundation needs to be reinforced strongly to build a strong organization. However, a strong organization is not possible without rock-hard pillars. The 12 pillars support the organization and create a bond between the foundation and the structure, and the roof is the focus of the organization. Figure 12.2 shows the Pinnacle House of Project Excellence in normal times.

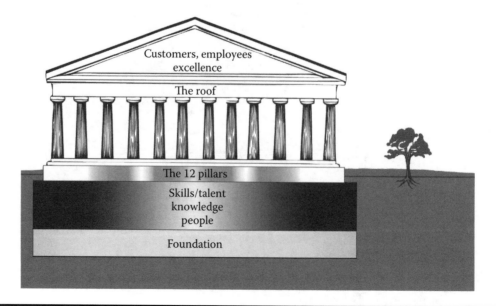

Figure 12.2   The pinnacle house of project excellence—in normal times.

12.5 Unique Philosophy—Dealing with Tough Economic Times

A heavy-duty foundation, solid pillars, and a well-supported roof are critical to designing a strong house that is resistant to extreme conditions. Similarly, an organization needs to be built to weather the extreme conditions of economy and problems. Bad economic situations make it tough on everyone. Very few companies are immune from the heat of the downturn in the economy. This downturn is affecting all corporations, big and small, and the budgets for projects are also shrinking. The easy solution is to go "slash, slash, slash—cut costs, cut staff, cut travel, cut benefits, cut this, cut that..." When the patient is suffering you cannot simply cut off the oxygen—now can you? Susan asks rhetorically. But that's exactly what some corporations are doing right now—taking the easy way out. Do they think their employees and their families do not have the same problems—rising costs and hurt in this economy? Can they stop feeding their children or call little 10-year-old Jimmy and 5-year-old Janice to their bedroom to tell them, "Sorry, we cannot afford you—you are fired."[2]

Today, employees are under pressures unknown to our previous generations. They are competing for jobs not only locally but globally—the pressure is intense to say the least. During downtimes, the employees do not only have the pressure of job security but are worried about their finances, mortgage, taxes, insurance, and other basic necessities.

When organizations are affected, the projects are affected. When projects are affected, project leaders make serious and unfortunate decisions. Organizations and project leaders are slashing their employees, cutting projects, and reducing their benefits to protect the organization from the impending burden. However, not knowingly, they are weakening the very foundation of the organization, the foundation that has been supporting the organization for many years. They are making the organization weaker by doing this, as shown in Figure 12.3. What should a dynamic project leader do when funding is reduced and employees are cut? What message should he send his higher-ups about the importance of taking critical projects? What should a sponsor, customer, or chief of an organization do to continue the core projects without really hurting employees? Pinnacle Process's way of thinking provides answers to these questions.

12.5.1 Strengthen the Foundation

Pinnacle Process's philosophy differs from the traditional approach, such as cutting jobs, in dealing with a downturn in business. We agree that sometimes, tough choices have to be made and layoffs are inevitable, but the decision to

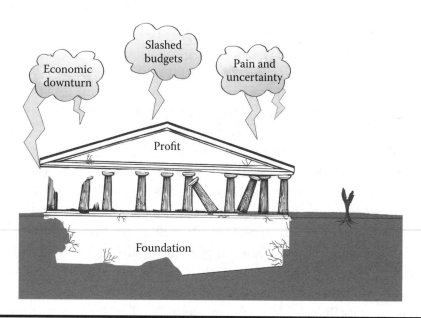

Figure 12.3   Normal organizations during economic downturns.

We strongly believe that downturns are not the time to push the employees down, but to pull them up.

A pull upward rather than a push downward can mean a lot to people during these times and is a very smart approach to motivating them.

reduce the workforce during a downturn should be an exception, not a rule. We strongly believe that downturns are not the time to push the employees down, but to pull them up. This is the time employees need to feel secure, motivated, and productive.[2] A pull upward rather than a push downward can mean a lot to people during these times and is a very smart approach to motivating them. Motivation need not be financial—it can simply be saying "You are an important asset to us and we value your skills and need them the most at this time" or enroll them in a class to help them deal with their stress or conduct motivational workshops on-site. Our employees know the business better than anyone else. When we invest in them, that is, provide the right environment for growth, free of stress and external pressures, they are able to provide results far better than we can ever imagine. People who are highly motivated tap into the core of their creativity and achieve results beyond their wildest dreams. Pinnacle Process' philosophy is not based on weakening the foundation, but strengthening foundations (people, knowledge, and skills/talents) to strengthen and raise pillars (principles of project leadership) to new heights by training, motivation, and enhancing employee skills by allowing them to undertake challenging projects, delight customers, and build a strong organization. Pinnacle Process's unique philosophy for overcoming tough economic times is shown in Figure 12.4.

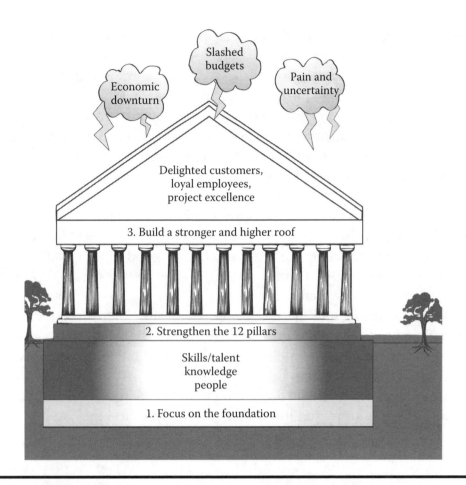

Figure 12.4   Pinnacle's unique strategy for overcoming tough economic times.

12.5.2 Low Tide Exposes All Sharp Edges

Our company has a completely different outlook on this economic situation or any issue that affects us significantly. We refer it to the "growing pains" or the "show me the rocks." Let me explain, says Susan. Have you ever seen a bird being hatched? Have you seen it struggling to break out of the shell? The struggle is nature's way of giving the bird an opportunity to strengthen its wings so it can face life and fly high for the rest of its life.[2] The honest truth, and advice that you will not hear often, is—"pain is good!" Yes, really—pain is not only a good teacher[2] but it is essential for survival and growth. We feel that taking on challenging projects is similar to the struggle necessary to expand our capabilities of creativity and innovation. The biggest advantage of taking challenging projects is the improvement of team skills

> **Really—pain is not only a good teacher[2] but it is essential for survival and growth.**

and their risk-taking capability. It is not usually easy for management to approve challenging projects in situations where money for the projects is limited and risk-taking can be considered as economic suicide. However, if project leaders truly believe that the project can be beneficial to the organization and will help the team expand their horizons, they should be able to convince the executives and senior management that taking on a challenging project will be the right thing to do for the entire organization. Thus, during tough economic times, we undertake challenging strategic projects as we feel our employees are at the peak of their productivity, innovation, and creativity and with a little focus, trust, and motivation, they can truly get some breakthrough results professionally and personally. Thus, using this unique philosophy, we not only withstand the storm of economic downturns better than most other organizations but also go beyond our performance during normal times and create a much stronger organization, as shown in Figure 12.5.

However, sometimes our issues and the resulting pain may also be due to some fundamental problems in certain areas of our business. Just like the high tide covers up the sharp edges on the rocks below, good times cover up a lot of issues. When the tide is low, it shows us all the sharp edges (issues). We use the "low tide" (tough times), which occurs during downturns to our advantage and use our assets to take care of these sharp edges and problems in our business. By eliminating these sharp edges (issues), we reduce the danger of potentially hurting ourselves (slowing down the business) when the tide comes back up again and covers up those sharp edges (issues).[2]

Our corporation always maintains a long-term vision and the bad times mostly act as a "burning platform" and motivate our employees to innovate and take our

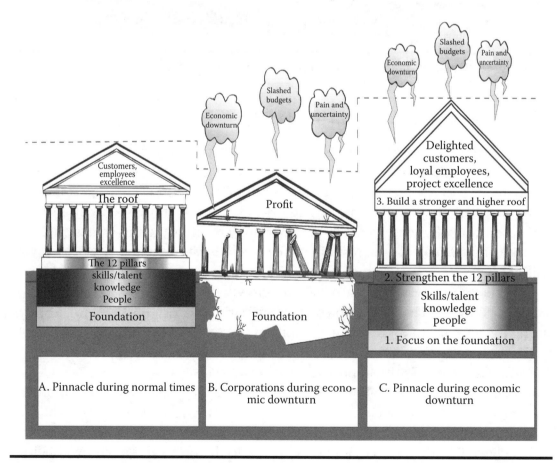

Figure 12.5 Shows how pinnacle house of project excellence excels during downturns.

corporation to the next level. I am sure you all have all heard this before—"when the going gets tough, the tough get going"—and we believe that our employees are tough and extremely responsible. Our entire executive team volunteered for a pay cut in order to be able to retain the personnel at risk of lay-offs due to lack of funds. The rest of the employees demanded that they should also be part of this pay-cut until the economic conditions improve and our corporate finances are stable again. They told us, if we have to bleed, we all must bleed together so we experience each other's pain and quickly find the most efficient way out of the painful situation. What better testament of loyalty and integrity can we ask for from our people?

Thus, we strongly believe that sustainable long-term growth can be realized in any economy without the traditional approach of slashing jobs. In fact, we believe that it is the best time for shedding some bad habits and fostering an increased sense of innovation and creativity within our employees.

Now, Susan is glancing at her watch and you see it as a signal to answer her last and final question—If you were to retire from this organization, what would you want the people who worked with you to say about you? Visualize yourself answering this question honestly to Susan. Visualize that after you are done, you are very anxious to hear from Susan about further insights within the culture of Pinnacle Process. You listen with complete attention as Susan begins talking.

12.6 Create Leaders and Leave a Legacy

At Pinnacle Process, "LEAD" stands for "Leave Everything Appreciated on Departure." We encourage our employees to "leave a legacy."

We do not want them to measure themselves by the short-term profit and loss statements, but by how many lives they have changed and how many leaders they have created for the organization. Here, leaders are considered successful only if their mentees are equal or more successful than themselves. We believe in the wise saying used by training within Industry: "If the worker hasn't learned, the instructor hasn't taught,"[4] as shown in Figure 12.6.[5]

L-Leave
E-Everything
A-Appreciated
D-(on) Departure

Leaders Leave a Legacy

Our Project Sensei's primary responsibility is to create leaders. In the process of teaching others, they themselves reach greater heights as Project Senseis—it is a win–win scenario for all of us.

As Peter Drucker points out, "Management is doing things right; leadership is doing the right things."[6]

Development of personnel is critical to our leaders, even more critical than the overall success of their projects or the success of the organization itself.

Figure 12.6   Job instruction card.

Our Senseis know that the time spent on developing individuals is the best investment of their time and effort.

Our Senseis know that the time spent on developing individuals is the best investment of their time and effort. It is true that developing project leaders is not an easy task. However, our Project Senseis provide the training and support required for project leaders to acquire the five powers required for leaders. They encourage the new dynamic project leaders to view their team as group of energized particles ready for reaction—all the project leaders need to do is to provide the initial energy thrust for the reaction to begin. Leaders teach by example, selecting the right individuals for the right jobs, delegating tasks to increase their confidence, and allowing them to make difficult decisions. Thus, our Senseis make sure that while they are developing project leaders, the project leaders are developing their team members to focus on their customer's needs while expanding their horizons, core capabilities, and confidence. Thus, our Senseis focus on their people, in turn, their people focus on the customers and get the required results on every project, making the organization successful. It is a simple formula—but it is too complex for today's complicated corporate world.

There is an immense amount of talent and passion within our employees. But sometimes, we are unable to utilize their talents in their current positions. Thus, the primary job of the leaders in our corporation is to find the brightest stars within their constellation and give them an opportunity to light up the path for the corporation. Our Sensei uses a simple technique to identify at least one talent or skill or passion in each team member that is not being utilized in their current position. Then, they find an opportunity or a project in which they allow the team member to utilize it. The team members automatically manage their time to complete their own jobs with enthusiasm and also have time left over to take on additional responsibilities in tasks they are excited about. If our employees are not getting opportunities to learn, grow, and apply what they are passionate about, how can they

Our Sensei uses a simple technique to identify at least one talent or skill or passion in each team member that is not being utilized in their current position.

be an asset to our organization? We give them a chance—just like a chance the TV show, *American Idol* gave to the unknown waitress from Texas, Kelly Clarkson, who is now an international star shining bright, or to the Alabama boy, Ruben Stoddard the *Velvet Teddy Bear*, who was nominated for a Grammy, or to unknown, Carrie Underwood, who went on to win a Grammy, and to Jennifer Hudson, who went on to win several awards for her acting role including an Academy Award, a Golden Globe Award, Screen Actor Guilds Award, and other coveted recognitions. Before American Idol, they were "nobodies," but now, we all know them as "talented stars." It's all about giving individuals an opportunity to grow and shine. Thus, our employees are given an opportunity to do what they are passionate about and it also helps our organization. We are pleasantly surprised by the results of this simple technique.

Although it may seem that our organization looks only for individual talent, our leaders also excel in promoting "teamwork." Our Project Sensei believes strongly in Nelson Mandela's words, "Leaders are important, but history is ultimately not made by kings and generals. It is made by the masses."[7] A successful project leader must learn the art of amalgamating the hearts, eyes, ears, voices, minds, and hands of several individuals and converging them into one superentity called the "project team," which uses it's amazing powers and talents to delight their customers. Thus, complex projects can never be completed solely by leaders; they require the project teams to work as one entity. Another way we encourage our leaders to "leave a legacy" is to show consistency of results. Our yardstick for measuring success is very different from most corporations, as we know that "if the yardstick is only 1 millimeter long, even a mouse can measure up to be a giant." Our fundamental yardstick for rewards is based on 3 to 5 years' consistent growth and not two or three quarters of 30% change that management got by cutting jobs, cutting corners on critical maintenance contracts, or reducing the budget for research innovation.

12.6.1 *Reward Consistency of Excellence*

Susan continued to explain the policy of Pinnacle Process that "the only index of success deserving rewards is consistent long-term growth, and not intermittent, short-term financial spurts."

Leaders and managers are measured and rewarded only on "consistency of excellence" over long periods. She explained that this was one of the key reasons the company grew from a small unknown business to a Fortune 500 company and leader in the industry as our leaders share the core principles of rewarding "consistency of excellence."

Susan continues. Just as leaders like Mahatma Gandhi, George Washington, Martin Luther King, and all other leaders lighted up the path for the rest of us with their brilliance, but at some point in their lives, were inspired and polished by other great leaders, our Project Senseis look at each individual on the team as a "diamond," some of which shine bright on their own accord, whereas others may need to be polished before their light can shine through. We believe that at Pinnacle Process, we are in the business of finding and polishing up diamonds, our people, who are the only appreciating assets we have. We are always looking for more "diamonds" and that is why you have been invited here today for this interview. Susan then picks up the beautiful pen from the penholder on the edge of her desk and gently writes three numbers on the sheet of paper in front of her. She then hands over the pen to you and with a smile, her kind eyes signal you to rate your answers from 1 (least fit for our culture) to 5 (best fit for our culture).

Visualize yourself taking the pen gingerly from Susan and writing an honest score for Questions 1, 2, and 3. How did you do? *Will you be the next Project Sensei at Pinnacle Process?*

Pillar XII Summary

Every successful project leader must invest in their appreciating assets—their people and find the stars and provide them opportunities to shine bright. They also need to find the optimal work–life balance. Pinnacle Process thinks that people, their knowledge, their skills, and talents are the real foundation of an organization. The 12 pillars consist of the principles of project leadership in which the organization lives by. The roof of excellence consists of delighted customers, excellent results, and employee loyalty.

Classic project managers who do not consider people as appreciating assets spend money on capital purchases and do not focus on the 12 pillars, thereby weakening the roof with their inability to delight customers, employees, and shareholders.

Every successful master project leader makes their organizations great by focusing on strengthening the foundation and raising the 12 pillars, thereby strengthening the roof by delighting customers, employees, and stakeholders. Their prime goal is to leave a legacy by appreciating their assets (people). Figure 12.7 represents the key principles of appreciating assets in organizations.

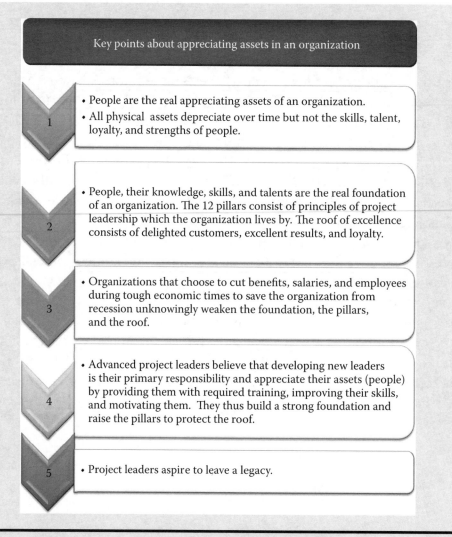

Figure 12.7 **Key points about appreciating assets in organizations.**

Pillar XII Case Study 1
Find "The Diamond" among Team Members

INTRODUCTION

This case study is about finding the "diamond" among the team members, polishing it, and providing the right opportunity for the diamond to shine bright.

CHALLENGE

During my career, I always made it a point to identify and utilize the passion of my team members and my direct-reports. At one point during my career at a Fortune 500 medical company, I was managing document control and marketing literature teams. On my team, I had a document clerk who confided in me that he was feeling underutilized in the documents control clerk position and may quit soon as wanted to be a web programmer as he had taken some classes and really enjoyed it. I already had plans to create an electronic service desk in my department but did not have a budget to hire a programmer. Although we were short-handed, I gave the employee permission to spend about 2 hours per day to build a web application that will help reduce walk-in traffic to the document control clerks.

SITUATION

Within a couple of months, with some support from internal IT staff, the document clerk had developed and tested a user-friendly web application. During this period, his motivation level was very high and he was somehow managing to complete all his work and also focus on the web application development. When we launched the application company-wide, the end-clients were delighted as they did not have to walk halfway across the building but could check on the status of their documents online. Also, the other clerks in the department were more productive as they could stay focused on completing their workload.

RESULTS

The document control clerk who was unhappy just 2 months ago and was planning to quit was recognized throughout the organization as a star for going the extra mile and accomplishing something not within his job description. He was truly thankful for being given the opportunity. It was a win–win situation for everyone involved.

Pillar XII: Case Study 2

Discover a "New Star"

I had another situation, while I was consulting with a company on a week-long kaizen event, where I got to discover a star. I had a chance to work with a very motivated individual during this event. Of all the members on my team, I identified an assembler as a star—she had the best attitude, was not afraid to think outside the box, and put in long hours to ensure that we got the results. A newly appointed plant manger was the sponsor of this event and wanted me to recommend someone who could be a "kaizen coordinator" for the organization. She mentioned that there were quite a few members on my team who had shown interest in this position. But she wanted my opinion as she knew that this position was a high-visibility managerial position with significant responsibilities. I told her candidly that others may be more qualified but I found this assembler to be the star—she had it in her to help their corporation take a leap into the lean journey. The plant manager interviewed her along with a few others on my team. By the end of that week, the plant manager agreed with my assessment and announced that the assembler would be the new corporate kaizen coordinator. Thus, on Monday, she stared on the kaizen event as an assembler; by Friday, she was the new kaizen coordinator—a very well-deserved promotion that allowed her to leap ahead by several grades. A star was born—or rather discovered and she did the corporation proud in her new role. Have you found some stars lately?

Pillar XII Force Field Analysis

PILLAR XII: FORCE FIELD ANALYSIS OF ORGANIZATIONAL ASSESSMENT

Table 12.1 shows force field analysis of organizational assessment. An organizational assessment is conducted to assess if the culture of the organization is in alignment with the principles of Pillar XII. Tables 12.2 through 12.4 are used to develop and implement an action plan to increase the impact of the organizational driving forces and decrease the impact of the organizational resisting forces.

PILLAR XII: FORCE FIELD ANALYSIS OF SELF-ASSESSMENT

Table 12.5 shows force field analysis of self-assessment. A self-assessment is conducted to assess if your own strengths are in alignment with the principles of Pillar XII. Tables 12.6 through 12.8 are used to develop and implement an action plan to increase the impact of the self-driving forces and decrease the impact of the self-resisting forces.

PILLAR XII: RECOMMENDATIONS FOR OPTIMAL RESULTS FROM FORCE FIELD ANALYSIS

For optimal results and actual transformation of culture and strengths conducive to the creation of advanced master project leaders, the following three steps are necessary:

1. Both the organizational and self-evaluation assessments must be completed.
2. A well-designed action plan must be created and implemented to increase the driving forces and decrease the resisting forces.
3. The principles of each pillar must be constantly practiced and improved.

It is highly recommended that both the organizational assessments and self-assessments be conducted every year and the action plan be updated at least every 3 months.

Note: The sum of scores for Organizational Driving Force and Organizational Resisting Force for each point must be less than or equal to TEN.

The sum of scores for Self Driving Force and Self Resisting Force for each point must be less than or equal to TEN.

Table 12.1 Pillar XII: Force Field Organizational Analysis

Team Name: _____   Date: _____

	Does My Organization Drive or Resist a Culture of Enhancing the Organizational Appreciating Assets?			
	0 Never	5 Sometimes		7 Mostly
	3 Rarely	ODF + ORF ≤ 10		10 Always
No.	Driving Forces	*Score Organizational Driving Force (ODF)*	*Score Organizational Resisting Force (ORF)*	Resisting Forces
1	My organization truly believes in the axiom "Things don't appreciate; people do."			My organization believes that investing in the latest technology and equipment is the secret to our success.
2	Our organization believes that our buildings and equipment can only provide an infrastructure, but only our employees can help define our culture.			Our organization believes that our infrastructure and systems help define our culture.
3	In our organization, in most cases, the success of any initiative depends on the people who execute it rather than on any equipment, consultant, software, or other tools and techniques.			In our organization, we believe that the success of any initiative depends on our equipment, consultants, software, or other tools and techniques.
4	Our leaders believe that "People generally perform at the level equivalent to the how much we value them at."			Our managers believe that "People generally need to be closely supervised in order for them to perform as expected."

5	A major factor differentiating us from the rest of our competitors is that our leaders optimize the human potential and the invaluable talent within our organization.			Our managers are skilled at getting maximum work out of their direct reports and we think that keeps us ahead of our competitors.
6	Our organization believes in truly caring for our employees at all levels and, in turn, the employees are very loyal to our organization.			Our organization makes people work very hard and employees get a paycheck; there is no need for loyalty in this simple business arrangement.
7	In our organization, we are all humans first, employees a distant second.			In our organization, all employees are just considered as dispensable resources.
8	Our leaders strongly believe that downturns are not the time to push the employees down, but to pull them up.			Our managers use layoffs as a primary and effective means to cut costs during downturns in the economy.
9	In our organization, we truly believe that employees who are highly motivated will tap into the core of their creativity and achieve results beyond their wildest dreams.			In our organization, we truly believe that employees, who are pushed to the maximum, get the required results.
10	In our organization, our leaders are expected to "leave a legacy" by the number of lives that have been changed positively, and the number of leaders that have been created in the organization.			In our organization, our managers are expected to focus on delivering profits and results.
	Total ODF Score			*Total ORF Score*

Result	Conclusion	Recommended Action Review and Update Every Quarter (3 months)
ODF ≫ ORF	My company culture strongly drives a culture of enhancing the organizational appreciating assets.	Use Tables 12.2 through 12.4 to set goals and create an action plan to preserve or continuously improve the culture of enhancing the organizational appreciating assets.
ODF > ORF	My company culture drives the culture of enhancing the organizational appreciating assets.	Use Tables 12.2 through 12.4 to set goals and create an action plan to increase ODF to create a culture of enhancing the organizational appreciating assets.
ORF ≫ ODF	My company culture strongly resists the culture of enhancing the organizational appreciating assets.	Use Tables 12.2 through 12.4 to set goals and create an action plan to increase the ODF and reduce the ORF to create a culture of enhancing the organizational appreciating assets.
ORF > ODF	My company culture resists the culture of enhancing the organizational appreciating assets.	Use Tables 12.2 through 12.4 to set goals and create an action plan to reduce the ORF to create a culture of enhancing the organizational appreciating assets.
ODF = ORF	My company culture does not drive or resist the culture of enhancing the organizational appreciating assets.	Use Tables 12.2 through 12.4 to set goals and create an action plan to increase the ODF to create a culture of enhancing the organizational appreciating assets.

Table 12.2   Pillar XII: Analysis of ODF and ORF Results

Result	Existing Organizational Culture	If the Goal is to Create a Moderately Strong Culture of Enhancing the Organizational Appreciating Assets	If the Goal is to Create a Very Strong Culture of Enhancing the Organizational Appreciating Assets
ODF			
ODF ≤ 25	No or minimal culture of enhancing the organizational appreciating assets	Focus on improving scores in at least 5 DF	Focus on improving scores in at least 7 DF
25 < ODF ≤ 50	Weak culture of enhancing the organizational appreciating assets	Focus on improving scores in at least 3 DF	Focus on improving scores in at least 5 DF
50 < ODF ≤ 75	Moderate culture of enhancing the organizational appreciating assets	Focus on improving scores in at least 1 DF	Focus on improving scores in at least 3 DF
ODF > 75	Strong culture of enhancing the organizational appreciating assets	N/A	Preserve or continuously improve the culture
ORF			
ORF > 75	No or minimal culture of enhancing the organizational appreciating assets	Focus on decreasing scores in at least 5 RF	Focus on decreasing scores in at least 7 RF
50 < ORF ≤ 75	Weak culture of enhancing the organizational appreciating assets	Focus on decreasing scores in at least 3 RF	Focus on decreasing scores in at least 5 RF
25 < ORF ≤ 50	Moderate culture of enhancing the organizational appreciating assets	Focus on decreasing scores in at least 1 RF	Focus on decreasing scores in at least 3 RF
ORF ≤ 25	Strong culture of enhancing the organizational appreciating assets	N/A	Preserve or continuously improve the culture

Table 12.3   Pillar XII: Action Plan to Increase Organizational Driving Forces (ODFs)

Team Name: _____   Date: _____

No.	Driving Force	Current Score	Goal (Target Score) ⬆	Action Plan to Increase DF Score	Complete by (Date)	Assigned to (Department Name or Initials of Person)
1	My organization truly believes in the axiom "Things don't appreciate; people do."					
2	Our organization believes that our buildings and equipment can only provide an infrastructure, but only our employees can help define our culture.					
3	In our organization, in most cases, the success of any initiative depends on the people who execute it rather than on any equipment, consultant, software, or other tools and techniques.					
4	Our leaders believe that "People generally perform work at a level equivalent to how much we value them at."					
5	A major factor differentiating us from the rest of our competitors is that our leaders optimize the human potential and the invaluable talent within our organization.					

6	Our organization believes in truly caring for our employees at all levels and, in turn, the employees are very loyal to our organization.					
7	In our organization, we are all valued as humans first, employees a distant second.					
8	Our leaders strongly believe that downturns are not the time to push the employees down, but to pull them up.					
9	In our organization, we truly believe that employees who are highly motivated will tap into the core of their creativity and achieve results beyond their wildest dreams.					
10	In our organization, our leaders are expected to "leave a legacy" by the number of lives that have been changed positively, and the number of leaders that have been created in the organization.					
	Total ODF					

Table 12.4   Pillar XII: Action Plan to Decrease Organizational Resisting Forces (ORFs)

No.	Resisting Force	Current Score	Goal (Target Score) ⬇	Action Plan to Decrease RF Score	Complete by (Date)	Assigned to (Department Name or Initials of Person)
1	My organization believes that investing in the latest technology and equipment is the secret to our success.					
2	Our organization believes that our infrastructure and systems help define our culture.					
3	In our organization, we believe that the success of any initiative depends on our equipment, consultants, software, or other tools and techniques.					
4	Our managers believe that "People generally need to be closely supervised in order for them to perform as expected."					
5	Our managers are skilled at getting maximum work out of their direct reports, and we think that keeps us ahead of our competitors.					

6	Our organization makes people work very hard and employees get a paycheck; there is no need for loyalty in this simple business arrangement.					
7	In our organization, all employees are just considered as dispensable resources.					
8	Our managers use layoffs as a primary and effective means to cut costs during downturns in the economy.					
9	In our organization, we truly believe that employees who are pushed to the maximum get the required results.					
10	In our organization, our managers are expected to focus on delivering profits and results.					
	Total ORF					

Table 12.5   Pillar XII: Force Field Self-Analysis

Name: _____   Date: _____

	Does My Behavior Drive or Resist the Principles of Enhancing the Organizational Appreciating Assets?			
	0 Never	5 Sometimes		7 Mostly
	3 Rarely	SDF + SRF ≤ 10		10 Always
No.	Driving Forces	*Score Self–Driving Force (SDF)*	*Score Self–Resisting Force (SRF)*	Resisting Forces
1	I truly believe that it is the "people" who make my projects successful.			My projects are successful because of our project management software and other tools available.
2	I believe that my projects provide a great opportunity to develop future leaders for my organization.			My projects only focus on getting the key project results using the assigned resources.
3	I feel that if I am not optimizing the human potential within my organization, I am literally throwing away talent and millions of dollars with it.			I feel that attempting to optimize the human potential is the responsibility of our human resources department.
4	I value the "loyalty" of my team members and I feel that if I take care of my team, they will .take care of the customers.			"Loyalty" is an outdated concept and is not something to be expected in organizations today.
5	I believe that my primary responsibility as a project leader is to create future leaders.			I believe that my primary responsibility as a project manager is to complete projects.
6	My philosophy is that people, knowledge, and skills/talents are the foundation of a strong organization and my role as a project leader is to strengthen the foundation by training, motivation, and enhancing employee skills by allowing them to undertake challenging projects and delight our customers.			My philosophy is that technology and infrastructure are the foundation of a strong organization and my role as a project manager is to invest in strengthening this foundation.
7	I encourage my team to embrace "pain" and undertake challenging projects to improve our skills as a team and fine-tune our risk-taking capability.			I encourage my team to only take on projects that we have experience with.

8	I use the economy downturn as a "burning platform" and motivate our employees to innovate and take our corporation to the next level.			I use the economy downturn as a perfect time to reduce my staff.
9	I believe that if one of my team member has not learned, I have not been successful in teaching.			I believe that if my team member has not learned, they are not capable of being members on the project team.
10	I intend to "leave a legacy" and measure my success by the number of lives I have positively affected, and the number of leaders I have created in my organization.			The measure of my success as a project manager is delivering profits and results.
	Total SDF score			*Total SRF score*

Results	Conclusions	Recommended Action Review and Update Every Quarter (3 months)
SDF ≫ SRF	My behavior strongly supports the principles of enhancing the organizational appreciating assets.	Use Tables 12.6 through 12.8 to set goals and create an action plan to continuously enhance the behavior to create a culture of enhancing the organizational appreciating assets.
SDF > SRF	My behavior supports the principles of enhancing the organizational appreciating assets.	Use Tables 12.6 through 12.8 to set goals and create an action plan to increase SDF to allow a stronger behavior toward creating a culture of enhancing the organizational appreciating assets.
SRF ≫ SDF	My behavior strongly resists the principles of enhancing the organizational appreciating assets.	Use Tables 12.6 through 12.8 to set goals and create an action plan to increase SDF and reduce SRF to allow a stronger behavior toward creating a culture of enhancing the organizational appreciating assets.
SRF > SDF	My behavior resists the principles of enhancing the organizational appreciating assets.	Use Tables 12.6 through 12.8 to set goals and create an action plan to reduce SRF to allow a stronger behavior toward creating a culture of enhancing the organizational appreciating assets.
SDF = SRF	My behavior does not drive or resist the principles of enhancing the organizational appreciating assets.	Use Tables 12.6 through 12.8 to set goals and create an action plan to increase the SDF to allow a stronger behavior toward creating a culture of enhancing the organizational appreciating assets.

Table 12.6   Pillar XII: Analysis of SDF and SRF Results

Result	Existing Behavior	If the Goal is to Create a Moderately Strong Behavior Toward Principles of Enhancing the Organizational Appreciating Assets	If the Goal is to Create a Very Strong Behavior Toward Principles of Enhancing the Organizational Appreciating Assets
SDF			
SDF ≤ 25	No or minimal activities in creating a culture of enhancing the organizational appreciating assets	Focus on improving scores in at least 5 DF	Focus on improving scores in at least 7 DF
25 < SDF ≤ 50	Weak activities in creating a culture of enhancing the organizational appreciating assets	Focus on improving scores in at least 3 DF	Focus on improving scores in at least 5 DF
50 < SDF ≤ 75	Moderate activities in creating a culture of enhancing the organizational appreciating assets	Focus on improving scores in at least 1 DF	Focus on improving scores in at least 3 DF
SDF > 75	Strong activities in creating a culture of enhancing the organizational appreciating assets	N/A	Preserve or continuously improve the behavior
SRF			
SRF > 75	No or minimal activities in creating a culture of enhancing the organizational appreciating assets	Focus on decreasing scores in at least 5 RF	Focus on decreasing scores in at least 7 RF
50 < SRF ≤ 75	Weak activities in creating a culture of enhancing the organizational appreciating assets	Focus on decreasing scores in at least 3 RF	Focus on decreasing scores in at least 5 RF
25 < SRF ≤ 50	Moderate activities in creating a culture of enhancing the organizational appreciating assets	Focus on decreasing scores in at least 1 RF	Focus on decreasing scores in at least 3 RF
SRF ≤ 25	Strong activities in creating a culture of enhancing the organizational appreciating assets	N/A	Preserve or continuously improve the behavior

Table 12.7   Pillar XII: Action Plan to Increase Self-Driving Forces (SDFs)

Name: _____   Date: _____

No.	Driving Force	Current Score	Goal (Target Score) ⬆	Action Plan to Increase DF Score	Complete by (Date)	Required Resources
1	I truly believe that it is the "people" who make my projects successful.					
2	I believe that my projects provide a great opportunity to develop future leaders for my organization.					
3	We feel that if I am not optimizing the human potential within my organization, I am literally throwing away talent and millions of dollars with it.					
4	I value the "loyalty" of my team members and I feel that if I take care of my team, they will take care of the customers.					
5	I believe that my primary responsibility as a project leader is to create future leaders.					
6	My philosophy is that people, knowledge, and skills/talents are the foundation of a strong organization and my role as a project leader is to strengthen the foundation by training, motivating, and enhancing employee skills by allowing them to undertake challenging projects and delight our customers.					

7	I encourage my team to embrace "pain" and undertake challenging projects to improve our skills as a team and fine-tune our risk-taking capability.					
8	I use the economy downturn as a "burning platform" and motivate our employees to innovate and take our corporation to the next level.					
9	I believe that if one of my team member has not learned, I have not been successful in teaching.					
10	I intend to "leave a legacy" and measure my success by the number of lives I have positively affected, and the number of leaders I have created in my organization.					
	Total SDF					

Table 12.8   Pillar XII: Action Plan to Decrease Self-Resisting Forces (SDFs)

Name: _____   Date: _____

No.	Resisting Force	Current Score	Goal (Target Score) ⬇	Action Plan to Decrease RF Score	Complete by (Date)	Required Resources
1	My projects are successful because of our project management software and other tools available.					
2	My projects only focus on getting the key project results using the assigned resources.					
3	We feel that attempting to optimize the human potential is the responsibility of our human resources department.					
4	"Loyalty" is an outdated concept and is not something to be expected in organizations today.					
5	I believe that my primary responsibility as a project manager is to complete projects.					
6	My philosophy is that technology and infrastructure are the foundation of a strong organization and my role as a project manager is to invest in strengthening this foundation.					

7	I encourage my team to only take on projects that we have experience with.					
8	I use the economy downturn as a perfect time to reduce my staff.					
9	I believe that if my team member has not learned, they are not capable of being members on the project team.					
10	The measure of my success as a project manager is delivering profits and results.					
	Total SRF					

Pillar XII   Exercises

PILLAR XII: ORGANIZATIONAL-LEVEL SKILL SET–ENHANCEMENT EXERCISES

GROUP EXERCISES

These exercises are best completed within a group of project managers, project leaders, executives, and stakeholders from within a department or an organization.

1. Using Table 12.9, identify at least five advantages to your organization in creating a culture of enhancing the organizational appreciating assets, rate them from 1 (least important) to 5 (most important), and explain the rating.
2. Using Table 12.10, identify at least five roadblocks within your organization in creating a culture of stress-free project leadership for your complex projects, rate them from 1 (least difficult to overcome) to 5 (most difficult to overcome), and explain the rating.
3. Identify a team within your organization which is a dynamic and high that performing (Team A). Request them to have a team meeting and use Table 12.11 to identify the following:
   a. What are the top three factors that contribute MOST to their success?
   b. What steps do they take to enhance these factors?

Table 12.9   Pillar XII: Five Advantages of Applying Principles of Pillar XII to Your Organization

No.	Advantages of Applying Principles of Pillar XII to Enhancing Your Organization Culture	Rating (from 1 = Least Important to 5 = Most Important)	Explain the Rating
1			
2			
3			
4			
5			

Table 12.10   Pillar XII: Five Roadblocks to Creating a Culture of Enhancing the Organizational Appreciating Assets Using Pillar XII

No.	Roadblocks to Applying Principles of Enhancing the Organizational Appreciating Assets as Described in Pillar XII to Your Organization	Rating (from 1 = Least Difficult to Overcome to 5 = Most Difficult to Overcome)	Explain the Rating
1			
2			
3			
4			
5			

Table 12.11   Pillar XII: Reflecting on Strengths of High-Performance Team and Identifying Principles of Pillar XII

Team A			
A. Top Three Factors Contributing Most to Success	B. Steps Taken to Enhance These Factors	C. Top Three Factors Contributing Least to the Success	D. Steps Taken to Reduce or Eliminate These Factors

    c. What are the top three factors that contribute LEAST to their success?

    d. What steps do they take to reduce or eliminate these factors?

4. Identify a team within your organization that is a low-performing team that is struggling to deliver results (Team B). Request them to have a team meeting and use Table 12.12 to identify the following:

    a. What are the top three factors that contribute MOST to their failure or struggle?

    b. How do these factors differ from the success factors identified by Team A?

    c. How can they apply these principles to be successful themselves?

5. Scenario Analysis: The CEO of your organization has read the *12 Pillars of Project Excellence* and is anxious to apply the principles to his organization. He wisely plans on applying the principles first to a pilot area and then roll it out to one division and then to the entire corporation. Your project team has been selected as a pilot to apply the principles of Pillar XII. Create a plan for the following for application within your team:

    a. Consciously building a culture where "people" are truly considered the only appreciating asset (use Table 12.13)

    b. Investing in the appreciating assets during economic downturns in order to strengthen your team (use Table 12.14).

Table 12.12   Pillar XII: Reflecting on a Team Performing Poorly and Learning to Apply Factors of Pillar XII from a High-Performance Team

Team B		
A. Top Three Factors Contributing MOST to Struggle or Failure	*B. How Factors Compare with Success Factors of Team A*	*C. Plan to Apply Success Factors of Team A to Make Team B Successful*

Table 12.13   Pillar XII: Scenario Analysis—Creating a Plan for Appreciating the Team Assets

Table 12.14   Pillar XII: Scenario Analysis—Creating a Plan for Appreciating Assets during Economic Downturns

PILLAR XII: PERSONAL-LEVEL SKILL SET–ENHANCEMENT EXERCISES

INDIVIDUAL EXERCISES

These exercises are to be completed individually after reviewing Pillar XII in detail.

1. Using Table 12.15, list at least five advantages of applying the principles of Pillar XII of enhancing the appreciating assets to your future projects. Rate the advantages from 1 (least important) to 5 (most important) and explain the rating.

2. Using Table 12.16, identify at least five roadblocks to applying the principles of enhancing the appreciating assets from Pillar XII on all your future major projects. Rate the identified roadblocks from 1 (least difficult to overcome) to 5 (most difficult to overcome) and explain the rating.

3. Using Table 12.17, select one individual from within your current project team or from within your organization. Fill in the following details:

   a. Evaluate existing motivation level and performance level on a scale of 1 (very low) to 5 (very high)

   b. Identify one talent/skill for that team member that is not being utilized within the organization

Table 12.15   Pillar XII: Five Advantages of Applying Principles of Pillar XII to Your Career

No.	Advantages of Applying Principles of Pillar XII of Stress-Free Project Leadership to All Future Projects	Rating (from 1 = Least Important to 5 = Most Important)	Explain the Rating
1			
2			
3			
4			
5			

Table 12.16   Pillar XII: Five Roadblocks to Applying Principles of Pillar XII

No.	Roadblocks to Applying Principles of Enhancing the Organizational Appreciating Assets Detailed in Pillar XII to All Future Projects	Rating (from 1 = Least Difficult to Overcome to 5 = Most Difficult to Overcome)	Explain the Rating
1			
2			
3			
4			
5			

Table 12.17   Pillar XII: Application of Talent among Team Members Using Principles of Pillar XII

Name of Individual Selected from the Project Team or Organization	
Their current role in the project/organization	
Current motivation level and performance levels from 1 (very low) to 5 (very high)	
One talent/skill possessed by the individual that is not being utilized within the organization	
Opportunities found within the organization to allow the team member to utilize their talents	
Has the performance of the selected individuals on existing project improved? (As evaluated after 3 months)	

    c. What opportunities can be found within the organization to allow the team member to utilize those talents?

    d. After 3 months, evaluate if the performance of the selected individual on the existing project has improved using a scale of 1 (very low) to 5 (very high).

4. Using Table 12.18, answer the following:

    a. Evaluate your existing motivation level and performance level on a scale of 1 (very low) to 5 (very high)

    b. Identify at least one talent/skill you possess that you are currently not using within the organization

    c. Request that your superiors identify an opportunity within your organization that will allow you to utilize the talent

    d. After 3 months, evaluate if your motivation level has increased or decreased after some progress by applying your talent in the identified area. Explain.

5. Scenario Analysis: There is an opening for a Project Sensei position within your organization. The competition for this coveted position is very high. The first step in the process is to answer two essay questions as a part of the application process for this position. Answer the following questions as if you are filling out an application form:

    a. What is the legacy you would like to leave as a Project Sensei? (Use Table 12.19)

    b. Which principles of Pillar XII will you apply to fulfill that legacy? How? (Use Table 12.20)

Table 12.18   Pillar XII: Application of Your Talent Using Principles of Pillar XII

Your Current Role in the Project/Organization	
One talent/skill you possess that is not being utilized within the organization	
Your current motivation and performance levels from 1 (very low) to 5 (very high)	
Opportunities found within the organization to allow you to utilize your talents	
Has your motivation level and performance levels on existing project improved? (As evaluated after 3 months)	

Table 12.19   Pillar XII: Scenario Analysis—Leaving a Legacy as a Project Sensei

What is the Legacy You Would Like to Leave as a Project Sensei?

Table 12.20   Pillar XII: Scenario Analysis—Application of the Principles of Pillar XII to Fulfill the Desired Legacy as a Project Sensei

Which Principles of Pillar XII Will You Apply to Fulfill That Legacy? How?

Pillar XII   References

1. Sensei—Definition. http://www.wordiq.com/Sensei (accessed November 11, 2010).
2. Dalal, A. F. (2007). *3 Tips for Corporations To Survive and Thrive In Any Economy*, pp. 1–3. Pinnacle Process Solutions, Intl. Ledar Park, TX 78613.
3. Minoura, T. (2003). *The Toyota Production System*, http://www.toyotageorgetown.com/tps.asp (accessed November 11, 2010).
4. Graupp, P. (2010). *The Human Element of Training within Industry*, http://www.reliableplant.com/Read/17267/human-element-of-training-within-industry (accessed November 11, 2010).
5. Huntzinger, J. (2010). *The Roots of Lean, Training within Industry: The Origin of Japanese Management and Kaizen*, Figure 3, TWI Job Instruction of card, http://twi-institute.com/pdfs/article_rootsofleanupdate.pdf (accessed December 6, 2010).
6. Drucker, Peter F. (1909–2005). http://quotationsbook.com/quote/22810 (accessed November 11, 2010).
7. Villa-Vicencio, C. (1996). *The Spirit of Freedom: South African Leaders on Religion and Politics*, p. 150. University of California Press.

Chapter 13

Summary of 12 Pillars

The 12 Pillars of Project Excellence is written with the hope to take the theory of project management from the age of command, control, and chaos to a solid practice of project leadership to bring about the dawn of the age of engagement, empowerment, and enlightenment in all organizations.

The 12 pillars are explained in this book and are shown in Table 13.1:

1. Be a Project Leader (Leadership)
2. Create a Balanced Project Structure (Structure)
3. Delight the Customers with a Project Vision Statement (Vision)
4. Sign the Charter (Charter)
5. Diffuse Your Passion (Passion)
6. Simplify Projects (Lean Thinking)
7. Minimize Meeticide (Meetings)
8. Take Risks (Risk)
9. Decode and Shield Your Data (Data)
10. Learn from Failures (Learning)
11. Make Projects Less Stressful (Environment)
12. Invest in Your Appreciating Assets (Assets)

Table 13.2 shows the key learning from each pillar that needs to be followed to progress from project manager to a master project leader.

Table 13.3 shows the key difference between a project manager before learning the principles of each pillar and a project leader after learning the principles of each pillar.

Figure 13.25 demonstrates the results after only applying the project management theory.

Figure 13.26 demonstrates success after applying the principles of the 12 pillars of project excellence along with the project management theory.

Table 13.1   The 12 Pillars of Project Excellence

Pillar I: Leadership	Pillar II: Structure
Be a Project Leader	Create a Balanced Project Structure
Pillar III: Vision	**Pillar IV: Charter**
Delight the Customers with a Project Vision Statement	Sign the Charter
Pillar V: Passion	**Pillar VI: Lean Thinking**
Diffuse Your Passion	Simplify Projects
Pillar VII: Meetings	**Pillar VIII: Risk**
Minimize Meeticide ™	Take Risks
Pillar IX: Data	**Pillar X: Learning**
Decode and Shield Your Data	Learn from Failures
Pillar XI: Environment	**Pillar XII: Assets**
Make Project Less Stressful	Invest in Your Appreciating Assets

Table 13.2 Key Points of the 12 Pillars of Project Excellence

Pillar I: Leadership *Be a Project Leader*	Pillar II: Structure *Create a Balanced Project Structure*

Project leadership is the key to success. Successful project leaders need to develop and use the following five powers:
 	
  i. Power of delegation
 	
  ii. Power of dynamic leadership
 	
  iii. Power of visualization
 	
  iv. Power of lean thinking
 	
  v. Power of humility
	One of the primary responsibilities of a project leaders on complex projects is to create a stable and balanced project structure consisting of
	
	  i. An air-support layer consisting of customers, steering committee, board of advisors, and project leader.
	
	  ii. A ground-support layer consisting of project leader, project subleader, team leaders, support team leaders, team members, and consultants/ vendors or subcontractors.

Pillar III: Vision *Delight the Customers with a Project Vision Statement*	Pillar IV: Charter *Sign the Charter*

Every successful project leader must develop and use a project vision statement that sets soaring standards and lays the foundation for ultimate success of the project by delighting the customers on each project. A project vision helps set the altitude of a project. A project vision statement is created by
  i. Forming a committee
  ii. Reviewing the charter
  iii. Interviewing the stakeholders
  iv. Identifying initial priority areas
  v. Preparing an initial project vision statement
  vi. Brainstorming the initial statement
  vii. Creating a powerful final project vision statement
 	
A personal vision statement can also help create a corporate fan club throughout the organization.
	Every successful project requires a completed and signed charter that acts as a shield against scope creep. A charter is a critical artifact to document all the key requirements of the project with clarity and without ambiguity. A project charter should be
	  i. Helpful in setting the longitude and the latitude of a project
	  ii. Containing information that is measurable and quantifiable
	  iii. Used as a legal contract between all the key stakeholders of the project
	  iv. Amended only when it is absolutely necessary
	  v. Used to proactively avoid any damage to the project results due to scope creep

Pillar V: Passion *Diffuse Your Passion*	**Pillar VI: Lean Thinking** *Simplify Projects*

In spite of a vast variety of communication methods in today's hi-tech world, projects are still failing primarily because of failure to communicate. Project leaders need to master the art of excellent communications and be a coach, salesperson, and motivator-in-chief to diffuse their passion across the project organization and lead their team to a successful finish on every project. Every successful project leader must master the following:
 	
  i. Vertical communications
 	
  ii. Lateral communications
 	
iii. Corporate communications
 	
True leaders use their own passion to tune their team members to their own frequency, creating a common mission for the project.
	Every successful project leader must practice the "Science of Simplicity™" while leading projects. A powerful, commonsense, and practical tool available to simplify projects is "Lean." Every project leader needs to be a lean thinker and identify the following:
	
	  i. Value-added activities
	
	  ii. Necessary non-value-added activities
	
	iii. Waste (*muda*)
	
	Muda or waste usually accounts for the greatest percentage of the three categories and can be of several types. There are eight types of *muda* known by the TIM E. WOOD. Project leaders should make efforts to eliminate or reduce these eight types of wastes to avert the resulting intellectual waste.

Pillar VII: Meetings *Minimize Meeticide™*	**Pillar VIII: Risk** *Take Risks*
Project leaders should look for opportunities to eliminate non-value-added, nonproductive meetings. If the meeting cannot be eliminated, project leaders should look for the options to reduce non-value-added time in the meetings. Every successful project leader must avoid loss of resource efficiency due to excessive meetings (Meeticide™) and keep the meetings to absolute minimum as required to get the results, so as to have an optimal project return of investment.	Dynamic risk leadership is the proactive assessment of risks and development of methods to resolve those risks. This approach focuses on "learn-and-apply" principles opposed to traditional risk assessment approach that focuses on "try-and-die" principles. Dynamic risk leadership involves the following three basic steps: 1. Creating a risk assessment team 2. Developing an assessment strategy 3. Creating a risk response plan

Pillar IX: Data *Decode and Shield Your Data*	**Pillar X: Learning** *Learn from Failures*

Today, we live in an age of data overload or too much information. It is very important for the project leader to categorize date into the following:
 	
    i. Value-added data
    ii. Necessary non-value-added data
    iii. Non-value-added data
 	
The following data elements are critical to consider when dealing with project data:
 	
    i. Data storage and retrieval
    ii. Data security
    iii. Data access
    iv. Data monitoring
    v. Data distribution
    vi. Data change management
 	
Every successful project leader must have a reliable system secure, monitor, distribute, control, access, and store project data
	Every successful project leader must learn from failures during the project, at the end of every phase, and at the end of each project so that he/she can continually fine-tune their leadership skills. There are three basic modes of failure:
	
	    i. System-level failure
	    ii. Process-level failure
	    iii. Human-level failure
	
	Project managers use a reactive approach and focus on human-level failures first, put in Band-Aid solutions, and create an environment of fear. Project leaders use a proactive approach and focus on system-level failures first to find and eliminate the root causes and create an open learning team environment.

Pillar XI: Environment *Make Project Less Stressful*	**Pillar XII: Assets** *Invest in Your Appreciating Assets*

As projects are more complex today, stress is very prevalent among project team members. Stress in the project can be avoided or reduced by eliminating ambiguous requirements, careful and proper planning, and project manager's emphasis on individual ability in the team. Every successful project leader must understand the unique nature of individuals on their team and give them appropriate roles and responsibilities and create a fun environment that allows them to stretch and grow without any adverse effects so that they completely transform themselves. Project managers should transform themselves into project leaders by changing their thinking from a "'one-size-fits-all" approach to "the enlightened" approach and try hard to keep the team in "zone of pinnacle performance."	"Things do not appreciate; only people do." The major factor differentiating great companies from their competitors is that every manager, leader, or executive of great companies is focused on optimizing the human potential within their organization. Great organizations focus on the following to survive and thrive during tough economic times:
	
	    i. Strengthening the foundation of people, knowledge, and skills/talents
	
	    ii. Strengthening and raising the 12 pillars (principles of project leadership) to new heights
	
	    iii. Strengthening the roof by delighting customers, employees, and shareholders

TABLE 13.3   Before and After Applying the Principles of 12 Pillars of Project Excellence

Before Applying Principles of Pillar I	After Applying Principles of Pillar I
Pillar I: Leadership	

A classic project manager who is focused on
 	
  i. Micromanaging project resources
 	
  ii. Directing resources using command and control techniques
 	
  iii. Constantly reacting to changes
	A master project leader who can
	
	  i. Lead the required project activities
	
	  ii. Create a shared project vision and coach and motivate team members
	
	  iii. Always proactive in avoiding issues

	1. Power of delegation 2. Power of dynamic leadership 3. Power of visualization 4. Power of lean thinking 5. Power of humility

Before Applying Principles of Pillar II	After Applying Principles of Pillar II
Pillar II: Structure	
A project manager who is facing failures because of poor communications and ambiguous requirements due to an imbalanced project structure with the following:	A master project leader who is highly successful because of a balanced project structure with the following:
i. No formal "air-support" structure from above	i. Formal "air-support" structure from above
ii. No input from voice of the customer	ii. Input from voice of the customer
iii. Demotivated ground troops	iii. Highly motivated ground troops
	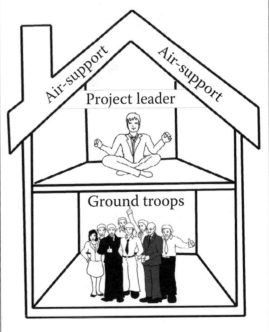

Before Applying Principles of Pillar III	After Applying Principles of Pillar III
Pillar III: Vision	

A project manager who does not create a project vision statement is at the risk of
 	
  i. Having blinders on the project
 ii. Being bogged down due to lack of direction
	A successful project leader who uses a project vision statement to
	
	  i. Set the altitude of a project
	 ii. Set personal standards for soaring high

Before Applying Principles of Pillar IV	After Applying Principles of Pillar IV
Pillar IV: Charter	
A project manager does not use a signed charter resulting in the following: i. No legal contract between stakeholders ii. Significant scope creep during project iii. Severe damage to the project and team	A successful project leader who uses a signed charter resulting in the following: i. A legal contract between stakeholders ii. No unnecessary scope creep iii. A proactive shield against any damage to project or to the team
	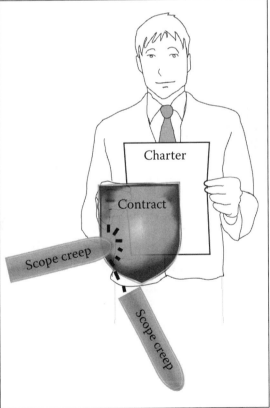

Before Applying Principles of Pillar V	After Applying Principles of Pillar V
Pillar V: Passion	
Classic project managers use traditional methods of communication and unable to inspire team resulting in i. Lack of interest ii. Confusion among team members iii. Project failure	Project leaders master the art of excellent communications and be a coach, a salesperson, and a motivator-in-chief to i. Diffuse their passion across the project organization ii. Lead their team to a successful finish on every project

Before Applying Principles of Pillar VI Pillar	After Applying Principles of Pillar VI
Pillar VI: Lean Thinking	
Classic project managers who do not use "lean thinking" resulting in i. Being overcome by the eight wastes or *muda* known by the acronym TIM E. WOOD ii. Succumbing to the resulting intellectual waste	Successful project leader practice the "Science of Simplicity™" while leading projects using "lean thinking." Project leaders learn to i. Identify and eliminate the eight wastes or *muda* known by the acronym TIM E. WOOD ii. Avert the resulting intellectual waste

Before Applying Principles of Pillar VII	After Applying Principles of Pillar VII
Pillar VII: Meetings	
Classic project managers who use traditional methods to run meetings resulting in i. Loss of resource efficiency due to excessive meetings (Meeticide™) ii. Excessive non-value-added, nonproductive meetings iii. Excessive non-value-added time in the meetings iv. Poor project return of investment	Project leaders who learn the art of running efficient meetings only as required to i. Avoid loss of resource efficiency due to excessive meetings (Meeticide™) ii. Reduce or eliminate non-value-added, nonproductive meetings iii. Reduce non-value-added time in the meetings iv. Gain optimal project return of investment

Before Applying Principles of Pillar VIII	**After Applying Principles of Pillar VIII**
Pillar VIII: Risk	

A classic project manager who uses
 	
  i. Traditional risk management techniques
 	
  ii. "Try-and-die" approach
 	
  iii. No calculations for consequences of risk
	A master project leader who uses
	
	  i. Dynamic risk leadership techniques
	
	  ii. "Learn-and-apply" approach
	
	  iii. Math to calculate the consequences of risk

 Try and die approach	 Learn and apply approach

Before Applying Principles of Pillar IX	After Applying Principles of Pillar IX
Pillar IX: Data	
A classic project manager who does not consider the importance of data management in projects resulting in data that is iv. Excessive v. Unreliable vi. Lost, unsecured, or corrupt Project manager does not use appropriate systems secure, monitor, distribute, control, access, and store project data.	A master project leader who uses dynamic data management and categorizes data into i. Value-added data ii. Necessary non-value-added data iii. Non-value-added data Project leader who uses reliable systems secure, monitor, distribute, control, access, and store project data.

Before Applying Principles of Pillar X	After Applying Principles of Pillar X
Pillar X: Learning Environment	
A classic project manager who does not discuss or learn from failures resulting in i. A reactive approach focusing on human-level failures first ii. Finding and blaming the people iii. Creating a team environment of fear iv. Continually repeating the same failures during other projects	A master project leader who is open to learn from failures resulting in i. A proactive approach focusing on system-level failures first ii. Finding and eliminating the root causes iii. Creating an open learning team environment iv. Continually fine-tuning leadership skills
	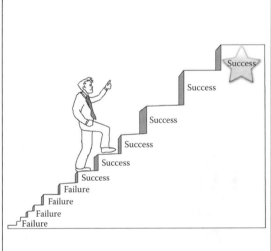

Before Applying Principles of Pillar XI	After Applying Principles of Pillar XI
Pillar XI: Environment	
A classic project manager who does not pay attention to project stress resulting in i. Boredom or ii. Fatigue, exhaustion, injury, or burnout iii. Project failures Managers who use a "one-size-fits-all" approach and do not know how to get the optimal performance from project resources	A master project leader who focuses on avoiding or reducing stress by i. Eliminating ambiguous requirements ii. Carefully planning the project iii. Customizing roles and responsibilities based on individual team member's abilities Leaders who use an "enlightened" approach to keep the team in zone of "pinnacle performance"

Before Applying Principles of Pillar XII	After Applying Principles of Pillar XII
Pillar XII: Assets	
A classic project manager who does not consider people as appreciating assests but iv. Spends money on capital purchases versus people development v. Does not focus on the 12 pillars (principles of project leadership) vi. Weakens the roof by inability to delight customers, employees, and shareholders	A master project leader who makes their organizations great by focusing on i. Strengthening the foundation of people, knowledge, and skills/talents ii. Strengthening and raising the 12 pillars (principles of project leadership) iii. Strengthening the roof by delighting customers, employees, and shareholders
Manager Unappreciated assets	Sensei Appreciated assets

Figure 13.25 Demonstrates results after applying the project management theory.

Figure 13.26 Demonstrates success after applying the principles of the 12 Pillars of Project Excellence along with the project management theory.

Chapter 14

Conclusions: The 12 Pillars of Project Excellence

Now, Go Do IT!

A conclusion can simply be the place where one got tired of thinking. However, in the case of the 12 pillars book, the conclusion is the place where adequate information has been provided in order for you to take steps in the direction of being a great project leader. There are a lot more details that can be provided, but this is definitely a good start.

The conclusion gives you the confidence and the five-step process to "now, go do it!"

The 12 pillars provide the formula for success and guidelines for "how to do it"; the conclusion gives you the confidence and the five-step process to "now, go do it!"

14.1 Five Simple Steps to "Now, Go Do It"

14.1.1 Know the Purpose—Pursue It!

A career in project management is like a career in golf; the fewer mistakes one makes, the more successful one can be.

A career in project management is like a career in golf; the fewer mistakes one makes, the more successful one can be. Also, just like golf, project management teaches us invaluable lessons in humility by taking us to the pinnacle of exhilaration in one task and plunging us in to the depths of frustration on the very next. However, one major difference between golf and project management is that whereas success in golf depends primarily on self-mastery, success in project management is much more challenging because in addition to self-mastery, one needs to master the art of empowering others.

What should be your key objectives while leading every project? If you cannot identify all the objectives correctly, the road to project leadership will be long and the success at the end of the journey will be eternally elusive. If you desire to be a master project leader, you need to pursue the following three key objectives while leading projects:

1. **Meeting or exceeding the objectives of the project charter:** Meeting or exceeding the objectives of the project charter is the basic requirement of any project manager. However, to be a project leader, you need to meet two more key objectives regarding your team and yourself.
2. **Developing your team members:** Great project leaders make developing their team members a primary objective while executing every project. They believe focusing on developing people will make the goal of exceeding the project charter objectives automatic and effortless and building the future generation of great project leaders is a great way to "leave a legacy" in the organization.
3. **Enhancing your own strengths:** Great project leaders make it a project objective to continually assess and enhance their own strengths and reduce or eliminate their flaws and blind spots. They aspire to be a better project leader than they were on the previous project.

Thus, successful project leaders know that on every project they undertake, it is important not only to define and pursue the basic expectations of the charter but it is also critical to focus on appreciating the organizational assets, including themselves.

14.1.2 Winning Is a Habit—Cultivate It!

Michael Phelps in his career as a U.S. Olympic swimmer has won a total of 16 Olympic medals—6 gold and 2 bronze medals at Athens Olympic games in 2004 and 8 gold medals at the Beijing Olympic games in 2008. Phelps dream of winning eight medals at the Beijing Olympics was almost shattered by his rival, Milorad Cavic, when competing in the 100-m butterfly competition. Cavic had beaten Phelps in the preliminaries, and Phelps was behind Cavic throughout the 100 m swim. Cavic was in the lead, and it seemed that he would finish big and win the gold. But Michael was in the habit of winning and in this race demonstrated how this habit made him superior to the best of his competitors of the world. His physical characteristics, natural abilities, and talents made him a great swimmer, but he became a world champion because of setting his heart on winning. Phelps managed to surge in the final 20 m and gradually gained on Cavic. But that did not seem enough and near the end, it was evident that Cavic would win. But Phelps's heart's desire was not a silver medal, and on the absolute last millisecond, the very final butterfly stroke, Phelps thrust forward to miraculously touch the finish first for his seventh gold medal at the Beijing Olympics, and Cavic was left to win the Silver medal. The difference between Phelps's and Cavic's times was that of a mere 1/100 of a second, the closest race in the history of the Olympic Games. Thus, 1/100 of a second or an "eyeblink" made the difference between winning the gold and the silver in the Olympics, and that final surge by Phelps would have been impossible for any athlete, if it was not for his habit of winning.[1]

According to the movie *212° the Extra Degree*, water gets hot at 211° but hot water cannot power anything. When the water is heated by just one more degree and the moment that it reaches 212°, the water transforms into steam via the process of boiling. That one extra degree gives the water the power to even move a steam locomotive weighing several tons. Thus, in life and in projects, that one extra degree can make a difference between a heart-warming victory and a heart-breaking failure.[2]

However, there is another important perspective to this that is important to remember. Without the 211° of heat, the steam would have been impossible to achieve. A clock chime is heard only when the minute hand reaches 60 minutes, but it takes 59 minutes 59 seconds of effort to reach that final second when the clock chime is heard. Thus, two critical lessons can be learned from this:

a. Do not give up if you do not see the results immediately. Just like steam is seen only when the temperature passes the final degree to reach the 212° and clock chimes are heard when the final second is reached to hit 60 minutes, victory will only be achieved by the last millisecond of effort, but do not get disappointed along the way as you never know when that final degree or that final millisecond will be for you.

b. Winning by itself is not enough—it is important on how you play the game to win. Let us take an example from the sport of ice skating. They are two people who really wanted to win and be at the pinnacle of this sport. On the male side, it was Scott Hamilton, who between 1980 and 1984 won the gold medal in every national and international competition he participated in, including Winter Olympics, World Figure Skating Championships, and U.S. and Canadian Championships. He battled testicular cancer and was operated for a brain tumor. He continues to be a champion and although physically of short stature, he is truly a giant in the sports of ice skating.

On the female side, someone who wanted to win at all costs was Tonya Harding; she had set herself apart from others by being the first ever to do a triple axel combination. However, in her desire to win, instead of pushing herself to achieve more, Harding plotted with her ex-husband and bodyguard to break her competitor Nancy Kerrigan's right leg so that she would be unable to skate and Tonya could win the competition in Detroit. This attack in 1994 on her competitor Nancy Kerrigan gained worldwide notoriety and resulted in ending Harding's career in skating and also led to several years of legal troubles after pleading guilty to the crime.

Thus, both Hamilton and Harding had a great desire to be winners, but Hamilton raised himself above his competitor by his tremendous talents and efforts, whereas Harding wanted to win by hurting her competition. Thus, there are two types of giants, one who rise in stature and stand tall among their competition by their own hard work and extraordinary efforts, and others who want to tower above their competition by chopping off their legs. One is a true winner and the other is just a cheater.

Thus, your attitude is the primary factor that determines your altitude. Winning is an attitude—develop it now. Be a true winner who stands tall based on personal virtues.

14.1.3 There Will Be Resistance—Face It!

Walt Disney is a fantastic example of one man with a great dream who influenced the entire planet in a wonderful way. Walt Disney's vision was so powerful, his strive for perfection so great, his risk taking ability so sound, his guidance to the employees so precise, and his execution so flawless that his dream continues to "delight" the masses of all ages and nationality.

Was Walt so special? Did Walt not face any issues in the execution of his dreams? Actually, Walt was like any "ordinary" boy but with an "extraordinary" ability to overcome any resistance he faced in making his dreams a reality. He grew up in Kansas delivering newspapers for his own father's newspaper distributorship business. His father did not support him in his dream to be a cartoonist. He left home and lived for many months looking for jobs, living in an old studio, and barely eating. Once his works like *Alice in Cartoonland, Oswald the Rabbit, Snow White*, and *Mickey Mouse* started being famous, he started being recognized as a genius. But he was still not there yet. When he began building Disneyland in Anaheim, California, his project was dubbed as "Disney's folly."[3] July 17, 1955, the opening day of Disneyland, was in fact known as "Black Sunday" and got very bad press because of the logistical nightmares faced when counterfeit tickets resulted in 33,000 people showing up versus the 22,000 invited. Was Disney broken? No, in fact he took this opportunity to overhaul his operations. After the debacle and overhaul, Disneyland was consistently getting crowds exceeding the initial calculations by 30%. Walt took this opportunity to add more rides. It was not only the outsiders who he had to stand up to; even after 40 years, and financial success, Walt had to argue with his elder brother Roy, a business partner, over Walt's spending and Roy's conservatism on money matters.

In my own career as a project manager, I had several instances where I felt that everything around me was dark and gloomy. There were some managers, peers, and other people who did not want me to succeed. I had one manager who clearly told me "You will never be a manager in this organization." I had several instances of managers feeling threatened by my success and throttling my project resources. I have had presidents of companies telling me that "This project will never be successful in this organization—you have just one chance to prove it works, else you are out!" I overcame all of these and was successful in each and every project I led. I used two analogies to help me through the tough times and allowed me to overcome the resistance—the sun analogy and the sandpaper analogy.

The Sun Analogy

Whenever all looked dark and gloomy, I thought of the sun. There are many days when because of dark clouds we cannot see even a single ray of sun reaching us. Does the sun say—well, nothing is getting past these clouds anyway, what's the use, let me stop shinning till I see an opening in the clouds? Does the sun ever stop shining? The answer is quite obvious. Thus, when in your career as a project leader you find obstacles, failures, unfairness, and a feeling of gloom, your course of action should be equally obvious—*just keep shining.* Do not let the intensity of your light decrease by even a single lumen. The dark clouds of obstacles will have to move out of your way for people to realize your passion, power, and intensity. You will always be able to see a silver lining on the dark clouds you encounter.

The Sandpaper Analogy

Whenever I encountered people who were rude and mean, I thought of them as sandpaper polishing me. I thought that they may scratch me and rub me the wrong way, but they will eventually end up polishing and shining me, while getting a little bit of my shine on themselves too. This helped me to look at the bright side of things.

Thus, if you are not facing resistance as a project leader, you are not doing your job of pushing the envelope and thinking out of the box very well. Resistance is to be expected, you will need to develop the tools not only to face this resistance but also to overcome it.

14.1.4 Passion Is a Requirement—Show It!

According to Mr. Jim Johnson of the Standish Group,[4] the top 10 project success factors are as shown in Figure 14.1. However, all surveys and reports on project management always miss the most critical factor for success—passion of project managers as it is very difficult to measure. However, the virtues that all executives are always looking for in leaders are passion and confidence in their abilities—this cannot be bought or taught but has to come from within them. For example, while leading the complete transformation of a medical business making endoscopic equipment from traditional manufacturing to flow manufacturing, the president of the division was "quite skeptical" at the start and he told me, in no uncertain terms, that, "I am quite sure you will be unsuccessful here as our business is different." However, considering the comment by the president as a warning of the

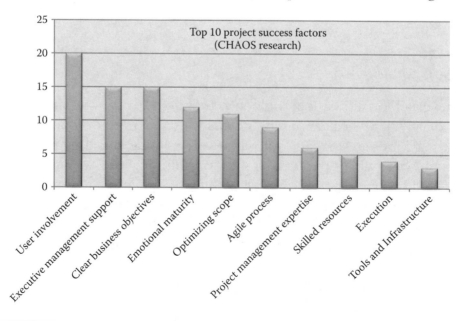

Figure 14.1   Top 10 success factors. (Based on Johnson, J., *CHAOS Report***, The Standish Group, Boston, MA, 2009.)**

challenges ahead, I encouraged my team to put in a significant effort in customization of the flow technology at this division. With the full support of the project sponsor and great effort on the part of the team, we forged ahead. Not only did we completely transform the division resulting in several million dollars in cost savings, but we created material management software that integrated seamlessly into our Enterprise Resource Planning (ERP) system and created simulation models for all business units—all in less than 1 year and $400,000 below the approved budget. The success of this project was mentioned in corporate magazine and even recognized by our CEO and other corporate executives during their rare visit to our manufacturing site. The reason I was successful is that I had unwavering faith in the ability of my team members and in my own abilities and confidence that I would find allies who would believe in my passion and give me a chance. Learn to develop this passion from the gold nuggets you can mine from the 12 pillars book and by visualizing yourself as a corporate superhero project leader who can solve any problem that exists.

Thus, great success in challenging endeavors is not achieved merely by dreaming, planning, and performing the assigned duties; one key success factor that is difficult to measure is true passion and a solid belief in one's abilities to succeed as shown in Figure 14.2.

14.1.5 Sky Is the Limit—Reach for It!

My company motto and personal belief for all individuals and businesses is "You are more than you can ever imagine!™" as shown in Figure 14.3. This is the truth—we do not understand our own true value. Both coal and diamond are the same fundamental material, carbon, but in different stages of refinement. Unless

"You are more than you can ever imagine!™"

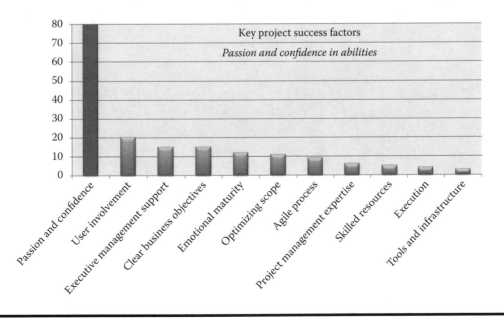

Figure 14.2 The most critical project success factor.

Figure 14.3   Philosophy of Pinnacle Process Solutions, Int.®

we put ourselves through the fire of refinement (undertaking challenging projects), we can never be recognized as superheroes, we truly are. Taking charge and successfully completing challenging, critical, and strategic projects demonstrate to us who we truly are. Let us not wonder how other leaders do it—let us go try it for ourselves and say "up, up and away!" as we begin our journey and soar to new heights of excellence.

I hope the 12 pillars book ignites in you and in your organization an undying bright fire of passion and desire for project excellence and provides a roadmap for success in your quest to be legendary leaders.

Summary

Figure 14.4 shows the five-step process to "now, go, do it" as follows:

1. Know the purpose—pursue it!
2. Winning is habit—cultivate it!
3. There will be resistance—face it!
4. Passion is critical—show it!
5. Sky is the limit—reach for it!

In summary, dream big and fly high to put the lessons from these 12 pillars into action. If you do this with zeal and passion and strive to keep a healthy balance between work and home life, success will be yours, and you will be well on your road to be recognized as corporate superheroes.

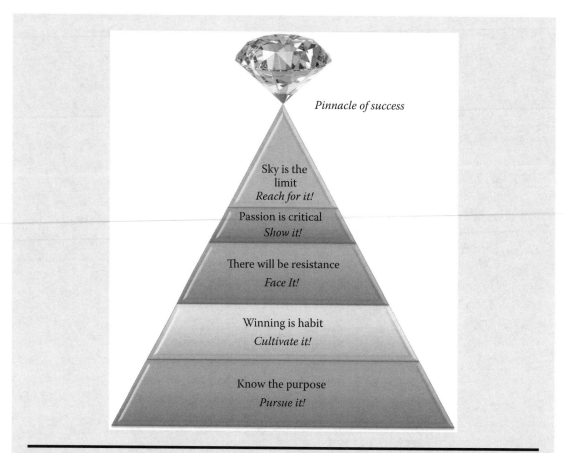

Figure 14.4   Five steps to "now, go do it!"

References

1. My Realty Television and the Lie Politic. (2008–2009). *Michael Phelps Wins 7th Gold in Closest Olympic Swim in History!! Wins Men's 100M Butterfly, Ties Spitz record!* http://myrealitytelevision.com/2008/08/michael-phelps-wins-7th-gold-in-closest-olympic-swim-in-history-wins-mens-100m-butterfly-ties-spitz-record/ (accessed October 27, 2010).

2. Parker, S. L. (1998–2010). *212° the Extra Degree,* http://www.just212.com/be212/?utm_source =google&utm_medium= cpc&utm_content=text_212-The-Extra-Degree&utm_campaign =google-cpc-212-brand (accessed October 27, 2010).

3. Sliger, M. (2010). *Sharing the vision,* http://www.stickyminds.com/sitewide.asp?Function=edetail&ObjectType =ART&ObjectId=12090 &tth=DYN&tt=siteemail&iDyn=2 (accessed October 27, 2010).

4. Johnson, J. (2009). *CHAOS Report 2009.* Boston, MA: The Standish Group International Inc.

INDEX

Author

Adil Dalal is the CEO of Pinnacle Process Solutions International®. Mr. Dalal is a keynote speaker, author and an internationally recognized expert and thought leader in project leadership and Lean/Advanced Flow Technology. He is well known for pioneering several key advances in project leadership and in Lean, including Lean Project leadership™, iLean® technology, Holistic Model (Lean + iLean)® and lean4kids®. Mr. Dalal's mission is to focus on enhancing the value of the "appreciating assets" and optimizing the human potential in addition to developing the necessary technical skills for ensuring the long term success of individuals and corporations.

Mr. Dalal holds several degrees: a MS in Engineering Management, a MS in Mechanical Engineering and a BS in Automotive Engineering. Additionally, he holds numerous certifications, including a Certified Project Manager (PMP), Certified Quality Engineer (CQE) and Certified Lean Bronze Professional (LBC). He is also a Certified Executive Coach.

Mr. Dalal has leveraged his expertise in Project Leadership and in Advanced Flow Technology to increase the performance of organizations around the world. His mastery has made Mr. Dalal a sought after strategic business partner and executive coach as he continues to drive excellence by implementing strategies for growth and long-term success.

Adil Dalal can be contacted at (512) 289 7080 or by e-mail at adil@pinnacle process.com.

Adil Dalal, PMP, CQE, LBC